TRUSTING YHWH

TRUSTING YHWH

Abiding Legacy of the Ancient Hebrew Psalms

Lorne E. Weaver

Foreword by
James A. Sanders

RESOURCE *Publications* · Eugene, Oregon

TRUSTING YHWH
Abiding Legacy of the Ancient Hebrew Psalms

Resource Publications
An Imprint of Wipf and Stock Publishers
199 W. 8th Ave., Suite 3
Eugene, OR 97401

www.wipfandstock.com

PAPERBACK ISBN: 978-1-4982-9043-2
HARDCOVER ISBN: 978-1-4982-9045-6
EBOOK ISBN: 978-1-4982-9044-9

Manufactured in the U.S.A.   FEBRUARY 28, 2019

Lord (Adonai), you have been our dwelling place in all generations.
Before the mountains were born, or ever you brought forth the earth and the world,
you are God (Elohim) from eternity to eternity.
Psalm 90:1-2

The one who dwells in the secret shelter of the Most High (Elyon),
and passes the night in the shadow of the God of Heaven (Shaddai), speaks:
'I will say of the LORD (YHWH), my refuge and my bulwark;
my God (Elohay) in whom I put my trust'.
Psalm 91:1-2

It is good to give thanks to the LORD (YHWH), and sing praises to your name,
O Most High (Elyon); to declare your loving kindness in the morning,
and your faithfulness in the night.
Psalm 92:1-2

Contents

Foreword

Fr. Lorne Weaver has crafted for the faithful believer an engaging read of the biblical Psalter. This is not just another scholarly book about the Psalms. It is a pastor's journey into the hymns and songs of the faithful in antiquity. And on that journey Weaver stops time and again to smell the "roses of Sharon" as he moves through psalm after psalm that move the reader to find expression after expression of trust in God even in the worst of circumstances.

Weaver finds in the Psalms amazing affirmations of trust in God in the midst of personal disasters that today drive many people away from the Church. While Weaver bases his readings on scholarship of the Book of Psalms he nonetheless pierces through the many conjectures about their forms, origins and provenances and finds what the lay person today faces who often lives on the boundaries of modern existence, the soul who quietly endures the worst that life can throw at a person. This book speaks to those who often quietly suffer pain and doubt to the point of despair. This is the book that speaks to those who ask the desperate question, "Why did God let this happen?"

Weaver has crafted out of his many years of ministry a reading of the Psalms that speaks directly to the individual believer who stumbles and staggers, even gropes for something stable on which to find his or her footing in a world that has lost the support of family and often finds her/himself alone and needing care, or is the care-giver for a loved one who literally absorbs all they have to give of themselves.

Weaver shows how biblical texts like those of the Psalms still speak loud and clear to those who read them needing sure help to get through life intact. Sure, they spoke to enough in antiquity to get on a tenure tract toward lodging in Jewish and Christian canons, but that is not Weaver's concern. Weaver's concern is for the soul out there who deeply needs spiritual succor. His confidence is that with the help this book can afford, even the sorely afflicted, the reader will find the true trust that fills the heart with the peace and solace that only God herself can provide.

James A. Sanders
Claremont, CA

Preface

TO MY KNOWLEDGE, THERE has not been a book written on the Psalms that deals solely with the genre of the songs of trust or psalms of confidence. The songs of trust are a sub-genre of the psalms of complaint or lament and there are roughly fourteen of them in the Psalter. Most scholars treat them within the broader genre of lament, although many psalms of complaint do have within them confessions of trust. But it is those psalms that are more brightly illumined in tone and mood by the dominant theme of trust which are commonly designated psalms of trust or songs of confidence.

These consist predominantly of affirmations of confidence and expressions of trust in YHWH, usually in the face of considerable troubles and severe adversity. These particular psalms are admittedly few in number in the Psalter. But their significance far outweighs their relatively small numbers. No two scholars agree completely on a specific list of psalms which are included in the genre of trust psalms but it is the dominance of the themes of trust and confidence that characterizes a particular psalm as warranting its classification as such. This book is not primarily focused on the genre of the psalms of trust although it does treat many of them. The book that treats solely the psalms of confidence genre is yet to be written.

I consider the following as fitting the genre of the psalms of confidence: Psalms 4, 11, 16, 23, 27, 46, 63, 73, 91, 115, 121, 125, and 139. Further, in my view, Psalms 90, 91, and 92, which open Book Four of the Psalter, are a literary unit and, when taken together, conform to the criteria of trust or confidence. Elements of thanksgiving and praise are evident, too, as well as notable didactic features. But the whole enterprise of form criticism—rewarding and instructive though it has been for Psalms studies over the past century—may be quite subjective and the lines of demarcation pertaining to particular psalm types ought not be drawn too finely. Strictly speaking, the entire book of Psalms is an ongoing dialog between Yahweh (יהוה) and the ancient people of Israel. It is in these pages where the voice of the people of God meets the voice of God; where the conversation has as its subject how life is to be lived this side of glory; when the very words spoken over and again instruct the faithful in the journey of faith.

Throughout I have chosen to use the Hebrew script for the sacred name YHWH, יהוה. The divine name is central to the book of Psalms, thematically and theologically, and therefore ought rightly be recognized and read as such. I have abandoned the Christian terms Old and New Testaments. Rather I choose to use the terms Hebrew Bible, Hebrew Scriptures and First Testament; and, the Second Testament and Christian Scriptures. I trust that these alterations may not prove too intrusive to the reader. In those places where I have used Hebrew and Greek script, an English translation is provided. Knowledge of Hebrew and Greek is not a prerequisite for reading this book.

Additionally, I have chosen to bracket the use of male pronouns such as *[he]*, *[him]*, *[his]* and *[himself]* and, frequently, the nouns *[man]* and *[men]* to show that, in fact, the usage of the language ought rightly embrace both male and female agency. This is not a perfect solution. However, it at least acknowledges the need for the use of an inclusive language model without resorting to the repetitious use of the word "God." There are other models out there which adopt a more drastic solution to a gender neutral rendering of the text (eg. The Saint Helena Psalter). I deem these models deficient in that they depart from the text by removing all references of the holy names of God in Hebrew, which are so central to the study of the Psalms. The repetitive use of the word "God" is in my view not at all helpful in seeking to achieve an inclusive model for a gender neutral text. The individual Hebrew Names for God are laden with rich theological meanings and nowhere moreso than in the book of Psalms.

Regarding the use of modern English versions of the Bible, I have relied on the New Revised Standard Version (NRSV), the Revised English Bible (REB), the Grail Psalter, and the Jewish Publication Society's Jewish Study Bible. Where no English version is indicated, I have supplied my own translation (LW). I have also used Mitchell Dahood's translation in certain few instances. I have distributed thirty Hebrew psalms, including three which lie outside the Psalter, throughout the text where I treat them as illustrative of having a particular relevance to the topic at hand. Nearly all of these psalms are my own translation. A few of them include the embellishment of paraphrase (e.g. 4, and 91).

I wish to acknowledge the good people of the Episcopal Church of the Advent, Sun City West, Az for their participation in a series of discussions on the Psalms which I led during the Lenten season of 2012. Also this book would never have seen the light of day were it not for the late Gerald Henry Wilson who encouraged me to put pen to paper in the days shortly before his untimely death. Additionally, I am indebted to my good friend Jim Sanders who perused the entire manuscript and offered valuable and helpful insights and suggestions along the way.

I also wish to extend my appreciation to the library staffs of the Claremont School of Theology Library, Claremont, CA, and the Hubbard Library, Fuller Theological Seminary, Pasadena, CA, for their help and assistance with the research part of this project. I was very fortunate to have these two excellent libraries at my disposal only separated by 30 miles of freeway—an easy commute. Finally, I dedicate this book, lovingly, to our family's three beautiful daughters. They are each gone now—far too soon, to be with the Good Shepherd, *"who on his shoulder gently lay, and home rejoicing brought them."*

+++

Merry Beth Davis October 09, 1963 – May 07, 1965

Cheryl Kay Weaver May 07, 1967 – November 13, 2005

Kimberly Noelle Weaver May 25, 1970 – October 07, 2006

+Pax Requiscant+

Lorne Edward Weaver,
Trinity Sunday, 2018
Upland, CA

Introduction

To OPEN THE BOOK of Psalms is to enter the world of God. To read the Psalms is to read the words of God and hear the words of the ancient people of Israel in response to this God who has graciously drawn them into an eternal covenant. The entire book of Psalms or, the Psalter, is one continuous conversation which ranges over many centuries–perhaps nearly a millennium-between the God of Israel and the people of Israel; or more accurately, the God of glory and this particular people who have been called to live life on the edge of glory as the people of God.

There is no mystery to this conversation. It is all an embroidery of grace. Specific words and phrases help us track the meaning of these 150 psalms down to our present day. It is this legacy—which is one of abiding trust—that mirrors a deep confidence in the *presence of YHWH* their God.[1] That is the subject of this book.

It would be an understatement to say that these particular poems emerged out of a longing and passionate faith. The many different poets of the Psalms were convinced that YHWH was their God and they belonged to the Just One. Through this poetic medium it became possible for ancient Israel to articulate its understanding and perceptions of the world that flowed from their long journey toward a realized monotheistic belief. These hymns and songs, complaints and laments, prayers and praises are compact verbal structures reflecting simplicity itself. But their message is anything but simple.

Hebrew psalms appear frequently in the guise of *cultic* [2] hymns and represent a common poetic genre that flourished throughout the ancient Near East in late

---

1. With the exception of the scriptural quotations and direct quotes from the works of others, I will be using the Hebrew script יהוה [Yahweh or YHWH] for the English, "LORD." The Hebrew language reads from right to left. An exact transliteration of the four consonants, or Tetragrammaton would be "HWHY." The pronunciation is only approximate. In ancient times, most scholars agree that it sounded something like Yah-way or, Yah-vay.

2. The term *cult (Ger. kultus)* as used here is an academic one. It refers to the "Sitz im Leben" or the real–life situation of a people–their corporate worshiping life, their rites and ceremonies and liturgical re-enactments as a faith community in the worship of their particular God. The "cultic life" of a people changes over time as that community wrestles with the practice of their belief system in new life situations. The use of the term *cult* here is to be distinguished from the more contemporary notion of *cult* that is usually understood negatively to connote the activities and secretive life of modern day separatist groups which are usually formed around a fanatical obeisance to a central autocratic

Bronze Age II, early Iron Age I. This genre and its forms were adopted by the Hebrew poets and became the instrument for expressing, in a collective voice, whether first person plural or singular, a radical new sense of time, space, history, and creation. Armed with the conviction that their God was the One and Only God of All, these poets and kings, singers and musicians, priests and teachers, braved the taunts and sarcastic affronts of their ancient neighbors and bet on the future and their life with יהוה. This psalmic character of individual and communal destiny found its greatest expression through these multiple liturgies that tracked their worship of יהוה and their celebrations of God's life with them, which were inextricably bound up in their common life.[3]

There is no question that the Psalter is preeminently the book of prayer and praise in the Hebrew scriptures.[4] Many of its songs, hymns, prayers, and laments have their setting in the cultic life of ancient Israel, which employed them daily in their individual and communal exercise of worship. We can seldom if ever be sure precisely what specific function each *psalm* [5] played in Israel's worship. This is a grievous loss to us. The Psalms are never the sole product of human ingenuity and genius. Rather, they reflect the particular modes of expression employed by all Israel in the various and manifold exigencies of their daily life and historical existence.

> *The book of Psalms is the Bible's book of the soul. In psalm after psalm, the human being turns directly to God, expressing his or her deepest thoughts and fears, asking for help or forgiveness, offering thanks for help already given. And so, for centuries and centuries, people have opened the book of Psalms in order to let its words speak on their behalf . . . These psalms–in fact, all the Psalms–open a direct line of communication between us and God. No wonder, then, that the pages of the book of Psalms tend to be the most worn and ragged in any worshiping family's Bible. And even Americans who know nothing else of Scripture often know Psalm 23 in the majestic language of the King James Version* [6]

---

personality. Modern examples abound.

3. cf. Muilenberg, *The Way of Israel.*

4. I will be using the terms "*Hebrew Bible,*" or "*Hebrew Scriptures,*" or, the "*First Testament*" rather than the Christian term, "Old *Testament.*" Some biblical scholars prefer the term, "*Tanakh*" (an acronym of the triadic parts of the Hebrew Bible: the Torah or Law or, Pentateuch; Nevi'im, or, Prophets; and the Ketuvim" or, The Writings; i.e. TaNaKh). Instead of using the term, "*New Testament*" I will make reference to the "*Christian Scriptures,*" or, the "*Second Testament.*" Such are my efforts to be respectful of both traditions although I am writing, of course, as a Christian.

5. Note: The word "psalm" is capitalized when referring to the book of Psalms or when it is followed by a number (e.g. Psalm 91); it is lower case in all other uses. The word "Psalter" is usually capitalized. cf. Weiser, *Psalms.* Old Testament Library. "The Psalter has been called 'the hymn-book of the Jewish Church', and that with some justification, for it contains various features that point to the cultic use of the psalms in the worship of the Temple and especially in the synagogue service in late Judaism." iv.

6. Kugel, *How to Read the Bible: A Guide to Scripture, Then and Now,* 459

In keeping with this complex and expressive purpose many of the psalms, upon closer scrutiny, prove to have a tensile and semantic structure that one would not expect from the conventionality of the Hebrew language. Israel, gathered, stood in the *presence* of יהוה her covenant-keeping LORD. It is יהוה who reigned as king on the royal throne of the ark, which was sequestered in the small asylum of the sanctuary. Israel had journeyed through the wilderness and the ark of יהוה would eventually come to rest in Solomon's temple at Jerusalem. Israel's early life was first of all characterized by pilgrimage and wandering. Her later sedentary life with the institution of the monarchy provided the historical context for the eventual development of her own inspired theology which achieved a fuller explication in her liturgical life and worshiping practices. The Psalter is the achievement of all Israel—over a period of about a thousand years—and its purpose is the praise and the glory of יהוה who is uniquely Israel's personal God.[7]

The Psalms represent the language of Israel's worship of יהוה. They are inexhaustible and they are timeless. They tell us how life is to be lived to its fullest-*shalom*. All statements about life are to be seen and understood in the primary context of Israel's Psalms, without losing sight of the fact that the Hebrew scriptures shared in the expressions and concepts of the religious world of the peoples around them. Life is a gift and a trust, like the land that was given in trust to God's people.

For those who are making an initial and serious inquiry into the Psalter, it is of fundamental importance to recognize this perspective at the outset: the psalms belong to a world which is no longer our world. But its themes and aspirations are as relevant to human life today as when they were first used in the worshiping life of Israel some thirty-three centuries removed from us.[8]

Although we can never fully understand much of that world, yet it is the book of Psalms that, unlike any other literature in the Bible, brings us into God's world. This is the world inhabited by יהוה and it is a soulful world full of wonder and awe. The particular world-view of the Hebrew poets is foreign to us, but their words still carry an amazing relevance which sometimes shocks our own postmodern sensibilities. This Hebraic *zeitgeist* reflected a wholesale affirmation of her life in God.

---

7. Miller, "Enthroned on the Praises of Israel," *Interpretation*. 39.1. (1985): 5-19. "To go through the Book of psalms is to be led increasingly toward the praise of God as the final word. While doxology *may* be the beginning word, it is clearly the final word. That is so *theologically*, because in praise more than any other human act God is seen and declared to be God in all fullness and glory. That is so *eschatologically*, because the last word of all is the confession and praise of God by the whole creation. And that is so *for the life of faith*, because praise more than any other act fully expresses utter devotion to God and the loss of self in extravagant exaltation of the transcendent Lord who is the ground of all." 8.

8. Anderson, *Out of the Depths*. ". . .the Psalter, though it received its final form three or four centuries before Christ, reflects a long history of worship, reaching back at least to the time of David and, in some instances, including forms of worship used by Israel in the early period of the settlement of the Land of Canaan. It may cover as much as a thousand years of the history of the worship of Yahweh." 13

But it clashes with the marketing, materialistic, militaristic world in which, most of the time, we have our being. Biblical poets use human speech metaphorically to portray a world in which God is related covenantly to a people, Israel, and through them to all peoples. It is a world in which our relation to God, whether in times of divine presence or apparent absence, is expressed creatively in this language of great power.[9]

The language of the Psalter does not contain abstract theological statements or anything approaching philosophical theology. What it does contain is some of the most erudite theological thinking and richness to emerge out of its deep sense of the knowledge of יהוה. This knowledge of God is rooted in relationship and the entire edifice is supported by the fact of the covenant. It elicits responses in prayer, praise and, frequently, laments or complaints which reflect the existential life situations of this people who have become, by the election of יהוה, the people of God. Israel's knowledge of יהוה is both a burden and a blessing. It defines the parameters of her long and historic relationship with and witnesses to the varied implications and meaning of that relationship.

No other literature in the Bible approaches the levels of intensity, pathos and promise as we find in the book of the Psalms. It tells us how life is to be lived this side of glory. It informs our spiritual formation, growth and maturity in faith. It teaches us life! G. W. Anderson enriches our introduction:

The Psalter is the supremely representative theological document of the Old Testament . . . and this book is, in its entirety, explicitly or by implication, confession. Its unity is not the formal unity of a carefully articulated statement, but the organic unity which is given to it by a worshiping community. Although it spans a considerable period in the life of that community, it does not present with any clarity the successive phases in the historical development of its religion, but gathers together those themes which were dominant throughout the development. It expresses them, not in some rarefied, quintessential abstraction of the faith of Israel, but in the prayers and praises in which, generation after generation, Israel confessed Yahweh, and in confessing [Him] encountered [Him].[10]

Some of the psalms have recognizable forms which help us to better understand the burden of their message and how we relate to them. Many of the individual psalms are heartfelt complaints which end in a reaffirmation of vows of trust. Some are songs

9. Anderson, Ibid, 9.

Prothero, The *Psalms in Human Life*. . . ."it [the Psalms] is presented as the anatomy of all parts of the human soul; in it, as Heine says, are collected 'sunrise and sunset, birth and death, promise and fulfillment—the whole drama of humanity.'" i.

10. Anderson, "Israel's Creed: Sung, Not Signed," *Scottish Journal of Theology* 16 (1963) 283. Note: The oft used masculine pronouns will be bracketed [ ] to indicate the embrace of both feminine and masculine agencies.

of pilgrims approaching the temple; some concern the bellicose utterances of warfare; some are hymns to creation; some are prayers of repentance; some are songs addressed to the king and others perhaps composed by the king. Not infrequently, the psalms seem disjointed to our literary sensibilities. To a very large extent this problem disappears when we view them as litanies of spontaneous prayer in which a limited number of themes are constantly repeated. What I am referring to here is a sense of the reader of the Psalter engaging a text that does not always seem inviting to modern ears. But once we have come to appreciate these select themes, it is not difficult to see how together they make up a coherent confession of faith.

This is confirmed by a small but invaluable publication by Jean-Pierre Prevost, in which he explains the significance of some forty key words that constitute the essential prayer vocabulary of the Psalter. *"Throughout the entirety of the psalms there is a great deal of repetition. The prayer vocabulary . . . is not extensive; the same words are used over and over again . . . They are the essence of the prayer, which lies in the relationship they presuppose and are there to deepen."* [11]

To enter the world of these psalms we must first appreciate the cultural milieu in which Israel's relationship with יהוה found expression. It is a world that is far removed from our experience. Its ideals are not abstractions, but rather reflect the realities of a *"concrete immediacy."* The conflict, bloodshed and oppression frequently referred to are not the products of metaphorical imagination, but the stuff of everyday experience. The Psalter is vibrant and alive because it is rooted in human and historical experiences of life.

The *rock*, for instance, is often spoken of—*"I love you, יהוה. . . my strength. יהוה is my crag, my fortress, my champion, my God, my rock, in whom I find shelter, my shield and sure defender, my strong tower"* (Ps 18:1, 2, REB). It is not a monument or a scenic tourist attraction but rather a riveting metaphor for Israel's personal God, *the Rock*. Note that the term *rock* occurs within a parade of metaphors that speak of refuge and strength, defense and shelter. These are recurring themes, all of which we will encounter over and over again in the pages just ahead.

The themes which the poet of Psalm 18 repeats make up the coherent confession of the faith of old Israel. The significance of this confession is not in its theological subtlety or inventiveness but in the daring with which it affirms the reality and practical implications of Israel's relationship with יהוה. This relationship is trusting, personal, and intimate. Such is the passionate trust that is characterized by the poets, again and again throughout the Psalter, in their efforts to articulate

---

11. Prevost, *A Short Dictionary of the Psalms,* 19.

cf. Tate, Psalms 51-100, Vol 20. "The psalm is intended for instruction and exhortation and is designed to challenge and strengthen the faith of those who trust in Yahweh." 450.

cf. Barth, *Introduction to the Psalms.* ". . . the common basis of all the psalms is a constant, total and exclusive trust in the God of Israel." 56.

cf. Muilenburg, Ibid, "In the Psalter, we listen to the way of Israel's speaking in the presence of the Holy One." 110.

clearly what it means to be in love with יהוה who is their Deliverer, their Salvation, their Refuge, their Redeemer![12]

The following section addresses fifteen broad contours that are reflected throughout the Psalter. The citing of these verses which are taken from many psalms provides a scriptural context for the remainder of this book. In order to immediately saturate the reader in the Psalms, and to enable the reader to read and hear them as sacred scripture, the reader is encouraged to patiently and quietly read the following section–uninterrupted if possible.

12. Murphy, "The Faith of the Psalmist," *Interpretation* 43.3 (1980): 229-39. "No one approaches the Psalter today without the recognition of two fundamental characteristics of these prayers . . .that the original locus or setting of these prayers is the temple liturgy, . . .and that the prayers that have been preserved in the Psalter are best appropriated by recognizing the various literary genres (hymns, laments, thanksgiving) which govern their structure and motifs." 230.

Irrepressible Gifts

IT IS SURELY ANCIENT Israel's daring trust and concrete realism that make it possible for the Christian church to affirm the Psalms as an essential part of its own confession, even as it celebrates the fulfillment of Israel's hopes. But in this book it is our intention to let the individual psalms speak for themselves and to pay close attention particularly to their uniquely Hebrew perspective. What are some of the themes related to trust that Israel so often celebrated? This section provides some fifteen examples of these celebratory, prayerful, and reflective tones. Each connotes a vibrant trust and confidence in יהוה and helps us to understand the vital burden of the message of the ancient poets. [1]

First, and central to Israel's confession, is the Psalms' witness to faith in the relationship-faith in the living God who has entered into covenant with Israel. *Magnalia Dei*, the great deeds God has done on Israel's behalf, in history, in deliverance, are constantly being recalled as the restorative acts of יהוה.

I will call to mind the deeds of יהוה and recall your wonderful acts of old . . . You are a God who works miracles; you have shown the nations your power. With your strong arm you rescued your people, the descendants of Jacob and Joseph (Ps 77:11,14, 15); When יהוה restores [his] people's fortunes, let Jacob rejoice, let Israel be glad (Ps 14:7); The coming generation will be told of יהוה; they will make known [his] righteous deeds, declaring to a people yet unborn: 'יהוה has acted!' (Ps 22:31); I shall exalt you, יהוה; you have lifted me up and have not let my enemies be jubilant over me (Ps 30:1); How great is your goodness, stored up for those who fear you (Ps 31:19); יהוה, your unfailing love reaches to the heavens, your faithfulness to the skies. Your righteousness is like the lofty mountains, your justice like the great deep (Ps 36:5, 6).

Israel rejoices in the praise of יהוה as practically expressed in her history. For Israel, God was active throughout their history and acted in their history by extraordinary saving events. The mighty deeds of יהוה were continually being celebrated. Their core experience as a people was the deliverance from slavery and oppression in Egypt.

---

1. The following biblical citations are taken from the REB, The Revised English Bible (1992). I have inserted the Hebrew script יהוה for "LORD." I am particularly indebted to William P. Brown, *Seeing the Psalms: A Theology of Metaphor* (2002) for the arrangement and discourse of some of the themes treated in this section.

These historic acts lie at the root of all praise, thanksgiving, and gratitude.[2] All praise and glory are always being addressed to the sacred name of יהוה.

Praise יהוה. *It is good to give thanks to* יהוה *for [his] love endures forever. Who can tell of the mighty acts of* יהוה *and make [his] praises heard? Happy are they who act justly, who do what is right at all times!* (Ps 106:1–3); *We have heard for ourselves, God, our forefathers have told us what deeds you did in their time* (Ps 44:1); *How awesome is* יהוה *Most High, great king over all the earth! [He] subdues nations under us, peoples under our feet; [he] chooses for us our heritage, the pride of Jacob whom [he] loves* (Ps 47:2–4); *Let all the earth acclaim God. Sing to the glory of [his] name, make [his] praise glorious* (Ps 66:1,2); *Awesome is God in your sanctuary; [he] is Israel's God. [He] gives might and power to [his] people. Praise be to God* (Ps 68:35).

Second, there are several primary attributes of יהוה that are particularly prized by the poets. Among these are God's compassion, God's love, and God's goodness. An overarching emphasis is on the graciousness of יהוה. The poets write of these attributes unerringly and with a directness and relentlessness that confront the serious reader full force. It is a worthwhile exercise to sit quietly and read this litany of love. As a preamble, Psalm 146:2 states: *As long as I live I shall praise* יהוה. *I shall sing psalms to my God all my life long.* This poet knows what [she/he] is talking about!

There is a transformational quality to the following psalms that, at once, serves to embrace and enfold the reader. This section (Books One to Five) is divided according to the traditional five books of the Psalter. This division gives a certain order and accessibility to these extraordinary themes of love, goodness and compassion. That יהוה is a personal, caring and involved God is the foundation of Israel's covenant relationship. יהוה is invested in Israel's life! I will be explaining later on in the book just why the Psalter is considered a collection of collections and how it is that the Psalms—as a book—is best understood as having an edited Introduction (Pss 1–2) and a summary Benediction (Pss 146–150) both of which cohere thematically to the overall book of Psalms and whose basic movement is from lament to praise.

Introduction (Pss 1–2)

Happy are all who take refuge in [יהוה] (Ps 2:11);

---

2. Note: I choose the terms *history, historic* and *historicity,* when referring to the Bible, very cautiously. The Bible is not essentially a book of history though it does tell the story of salvation by יהוה assuming a human historical context. For instance, when Israel rejoices in Yahweh's intervention in the event of the Exodus, the writers are relying on the memory of Yahweh's objective action in history *as it is remembered* by Israel's story-tellers. The Exodus story of her deliverance is recounted down to the present day and marks the *regenerative continuance* of Israel's own unique experience of God's mighty acts, retold in history, in time, from generation to generation. cf. Walter Brueggemann in *Abiding Astonishment,* writes: "Israel's normative response to Yahweh's rescuing fidelity is one of praise and gratitude. Gratitude (*hodu*) sets the parameters of Israel's life with God, and there is in Israel a great deal for which to be grateful. Gratitude stands at the beginning and the end of Israel's life." 18

Book One (Pss 3–40)

Return, יהוה, deliver me; save me, for your love is steadfast (Ps 6:4);

. . . for the king puts his trust in יהוה; the loving care of the Most High keeps him unshaken (Ps 21:7);

Goodness and love unfailing will follow me all the days of my life (Ps 23:6);

All the paths of יהוה, are loving and sure (Ps 25:10);

Well I know that I shall see the goodness of יהוה, in the land of the living (Ps 27:13);

Blessed be יהוה, whose unfailing love for me was wonderful (Ps 31:21);

*. . . the earth is filled with the unfailing love of יהוה, (*Ps 33:5);

יהוה, who saves both [man] and beast, how precious is your unfailing love! (Ps 36:7);

It is יהוה who directs a person's steps; [he] holds [him] firm and approves of [his] conduct (Ps 37:21);

You, יהוה, will not withhold your tender care for me; may your love and truth forever guard me (Ps 40:11);

Book Two (Pss 41–72)

By day יהוה, grants [his] unfailing love; at night [his] praise is on my lips, a prayer to the God of my life (Ps 42:8);

Arise and come to our aid; for your love's sake deliver us (Ps 44:26);

God, within your temple we meditate on your steadfast love (Ps 46:9);

. . . [he] chooses for us our heritage, the pride of Jacob whom [he] loves (Ps 47:4);

God, be gracious to me in your faithful love; in the fullness of your mercy blot out my misdeeds (Ps 51:1);

For I trust in God's faithful love for ever and ever (Ps 52:8);

May God send [his] love, unfailing and sure (Ps 57:3);

My God, in [his] unfailing love, will go before me; (Ps 59:10);

'Power belongs to God' and 'Unfailing love is yours, Lord' (Ps 62:12);

Your unfailing love is better than life; (Ps 63:3);

Blessed is God who has not withdrawn from me [his] love and care (Ps 66:20);

Book Three (Pss 73-89)

Assuredly God is good to the upright, to those who are pure in heart (Ps 73:1);

Has God forgotten to be gracious? Has [he] in anger withheld [his] compassion (Ps 77:9);

יהוה*, show us your love and grant us your deliverance* (Ps 85:7);

Lord, you are kind and forgiving, full of love towards all who cry to you (Ps 86:5);

But you, Lord, our God, are compassionate and gracious (Ps 86:15);

The source of all good is in you. (Ps 87:7);

I shall sing always of the loving deeds of יהוה*; I said: "Your love will stand firm forever;"* (Ps 89:1,2);

Book Four (Pss 90-106)

*[*יהוה *speaks]:'Because his love holds fast to me, I shall deliver him'* (Ps 91:14);

It is good to give thanks to יהוה*, to declare your love in the morning and your faithfulness every night* (Ps 92:2);

If I said that my foot was slipping, your love, יהוה*, continued to hold me up* (Ps 94:18);

יהוה *loves those who hate evil; [he] keeps [his] loyal servants safe* (Ps 97:10);

יהוה *has remembered [his] love for Jacob, [his] faithfulness towards the house of Israel* (Ps 98:3);

יהוה *is good and [his] love is everlasting* (Ps 100:5);

As the heavens tower high above the earth, so outstanding is [his] love towards those who fear [him] (Ps 103: 11);

It is good to give thanks to יהוה*, for [his] love endures forever* (Ps 106:1);

Book Five (Pss 107-145)

Let them give thanks to יהוה *for [his] love* (Ps 107:8, 15, 21, 31,);

Help me, יהוה*, my God; save me by your love* (Ps 109:26);

יהוה *is gracious and compassionate* (Ps 111:4);

Not to us, יהוה, not to us, but to your name give glory for your love, for your faithfulness! (Ps 115:1);

Gracious is יהוה and righteous; our God is full of compassion (Ps 116:5);

Praise יהוה, all the nations, extol [him], all you peoples; for [his] love protecting us is strong, the faithfulness of יהוה is everlasting. Praise יהוה (Ps 117);

Let your love comfort me, as you have promised me, your servant (Ps 119:76);

In your love hear me, and give me life, יהוה, by your decree (Ps 119:149);

For in יהוה is love unfailing, and great is [his] power to save (Ps 130:7);

It is good to give thanks to יהוה, for [his] love endures forever (Ps 136 = the entire psalm);

For your love and faithfulness, I shall praise your name; your love endures forever, יהוה (Ps 138:2, 8);

In the morning let me know of your love, for I put my trust in you (Ps 143:8);

יהוה is gracious and compassionate, long-suffering and ever faithful. יהוה is good to all; [his] compassion rests upon all [his] creatures (Ps 145: 8,9).

Concluding Benediction (Pss 146–150)

יהוה does not delight in the strength of a horse and takes no pleasure in a runner's fleetness; [his] pleasure is in those who fear [him], who wait for [his] steadfast love (Ps 147:10, 11).

Three, the God who intervened in Israel's history is praised as the guarantor of the weak. The covenantal demands instruct Israel in the ways of God and the Psalms confess יהוה, their God, to be eternally on the side of the oppressed–*Though you would frustrate the counsel of the poor, יהוה is their refuge. If only deliverance for Israel might come from Zion! When יהוה restores [his] people's fortunes, let Jacob rejoice, let Israel be glad* (Ps 14:6–8);

יהוה is exalted, yet cares for the lowly and from afar [he] takes note of the proud . . . יהוה will accomplish [his] purpose for me. Your love endures forever, יהוה; do not abandon what you have made (Ps 138:6,8).

This confidence in God's covenant faithfulness is often remarkably intimate–*As the eyes of the slaves follow their master's hand or the eyes of a slave-girl the hand of her mistress, so our eyes are turned to יהוה our God, awaiting [his] favour* (Ps 123:2); *יהוה is my shepherd . . . goodness and mercy unfailing will follow me all the days of my life* (Ps 23);

Guard me as the apple of your eye; hide me in the shadow of your wings (Ps 17:8).

Four, the love so often proclaimed in the Psalms is the practical faithfulness of יהוה in the covenant relationship. Through her covenant with יהוה, Israel finds herself caught up in the great redemptive plan of God and its boundless expectations. When one considers the harsh exclusiveness—which was to become Israel's greatest temptation–even as it remains ours today, it is utterly remarkable how frequently the Psalms speak of God's plan as embracing all peoples– *Let all the ends of the earth remember and turn to* יהוה; *let all the families of the nations bow before [him]. For kingly power belongs to* יהוה ; *dominion over the nations is [his]* (Ps 22:27);

> *Of Zion it will be said, 'this one and that one were born there.' The Most High [himself] establishes her.* יהוה *will record in the register of the peoples: 'this one was born there'* (Ps 87:5,6).

As Israel's faith developed and matured, the unique power and authority of the God of the covenant and of the nations comes to be celebrated as the Creator of the universe–the One God of All.[3] Many times, as a consequence, the Psalms celebrate the Creator's greatness as manifest in the power and wonder of the material universe. At the word of the Creator all things came to be. *The heavens are yours, the earth yours also; you founded the world and all that is in it* (Ps 89:11); *Before the mountains were brought forth, or the earth and the world were born, from age to age you are God.* (Ps 90:2);

> *When I look at your heavens, the work of your fingers, at the moon and the stars you have set in place, what is a frail mortal, that you should be mindful of [him], a human being, that you should take notice of [him]?* (Ps 8:3,4);

> *The heavens tell out the glory of God, heaven's vault makes known [his] handiwork* (Ps 19:1);

> *The word of* יהוה *created the heavens; all the host of heaven was formed at [his] command. [He] gathered into a heap the waters of the sea, [he] laid up the deeps in [his] store-chambers* (Ps 33:6,7);

> *Long ago you laid earth's foundations, and the heavens were your handiwork. They will pass away, but you remain* (Ps 102:25).

One of the more complementary features of the Psalter is the way in which it speaks of Israel's experience in the on-going drama of the covenant relationship. The Psalms are an unconscious disclosure of how Hebrew faith understood the human condition. We could describe this awareness as a personalism of concrete immediacy. Its ideals are not mere abstractions. It has no concept of immateriality. Transcendence is known in the incomparable otherness of the divine. In some mysterious way this

---

3. Harkness, *The Providence of God.* "God remains Lord of all that [He] has made. This is stated with marvelous beauty and power in the nature poetry of the Psalms, but it is implied throughout the whole Bible . . . and this is basic to our own understanding of God's wonderful works . . . the biblical writers were not tempted to devise ideas of a deistic intervention . . . they saw the immanent *presence* of the transcendent God throughout [His] world." 159.

divine greatness is shared intimately through the awareness of the covenant and the presence of יהוה in temple worship—*By day יהוה grants [his] unfailing love; at night [his] praise is upon my lips, a prayer to the God of my life* (Ps 42:8);

> *Send out your light and your truth to be my guide; let them lead me to your holy hill, to your dwelling-place* (Ps 43:3);

> *Happy are those who dwell in your house; they never cease to praise you* (Ps 84:4);

> *Let me hear the words of God–יהוה; [he] proclaims peace to [his] people* (Ps 85:8);

> *יהוה, teach me your way, that I may walk in your truth. Let me worship your name with an undivided heart* (Ps 86:11).

Five, the power of the personalism of the Psalms may be described as visceral. The whole person is involved, bodily, in the drama of personal existence. For example, this is reflected in two terms frequently occurring in our versions, heart and soul. Beyond its purely physical association with strong emotions, the heart (לב *leb*) designates the interior mystery of the person where intentions, decisions, feelings and speech take form; where the human person experiences the *presence* of God who knows her or him profoundly and gives support throughout life.[4]

> *Examine me, God, and know my mind; test me, and understand my anxious thoughts. Watch lest I follow any path that grieves you; lead me in the everlasting way* (Ps 139:23);

> *The precepts of יהוה are right and give joy to the heart. The commandment of יהוה is pure and gives light to the eyes. The fear of יהוה is unsullied; it abides forever* (Ps 19:8,9);

> *'Come,' 'my heart has said, 'seek [his] presence.' I seek your presence, יהוה* (Ps 27:8);

> *My heart is steadfast, God, my heart is steadfast. I will sing and raise a psalm* (Ps 57:7).

Soul (נפשי *nephesh*) refers to the innermost, volitional being of a person where conscious decisions and choices are made. In Hebrew it is the noun that refers bodily to the gullet or the neck. Like heart, its significance expands to refer to more than bodily hunger, thirst and taste; it stands in sharp relief to the human being in a situation of want and necessity as a desiring being-*How long must I suffer anguish in my soul, grief in my heart day after day?* (Ps 13:2);

---

4. Eaton, *The Psalms: A Spiritual and Historical Commentary,* "The faithful person turns to prayer and also witnesses to the good way, where there is awe of God, turning from sin, stillness and meditation, worship that finds and holds to God, and above all, trust in [him]. In such trust the psalmist concludes, confident that the Lord in [his] own time will fill the heart again with rejoicing, and make [his] peace known in every danger." 72.

The law of יהוה is perfect and revives the soul (Ps 19:7);

As I pour out my soul in distress, I call to mind how I marched in the ranks of the great to God's house (Ps 42:4);

God, you are my God; I seek you eagerly with a heart that thirsts for you and a body wasted with longing for you (Ps 63:1);

I pine and faint with longing for the courts of the temple of יהוה; my whole being cries out with joy to the living God (Ps 84:2);

Bless יהוה, my soul; with all my being I bless [his] holy name. Bless יהוה, my soul (Ps 103:1,2);

For the poets, the eyes also are closely associated with the movements of the heart.—*My strength, I look to you; for God is my strong tower. My God, in [his] unfailing love, will go before me (Ps 59:9, 10);*

Come, see what יהוה has done, the astounding deeds [he] has wrought on earth (Ps 46:8);

My eyes are worn out with waiting for my God (Ps 69:3);

Look to יהוה and be strong; at all times seek [his] presence (Ps 105:4);

Turn my eyes away from all that is futile; grant me life by your word (Ps 119:37);

I lift up my eyes to the hills; from where is my help to come? My help comes from יהוה, the Maker of heaven and earth (Ps 121:1);

יהוה, my heart is not proud, nor are my eyes haughty (Ps 131:1);

But my eyes are fixed on you, יהוה God; you are my refuge; do not leave me unprotected (Ps 141:8);

I will not give sleep to my eyes or slumber to my eyelids, until I find a place for יהוה, a dwelling for the Mighty One of Jacob (Ps 132:4, 5);

I lift up my eyes to you whose throne is in heaven (Ps 123:1);

My eyes are ever on יהוה, who alone can free my feet from the net (Ps 25:15).

Six. The Psalms' personalism of *concrete immediacy* is frequently expressed in a narrative form which captures the drama of the poets' present moment within the totality of their on-going story. Vivid images abound. Human life is the walking of paths, but only one path is secure and therefore desirable; the path of יהוה—*You will show me the path of life; In your presence is the fullness of joy, at your right hand are pleasures for evermore (Ps 16:11);*

My steps have held steadily to your paths; my feet have not faltered (Ps 17:5);

What god is there but יהוה? What rock but our God? It is God who girds me with strength and makes my way free from blame, who makes me swift as a hind and sets me secure on the heights (Ps 18:31,32);

יהוה revives my spirit; for [his] name's sake [he] guides me in the right paths (Ps 23:3);

Teach me your way, יהוה; . . . lead me by a level path (Ps 27:11);

Whoever fears יהוה will be shown the path he should choose (Ps 25:12);

It is יהוה who directs a person's steps; [he] holds firm and approves of [his] conduct. Though [he] mayfall, [he] will not go headlong, for יהוה grasps [him] by the hand (Ps 37:23, 24);

For you have rescued me from death and my feet from stumbling, to walk in the presence of God, in the light of life (Ps 56:13);

I have chosen the path of faithfulness; I have set your decrees before me (Ps 119:30);

יהוה, teach me your way, that I may walk in your truth (Ps 86:11);

When my spirit is faint within me, you are there to watch over my steps (Ps 142:3).

God is a very real companion and stronghold, a high tower and refuge to the poets.[5] This is a recurring theme in the Psalms and is especially appropriated in the psalms of trust– *But let all who take refuge in you rejoice, let them forever shout for joy* (Ps 5:11);

יהוה my God, in you I find refuge (Ps 7:1);

May יהוה be a tower of strength for the oppressed, a tower of strength in time of trouble (Ps 9:9);

Keep me, O God, for in you have I found refuge (Ps 16:1);

יהוה is my shepherd: I lack for nothing (Ps 23:1);

יהוה is my light and my salvation; whom should I fear? יהוה is the stronghold of my life; of whom then should I go in dread? (Ps 27:1);

In you, יהוה, I have found refuge; let me never be put to shame (Ps 31:1);

Taste and see that יהוה is good. Happy are they who find refuge in him! (Ps 34:8);

---

5. Brown, *Seeing the Psalms*, ". . . the metaphor of 'refuge' bears not only salvific weight, namely, blessing and protection, but also moral import. God's refuge constitutes both home and destiny for the righteous, and *seeking* refuge connotes trust in and allegiance to YHWH to the exclusion of things that do not warrant ultimate reliance, from idols to riches" 31. Note: The term occurs in the Introduction to the Psalter (Ps 2:12b) and signals its recurring prominence in what is to follow: "*Happy are all who find refuge in יהוה (him)*" 75. cf. Jerome F. D. Creach, *Yahweh as Refuge and the Editing of the Hebrew Psalter.*

Deliverance for the righteous comes from יהוה, their refuge in time of trouble (Ps 37:39);

יהוה will save him in time of trouble; יהוה protects him and gives him life (Ps 41:1,2);

God is our refuge and our stronghold, a timely help in trouble (Ps 46:1);

The mountain of Zion. . .is the city of the great king. God in her palaces is revealed as a tower of strength (Ps 48:2,3);

God has rescued me from every trouble (Ps 54:7);

I shall raise a psalm to you, my strength; for God is my strong tower. [He] is my gracious God (Ps 59:7);

I am safe in the shadow of your wings. I follow you closely and your right hand upholds me (Ps 63:8);

With יהוה on my side, as my helper, I shall see the downfall of my enemies (Ps 118:7);

God, be gracious to me; be gracious, for I have made you my refuge. I shall seek refuge in the shadow of your wings until the storms are past (Ps 57:1);

But יהוה has been my strong tower, and my God is my rock and my refuge (Ps 94:22).

Seven, there are remarkable notes of intimacy with which Israel addresses her God. They speak too in the language of the formidable and address God in wondrous titles. יהוה is addressed as:

The Praise of Israel: *You, the Praise of Israel, are enthroned in the sanctuary* (Ps 22:3);

The Shepherd of Israel: *Hear us, Shepherd of Israel, leading Joseph like a flock* (Ps 80:1);

The Holy One of Israel: *. . . on the lyre I shall sing to you, the Holy One of Israel* (Ps 71:22);

Again and again they tried God's patience and provoked the Holy One of Israel (78:41);

To יהוה belongs our shield, to the Holy One of Israel our king (89:18).

Israel's God: *But you, Lord God of Hosts, Israel's God . . .* (59:5);

Awesome is God in your sanctuary; [he] is Israel's God (68:35);

God of Israel, let none who seek you be humiliated through me (Ps 69:6);

Blessed be the Lord God, the God of Israel (Ps 72:18;);

Blessed be יהוה *the God of Israel, from everlasting to everlasting (Ps 106:48).*

Israel's hiding-place and shield: *But you,* יהוה, *are a shield to cover me (Ps 3:3);*

For you, יהוה, *will bless the righteous; you will surround them with favour as with a shield (Ps 5:12);*

I rely on God to shield me; he saves the honest of heart (Ps 7:10);

Guard me like the apple of your eye; hide me in the shadow of your wings (Ps 17:8);

the word of יהוה *has stood the test; [he] is a shield to all who take refuge in [him] (Ps 18:30);*

יהוה *is my strength and my shield; in* יהוה *my heart trusts (Ps 28:7);*

. . . you are a hiding-place for me in distress; you guard me and enfold me in salvation (Ps 32:7);

You will hide me under the cover of your presence (Ps 31:20);

O Lord, my shield (Ps 59:11);

In your tent I shall make my home forever and find shelter under the cover of your wings (Ps 61:4);

To יהוה *belongs our shield (Ps 89:18);*

You have made the Most High your dwelling-place (Ps 91:9);

Those who fear יהוה *trust in* יהוה: *. . . [he] is their help and their shield (Ps 115:9–11);*

יהוה *God, my strong deliverer, you shield me on the day of battle (Ps 140:7);*

Blessed be יהוה, *my rock, . . . my shield in whom I trust (Ps 144:2).*

Israel's rock:[6] *God only is my rock of deliverance, my strong tower, so that I stand unshaken (Ps 62:2);*

יהוה *lives! Blessed is my rock! High above all is God, my safe refuge (Ps 18:46);*

To You, יהוה, *I call; my Rock, do not be deaf to my cry (Ps 28:1);*

Be to me a rock of refuge, a stronghold to keep me safe. You are my rock and my stronghold (Ps 31:2,3);

God only is my rock of deliverance, my strong tower, so that I stand unshaken (Ps 62:2);

---

6. Israel's poets characterize the solidity of faith and trust in יהוה as the "rock." It is a metaphor both of prominence and eminence.

Do not vaunt yourself against heaven or speak arrogantly against the Rock (Ps 75:5);

God is the rock of my heart (Ps 73:26);

יהוה *is upright; he is my rock, and there is no unrighteousness in him* (Ps 92:15).

Blessed be יהוה, *my rock, who trains my hands for battle* (Ps 144:1).

יהוה **God of Hosts:** יהוה *of Hosts, [he] is the king of glory* (Ps 24:10);

יהוה *of Hosts is with us* (Ps 46:11);

יהוה *God of Hosts, Israel's God, arouse yourself to come to me and keep watch* (Ps 59:4);

יהוה *God of Hosts, how long will you fume at your people's prayer?* (Ps 80:4);

יהוה *God of Hosts, let none of those who hope in you be discouraged* (Ps 69:6);

יהוה *God of Hosts, restore us, and make your face shine on us, that we may be saved* (Ps 80:7; 19);

יהוה *of Hosts, how dearly loved is your dwelling-place* (Ps 84:1);

יהוה *God of Hosts, hear my prayer* (Ps 84:8);

יהוה *God of Hosts, who is like you? Your strength and faithfulness are all around you* (Ps 89:8);

The Most High: *I shall rejoice and exult in you, the Most High* (Ps 9:2);

Yet they provoked and defied God Most High (Ps 78:56);

. . . all sons of the Most High (Ps 82:6);

I put my trust in you, the Most High (Ps 56:3);

I shall call to God Most High (Ps 57:2);

Does the Most High know or care? (Ps 73:11);

Has the right hand of the Most High changed? (Ps 77:10);

The Most High establishes her (Ps 87:5);

[He] who lives in the shelter of the Most High . . . (Ps 91:1);

You have made the Most High your dwelling-place (Ps 91:9);

It is good to give thanks to יהוה, *to sing praises to your name, O Most High* (Ps 92:1).

The God of Jacob: *May the name of Jacob's God be your tower of strength* (Ps 20:1);

. . . such is the fortune of those who seek [him], who seek the presence of the God of Jacob (Ps 24:6);

. . . the God of Jacob is our fortress (Ps 46:11);

Sing out in praise of God our refuge, acclaim the God of Jacob (Ps 81:1);

God of Jacob, listen . . . (Ps 84:8);

Earth, dance at the presence of the Lord, at the presence of the God of Jacob (Ps 114:7);

. . . a dwelling for the Mighty One of Jacob (Ps 132:2);

Happy is he whose helper is the God of Jacob (Ps 146:5).

יהוה my God: *יהוה my God, in you I find refuge; (Ps 7:1);*

Look now, יהוה my God, and answer me (Ps 13:3);

יהוה my God, to you I lift my heart (Ps 25:1);

But in you, י׳, I put my trust; I say, 'You are my God.' (Ps 31:14);

Judge me, יהוה my God, as you are righteous (Ps 35:24);

On you, יהוה, I fix my hope; you, יהוה my God, will answer (Ps 38:15);

יהוה my God, great things you have done (Ps 40:5);

יהוה , my God, by day I call for help, by night I cry aloud in your presence (Ps 88:1);

יהוה has been my strong tower, and my God is my rock and refuge (Ps 94:22);

יהוה my God, you are very great (Ps 104:1);

You, יהוה my God, deal with me as befits your honour (Ps 109:21);

Help me, יהוה my God; save me by your love (Ps 109:26);

I say to יהוה, 'You are my God (Ps 140:6).

Eight, since there is not an actual Hebrew word for the *presence* (of God), the poets speak anthropomorphically of "the face" (לפניך *lepanim*) of יהוה; they speak too in potent images and language concerning the nearness and dearness, and the grandeur and intimacy of יהוה. When the poets are in trouble, they persist in the conviction that the *presence* of יהוה is ever near—as before the face or in the the *presence* of יהוה; to dwell in the *presence* of God is the singularly longed for experience of the one who hungers after a life of friendship with God. It is, for Israel, the highest good.[7]

7. Murphy, "The Faith of the Psalmist: 229–39 "It is indeed remarkable, and one marvels at the ability of the psalmists to repeat, *without* monotony, . . .This was possible because theology was not locked into an abstract system but found expression in images and metaphors—drawn from daily experience—without which prayer must remain quite jejune indeed." 231, 32.

Let the light of your face shine on us, יהוה (Ps 4:6);

For יהוה *is just and loves just dealing; [his] face is turned towards the upright* (Ps 11:7);

[He] asked of you life, and you gave it to [him], . . . for you bestow everlasting blessings on [him], and make [him] glad with the joy of your presence (Ps 21:4, 6);

For יהוה *is just and loves just dealing; [his] face is turned towards the upright* (Ps 11:7);

יהוה *has not scorned [him] who is downtrodden, . . . nor hidden [his] face from [him]* (Ps 22:24);

'Come,' my heart has said, 'seek [his] presence.' I seek your presence, יהוה (Ps 27:8);

How long, יהוה, *will you leave me forgotten; how long will you hide your face from me?* (Ps 13:1,2);

I thirst for God, the living God; when shall I come to appear before [his] presence? (Ps 42:2);

Do not drive me from your presence or take your holy spirit from me (Ps 51:11);

May God be gracious to us and bless us, may [he] cause [his] face to shine on us (Ps 67:1);

Do not hide your face from me, your servant; answer me without delay, for I am in dire straits (Ps 69:17);

You are awesome, Lord; . . . who can stand in your presence? (Ps 76:7);

God of Hosts, restore us, and make your face shine on us, that we may be saved (Ps 80:3,7, 19);

Worship יהוה *in gladness; enter [his] presence with joyful songs* (Ps 100:2);

יהוה, *hear my prayer and let my cry for help come to you. Do not hide your face from me when I am in dire straits* (Ps 102:1,2);

Look to יהוה *and be strong; at all times seek [his] presence* (Ps 105:4);

Earth, dance at the presence of the Lord, at the presence of the God of Jacob (Ps 114:7);

Let your face shine on your servant and teach me your statutes (Ps 119:135);

Where can I escape from your spirit, where flee from your presence? (Ps 139:7);

Do not hide your face from me or I shall be like those who go down to the abyss (Ps 143: 7).

Nine, it is moving to reflect on how this astounding confidence and trust of which we are speaking co-exists with a tragic realism. The psalmists are profoundly aware of the precariousness and transience of human existence. The parameters of human life and existence are strikingly apparent when the poets speak of human mortality–which they do often. Here are but a few examples–

All our days pass under your wrath; our years die away like a murmur (Ps 90:9);

I know you have made my days a mere span long, and my whole life is as nothing in your sight. A human being, however firm [he] stands, is but a puff of wind (Ps 39:5).

[He] remembered that they were but mortal, a breath of air which passes by and does not return (Ps 78:39);

Remember how fleeting is our life! Have you created all [mankind] to no purpose? (Ps 89:47).

And the endless blackness of death's pit is never far away—

What profit is there in my death, is my going down to the pit? Can the dust praise you? Can it proclaim your truth? (Ps 30:9);

Will it be for the dead you work wonders? Or can the shades rise up and give you praise? Will they speak in the grave of your love, of your faithfulness in the tomb? (Ps 88: 10, 11);

Who can live and not see death? Who can save [himself] from the power of Sheol? (Ps 89:49).

Even so, confidence in יהוה is so remarkably expressive that commentators are often uncertain whether some of these psalms are looking forward to something more than simply knowing the joy of God's *presence* in the temple worship. They take us to the threshold of the Christian gospel when they insist–

For you will not abandon me to Sheol or suffer your faithful one to see the pit (Ps 16:10);

For you have rescued me from death and my feet from stumbling, to walk in the presence of God, in the light of life (Ps 56:13);

But God will ransom my life and take me from the power of Sheol (Ps 49:15);

Yet I am always with you; you hold my right hand. You guide me by your counsel and afterwards you will receive me in/to/with glory (Ps 73:23, 24).

Ten, there is a vibrant social conscience exhibited throughout the Psalter. The covenant experience gives rise to derivative themes which have an important place in the Psalms' confession of faith: the challenge brought to the plan of God by the abuse of human freedom, and the tangible ways in which God's *presence* is mediated in the midst of Israel. Israel's life is undermined when the unjust and the powerful oppress those who are defenseless. The true faith of Israel is learned from the God who intervenes in their history as the champion of the oppressed. יהוה is the Just One who demands justice for the weak and the powerless. It is in her living that this faith is reaffirmed and deepened.—

> יהוה *hears the cry of the poor; They crush your people,* יהוה, *and oppress your chosen nation; they murder the widow and the stranger and put the fatherless to death* (Ps 94:5f.);

> *'Now I will arise,' says* יי, *'for the poor are plundered, the needy groan; I shall place them in the safety for which they long.'* (Ps 12:5);

> *When the righteous cry for help,* יהוה *hears them and sets them free from all their troubles* (Ps 34:17);

> *For* יהוה *crowns the lowly with victory* (Ps 149:4);

> יהוה *lifts the weak out of the dust and raises the poor from the rubbish heap* (Ps 113:7).

The Psalms reflect both the blessings of the temple and the bitter lessons of national defeat and subsequent forced exile—

> *By the rivers of Babylon, we sat down and wept as we remembered Zion* (Ps 137:1);

> *I shall say to God, my Rock, 'Why have you forgotten me?' Why must I go like a mourner because my foes oppress me?* (Ps 42:9);

> *Restore now what has been altogether ruined, all the destruction that the foe has brought on your sanctuary* (Ps 74:3).

With humility, the Psalms recognize that opposition to God's designs come also from the depths of Israel's own sinful heart. This recognition of culpability and accountability before יהוה—by Israel's ancient poets–is acute, even uncanny. [8]

> יי, *do not rebuke me in your anger, do not punish me in your wrath* (Ps 6:1);

> *Who is aware of his unwitting sins? Cleanse me of any secret fault.* (Ps 19:12);

> *Test me,* יהוה, *and try me, putting my heart and mind to the proof;* (Ps 26:2);

8. VanGemeren, Psalms, Vol. 5. *The Expositor's Bible Commentary.* "The Psalms thereby invite us to make a frank appraisal of how the promises of God are evidenced in reality and to bring our feelings of disappointment to God . . . We do so because [he]—after all—is the one who can resolve our dilemma, whether by changing circumstances or by changing our understanding and redirecting our expectations. As a result of this encounter, our relationship with God is enhanced, not diminished. Other OT characters, such as Habakkuk and Job, have taken similar pilgrimages." 304.

> *. . . for my iniquities tower above my head; they are a heavier load than I can bear* (Ps 38:4);

> *God, be gracious to me in your faithful love; in the fullness of your mercy blot out my misdeeds* (Ps 51:1).

Eleven, it has been noted that there is no parallel in ancient world literature to the Hebrew Scripture's acknowledgment of national apostasy and communal failure. Through its regression and failure to honor the dictates of the covenant, and its struggles to live in fidelity and trustful obedience, Israel came to the profound knowledge of God's mercy and forgiveness which is often echoed in the confession of the psalms–

> *When I acknowledged my sin to you, when I no longer concealed my guilt, but said, 'I shall confess my offense to* יהוה*' then you for your part remitted the penalty of my sin* (Ps 32:5);

> *God, be gracious to me in your faithful love; in the fullness of your mercy blot out my misdeeds. Wash . . . away all my iniquity and cleanse me from my sin* (Ps 51:1);

> יהוה *is righteous in all [he] does . . .* יהוה *is compassionate and gracious, long-suffering and ever faithful . . . As far as the east is from the west, so far from us has [he] put away our offenses* (Ps 103:8, 12).

Twelve, symbols and imagery play an indispensable function in human existence. It is not surprising then that these too have a place in Israel's confession of faith. God's *presence* came to be mediated in the life of the nation in different ways: in the common confession in the Jerusalem temple, and through the line of David, envisioned as the lineage from whom God's anointed will come. The *presence* of יהוה was mediated by the nation's common confession of faith. This confession is a profoundly personal one. Yet it is also communal. For centuries scholars interpreted the "I", which is so prevalent throughout the Psalter, as finding a voice in an individualized piety, an inner ethic seeking expression for itself.[9] Today it is understood more and more that in the Psalms—as is the case for the Hebrew Scriptures as a whole—it is primarily the communal faith of Israel that is being expressed.

It is this faith that resonates throughout the multi-faceted contributions of the Hebrew poetic genius. When we read the "I" as also a "we", and understand "servant" as also applying to Israel, we find there is a common embrace of both the personal and the communal. The personal/individual and the communal/corporate are held

---

9. Koch, "*Is there a Doctrine of Retribution in the Old Testament?*" in Theodicy in the Old Testament, IRTh vol. 4 ". . . the Israelite does not speak of 'practicing' faithfulness or 'traveling down the road of wickedness. According to the Hebrew way of expressing this, good actions or evil actions are 'created'. . . . Good actions and wickedness do not have a spatial quality like other 'things' which can be held and viewed. The characteristic of the relationship between the person who does something and what that person does is highlighted by the use, throughout the Old Testament, of the preposition *be* in its original locative sense, meaning 'in'. A person finds oneself 'inside' one's actions." 71.

throughout in dialectic tension. We can hear them, then, as the liturgies of the temple in Jerusalem, which was the central locus of Israel's worshiping life. This neither means that the Psalms are impersonal nor does it exclude their adaptive power to speak personally to the individual seeking a connection to יהוה.

What it does mean is that all Israel, gathered in the temple at Jerusalem or in other shrines, sanctuaries, and assemblies, as in old Israel, appropriated both dimensions: the personal and the corporate in worship, much as we experience worship and liturgy today in our common gathering and individual exercise of prayer and praise in our worship of God. All Israel's worship and praise is addressed to יהוה. Again we will follow the Psalter's five book arrangement as we track the Psalter's representation of Israel as the worshiping people who are in love with יהוה and with the place of worship—the temple.

Book One

Through your great love I may come into your house, and at your holy temple bow down in awe (Ps 5:7);

My God who ordered justice to be done, awake. Let the peoples assemble around you; take your seat on high above them (Ps 7:6,7);

Sing to יהוה enthroned in Zion; proclaim [his] deeds among the nations (Ps 9:11);

יהוה is in [his] holy temple; the throne of יהוה is in heaven (Ps 11:4);

יהוה I shall praise you among the nations and sing praises to your name (Ps 18:49);

 May the name of Jacob's God be your tower of strength. May [he] send you help from the sanctuary (Ps 20:1,2);

Be exalted, יהוה, in your might; we shall sing a psalm of praise to your name (Ps 21:13);

Let all the ends of the earth remember and turn again to יהוה; let all the families of the nations bow before [him] (Ps 22:27);

Lift up your heads, you gates, lift them up, you everlasting doors, that the king of glory may come in (Ps 24:9);

יהוה, I love the house where you dwell, the place where your glory resides (Ps 26:8);

יהוה will give strength to [his] people; יהוה will bless [his] people with peace (Ps 29:10);

Sing a psalm to יהוה, all you [his] loyal servants; give thanks to [his] holy name (Ps 30:4);

Shout for joy to יהוה, you that are righteous; praise comes well from the upright (Ps 33:1);

Rescue me from those who would destroy me, save my precious life from the powerful. Then shall I praise you in the great assembly, I shall extol you in a large congregation (Ps 35:17, 18);

In the great assembly I have proclaimed what is right; I do not hold back my words, as you know, יהוה (Ps 40:9).

Book Two

Send out your light and your truth to be my guide; let them lead me to your holy hill, to your dwelling-place. Then I shall come to the altar of God, the God of my joy and delight, and praise you with the lyre, God my God (Ps [43:3,4]); [10]

God, within your temple we meditate on your steadfast love. God, the praise your name deserves is heard at earth's farthest bounds (Ps 48:9, 10);

I am like a spreading olive tree in God's house, for I trust in God's faithful love for ever and ever. I shall praise you forever for what you have done, and glorify your name among your loyal servants, for that is good (Ps 52:8,9);

My heart is steadfast, God, my heart is steadfast. I shall sing and raise a psalm (Ps 57:7);

I shall raise a psalm to you, my strength; for God is my strong tower, [He] is my gracious God (Ps 59:17);

So I shall ever sing psalms in honour of your name as I fulfill my vows day after day (Ps 61:8);

With such longing I see you in the sanctuary and behold your power and glory. Your unfailing love is better than life; therefore, I will sing your praises. Thus all my life I bless you; in your name I lift my hands in prayer (Ps 63:2, 3);

Let all the earth acclaim God. Sing to the glory of [his] name, make [his] praise glorious. Say to God, 'How awesome are your deeds!' (Ps 66:1,2);

Your processions, God, come into view, the processions of my God, my King in the sanctuary; in front the singers, with minstrels following, and in their midst girls beating tambourines. Bless God in the great congregation; let the assembly of Israel bless יהוה (Ps 68:24–26);

Awesome is God in your sanctuary; [he] is Israel's God. [He] gives might and power to [his] people. Praise be to God (Ps 68:35).

10. Psalms 42 and 43 make up a single complaint or lament. They comprise one psalm; note the repeated refrain in 42:5, 11 and 43:5. The REB brackets Ps 43 and adds an explanatory footnote in the Oxford Study Bible edition.

Book Three

Hear us, Shepherd of Israel, leading Joseph like a flock. Shine forth, as you sit enthroned on the cherubim. Leading Ephraim, Benjamin, and Manasseh, rouse your might and come to our rescue. God, restore us, and make your face shine on us, that we may be saved (Ps 80:1–3);

Sing out in praise of God our refuge, acclaim the God of Jacob. Raise a melody; beat the drum, play the tuneful lyre and harp (Ps 81:1,2);

יהוה *of Hosts, how dearly loved is your dwelling-place! I pine and faint with longing for the courts of the temple of* יהוה; *my whole being cries out with joy to the living God* (Ps 84:1,2);

יהוה *teach me your way, that I may walk in your truth. Let me worship your name with an undivided heart. I shall praise you, Lord my God, with all my heart* (Ps 86:11, 12);

The city of יהוה *founded stands on the holy hills. [He] loves the gates of Zion more than all the dwellings of Jacob. Glorious things are spoken about you, city of God* (Ps 87:1–3).

Book Four

It is good to give thanks to יהוה, *to sing praises to your name, Most High, to declare your love in the morning and your faithfulness every night to the music of a ten-stringed harp, to the sounding chords of the lyre* (Ps 92:1–3);

Come! Let us raise a joyful song to יהוה, *a shout of triumph to the rock of our salvation. Let us come into [his] presence with thanksgiving and sing psalms of triumph to [him]* (Ps 95:1,2);

Enter in! Let us bow down in worship, let us kneel before יהוה *who made us, for [he] is our God, we are the people [he] shepherds, the flock in [his] care* (Ps 95:6,7);

Sing a new song to יהוה. *Sing to* יהוה, *all the earth. Sing to* יהוה *and bless [his] name; day by day proclaim [his] victory* (Ps 96:1,2);

Ascribe to יהוה, *you families of nations, ascribe to* יהוה *glory and might; ascribe to* יהוה *the glory due to [his] name. Bring an offering and enter [his] courts; in holy attire worship* יהוה (Ps 96:7–9);

יהוה *has become King; let peoples tremble. [He] is enthroned on the cherubim; let the earth shake.* יהוה *is great in Zion; [he] is exalted above all the peoples. Let them extol your great and terrible name. Holy is [he]* (Ps 99:1–3);

Let all the earth acclaim יהוה! Worship יהוה in gladness; enter [his] presence with joyful songs. Acknowledge that יהוה is God; [he] made us and we are [his], [his] own people, the flock which [he] shepherds. Enter [his] gates with thanksgiving, [his] courts with praise. Give thanks to [him] and bless [his] name; for יהוה is good and [his] love is everlasting, [his] faithfulness endures to all generations (Ps 100);

I shall sing of loyalty and justice, as I raise a psalm to you, יהוה. (Ps 101:1);

As long as I live I shall sing to יהוה; I shall sing psalms to my God all my life long. May my meditation be acceptable to [him]; I shall delight in יהוה (Ps 104:33, 34);

Give thanks to יהוה, invoke [him] by name; make known [his] deeds among the peoples. Pay [him] honour with song and psalm and tell of all [his] marvelous deeds. Exult in [his] hallowed name; let those who seek יהוה be joyful in heart. Look to יהוה and be strong; at all times seek [his] presence (Ps 105:1–4).

Book Five

It is good to give thanks to יהוה, for [his] love endures forever ... Let them give thanks toיהוה for [his] love and for the marvelous things [he] has done for [hu] mankind ... Let them give thanks toיהוה ... Let them give thanks to יהוה ... Let them offer sacrifices of thanksgiving and tell of [his] deeds with joyful shouts ... Let them give thanks to יהוה for [his] enduring love and for the marvelous things [he] has done for [hu]mankind]. Let them exalt [him] in the assembly of the people and praise [him] in the elders' council (Ps 107:1, 8, 15, 21, 22, 31);

My heart is steadfast, God, my heart is steadfast. I shall sing and raise a psalm. Awake, my soul. Awake, harp and lyre (Ps 108:1, 2);

I shall lift up my voice to extol יהוה, before a great company I shall praise [him] (Ps 109 30, 31);

With all my heart I shall give thanks to יהוה in the congregation, in the assembly of the upright, Great are the works ofיהוה (Ps 111: 1,2);

Praise יהוה! (Ps 112:1; 113:1; 117:1);

Blessed is [he] who enters in the name of יהוה; we bless you from the house of יהוה (Ps 118:26);

I rejoiced when they said to me, 'Let us go to the house ofיהוה' Now we are standing within your gates, Jerusalem; Jerusalem, a city built compactly and solidly ... Pray for the peace of Jerusalem ... I shall say, 'Peace be within you.' (Ps 122:1–3, 6);

Lift up your hands towards the sanctuary and bless יהוה. May יהוה, maker of heaven and earth, bless you; May יהוה, maker of heaven and earth, bless you from Zion! (Ps 134:2, 3);

I shall give praise to you, יהוה, with my whole heart; in the presence of the gods I shall sing psalms to you. I shall bow down towards your holy temple; for your love and faithfulness I shall praise your name, (Ps 138: 1, 2);

I shall sing a new song to you, my God, psalms to the music of a ten-stringed harp (Ps 144:9);

I shall extol you, my God and King, and bless your name for ever and ever. Every day I bless you and praise your name for ever and ever (Ps 145:1, 2).

Concluding Benediction (Pss 146–150)

Praise יהוה. My soul, praise יהוה. As long as I live I shall praise יהוה; I shall sing psalms to my God all my life long (Ps 146:1,2);

יהוה will reign forever, Zion, your God for all generations. Praise יהוה! (Ps 146:10);

Praise יהוה. How good it is to sing psalms to our God! How pleasant and right to praise [him]! (Ps 147:1);

Sing to יהוה a song of thanksgiving, sing psalms to the lyre in honour of our God (Ps 147:7);

Jerusalem, sing to יהוה; Zion, praise your God, for [he] has strengthened your barred gates; [he] has blessed your inhabitants (Ps 147:12, 13);

Praise יהוה. Praise יהוה from the heavens; . . . Praise יהוה from the earth . . . let them praise the name of יהוה, for [his] name is high above all others, and [his] majesty above earth and heaven, [He] has exalted [his] people in the pride of power and crowned with praise [his] loyal servants, Israel, a people close to [him]. Praise יהוה (Ps 148 :1, 7, 13, 14);

Praise יהוה. Sing to יהוה a new song, [his] praise in the assembly of [his] loyal servants! Let Israel rejoice in their maker; let the people of Zion exult in their king. Let them praise [his] name in the dance, and sing to [him] psalms with tambourine and lyre . . . Praise יהוה (Ps 149:1–2, 9).

Thirteen, communal solidarity holds a fundamental place in the Hebrew's aware-ness of the corporate personality paradigm. This is reflected continuously throughout the Bible. The "I" of the psalms is now commonly recognized as "we," the community of Israel confessing its faith through a variety of spokes-persons. Clearly, individual contributions were not lacking for leaders such as Levites, prophets or kings and their associates. The various poets who contributed to the Book of Praises, too, articulated this common faith from within their own particular and unique perspectives.

The shared nature of the Psalms' confessions however is made clear when we reflect on the fact that they were commonly chanted, as their many references to singing make clear and their frequent use of simple refrains in which all could join. We have in the Psalms an example of the *sensus fidelium*, functioning with health and vigor in the life of the people of God.

> *You, the praise of Israel, are enthroned in the sanctuary. In you our fathers put their trust; they trusted, and you rescued them* (Ps 22:3);

> *How good and how pleasant it is to live together as [brothers] in unity! It is like fragrant oil poured on the head and falling down upon the beard* (Ps 133:1,2).

The *presence* of יהוה was most acutely mediated throughout ancient Israel's temple liturgy in which all the people gathered and participated–

> *The nations will revere your name, יהוה, and all earthly kings your glory, when יהוה builds Zion again and shows [himself] in [his] glory* (Ps 102:15, 16).

The immense significance of the temple as the locus of the *presence* of יהוה in the midst of Israel is reflected in countless references throughout the Psalms–

> *יהוה, who may lodge in your tent? Who may dwell on your holy mountain?* (Ps 15:1);

> *Great is יהוה and most worthy of praise in the city of our God. [His] holy mountain is fair and lofty, the joy of the whole earth* (Ps 48:1,2);

> *יהוה of hosts, how dearly loved is your dwelling-place! . . . Happy are those who dwell in your house; they never cease to praise you! Happy those whose refuge is in you, whose hearts are set on the pilgrim's way! Better one day in your courts than a thousand days in my home* (Ps 84: 1, 4, 5, 10).

The joyful faith of those journeying up to the temple rings out in a series of fifteen remarkable psalms, commonly referred to as the Psalms of Ascents or Steps, or simply, the Pilgrim Psalter (Pss 120–134).

> *I rejoiced when they said to me, 'Let us go to the house of יהוה* (Ps 122:1);

> *I lift my eyes to you whose throne is in heaven* (Ps 123:1);

> *As the mountains surround Jerusalem, so יהוה surrounds [his] people both now and evermore* (Ps 125:2);

> *When יהוה restored the fortunes of Zion, we were like people renewed in health* (Ps 126:1);

> *Unless יהוה builds the house, its builders labour in vain* (Ps 127:1);

Happy are all who fear יהוה, *who conform to [his] ways* (Ps 128:1);

The blessing of יהוה *be on you! We bless you in the name of* יהוה (Ps 129:8);

For יהוה *is love unfailing, and great is [his] power to deliver* (Ps 130:7);

Israel, hope in יהוה, *now and for evermore* (Ps 131:3);

Arise, יהוה, *and come to your resting-place, you and your powerful Ark* (Ps 132:8);

Lift up your hands towards the sanctuary and bless יהוה, *may* יהוה, *maker of heaven and earth, bless you from Zion!* (Ps 134:2,3).

Fourteen, the Davidic dynasty, too, came to be seen as the agent of God's designs and the bearer of God's promises. For the ancient cultures of the world of the Hebrew Bible, the king or ruler–the sovereign—was commonly viewed as embodying the *presence* of the divinity being worshiped. It is not surprising therefore that with important modifications reflecting Israel's faith in the divine mystery, the nation's royal line is celebrated in several psalms as having received a kind of divine adoption:

I shall announce the decree of יהוה: 'You are my son,' he said to me; 'this day I become your father. Ask of me what you will; I shall give you the nations as your domain, the earth to its farthest ends as your possession* (Ps 2:7);

יהוה, *the king rejoices in your might: well may he exult in your victory* (Ps 21:1);

God has enthroned you for all eternity; your royal sceptre is a sceptre of equity. . . . I shall declare your fame through all generations; therefore, nations will praise you for ever and ever (Ps 45:6f.);

I shall establish your line for ever; I shall make your throne endure for all generations (Ps 89:4);

יהוה *says to my lord, 'Sit at my right hand until I make your enemies my footstool'* (Ps 110:1).

Fifteen, there is the height of irony and ambiguity which attaches to the biblical tradition since the kings and their officials were often the very oppressors of the people. This oppression by the kings of Yhwh brought the continued judgment of the prophets—and Yhwh! It was only when the Davidic line no longer ruled in postexilic times that this theme could more fully establish itself as part of the nation's confession of faith and hope. During this period, the theme of God's kingship over all creation emerged-

Sing a new song to יהוה. *Sing to* יהוה, *all the earth. Sing to* יהוה *and bless [his] name; day by day proclaim [his] victory* (Ps 96:1, 2);

יהוה has become king; let the peoples tremble; יהוה is enthroned on the cheru-bim; let the earth shake. יהוה is great in Zion; [he] is exalted above all the peoples (Ps 99:1,2);

It is good to give thanks to יהוה, to sing psalms to your name, Most High, to declare your love in the morning and your faithfulness every night (Ps 92:1,2).

Israel's self-understanding of its covenant with יהוה was beginning to extend to all the world. This is one of the Psalter's greatest legacies. The various poets of the ancient psalms are of one mind. This is all the more amazing when one remembers that we are dealing with many texts, some of which are separated by nearly a millennium of history—from oral transmission, to their composition, to final editing and reception into the Hebrew biblical canon.

> *The little nation of Israel, which entered the world of the great religions of the Near East as a novice, had, with its faith in the one, true God, unflinchingly made its way against the primitive traditions of its environment. It took up many various themes from the other religions, but it fused them all and made them useful to its avowal that only this one God existed and that he alone was the Lord. Here again it becomes clear how much the history of Israel's religion is our history. We stand quite obviously on this ground which Israel had created in its encounter with the other religions.*[11]

There is a unanimity of purposeful reflection, theologically, throughout the various texts of the Psalter. One common and unifying theme is the idea of God as refuge, whereby the individual poet expresses an inherent trustingness toward יהוה; this is an abiding astonishment [12] to the poets and the following section serves to illustrate this phenomenon.

---

11. Rendtorff, *God's History: A Way Through the Old Testament*, 56.

12. This is a term that is borrowed from the title of Walter Brueggemann's little book, the full title of which is: *Abiding Astonishment: Psalms, Modernity, and the Making of History.* Louisville: Westminster/John Knox Press, 1991.

Anthology of Refuge

BEFORE WE GET INTO the text of the book and the theme of ancient Israel's legacy of trusting YHWH, I want to provide you with a sample of some of the usages of refuge that are dominant throughout the Psalter. Ancient Israel's legacy of trusting יהוה is grounded in the metaphors of protection—*refuge, fortress, shelter, stronghold, shield, shadow of your wings*, etc. The *concrete realism* of Israel's trusting faith in יהוה alone is heightened and emphasized throughout the book of Praises. That this is the language of the heart and soul of the penitent, the suppliant, is undeniable: Israel's voice, many times filtered through the language of bitter complaint, is ever one that issues forth in the resolution of a confident trust! [1]

> *All those you protect shall be glad and ring out their joy. You shelter them; in you they rejoice, those who love your name (5:12);*

> *Yhwh, my God, I take refuge in you. From my pursuers save me and rescue me (7:2);*

> *For the oppressed let Yhwh be a stronghold, a stronghold in times of distress (9:10);*

> *In Yhwh have I taken my refuge (11:1);*

> *Preserve me, God, I take refuge in you. I say to you, Yhwh: "You are my God. My happiness lies in you alone" (16:1);*

> *Guard me as the apple of your eye. Hide me in the shadow of your wings (17:8);*

1. The psalms selections that follow are taken from *The Grail Psalter*. Its Introduction captures nicely the essence of the Psalter. "Rightly have the Psalms been called 'a school of prayer.' As these prayers give voice to so many of the experiences presented in the stories of the Bible, they come to us as words that have already been cried, shouted, and sung by people of faith throughout the centuries. Facing the human struggles of illness, imminent death, bigger-than-life enemies, and warring nations, the psalmist gave expression to the fears and uncertainties that troubled the present situation. Similarly, the joy of victory, the gratitude for prayers answered, and wonder at the marvels of creation all become part of the praise that is lifted up to the God who rules the world and brings all life into being. The psalmist attests with unshakable conviction that the One and Almighty God who touches every movement of history and each human life is the focus of all praise, the healer of every ill, and the source of all blessing" *Introduction*, xv.

Note: This anthology of protective songs of trust and confidence, from the *Grail Translation*, is provided with one exception: The name "Yhwh" has been inserted in place of "LORD."

For who is God but you, Yhwh? Who is a rock but you, my God? You who gird me with strength and make the path safe before me (18:32–33);

May the spoken words of my mouth, the thoughts of my heart, win favor in your sight, O Yhwh, my rescuer, my rock! (19:15);

Yhwh is my light and my help; whom shall I fear? Yhwh is the stronghold of my life; before whom shall I shrink? (27:1);

You, Yhwh, are my strength and my shield; in you my heart trust . . . Yhwh, you are the strength of your people, a fortress where your anointed finds refuge. (28: 7–8);

In you, O Yhwh, I take refuge. Let me never be put to shame. In your justice, set me free, hear me and speedily rescue me. Be a rock of refuge for me, a mighty stronghold to save me, for you are my rock, my stronghold. (31:1–3);

Our soul is waiting for Yhwh. The Lord (Adonai) is our help and our shield. Our hearts find joy in the Lord (Adonai). We trust in God's holy name. May your love be upon us, O Yhwh, as we place all our hope in you (33:20–22);

The angel of Yhwh is encamped around those who fear God, to rescue them. Taste and see that Yhwh is good. They are happy who seek refuge in God (34:8, 9);

The salvation of the just comes from Yhwh, their stronghold in time of distress. Yhwh helps them and delivers them and saves them, for their refuge is in God (37:39–40);

God is for us a refuge and strength, a helper close at hand, in times of distress, so we shall not fear, though the earth should rock, though the mountains fall into the depths of the sea; (46:1);

Yhwh of hosts is with us; the God of Jacob is our stronghold (46:12).

But I have God for my help. The Lord (Adonai) upholds my life. (54:6);

Have mercy on me, God, have mercy, for in you my soul has taken refuge; In the shadow of your wings I take refuge until the storms of destruction pass by. (57:1);

O my Strength, it is you to whom I turn, for you, O God, are my stronghold, the God who shows me love (59:18);

On a rock too high for me to reach set me on high, O you who have been my refuge, my tower against the foe. Let me dwell in your tent forever and hide in the shelter of your wings. (61:3, 4);

In God alone is my soul at rest; from God comes my help. God alone is my rock, my stronghold, my fortress; I stand firm (62:1–2);

The just will rejoice in Yhwh and fly to God for refuge. All the upright hearts will glory (64:11);

In you, O Yhwh, I take refuge; let me never be put to shame. In your justice rescue me, free me; pay heed to me and save me. Be a rock where I can take refuge, a mighty stronghold to save me; for you are my rock, my stronghold (71:1–3);

To be near God is my happiness. I have made Yhwh God my refuge. I will tell of all your works at the gates of the city of Zion (73:28);

They remembered that God was their rock, God, the Most High (Elyon) their redeemer (78:35);

O Lord (Adonai), you have been our refuge from one generation to the next. Before the mountains were born or the earth or the world brought forth, you are God, without beginning or end (90:1, 2);

Those who dwell in the shelter of the Most High (Elyon) and abide in the shade of the God of Heaven (Shaddai) say to Yhwh, "My refuge, my stronghold, my God (Elohay) in whom I trust!" (91:1, 2);

As for me, Yhwh will be a stronghold; my God will be the rock where I take refuge (94:22);

You who fear Yhwh, trust in Yhwh; [he] is your help and your shield. Yhwh remembers and will bless us; (115:11f.);

I have no love for the halfhearted; my love is for your law. You are my shelter, my shield; I hope in your word (119:113, 114,);

Yhwh will guard you from evil, and will guard your soul. Yhwh will guard your going and coming both now and forever (121:7–8);

To you, Yhwh God, my eyes are turned; in you I take refuge; spare my soul! (141:8);

In the morning let me know your love for I put my trust in you. Make me know the way I should walk; to you I lift up my soul. Rescue me, Yhwh, from my enemies; I have fled to you for refuge (143:8, 9);

God is my love, my fortress; God is my stronghold, my savior, my shield, my place of refuge, who brings peoples under my rule (144:2).

These verses bear the hallmark of a consummate skill in compositional poetry. The poets convey a deep awareness of the inner life and a commensurate knowledge of self which is conveyed in marvelous language replete with striking images. These magnificent and ancient poems reflect the Hebraic poets' mastery of metaphor—images of protection, refuge, intimacy and security. For them there is no place in the cosmos where יהוה is not present. In fact, יהוה is described as being in heaven and on earth at the same time. It is this language of immanence and transcendence that permeates the Psalter. It is a tension that is expressed repeatedly when speaking of a relationship with this God of Israel. The poets of the Psalms accept this as fact.

Israel's God is the God of omnipresence. There is no place in the cosmos that is foreign to יהוה yet יהוה is also personal, a deity who makes connections with humans, who enters into relationship with those who seek after יהוה. This is the most profound reality for the Hebrews in that it makes יהוה incomparable by any standard in terms of the other gods worshiped throughout the ancient world. יהוה has no rivals and is peerlessly invested in human life. All creation is blessed of יהוה. John Day writes:

> The Hebrews conceived of Yhwh as both transcendent and immanent, and this is
> reflected in the Psalter. [He] is regarded as dwelling at once in heaven and in the
> temple on Mt. Zion. Ps.11.4, ' The Lord is in [his] holy temple, the Lord's throne
> is in heaven. [His] eyes behold, [his] searing gaze scrutinizes humankind.' [2]

This ancient psalm (Psalm 11) serves as our first example of a song of trust wherein the poet appeals directly to יהוה in the face of his pursuers.[3]

Psalm 11

For the director. Of David

In יהוה I take refuge.

How can they lie in wait for my life,

and pursue me like a bird saying,

"Fly back to your mountain and hide!"

For look, the violent ones are bracing the bow,

placing their arrows upon the taut string,

to ambush and shoot the upright of heart.

When the foundations are being torn down,

what can a just person do?

יהוה—in the temple's holy seat,

יהוה—in heaven's throne.

The eyes of יהוה inspect;

the pupils of יהוה scrutinize humankind.

יהוה is the Just One

2. Day, Psalms in *Old Testament Guides*, 128.

3. Bellinger. "The Interpretation of Psalm 11," *Evangelical Quarterly 56*. ". . . the psalm (11) had come to be viewed as a strong spiritual affirmation of trust in the midst of difficulty: God will protect the faithful. The language has no mythical component but both a literal and a figurative element are present. Perhaps it has been reinterpreted and 'redacted' as it was used through the years in worship to allow a more metaphorical, 'spiritual' meaning. However, any editing would only have been slight and gradual. Thus, it may very well be that at least two levels of meaning are still present in the text as we have it—the cultic and spiritual or figurative." 100.

who will indeed assay the deeds of the wicked;

[He] stands against the lovers of injustice and their hatred of life.

Send upon the ruthless bellows of fire, and sulfur,

with scorching wind their lot.

For the Just One, יהוה, loves just actions;

the upright shall gaze upon the face of יהי.

יהוה is the Just One, for the poet of Psalm 11,[4] and יהוה is a God who is intimately involved with humankind. יהוי is a God who is attentive and who carefully scrutinizes all humanity; who is aware of human behavior and stands against those who would "draw the bow" against the faithful one.

Contradicting the counsel of his "friends" to flee, the poet recognizes that his sufficient protection is in fully trusting יהי. He instinctively seems to know where true righteousness lies. Claiming his own righteousness, he trusts in the Just One to determine who is innocent and who are the wicked ones.

When the very foundations and institutions of the social order are shaken, when the violent seek to ambush and destroy the just, the righteous flee to יהוי for refuge and reside within the *presence of* יהוי. *The salvation of the righteous is from* יהוה; *he is their refuge in the time of trouble* (37:39 NRSV).

This type of psalm, an example of a psalm of trust, finds expression out of a particular lament, initially a complaint against יהוה that ultimately surrenders into expressions of confidence. Trust then becomes the dominate feature of these particular psalms. It extends to the limits of human life and touches on the eternal hope that; *the Lord is righteous; he loves righteous deeds; the upright shall behold his face* (11:7. NRSV). Such a declaration of trust in יהוי is altogether predominant in some other psalms of the trust/confidence genre. Dahood reckons how Psalm 11 has a wider vista; that

> *the version proposed here is a statement of belief in the beatific vision in the afterlife; The vision of God mentioned here is doubtless that of Pss 16.11; 17.15; 41.13; 73. 24, which suggest a belief in an afterlife in the presence of Yahweh. If perfect justice is not attained in this life, it will be in the next; this seems to be the ultimate motive for the psalmist's confidence.*[5]

It is the firm conviction of these poets of trust that in the final analysis, יהוי is the One on whom factual reliance is founded. There is no doubt that יהי is the ground of hope on which all else depends. The Hebrew conception of יהוי is complex as God is both the transcendent and the immanent reality; at once removed and far off, and yet both near—very near—and close at hand. We will be considering the subject of

4. Dahood, *Psalms*, "Since Yahweh is the Just One, the psalmist is confident that justice will ultimately prevail. This type of psalm may have developed from the laments, in which expressions of confidence are a common feature."68.

5. Dahood, *Ibid.*

the Psalms and the afterlife later on in this book. For now, we turn to exploring the hallowed names that are used by the psalmists as appellatives for God, remembering that the term "God" is a symbol, a concept, not a name.

Hallowed Names

THROUGHOUT THIS BOOK WE will be treating Psalms 90, 91 and 92 as a specific literary unit in the Psalms. There is much evidence to support its supposition. We focus first on Psalm 91 where only here in the Psalter, the poet employs four different names for God, each of which is intended to emphasize the total sovereignty and power and incomparability of the Hebrew God.

The one who dwells in the secret shelter of the Most High (עליון), and passes the night in the shadow of Shaddai (שדי) speaks: 'I will say of the LORD (יהוה), my refuge and my bulwark; my God Elohay (אלהי) in whom I put my trust' (91:1,2, LW). Here עליון (*Elyon*) is God Most High.[1] עליון (*Elyon Most High*) also occurs in certain other psalms identified with Zion and is often times used with the prefix אל (*El*)

In Psalm 78:56, it is the continued sin of the people that is met by divine anger, but it is anger tempered with compassion. *For they tested the Most High God, and were in utter rebellion. They did not observe the divine decrees, but turned away and were faithless like their ancestors.* Again it is used in its plural form אלהים (*Elohim, gods*) in Psalm 57:3. *I cry to God Most High, to God (אלהים) who fulfills [his] purpose for me. God will send from heaven and save me; God will put to shame those who trample me under foot. God will send forth [his] constant love and faithfulness* (LW). God as the exalted ruler of the universe vindicates the innocent and confronts the faithless.

In Psalm 113, we read how the personal, intimate יהוה is high above all nations, and his glory above the heavens. *Who is like יהוה our God, who is seated on high, who looks far down on the heavens and the earth?* אלהי (*Elohay, my God*), which only occurs in three other places in the book of Psalms, is the singular, feminine form of אלהים , the plural (*Elohim, gods*). Both אלהים (*Elohim*) and אלהי (*Elohay*) are derivations of the broader prefix אל (*El*) the chief god in the Canaanite pantheon.

---

1. Kraus, *Theology of the Psalms,* "The divine name *Elyon* suggests the idea of 'ascend' and connotes 'the Highest'. The name indicates the exalted status and power of God (e.g. Pss 47:2, 6–7; 82:6; 83:19; 91:1, 9; 97:9). It is an epithet of kingship." 461.

cf. Mettinger, *In Search of God: The Meaning and Message of the Everlasting Names.* "The biblical names of God are symbols. On the pump-organ of human language, these symbols perform the music that speaks about God. The symbols are not a direct reproduction of the original tones, but are a downward transposition with a supposedly analogical relationship to them. The symbols are names that speak of the Ineffable through categories deriving from the world of human experience." 201

With the conjunctive יהוה עליון, *YHWH* and *Elyon* are also used in apposition in several other psalms.

I will give thanks to יהוה *with my whole heart; . . .I will sing praises to your name, O* עליון (Ps 9:2); *For* יהוה *thundered in the heavens, and* עליון *(elyon) raised [his] voice* (18:13); *For the king trusts in* יהוה *and through the constant love of* עליון *(elyon) he shall not be moved* (21:7, NRSV). This close association between the two names is found throughout the Hebrew Bible and is particularly noteworthy in the Psalms. *Elyon* (עליון) connects Psalm 92 to Psalm 91. *It is good to give thanks to* יהוה *and to sing praises to your name, O* עליון *(elyon).* cf. 92:1, 4, 5, 8, 9, and 15. Psalm 92 is a thanksgiving hymn for the just order. It speaks to the deliverance by יהוה of Israel out of the hands of her enemies and oppressors. It is a resounding hymn which builds on the majestic confidence and trust of Psalm 91.

In Psalm 91:4 a distinctly unique metaphor for refuge is employed. יהוה *will cover you with [his] pinions, and under [his] wings you will find refuge.* The Hebrew noun סֹחֵרָה (*sokherah*), which occurs only here in the Hebrew Bible, refers to a surrounding enclosure, a rampart, or an enveloping and rounded shield. This metaphor is intended to evoke the powerful image of יהוה encompassing the poet with complete protection against all assaults. Included in this imagery is the understanding of the life of faith and trust as one that is embattled, requiring the unfailing assistance and continuously abiding protection of the *presence* of יהוה throughout one's life. Assurance of the *presence* of יהוה is appealed to by the poets over and over again and is a constant theme in the life of faith for the ancient people of God.

Psalm 91 uses two names for the deity which are typically associated with pre-Mosaic religion: עליון (*Elyon, Most High*) and שדי (*Shaddai, the God of Heaven*) which are both names of great antiquity.[2] *Shaddai* is usually translated *the Almighty* in the LXX. יהוה is referred to in the prophet Hosea as "*the living God.*" Moses is told in Exodus 6:2–8 that שדי (*Shaddai, Almighty*) is the name by which the patriarchs knew God. The most likely meaning of this divine appellative is *god of the fields,* or *mountain,* but the name יהוה was possibly unknown to them. What we have in the name אל שדי (*el shaddai*) is an ancient divine appellative with roots deep in the Semitic past. The derivation and meaning of אל שדי (*el shaddai*) is mostly translated (*Almighty*) in the *Septuagint*—whose interpreters themselves were unfamiliar with the original meaning of the name.

Another feature of the *LXX (Septuagint)* [3] is the reference to the God of Israel, translated *the Lord of all the earth.* In Psalm 97:5 it states: *The mountains melt like*

---

2. A. A. Anderson, *Psalms, New Century Bible Commentary, vol. II.* "Shaddai possesses not only a protective character but also a fearsome aspect. It is very likely an early Canaanite divine epithet usually rendered 'the one of the mountains;'" 656.

3. Note: The Septuagint, or *LXX,* (the term *Septuagint* meaning seventy) is the first Greek translation of the text of the Hebrew Bible. Tradition says it was the product of seventy-two Jewish scholars convened sometime in the third century BCE in Alexandria. According to an ancient document, *the Letter of Aristeas,* legend states how seventy-two Jewish scholars were commissioned during the reign

wax before יהוה *before the Lord of all the earth;* and 98:4: *All the ends of the earth have seen the victory of our God. Make a joyful noise to* יהוה, *all the earth.* In a non-biblical reference, it is used of the Greek god, Zeus and the Egyptian god, Osiris, specifically by Plutarch (cf. *Isis and Osiris 355e*).

The origin of the sacred name, יהוה, goes something like this. In its classical form the traditional *Kenite* hypothesis postulates the view that the Israelites became acquainted with the worship of יהוה through Moses. Jethro, Moses' father-in-law in one account was, according to an old tradition, a Midianite priest (Ex 2:16; 3:1; 18:1) who worshiped יהוה (e.g. Ex 18:10–12). In two other accounts Hobab is referred to also as Moses' father-in-law (in Judg 1:16; 4:11; Num 10:29) and belonged to the Kenites (Judg 1:16; 4:11) a branch of the Midianites. By way of Hobab and Moses, then, the Kenites were the mediators of the cult of יהוה.

Dependency on the historical role of Moses, moreover, is problematic. It seems more prudent not to put too much weight on the figure of Moses—to say nothing of the discrepancy that is found in scripture regarding the actual identities of Jethro and Hobab who are each cited as Moses's father-in-law (perhaps Moses had two fathers-in-law?). It is only in a much later tradition that Moses came to be regarded as the legendary ancestor of the Levitical priests and a symbol of the "יהוה *alone* movement." That יהוה is known as the God of deliverance and grace is attested in the Exodus 18 strata; *Moses said to Hobab . . . We are setting out for the place of which* יהוה *said, 'I will give it to you'; come with us, and we will treat you well; for* יהוה *has promised good to Israel.* (cf. Num.10:29).

A major flaw in the classical *Kenite hypothesis*, however, is its disregard for the Canaanite origins of Israel (ca. early to mid thirteenth-century BCE) near the end of the Late Bronze Age. The view that under the influence of Moses, the Israelites then became Yahwists during their journey through the desert, and brought their newly acquired religion to the Palestinian soil, neglects the fact that the majority of Israelites were already firmly rooted and established in Palestine. It is most likely, and it is accurate, I think, to say that Moses first learned the name יהוה in the low desert area separating Canaan and Egypt. This is roughly the geographical location of the Exodus 3 tradition—the Name of the Hebrew God is given to Moses, the Tetragrammaton, YHWH, יהוה Numerous biblical references specifically associate the God of Israel, יהוה, with one or more of the southeastern desert regions of Sinai, Paran, Seir/Edom, Midian, Cushan, and Teman (Dt. 33:2; Jud. 5:4, 5; Hab. 3:3; Ps 68:8,17). The appellative, *elyon, Most High,* is the name that Moses used for the divine in one of his last

of Ptolemy Philadelphus of Egypt to carry out the task of translating the Hebrew Bible into Greek. Widely used among Hellenistic Jews, this Greek version of the Hebrew Bible was called forth as many Jews who were dispersed throughout the far-flung Roman world were beginning to lose contact with their Hebrew roots and language. One of the fascinating results of translating the Hebrew Bible into Greek is that it gave non-Jews a window into viewing Judaism and its ancient traditions. The *LXX* had an enormous influence on the early church, most particularly among the first century CE writers of what would become the Christian scriptures. The LXX WAS the "Old Testament" for the early church.

speeches. *When the Most High apportioned the nations, when he divided humankind,* *[he] fixed the boundaries of the peoples according to the number of the Israelites; the* *portion of* יהוה *was [his] own people, Jacob his allotted share (Dt. 32:8 NRSV).*[4] *Elyon* (עליון) is a richly textured term connoting the idea of *the Most High or Highest God.*

By openly proclaiming that God is known as (עליון) *Elyon,* (שדי) *Shaddai,* (יהוה) *Yhwh,* and (אלהי) *Elohay,* the poet of Psalm 91 appropriates this combination of divine names which seems intended to evoke supreme confidence in and a deep inner consciousness of the Holy.[5] This aggregate of appellatives connotes the power of the Creator-God as well as the enduring love of the Deliverer God in whom Israel lives and moves by virtue of the eternal covenant. Both transcendence and immanence are attributed to the Hebrew God יהוה, and this God יהוה is the personal and incomparable deity. The use of the sacred name יהוה in Psalm 91 then, in this line of thought, is intended to gather up into completion all the meanings of the other three names. It was then fused with the older deity, *El* or *Elohim,* and is associated with the land of Canaan.[6]

This is Moses' greatest contribution to Israelite religion and the psalmists make conscious decisions to employ the Name numerously. יהוה is by far the most prevalent designation of the deity in the Psalms. The covenantal Name יהוה—which occurs nearly 700 times throughout the Psalter–along with the abbreviated יה (*yah*)–is, by far, the most conspicuous. The Psalter is predominately a Yahwist Book! The only exception to its prominence throughout the book is found in the common usage of אלהים (*elohim*) in what is now usually referred to as the *Elohistic Psalter* (Pss 42–83). We will consider this phenomenon in another chapter.

The richness of ancient Israel's religious experience and practice is reflected in the interface between יהוה and the people of God. It is יהוה who revealed to Israel (Moses) the holy and ineffable Name (Ex 3). For Israel to be given the name יהוה was an extraordinary thing.[7] It is a basis for confidence therefore that the giving of the

---

4. Wallace, *The Narrative Effect of Book IV of the Hebrew Psalter.* "The faithful in Ps 91 will also find protection of Yahweh's 'pinions' (v. 4). This word is also used in Dt. 32:11. When the divine does speak in Ps. 91, in the oracle, Yahweh states in 14b that '*I will protect those who know my name.*' The phrase is conspicuous when read with Dt. 32:3 '*I will call on the name of Yhwh*.'" 23.

Note: There are various similarities between the Song of Moses (Deut 32) and Psalm 91. cf. Andre Caquot, "Le Psaume XCI" *Semitica* 8 (21–37).

5. Ps 91:1, 2. יהוה (*Yahweh*) occurs in the Psalms close to 700 times, of which the abbreviated form *yah* occurs 43 times; *elohim,* 365 times; *El,* 79 times; *Adonai,* 54 times; *Elyon,* 22 times; *Elohay,* 4 times; and *Shaddai,* twice, in Ps 68 and Ps 91.

6. Note: The fact that there remains a very close linkage between our psalms (Pss 90, 91, 92) and the seventh-sixth century BCE deuteronomistic historians—editors, tells us even more about the very long process of time that passed in bringing the Psalter to its present form, approximately in the second century CE. cf. M. Segal, "El, Elohim, and YHWH in the Bible," in *Jewish Quarterly Review* 46 (89–115).

7. Vriezen, *The Religion of Ancient Israel.* It is an extraordinary thing because it is also a "clear case of a personal relationship with the Most High God, with Israel's only God in person. [He] is directly accessible. Not only kings (like David, in 1 Sam. 30:6) may call upon [him], but all who are in distress

divine Name is rooted in the character of God. In most current English Bible versions (NRSV, REB, Grail, and JPS), יהוה is rendered LORD, in four capital letters; it is thus distinguished from "Lord", or Adonai, meaning sovereign. יהוה was mistakenly trans-literated Jehovah in the 19th century. YHWH, the tetragrammaton or the four Hebrew consonants יהוה, is identified with the I am who I am, or, I will be who I will be in the pentateuchal narrative. Most scholarship today understands יהוה to be a pun which plays on the Hebrew verb, to be.[8]

This is the name of the personal, intimate God and it is this name that was com-municated directly to Moses—according to the Exodus 3 narrative tradition. It is fre-quently insufficiently recognized that, at the beginning of Iron Age I, the role of the god El—king of the pantheon of the Canaanite gods—had become largely nominal. By the end of Iron Age I, the cult of El had survived only in some border zones of the Near East. In most regions, including Palestine, El's career as a living god (i.e. as a cultic reality and an object of actual devotion) had ended.

The name survived in such expressions as 'the council of El' and 'sons of El', but this was survival in name only. This fact explains why there are no traces of polemic against El in the Hebrew Bible. The name was increasingly used either as a generic noun meaning 'god' or, more specifically, as a designation of the personal god. In both cases, יהוה could be called El. Along with the name, יהוה inherited various traits of El. One of them is divine eternity. Ugaritic texts refer to El as the "father of years" while יהוה is called "Ancient of Days" (Dan 7). Power and compassion are commonly attributed traits of both El and יהוה.

Other references where עליון (elyon) occurs on its own are: And I say, 'It is my grief that the right hand of the Most High (elyon) has changed' (77:10); and, I say, 'You are all gods, children of the Most High, עליון (elyon) all of you; nevertheless, you shall all die like any mortal-fall like any prince (82:6, LW); And of Zion it shall be said, 'This one and that one were born in it'; for the Most High עליון (elyon) himself will establish it (87:5, LW) and 92:1. Of these examples, עליון (elyon), as a term for the God of Israel, must have been interpreted early on as an allusion to Zion. The latter redactors and editors of the Psalter

---

(Pss. 25, 35, 69, 71, 84, 86, 143, passim); . . . In other words, there is in Israel an absolute immediacy about the relationship between God [himself], in the highest sense of that term, and the individual human being." 27.

8. Freedman, "The Real Formal Full Name of the God of Israel" In Sacred History, Sacred Literature, "If the Tetragrammaton, YHWH, is a verb in the earliest biblical tradition, then it has a pronominal subject that is expressed, and behind it a subject-noun. From the passages of Exod 3:6; 6:2–3, and 34:6 -7, it seems clear that Yahweh was originally a verb for which the subject was El" 119. cf. Albertz, Israelite Religion. "Attempts have been made time and time again to learn something about the nature of Yahweh from the explanation of [his] name. The divine name appears in different forms, in the Old Testament mostly in the long form (tetragrammaton) YHWH; because of the reluctance to utter the divine name which began in the Hellenistic period, its pronunciation is not completely certain. When the Massoretes laid down the pronunciation of the Hebrew consonantal text in the early Middle Ages, they vocalized the tetragrammaton by the words which were read in its place, 'adonay ('Lord') or 'elohim (God); this gave rise to the false reading 'Jehovah' which was popularized by the nineteenth century." 49, 50.

gave expression to this allusion in its final shaping. The God of the psalmists is an active God who intervenes for the benefit of, and on behalf of, [his] worshipers.

The joy of the worshiping psalmist at the intervention of יהוה is not a quiet feeling of happiness which he keeps to himself; rather the words of worship that are employed are usually associated with the praise of God in hymns or with the festive joy of the celebrations in the temple. The divine epithets speak of praise and majesty, honor and power. All these are compressed into the first two verses of Psalm 91. The names of יהוה that occur in the Psalms are derived in all likelihood from the cultic tradition of the old Jebusite city–Jerusalem. Evidence also exists which seems to suggest how very early on, יהוה was venerated as אל עליון (*El Elyon*) at Shiloh in the pre-monarchical period. This is a sacred name of great antiquity and Israel believed that only Yahweh is *El Elyon* ("*God Most High*" cf. Gen 14:22).

> "*The psalmists, too, use the epithet 'Elyon' to refer to Yahweh, and their use has no mythological overtones. Whatever they may say about Elyon is completely adapted to the bounds of revelation from Sinai: 'For you, O Lord, are the Most High [Elyon] over all the earth; you are exalted far above all gods' (97:9). [He] is Yahweh Elyon, and there is no other Elyon than Yahweh! Therefore, the psalmist prays, 'Let them know that you, whose name is the LORD–that you alone are the Most High [Elyon]over all the earth' (83:18)."[9]*

Though יהוה was known and worshiped among the Israelites before 1000 BCE, [he] did not become the patron, national god until the monarchic era. Due to the religious politics of Saul, יהוה only became the patron deity of the Israelite state following its origination in the south–primarily the tribe of Judah. As David and Solomon inherited and enlarged Saul's Kingdom, they acknowledged the rightful position of יהוה as Israel's national God. David brought the Ark of יהוה from Benjamin to Jerusalem (2 Sam 6). Solomon sought the blessing of יהוה at the sanctuary of Gibeon, the national temple of the Saulide state (1 Kgs 3:4). Evidence of the predominant role of יהוה in the official cult during the Monarchic Era are the theophoric personal names, the biblical names, and the epigraphical ones.

> *. . . there is not a single derivation of the word 'Yahweh' from a native Hebrew root; they are all from foreign roots, most of them Arabic, indicating quite clearly that Yahweh was a foreign god, most probably originating in Arabia. [He] was anything but a native Hebrew god, and on that particular point practically all scholars are agreed. They agree, too, that [he] originated in the south. They differ only as to whether [he] was of Arabic or Kenite origin.* [10]

---

9. VanGemeren, *Psalm 131:2*, 153.

10. Meek, *Hebrew Origins*. 109–110. cf. Albertz, *A History of Israelite Religion*, "So the god Yahweh is older than Israel; [he] was a southern Palestinian god before [he] became the god of liberation for the Moses group. It was important here that [he] was a god who came from outside, an alien god who had not yet been incorporated into the structure of the Egyptian pantheon and was thus in a position to break up this religious system which gave political stability to society." 52.

The divine name, יהוה is by far the most common theophoric element. The practical henotheism of יהוה should not be taken for a strict monotheism. Far from it! Not only did the Israelite's continue to recognize the existence of other deities besides יהוה, for a very long time, they also knew more than one הוה ! Though at the mythological level there is only one, the cultic reality reflected a plurality of יהוה gods. Non-biblical evidence mentions a "יהוה from Samaria" and a "יהוה of Teman"; it is possible that the two names designate one god, the official god of the northern Kingdom ("Samaria", after its capital). Yet the recognition of a northern יהוה is mirrored by the worship of a "יהוה of Hebron" and a "יהוה of Zion" (2 Sam 15:7) all of which should be understood as references to local forms of יהוה worship centered in regional shrines dating back to the earliest days before the monarchy and reminiscent of the days of the tribal confederation. In the Hebrew Bible, the name יהוה is written in two different ways when standing by itself, יה (yah) and יהוה and, in three different ways, when used in personal names, יהו, יה, and יו, but never as יהוה. Outside the Hebrew Bible, it is found in only two other places as יהוה—*on the Moabite Stone and the ostraca from Lachish.*[11]

Indicators all point to there being an early epithet of על (el) who, as the dominant god in the surrounding Semitic cultures, undoubtedly posed challenges to ancient Israel when the newly arrived Hebrews gained entrance into Canaan in the fourteenth-century BCE. The name *elyon* connects our three Psalms, 90, 91, and 92. There is also evidence to suggest that the inhabitants of the old Jebusite city (pre-Israelite Jerusalem) already entertained religious and cultic conceptions of the *Highest God* or *el Elyon*. Consequently, a qualitative distinction was formidably drawn between the worshiping practices in Israel and that of her surrounding neighbors.

This distinction is critical to any right understanding of the Hebrew conception of the incomparability of יהוה when contrasted to other gods. The religious situation in early Israel, therefore, was extremely complicated. For much of the period of old Israel, it faced a daunting reality that was not merely one of a rampant polytheism, but also of poly-yahwism. The Deuteronomic emphasis, of course, is on the unity of יהוה amid these complexities and ought to be so understood against this background.

11. Wurthwein, *The Text of the Old Testament: An Introduction to the Biblia Hebraica.* 122–124. Note: The inscribed Bowl from Lachish was discovered in 1935 and a date has been proposed to the second quarter of the fourteenth century BCE. The inscription consists of eleven signs or letters. Seven of these are well preserved. Most scholars agree that the identity of the first five signs are the Hebrew letters b, s, l, s, t (i.e. a form of the number "three" with the prepositional prefix, b). The sixth symbol is probably a division mark and the seventh, the beginning of another word, is now illegible. The Moab Stele was discovered in 1868 by a missionary, F. A. Klein, in Dhibon, Jordan. It is a victory inscription on black basalt consisting of thirty-four lines in Phoenician-Old Hebrew script with twenty-seven lines preserved entirely. They celebrate the victory of Mesha, King of Moab, over Israel after a period of Moabite submission (cf. 2 Kgs 3: 4—27) and are a record of a program of city building. The stele is of great importance as it is the sole historical monument of the Moabite kingdom and a record of historical relations between Moab and Israel, which are glossed over or omitted from the "Old Testament." It dates from the ninth century BCE.

Israel's journey to monotheism was a long, complicated and arduous one and was never arrived at easily.

> *The question of the origin and age of biblical monotheism has again been vigorously discussed in recent times [c. 1994]. Whereas earlier scholars generally saw the exclusiveness of Israel's worship of Yahweh as an old legacy of the early period, which in the crises of the settlement and formation of the state was gradually developed into the express requirement of monolatry (sole worship) in the face of the threat of 'Canaanite' infiltration, and finally, during the exile, into theoretical monotheism (the assertion of a sole God and the denial of all others), in more recent scholarship the exact opposite has been maintained, that throughout its pre-exilic phase the religion of Israel had been a 'polytheistic religion which was no different from the religions of the surrounding world'. The propagation of the sole worship of Yahweh is said to have begun only at a late stage, at the earliest with Elijah in the ninth century, but really only with Hosea in the eighth century, and to have been the concern of only small opposition groups (the 'Yahweh alone movement'). According to this view, this movement was only able to influence society for a short period under Josiah, but then finally helped monotheism to victory in the exilic and early post-exilic period.*[12]

The Hebrew text—which the *LXX* translated into Greek—differed from the *MT (Masoretic Text)* to some extent. The condition of that earlier text was quite variable and in some cases was doubtless superior to our present Hebrew text. But in other instances it was clearly inferior. Our conclusion here is that the *LXX*, while certainly indispensable to the study of the Psalms, must be handled with care. Diligence therefore must be exercised in weighing its evidences and appropriating its conclusions to our reading and interpretation of the text. [13]

The *MT (Masoretic Text)* is the earliest Hebrew text available to us and dates from the ninth-century CE. In the *MT* the term שדי (*Shaddai, Almighty*) also appears only twice in the Psalter (91:1 and 68:14) but over thirty times, for instance, in the book of Job. Biblical references to שדי (*Shaddai*) in their present form, are most likely of post-exilic origin. In the *LXX Shaddai* has been rendered variously, but the predominant rendition was *Almighty* and it issued forth in the eastern Christian church, eventually, by the Greek title *pantokrator* or Lord of all worlds.

> *Pantokrator-as a Greek title of the divine and cosmic Lordship of Christ first appeared in the Eastern church in the 4th -5th centuries CE. That Jesus was the Christ of God and the one promised in the Old Testament was the central*

---

12. Albertz, *A History of Israelite Religion*, 61. cf. For an excellent discussion of the long process toward monotheism in ancient Israel, please see James A. Sanders, *The Monotheizing Process: Its Origins and Development*, 2014.

13. Note: The findings of the psalms scroll at Qumran have reinvigorated and renewed confidence in the reliability and accuracy of the Hebrew of the ninth century CE Masoretic text (MT). This is one of the greatest contributions of the Dead Sea Scrolls for research and study of the Psalter.

conviction with which Christianity had arisen out of Judaism. The conviction had been worked out in early Jewish -Christian debates, but Byzantine theology expanded the case for this identification of the Christ . . . It was the theme and purpose of Christian writings against Judaism to show 'from the Scriptures and from the truth itself [that various passages of the Old Testament] speak about the incarnate economy of the Son of God.' These passages had been fulfilled before the eyes of the entire cosmos, proving [to those who believed in his name] that Jesus was the promised one.[14]

In the early apostolic church, the confession (ἐστιν πάντων κύριος)—("he is Lord *of all")* in Acts 10:36, conveys the core conviction of the lordship of the risen Christ through this parenthetical remark by Luke. It is obvious that the early Christian writers utilized the *LXX.* Luke was certainly familiar with it. The theological significance to the speech by Peter is that the risen Jesus is become Christ, and, by Christians, is subsequently to be proclaimed as the Lord of all worlds. The gospel of the risen Christ—from the beginning of the Christian tradition–was understood, by implication, to have cosmic significance.

There has been considerable debate about the appearances of the name יהוה in the Pentateuch, primarily because of various theories asserting that the name יהוה was unknown in antiquity. The idea that the name יהוה was revealed here only raises the question of how God was known earlier. *God* is not a name but rather a concept. אל שדי (*el shaddai*) is used only a few times in Genesis. Israel would not have had a nameless deity–especially since Genesis says that from the very beginning people were making proclamation of, and erecting altars in the name of יהוה (Gen 4:26; 12:8). It is possible that they did not always need a name if they were convinced that there was only יהוה and there were no other gods.

Probably what Moses was anticipating was the Israelites' needing assurance that he came to them with a message from their God and that some sign would serve as verification of the fact that the *presence* of יהוה was indeed with them. They would have known the Name and they would have known the ways in which יהוה had been manifested. It would have done no good for Moses to come to the people with a new name for God for that would be like introducing them to a new god. It would in no way authenticate to them Moses's call, only confuse; after all, they would not be expecting a new name since they had been praying to their God all along. They would want to be assured that their God actually had sent Moses to lead them.

To satisfy the Israelites Moses would had to have been familiar with the name יהוה—if nothing more than to convey to them the reality of the divine *presence* among them; that this indeed was the self-revealing God who had appeared to him in the Exodus 3 theophany. They would also have wanted to know if יהוה had sent Moses and how this was going to work in their deliverance—for they had been crying out to their God for rescue for a very long time. As it turned out the Israelites had less problem

14. Pelikan, The Spirit of Eastern Christendom (600–1700) In *The Christian Tradition,* Vol. 3. 208.

with this than Moses anticipated. Indeed, they were delighted when he came. It is likely that much of this concern was Moses's own need for assurance that this was the God of their ancestors. The promised deliverance was now to take place. Israel's long communion and worship of יהוה as the covenanted and covenantal people begins at Sinai. This marks the beginning of the Sinai theology tradition which can be traced with clarion accuracy through the Asaphite psalms (50, 73–83) which are songs originating in the north (Israel or Ephraim).[15]

In the Hebrew Bible, *the Name (Heb. hashem),* is used in place of יהוה in reverence of the holy Name. This reverence for יהוה is still maintained in various expressions of modern day Judaism. There is a reluctance to appropriate its usage aloud—this in sobering contrast to much of contemporary Christianity's casual references to the holy One. The only appropriate stance is to tread carefully with awe and worship in the *presence* of the Holy.[16] The acknowledgment of the activity and attributes of יהוה, particularly immanence and transcendence, frequently come to expression through the various images used to describe God's actions in the Psalms. The more frequent Hebraic images express a knowledge of the nearness and awareness of the *presence* and help and deliverance of יהוה. It is the *presence* of יהוה that is, for ancient Israel, the primary locus of divine activity.

A deep trust and confidence in יהוה emerges out of each of these texts. This trust is rooted in ancient Israel's common life and work and, most of all, worship. Our three psalms represent some of the highest expressions of trust in the Psalter. In this respect Psalm 91 marks the zenith of the book of Psalms. The entire book is the subject of a people's growth in faith and trust in יהוה their God. יהוה is the sacred name of the God of Israel, both in the northern kingdom and in Judah. Before ca. 1200 BCE, the name is not found in any semitic texts. יהוה was never known at Ugarit according to the findings. But it is in the Psalms where we may eavesdrop on the way God's ancient people conversed in the *presence* of the sacred Name. Nowhere is the transaction of the divine-human drama expressed more convincingly than in ancient Israel's ongoing dialogue with יהוה, the God of history. The results of this dialog bear the hallmarks of the book of Praises.

James Muilenburg's observation made a half century ago, still remains an accurate assessment of ancient Israel's uniqueness: *The way of Israel is historical. It is historical to a maximum degree because its history belongs to God. History is God's gift to Israel and to the world.*[17] That יהוה will one day come to be recognized by all as the

---

15. cf. Cook, *The Social Roots of Biblical Yahwism*, Society of Biblical Literature. 2004.
Note: Cook cites often the connection that exists between the Psalms of Asaph (50, 73–83) and the Sinai theology tradition which is the monotheistic Yahwist belief and which becomes the subsequent confession of ancient Israel.

16. cf. Tozer, *The Knowledge of the Holy,* 44.

17. Muilenburg, *Psalm 4:7,* 44.
cf. Rendtorff, *Canon and Theology,* ". . . the historical experiences of Israel are reflected in the Psalms in various ways. The personal religion that finds its expression here is rooted in God's action in

God of all the earth is attested in Psalm 83:18–*Let them know that you alone, whose name is* יהוה, *are* עליון *(elyon) over all the earth.*

> ... *it is important to note the close association between the idea of Yahweh's incomparability and the idea that not only Israel, but also the heathen had to acknowledge Yahweh as God ... it cannot be denied that, at least to a certain extent, the concept shows trends of universalism ... in connection with the idea of [His] incomparability it means that other peoples will recognize not only this, but also [His] uniqueness. Should universalism be seen as one of the requirements for pure monotheism, then this confession undoubtedly met this requirement, for right from the beginning it transcended national limitation in showing a universalistic trend.*[18]

The identity and the universality of Israel's God is firmly rooted in the prophets, particularly Isaiah: *Only in* יהוה *it shall be said of me, are righteousness and strength; all who were incensed against him shall come to him and be ashamed. In* יהוה *all the offspring of Israel shall triumph and glory* (Is 45:24, NRSV). The broad parameter of the use of the divine names is illustrated abundantly throughout the book of Praises. Israel's very existence bears witness to the promises of the covenant which she entered into with יהוה. Israel's conversation with יהוה is Israel's gift to us. Here we witness the mighty deeds *of* יהוה, Israel's words *to* God, and God's words *to* Israel. This is, theologically speaking, a new horizon in Israel's faith development. When meditating on the Psalter we too may step into the historic stream -this remarkable legacy of trusting יהוה in faith—whether in times of lamentation and desolation or times of celebration and praise. The unique and primary locus of these hymns of praise in the Hebrew Bible is found in the Psalter.

In the *LXX* the word *psalm* is derived from the Greek (ψαλμοῖς, *psalmois*) which in turn translates the Hebrew מזמור (*mizmor*, root meaning *to pluck*) and is the most common title. It is used in the superscriptions of 57 psalms.[19] מזמור (*mizmor*) refers to a song accompanied by a stringed instrument.

The term *Psalter* is derived from the Latin, *psalterium*, or stringed instrument. Many of the psalms that have come down to us clearly denote musical accompaniment (lyre and harp, zither, trumpets, tambourines and drums) in a particular liturgical setting—but reaching anything like exact dates when these titles were first appropriated is only ill-advised speculation.

---

the past; but it directs itself ever and again to the yet imminent future deeds of God." 64.

18. Labuschagne, *The Incomparability of Yahweh in the Old Testament*, 146.

19. Note: The superscriptions or titles are headings that appear at the beginning of 116 psalms (the opening verse or verses in Hebrew). They provide ancient, though not original, information in a variety of forms: authorial attribution, historical setting, instrumental accompaniment, poem-prayer types, etc. The remaining psalms which have no titles are sometimes referred to as "orphans." The psalm titles are late editorial additions to the collections and may most certainly be dated in the late postexilic era.

> *. . . there is the attempt to place various psalms on a continuum according to their theological perspective. The interpretation of the Old Testament has been plagued by this necessity to argue from the development of religious thought to history and from historical context to the date of the literature. For this reason, all judgments about the relative dates of biblical texts are hazardous. Naturally, this approach assumes that religious ideas progressed ever more in ancient Israel, and the purest teachings necessarily came later than others less refined. Of course, we know that societies do not evolve in this fashion and pockets of a culture invariably preserve older values.*[20]

The *LXX* remains an immensely important translation and has served as an invaluable resource to all subsequent studies of the Hebrew Scriptures for more than two millennia. Since the *LXX* is a translation, scholars speculate as to what degree it accurately reflects the Hebrew text of the third-century BCE. On closer examination of both the *LXX* and the ninth-century CE Masoretic Text (*MT*) there do occur, understandably, some variations. Were these due to errors in translation, transcription, or are the *LXX* and *MT* based on two different Hebrew manuscripts? The discovery of the Dead Sea Scrolls has certainly helped shed light on some of these questions.

The inhabitants of Judea and Israel in the time of the monarchy were constantly tempted to forsake יהוה and to engage in the ancient cults of the neighboring nature deities. Israel's God, by any name, is holy and awe-filled. But it was the constant allurement of the prolific nature deities of Canaan that remained a continuing enticement to Israel to abandon the worship of "יהוה *alone.*" The influence of Canaanite religion played a significant role in these developments. Our knowledge of the religions of Canaan has been much advanced by archaeological discoveries of documents and potsherds, especially from Ugarit (Ras Shamra) which date from the middle of the second millennium, ca.1420 BCE.

These Bronze Age religions had a powerful impact on the Iron Age Israelites, particularly during the time of the divided kingdom and they gained entry into Israel's life especially under the program and policies of Jeroboam I, the first king of the northern kingdom (Israel). But it was later, under Ahaz and his Sidonian princess wife Jezebel, that a particularly noxious and virulent strain of Canaanite religion was introduced in the north and was practiced openly.[21] This threatened the very future of Yahwism in both North and South. The early prophets of the north, Elijah and Elisha in the ninth century BCE, continually castigated the northern kings for their polytheism. The eighth-century BCE prophets railed against these cultural accretions, particularly Amos and Hosea in the north, beginning in the mid-eighth century.

---

20. Crenshaw, *A Whirlpool of Torment*, 95.

21. Admittedly what we know of the monarchy in the northern kingdom of Israel—at least what is in the Bible— is filtered through the 7th century BCE Deuteronomist historians who view Israel's monarchy through the prism of the southern kingdom perspective. This royal propaganda considered all the kings of northern Israel bad—in their view.

Somewhat later in the century, in the south, Micah–and still later on, Jeremiah in the late seventh and early sixth-centuries BCE continued to warn the southern kingdom of Judah of impending disaster.

The contrast and movement from *polytheism* and *henotheism* to *monotheism* run like a continuous thread through ancient Israel's history.[22] Israel never arrived at a pure monotheism easily. There is no evidence for this transition from henotheism to monotheism having occurred abruptly. Rather, it appears to have been a lengthy process that continued through much of pre-exilic Israel's life.

The arrival of a belief in the form of a distinct monotheism as central to ancient Israel's life, is thus postulated as having arrived in the post-exilic years. Psalm 82 is frequently cited as marking the moment that Israel adopted a thorough-going monotheism.

A comparison between Psalm 91:1, 2 and Psalm 18:1–3 and its hymnic praise to יהוה by heaping metaphor upon metaphor underscores the centrality of the "יהוה *alone movement*" as it may be tracked throughout the Psalter. It may be said that *metaphorical monotheism* characterizes much of the these psalms. But the worship of יהוה did not mean that Israel was immediately transformed into a monotheistic culture. This process would take centuries. The form and fact of henotheism weaves a pattern throughout Israel's history and is the subject of the constant judgment of יהוה on the people of God. Israel's God, יהוה, is a jealous God. Much of this language may be found throughout the Psalter.

Many scholars understand monotheism as a solely post-exilic phenomenon which began to flourish during the "Babylonian Captivity." In exile, Israel–or Judah—was forced to come to terms with her recent debasement and central to this core belief was the recognition that יהוה was the One God of All, having chosen Israel's' oppressors as instruments of correction to call the people back to the true meaning of their life as the people of God. This radical movement took root during the seventy years the people were in exile. It was to be the harbinger of new life that infused the exiled community, upon their return, to begin to understand the universal meaning of their election by יהוה in dramatically new and fundamentally altered ways. The prophetic words uttered by Amos and Hosea in the eighth-century BCE, and the message of Jeremiah in the seventh and sixth centuries, and of the later prophets, Habakkuk and Zechariah, had not been heeded. Their words now came back to haunt the defeated people. They purposed to reconstruct their lives under יהוה and the end result was the miracle of Judaism whereby the Jews became the people of the book, or Torah meaning the way of instruction (cf. Psalm 119).

Some of the post-exilic psalms reflect this fundamental shift in understanding (96, 97, 103, 107, 113, 115, 123, 138, etc.). יהוה as sheltering *presence* and protecting refuge serve as core monotheistic metaphors. These are stirring descriptions. Psalm 18, an early

---

22. Polytheism is the devotion to and worship of a plurality of gods; Henotheism is the worship of one God per tribe or nation among other gods; Monotheism is the worship of the One and Only God of All. Monolatry is a synonym of henotheism.

psalm considered by many scholars as most likely a Davidic poem, is well known for its exceedingly rich metaphorical flourishes in the opening verses: *I love you, O יהוה, my strength. יהוה is my rock, my fortress, and my deliverer, my God, the Rock in whom I take refuge, my shield, and the horn of my salvation, my stronghold* (18:1–2, NRSV).

But it is only in Psalm 91 that we find this compact formula consisting of four divine appellatives—in just two verses. In Psalm 90 the poet quickly picks up on the image of *refuge* proclaiming יהוה as מחסי (*machasa, to hide or shelter*); it is the principal word for refuge, which occurs twice in Psalm 91 (vss 2, 9). Psalm 115 is considered a communal song of trust to be sung and celebrated by the whole people. The alternating pronouns suggest antiphonal responses throughout the recitation or singing of the prayer. All praise is attributed to the Name, יהוה. The poet is attuned to the complaints on the part of the people. Their situation is understood to be a challenge to the glory and honor of יהוה. The poet reinforces the power and demonstration of the glory of the Name יהוה in the face of the taunts of the surrounding nations. The entire poem is a call to monotheistic Yahwism. As a response to such charges, the poet declares the vitality and power of the God of Israel, יהוה. The idols of the nations are reduced to the futility of their makers while the people of Israel are encouraged to trust in יהוה alone and express their confidence in God's rescue and deliverance of them.

At the very outset of Psalm 115, glory to the Name of יהוה is expressed and the situation of the people in the face of their enemy Egypt is taken to be a challenge to the glory and honor of יהוה. The poem's representative voice declares the awesome power and strength of Israel's God over and against all other gods. The stress is on the transcendence of God. *For our God is in the heavens; whatever God wills, God does.* The word of finality is expressed in the final strophe: *Praise YHWH!* This psalm, a liturgical communal prayer of the people in Jewish tradition, is one of the *Egyptian Hallel* (*"praise"*) psalms (113–118)—sung before (Pss 113–114) and after (Pss (115–118) the Passover meal in praise of the deliverance out of Egypt by the hand of יהוה.

Psalm 115

Not to us, O יהוה, not to us,

but to your Name give the glory

for the sake of your constancy and your truth,

lest the heathen say: *"Where is their God?"*

For our God is in the heavens;

whatever God wills, God does.

The idols of the heathen are silver and gold,

the work of their hands.

They have mouths but they cannot speak;

they have eyes but they cannot see;

they have ears but they cannot hear;

they have nostrils but they cannot smell.

With their hands they cannot feel;

with their feet they cannot walk.

No sound comes from their throats.

Their makers will become like themselves

and so will all who put their trust in them.

O Israel's family, trust in יהוה;

יהוה is your help and your shield.

Aaron's family, trust in יהוה;

יהוה is your help and your shield.

You who fear יהוה trust in יהוה;

יהוה is your help and your shield.

יהוה remembers and will bless us;

will bless the family of Israel,

will bless the family of Aaron.

יהוה will bless those who fear him,

the little no less than the great;

The heavens belong to יהוה

but God has given the earth into our keeping.

Those who go down to the grave shall not praise יהוה,

nor the dead who, in silence, know only oblivion.

But we will bless יהוה

both now and forevermore.

Praise יהוה!

This psalm functions as a potent discourse on the close relationship that exists between the family of Israel and her God, יהוה. As has already been noted, the Psalter is first and foremost an account of the relationship between יהוה and Israel—God's word to God's people and their words as a response to יהוה. There is a continuing conversation between יהוה and the covenantal people throughout the Psalter. This is the hallmark of its many themes and features. It is little wonder then that the rabbis call the Psalter *sepher tehillim*, formed from the same root as the word הללויה (*hallelujah*), thus the title *The Book of Praises*.

> *The Hebrew title of the book of Psalms is tehillim, 'Praises.' Although the hymns or songs of praise are outnumbered in the Psalter by the prayers of lament or complaint, the title 'Praises' is appropriate. Even the prayers of lament or complaint move toward praise. So does the Psalter as a whole. Whereas prayers of*

lament or complaint dominate Books I-III, hymns or songs of praise are domi-
nate in Books IV-V. Thus praise becomes the goal of the Psalter in the same way
that praise is the goal of human life. Praise is fundamental.[23]

Although the songs of praise and thanksgiving are outnumbered, dominantly so, by the prayers and songs of lament-complaint, the title *book of Praises* is still appropriate. For these and other reasons the Psalter is sometimes referred to as the *Hymnbook of the Second Temple.*[24] This would be appropriate if the book of Psalms was viewed primarily as a post-exilic book, which was commonly held a century ago. But this, too, is inaccurate and misleading as we now understand that not a few psalms likely predate by at least one hundred years the first temple's Iron Age construction in the mid-tenth-century BCE.

It is important to remember that these early psalms would have begun their life in the worship of יהוה following the event of the exodus; in their journey through the wilderness, shrines and altars were erected in order for the people of יהוה to continue their sacrificial rites and ceremonies. These psalms would travel far and wide before coming to rest in the liturgy of the temple beginning in the tenth century BCE. It is fair to say that ancient Israel's psalms became, over time, the voice of the people of יהוה communing with their God. This is substantiated by the repeated pleas that the *presence* of their God would remain and abide with them forever.

23. Craigie, Psalms 1–50, vol. 1 *Word Biblical Commentary,* 53. cf. Curtis, Psalms in *Epworth Commentaries* "The Hebrew name *sepher tehillim* means 'Book of Praises' and the title is most appropriate. Many psalms are hymns of praise to God, while others praise [him] indirectly, e.g. by praising Zion where [his] presence was believed to dwell." xxi.

24. Kraus, Psalms 1–59, vol. 1. *A Continental Commentary,* 11. Kraus prefers the designation, "the Hymnal of the Jewish Community," as, in his view, "the title *Sepher Tehillim* is not at all suitable to serve as a general title that is exhaustive and at all adequate for the contents of the 150 psalms." 5. Note: However, even the prayers of lament or complaint, by their structure and occurrences throughout, demonstrate the inexorable movement toward praise.

Deep Memory

THE PSALTER IS DIVIDED into five distinct books, each of which, excepting Psalm 145, concludes with a benediction: Book I (3–41: *Blessed be* יהוה, *the God of Israel, from eternity to eternity. Amen and Amen*); Book II (42–72: *Blessed be* יהוה, *the God of Israel, who alone does wondrous things. Blessed be his glorious name forever; Amen and Amen*); Book III (73–89: *Blessed be* יהוה *forever. Amen and Amen*); Book IV (90–106: *Blessed be* יהוה, *the God of Israel, from eternity to eternity. And let all the people say, "Amen." Praise* יהוה); and Book V (107–145). Psalms 146 through 150 serve as the postscript and the unitive doxology of praise to the entire Psalter. Each begins "Alleluia" or *Praise* יהוה! In these schema we take also Psalms 1 and 2 as the *Introduction to the Psalter*.

In Hebrew, Psalm 1 begins with *aleph*, the first letter of the alphabet; its final word begins with the letter *taw*, the last letter of the alphabet. Consequently, the letters *aleph* and *taw* are intended to symbolize all the letters and words in between, thereby embracing the entire Psalter. Psalm 2 alerts all readers who approach the book of Praises to listen carefully to what follows and meditate on it day and night for what they will encounter there reaches beyond time!

> *Psalm 2 is the second panel of the introduction to the Book of Psalms. It is united to the first psalm by the inclusion of the . . . ("Blessed," or "How happy") which open the first [Psalm] and conclude the second [Psalm], and by the repetition of themes from the first (1:6) in the second (2:12). Together Psalms 1 and 2 introduce major topics and terms that are woven through the texture of the entire book. The piety represented by these psalms is beset by the problems of the wicked and the nations. The reader is asked to take both psalms as the voice of the speaker, who identifies himself in 2:7 by an identity given him by God. ' The son' pronounces the beatitude of Psalm 1 about the wicked and the righteous and discloses the policy of heaven concerning the nations in Psalm 2.* [1]

Likewise, *the doxology*, Psalms 146–150 is a collection of "Hallelujah Psalms" that constitutes the conclusion of the Psalter in a crescendo of praise. In this manner we are then left with one hundred and forty-three psalms (3–145). These are divided into two segments (3–89 and 90–145). With these divisions we are able to recognize

---

1. Mays, "The Portrayal of the Messiah in the Psalms," 2.

48

more clearly the definitively intentional organizational structure and shaping of the book of Psalms. This lends the view that the Psalter in its final form is the result of a collection of collections, purposeful editing and arranging, resulting in a distinct shape. These sets of markers are, however, not immediately recognizable to us. What gives a distinct shape to the corpus as a whole, from the *Introduction* of Psalms 1 and 2, to the corporate *Doxology* of Psalms 146 to 150, is a consciously intentional ordering of a "*collection of collections*" and assumes a deliberate editorial arrangement.[2] We tentatively posit a final, settled arrangement of the Psalter before the end of the first-century CE (ca. 90) or even into the early second-century. We know that the psalms were widely read and sung by the first-century Christian churches and in the Jewish synagogues that were scattered throughout the ancient Roman world.

This conscious arrangement of the Psalter, and its ready inclusion into the Hebrew canon, may be asserted as having come about rather early in the canonical process. We posit a second-century BCE time frame. The canon–as we now have it in our bibles—was not yet closed for all Judaism in the first-century BCE. Some of the psalms found at Qumran show that the last third of the Psalms was the section with the greatest textual fluidity. These manuscripts (4QPsf = 4Q8811; Qps a-b = 11Q 5–6)[3] include additional apocryphal psalms, some of them known from the Greek Psalter (Ps 151) or the Syriac Psalter (Pss 151, 154, and 155). Some scholars view these Qumran psalters as biblical or "canonical," all of which suggest that the number and sequence of the canonical psalms had not yet been definitively established in the Qumran period. Others view these scrolls as a secondary compilation for liturgical use or as library editions.[4] However, this arrangement hinges on several other considerations relevant to our study.

The implication that follows is that both Psalms 1 and 2, the *Introduction*, and Psalms 146–150, the final *Doxology*, were added late in the development of the entire book. A late post-exilic setting in the Persian period of the restoration and the rebuilding of the walls of the temple under Ezra-Nehemiah can reasonably be postulated. This does not mean, however, that they were the last of the compositions to be included in the collection. Psalm 2 alone can reasonably be set in the tenth-century BCE and Psalm 1 "*is more than an introduction to the Psalter; it is a precis of the Book of Psalms.*[5] This assessment of the *shaping of the Psalter* implies that the canon of the Hebrew scriptures was open for a very long time. We know now that the Hebrew canon was still quite fluid at the time of the *LXX* and included the book of Daniel, thought

2. cf. Wilson, "The Shape of the Book of Psalms," 129–142. cf. McCann, *Theological Introduction to the Book of Psalms*. "It is interesting to consider the possibility that an earlier form of the Psalter may have consisted of Psalms 1–119. If so, this would mean that at one stage of its existence the Psalter itself was encompassed by what Psalms 1 and 119 affirm is all-encompassing—the instruction of the Lord. It would be yet another instance of how literary structure reinforces content and theology."32.

3. These are simply the symbols that are used to catalog the Dead Sea findings.

4. cf. *The New Interpreter's Bible*, Vol. IV, 554.

5. Dahood, *Psalms*, 1.

to be one of the last entries into the Hebrew canon. This is significant for determining a relative time of the closing of the canon of Hebrew scripture by the community of scribal authorities, toward the end of the first-century CE.

> *The earliest attestations of the Hebrew canon as a list come from the second half of the first century C. E. Between 250 B.C.E. and 50 C. E., it seems that there was no canon in the sense of a numerus fixus of holy books. The widely accepted doctrine of the era of revelation permitted discussion about the authenticity, antiquity, and authorship of specific books.*[6]

But the closing of the Hebrew canon, which we postulate as ca. 90 to 125 CE does not preclude the Psalter's continued shaping and editing right up to that time. Final canonization and the editing of the texts are two very different activities; and the consideration of the text of the Hebrew Bible as being in some sense sacred prior to canonicity is not a contradictory position.

The Psalms did not become "inspired scripture" the moment they were canonized. Indeed, they had functioned in the community as sacred songs for a very long time. They were received into the ancient canon as the primary witness to the great deeds of יהוה by a people who had sung and prayed them over many centuries. Indeed, they had functioned liturgically long before they were written compositions; before they were read, they were sung; before they were collected; before they were arranged; before they were edited; indeed, before they were text, they had nurtured and consoled the wider community of the faithful. Inspiration is implied in the Hebrew bible.

It only became a focus of the Christian church in the second and third centuries CE as it struggled with establishing its own criteria as to what constitutes an "inspired text." Determining just how specific words come to be "enscripturated" is a process that takes place over an extended period of time. What is clear is that the early Christian church understood the Hebrew bible to be sacred scripture by its repeated use of the moniker "*it is written.*" That the Psalms were used widely throughout early Christian worship is attested by no less than Luke, Peter, Paul and the other evangelists. The Hebrew bible translated into Greek (LXX) was, for the early church, the book of the "law and the prophets."

That the psalms were considered authoritative witness by the Jews prior to the closing of the canon, is widely attested. The word *canon* means a *reed* or *rule*; a standard to be agreed on; a *settled text.* An early version of the book of Psalms (second-century BCE) gives every appearance of having been readily received into the Hebrew canon as sacred text of Scripture. It quickly secured the mantle of unparalleled authoritative and faithful witness to the historic acts and words of יהוה in the life of the ancient people of God. This is thoroughly demonstrated and it's witnessed throughout the Christian scriptures in the church. Indeed, the first scriptures of the early Christians was the Hebrew bible. Its searching use of the Psalms bore witness to Jesus as the fulfillment of God's promises

---

6. van der Toorn, *Scribal Culture and the Making of the Hebrew Bible,* 261.

to all humanity. The promised Messiah was the subject of their investigations. Without the witness of the Psalms as scripture, this pattern of promise and fulfillment would not be nearly so transparent to the new community of God.

The two major Greek translations of the "Old Testament", the *LXX* third-century BCE and the ninth-century CE *Theodotion Text,* [7] both include additional materials taken from the book of Daniel, and others which were relegated to the Apocrypha. In both the Hebrew and Protestant bibles, the First Testament books consist of 39 entries. Although they are arranged in a differing order, both canons contain exactly the same authorized books. These differ from their Roman Catholic and Eastern Orthodox counterparts, both of whom admit deutero-canonical books into their canons of Holy Scripture. The Protestant Anglican Communion admits some few apocryphal books for the purpose of reading and edification, but not for the constructing and establishing of any doctrine. This is a position that is theologically unique to the Anglican Communion—and in turn, the Episcopal Church in the United States.

Additionally, manuscript fragments of the prophecy of Daniel were also found among the Dead Sea Scrolls in three caves at Qumran including apocalyptic texts that employ language reminiscent of Daniel 7 and 12. The earliest date of the Dead Sea Scrolls is placed in the second-century BCE. The inclusion of sacred scriptures into the Hebrew canon occurs later than the *LXX*, which includes both of these books and is relatively fixed by the time of the council at Jamnia, ca. 90 CE.[8] There are substantial differences in the Hebrew biblical canon, and that found in the Greek and Latin and modern Roman Catholic Bibles regarding the status and use of apocryphal books and their inclusion into the Hebrew canon of sacred scripture. These so-called deutero-canonical writings, with only one or two exceptions, are extant only in Greek and do not form part of the Hebrew canon. Further support may be garnered from the Dead Sea Scrolls where one may compare the arrangement of the Psalter to that found in the Masoretic Text (*MT*), the stabilization of which appear to take place in two distinct stages:

> *Psalms 1–89 (or thereabouts) prior to the first century BCE, and Psalms 90 on-wards toward the end of the first century CE. The scrolls strongly suggest that during the entire Qumran period Psalms 1–89 were virtually finalized as a collection while Psalms 90 and beyond remained much more fluid.* [9]

7. The Theodotian Text (9th century CE) is a thorough revision of the LXX, bringing it to some extent into harmony with the Masoretic Text as current in the translator's time.

8. The historical significance of the so-called "council of Jamnia" otherwise called Yabneh, has been called into doubt increasingly by scholarship in recent years and has been abandoned in some quarters. "But the impression has persisted that, so far as the establishment of the Old Testament canon is concerned, this may be something of a quibble. Council or no council, it was among the rabbinic authorities gathered at Yabneh after the destruction of the Temple that disputes about the exact limits of Scripture began to be settled." John Barton, *Holy Writings Sacred Text*, 108. Note: A late first or early second century CE date at which time the Hebrew canon was largely "stabilized" is most likely.

9. Flint, *The Dead Sea Scrolls and the Book of Psalms*, 148. Note: In this respect, James Sanders interprets, and I think rightly, that the evidence taken from the findings in the Dead Sea Scrolls indicates that the first two-thirds of the Psalter, i.e. Books I, II, III (Pss 3–89), had reached a state of relative

For Christians, the value of the Psalter of course, lies chiefly in the relationship between the Hebrew bible and the Christian scriptures. Rather than resorting to analysis alone, the Psalms call for synthesis and constantly challenge the mind and the heart of the serious reader. Discussion of the shape of the book of Psalms cannot afford to overlook what this combination of earlier and later segments into a final form was intended to signify. An intentional and purposeful editorial arrangement and *a collection of collections* in the final shaping of the Psalter is clearly at work, bringing it to the final form we have today. The Psalms are normally assumed to be the poetic constructions of some of the more famous individuals in Israel's history. But this is not necessarily accurate because the authorship of the various psalms is now thought to be a largely anonymous enterprise and the actual identity of any of the individual poets is now considered highly speculative.

These particular 150 poetic compositions (there were thousands of psalm compositions produced in ancient Israel) are filled with songs and hymns, prayers and praises, laments and thanksgiving. Whereas prayers of lament or complaint psalms dominate *Books I-III*, the hymns and songs of praise are more numerous in *Books IV-V*. Broadly speaking, most of the psalms in *Books I-III* are thought to be of pre-exilic origin while the latter *Books IV and V* are usually considered to be mostly postexilic in origin. In this same manner praise becomes the goal of the Psalter in the way that praise is the goal of human life.

Praise is fundamental to any right understanding of the Psalms. A dialogical relationship between God and the people of God reflects the faith experience of the community that cries out in hope for the plenitude of God's mercy, deliverance and redemption. The Psalms speak directly to the human heart. This dynamic element lies more often than not in an inherent ambiguity which is the subject of the Psalter: יהוה, who in love or anger, forgiveness or punishment, seeks to be the God of Israel, and Israel, which can only exist as the people of this God, in each historic moment, seeks to hear and respond to God's call to them. It is YHWH who gives this particular people their corporate identity.

The compositions of the Psalms are primarily poetic but certainly not in the way we have come to understand poetry. Biblical prose is highly linear and sequential, moving from one event in time to the next through the ever present *and* in our English Bible versions. Prose is much more accessible to the contemporary reader, encouraging and inviting a dynamic interaction with the text. But the various poetic forms of the Psalms do not move so smoothly. Hebrew poems don't typically tell a story so they lack the connective sinew which ties prose together. The short half-verses are bonded together in verbal parallelism and in turn mark the transition from one line to the next -a relatively tenuous exercise. Each line in Hebrew poetry functions more like a brick

---

stabilization and fixity at a time when the last third, Books IV and V (Pss. 90–145), was still in a state of editorial flux. This "window" would most likely have been opened between the second-century BCE and the late-first century CE. cf. Sanders, *The Qumran Psalms Scroll*.

in a wall than it does a length of rope or a cable. However, very few languages are better suited to the form of noble poetry than is biblical Hebrew. In part, this is due to its very great strength of accent which normally falls on the last syllable, thus bearing the weight of sound and meaning carried by the word. The result is such that even Hebrew prose has a very strongly marked cadence or rhythm. Although our efforts to reproduce the sounds of the sung psalms it in its ancient and original state are completely futile, its sung sound must have been melodious–even ethereal–and exceedingly pleasant to the human ear. Because of this style of composition, and combined with the fact that Hebrew is a terse, pithy language all make the poetry of the psalms more difficult to access than the "friendlier" prose to which we are accustomed in the Bible.

When it comes to the translation of the Hebrew text into English the terseness of the original is almost always lost. Translation is more art than science and translators typically elongate and smooth out features of Hebrew poetry making it more challenging to access the original meaning of the text.

Nevertheless, we are not without a relatively high degree of confidence that—with some very few exceptions—the text of the Psalter is fundamentally reliable. In conveying accurately, the essence of these poetic compositions, they are affirmed as a whole and contribute to some of the most deeply intimate, moving and affective language in the entire Bible. The Psalms are the product of a community of faithful and observant worshipers. Together they sang and prayed what would gradually become, over a very long period of time, these unparalleled poems, songs, and prayers in praise of יהוה. Taken as a whole, they tell us that this is the way of Israel's life and standing before יהוה.

This too is the genius of the Psalter. Its poetry speaks the language of every person because it mirrors not only the general and the typical, but also the particular and the specific. The first word is very often the personal divine name of God, יהוה. In the Book of Common Prayer, and in most English Bible versions as well, the name יהוה is translated *LORD* (all upper case); אדני *Adonai,* or *Lord* (lowercase), is translated as the epithet meaning *Sovereign.* This feature again represents the psalmists' concern to preserve the sanctity of the holy and sacred Name: יהוה. In the use of this one word so much is compressed, especially allusions to the personal relationship with יהוה and the confession that [he] alone can save. Claus Westermann explains the structure of Hebrew poetry and rhyme in this way:

> It is a feature of the Hebrew language (as well as the neighboring Semitic languages) that sentences rather than words or syllables are rhymed. The rhyme occurs neither in sound nor in the number of words but in the meaning of the sentences. In this feature the ancient idea is kept alive that all human speech consists not of words, but sentences. Not the single word but the sentence as a whole is the basic unit.[10]

10. Westermann, *The Living Psalms,* 123.

It is from this perspective that thought-rhymes or sentence-rhymes called *parallelism* are to be understood. In the Psalms, singing and praying are still united; psalms are sung prayers or prayed singing. As songs they are at the same time what we call poetry but in a different sense than our modern poetry. The Psalms unite in themselves three separate types of word formulations: *prayers* (words directed to God in petition or praise), *poetry* (poetically formulated language), and *songs* (that go beyond the speaking or recital of a poem and become music). Poetic language, then, becomes the *voice* of the Hebrew Bible. This *voice* calls out to us from the distant vistas of history and is the community's witness to ancient and foreign encounters with the Holy. It is never easy to determine the exact meaning of the text amid its many layered forms.

> *The full hearing of the psalms will be greatly enhanced when the familiar tendency to abstract content from form or to empty form of its content is overcome. To know the psalms are poetic is not to forget that they are Scripture. To read and hear them as Scripture requires that one receive them also as poetry. From either direction, understanding is all.* [11]

Establishing the *historical* context of a given psalm is all but impossible. The titles, where provided, are considered to be later additions. They are not part of the early text, and are thought not to be reliable for establishing any historical frame of reference. So at best we are confronted with material that is book-ended by the Babylonian exile–pre-exilic and post-exilic.

A critical and essential component of the hermeneutical task then involves interpreting the Psalms through a continuous *reinterpretation* as a method of studying how each psalm may be understood. Interacting with the texts themselves and paying close attention to the details of the language is demanded. Discerning the shape and shaping of the Psalter can provide the serious exegete with an interpretative vantage point. This is no modest task, as Klaus Seybold remarks:

> *In the practical work of exegesis on the Psalms it proves useful to begin by seeing how a psalmist opens his psalm, and how he closes it. In all speech, the first word is of paramount importance, as it marks the speaker's point of attack, where he himself stands or professes to stand, from where he makes himself heard, in which direction he speaks or calls, and where he knows or presumes the listener to be.* [12]

An added complexity to early biblical Hebrew was the absence of vowel markings, punctuation, and cases. Sentence divisions—as we know them—as well as a system of notation indicating grammar were only added to the Hebrew text in the Middle Ages. The present division of the biblical text was adopted by Stephen Langton (1150–1228 CE) and was incorporated into the Hebrew text in the fourteenth-century CE. These divisions do not reflect the text's original arrangement. With precious few

---

11. Patrick D. Miller, Jr. *Interpreting the Psalms*, 17.

12. Klaus Seybold, *Introducing the Psalms*, 39.

exceptions, the dates and relative setting at which the hymns and prayers as they are now preserved in the Psalter, were originally composed, cannot be determined with anything like precision. It clearly appears that the great majority of them, like the proverbs and hymnic poems later collected in the wisdom literature of the Hebrew Bible, surfaced orally and were chanted or sung in communal worship in the temple before the fall of Jerusalem in the early sixth-century (587 BCE).

It is likely that some of them may come from David himself; others, not so likely. For example, we know that the psalms of Korah (Psalms 42, 44–49; 84–85; 87–88) most likely originated in at least the early eighth-century BCE near the ancient sanctuary of Dan in the far northern frontier of Israel. The head-waters of the ravines and torrents in the foothills of Mount Hermon is the most probable geographic location for many of these psalms. These "northern songs" most likely made their way south in the latter part of that century under the pressure of Assyrian incursion and the subsequent invasion of the territory of the northern tribes of Israel resulting in the wholesale destruction of Samaria in 722–21 BCE.

Our interpretive challenge in understanding so many of the psalms is a multi-layered one. The psalmists' close bonds with יהוה are spelled out in striking images; the affirmation that each of the psalmists live in the grace of יהוה; that the cup of salvation comes only from יהוה (Ps 116:13); that each psalmist perceives their own individual identity and destiny; that all that makes up life in God is in the hands of יהוה to give and to shape. The gift is the *presence* of יהוה who will never abandon to death and nothingness [his] covenant-partner. Bonded in a love of extraordinary fidelity, the emphasis is on total devotion to יהוה and trust in [his] abiding *presence*.

The Hebrew *"gospel"* can be summed up as follows: *You will show me the path of life. In your presence there is fullness of joy; in your right hand are unimagined glories forevermore* (Ps 16:11, LW). The *path of life* (ארח חיים) is none other than יהוה who is the journey and the journey's end. Life is a gift to be held in trust—like the land that was held in trust to God's people. All statements about life are to be seen and understood in the liturgical context of Israel's psalms without losing sight of the fact that Israel shared widely in the expressions and concepts of the ancient religious world and the neighboring peoples surrounding her.

The relative antiquity of psalms can be traced to their origins in Late Bronze Age II. We assess these relative dates by assigning to Israel's origins some pertinent archaeological data. Important non-biblical sources for establishing Israelite origins in Palestine are the *Merneptah Stele* (ca. thirteenth-century BCE), which mentions an Egyptian defeat of "Israel" in Canaan, dated to ca. 1207 BCE, and the *Amarna Letters,* which disclose extensive political and social upheaval in the Canaanite city-states during the approximate period 1390–1362 BCE. The stele's reference to Israel gives us a valuable chronological horizon for establishing the presence of Israel in Palestine by *at least* 1230 BCE, the beginning of Early Iron Age I. It is altogether probable that

Israel—by the late thirteenth century BCE—was first a loosely confederated group of clans, and then, of tribes.

> *Merneptah's inscription is hardly sober fact, but royal propaganda. There are many points of dispute in its interpretation. Nevertheless, it establishes that a group called Israel had a recognized presence in Palestine around 1200 and was important enough for an Egyptian monarch to brag about defeating them. It is significant that Israel is not simply given the standard label Shasu or sand dwellers, stock terms for despised Asiatic folk in Egyptian materials. Instead, Israel is referred to by name as a foe worthy of mention. Israel must have been prominent enough to serve the inscription's propaganda purpose of honoring the king and to be recognized by its intended readership.*[13]

Although the stele does not locate the geographical site of the battle or tell us anything about the strained and often duplicitous relations between the Egyptian court and its Canaanite vassals, it enlightens us about the internecine struggles that occurred among the vassal states. They attest to social unrest and rebellion within some of the city-states that seem to display early stages in the decline of the power centers in Canaan. In the absence of regional powers, this political vacuum would have allowed Israel to emerge in the same region more than a century later. We presume, based on this data then, that Israel emerged as an amphictionic tribal formation somewhere toward the end of Late Bronze Age II extending into Early Iron Age I. This then positions Israel's origins and beginnings in Late Bronze Age II and her subsequent emergence as a national state with the inception of the monarchy which may be dated from Iron Age I, ca. 1030 BCE. [14]

A delicate balance must be struck, then, when engaging the task of interpreting the psalmic texts. For a long time, that is, a very long time, perhaps nearly a thousand years before the Psalter was received into its final canonical form, and before the principal parts of its contents were written, there existed a tradition of psalmody in ancient Israel. The evidence for this tradition is found in the poetic texts themselves, which are part of a few prose narratives concerning Israel's earliest era. The body of this ancient poetic material—in the form of ancient books—is actually quite small. It is important to recognize and appreciate that the Psalter is situated within the larger

13. Nelson, *Historical Roots of the Old Testament (1200–63 BCE)*, 15.

14. Note: This historical perspective contravenes the "minimalist" historians view who hold that the Bible has little or no historical connection to the events described and therefore is of little value as a "historical" document. Their position is that the composition of the Bible takes place long after the exilic and post-exilic periods and assigns it somewhere in the Hellenistic era, that is ca. 332–167 BCE. I place more confidence than that in the Bible's early witness to an ancient pre-exilic period–even a pre-monarchical period going back to "old Israel" in the amphyctionic era in the 13th and 12th centuries BCE. In this historical pedigree, I believe the case can even be made for some pre-monarchic psalms, and, of course, many pre-exilic ones. Israel's covenant with Yahweh begins at Sinai, following an exodus from Egypt. This is, I believe, the solid witness of the Psalter which is a Yahwist book! Additional archaeological data suggest a similar view. cf. Yosef Garfinkel, "The Birth and Death of Biblical Minimalism," *Biblical Archaeology Review*, Vol. 27. 3, 47–53.

literary context of the Hebrew Bible. Israel's worship of יהוה only reached its climax in the praises of the Psalter. It is undeniable that some of these poems were broadly influenced by Canaanite literary style and mythical imagery.

By way of example, two ancient books, *The Book of Jashar (the Book of the Upright)* and *The Book of the Wars of Yahweh,* had survived from the dawn of Israel's collective memory. The Hebrew bible offers us little information about these two ancient anthologies.

> *It is likely that many if not most of the poems . . .appeared in one or the other of two early anthologies which are mentioned in the Bible: The Book of the Wars of Yahweh (Num 21:14), and the Book of Jashar (Josh. 10:13; II Sam. 1:18). The earliest editions of these collections may well go back to the time of the Judges, but the final published form must be dated to the monarchic period. In fact, there is a reference to the Book of Jashar in the LXX of I Kings 8:13, as the source for a poetic utterance attributed to Solomon at the dedication of the temple.[15]*

The applicable historical-political context for these extra-biblical *books* is the time of the Judges–around the time of the *amphictyony* where the various clans of Israel coalesced together and remained loosely knit for nearly two centuries in Canaan. The term *amphictyony* refers to regional worshiping communities that dwelt in close physical proximity around individual shrines and who conducted cultic rituals and celebrations in the worship of ancient Israel's God. Such observances were conducted in a number of local sanctuaries: Hebron, Shechem, Dan, Bethel, Gilgal, Shiloh, Kadesh, Gibeah, and Sinai. In the major central amphictyonic shrines of Hebron and Shechem—and probably Shiloh—the historical traditions of Israel had been gathered and collected. Whether the northern traditions which had collected around the ark, were brought to Jerusalem during the united monarchy is uncertain, but it is also unlikely.

Whatever the content of these two ancient *books* may have been—apart from the few scant passages explicitly identified as having been drawn from them—both *may* indicate the earliest collection and preservation of some of the *oral* poetry of Israel. They may also have been a part of the earliest collections and served as examples of the rudimentary beginnings of the first psalms of ancient Israel (e.g. Ps 18, 29, 68) which were later incorporated into some final collections of the book of Psalms. Whether there existed any other "books" of Israel's earliest poetic compositions is unknown and is currently unknowable.

What can be asserted with some degree of confidence is that there existed an early tradition of collecting songs and poetry. It follows then that in all probability there were various traditions and customs—unknown to us–which contributed to and culminated in the formation that resulted in the eventual book of Psalms. These types of poetry were the natural medium through which Israel gave expression to its

15. cf. David Noel Freedman, "Divine Names and Titles" in *Magnalia Dei,* 99.

most profound human feelings, aspirations and insights so obviously apparent in the compositions which comprise the book of Praises. Expressions of joy and celebration were intrinsic to their response to God's mighty acts on their behalf. Some scholars find in the Song of Deborah and Barak (Judg 5) the original life-setting of *theophany* in the Hebrew bible.

A *theophany* is the human experience of a divine self-disclosure initiated solely by the deity. There is no human initiative undertaken nor are any special qualifications or preparation required. In the Bible the human response is always one of fear and awe. There is never a sense of entitlement or privilege in the person's retrospect. Theophanies are manifested as temporal events; they are not permanent reality. Rather these momentary encounters with the divine occur in a particular place and at a particular time. A theophany is a transient happening. It impacts the totality of the human person who encounters it at a profoundly life-altering level. Nothing thereafter remains the same. This poem of Deborah and Barak, then, is one of a number of representative psalms that lie outside the Psalter; it is a victory song over an oppressive enemy and is regarded as the oldest poetry of ancient Israel. It is the sort of poem that an oppressed people might delight to recite, as it tells about the defeat of a despised enemy. This poem is the earliest extant writing found in the Hebrew Bible![16]

Judges 5

Then Deborah and Barak son of Abinoam sang on that day, saying:
"When locks are long in Israel,
when the people offer themselves willingly -
bless יהוה!
"Hear, O kings; give ear, O princes;
to יהוה I will sing,
I will make melody to יהוה,
the God of Israel.
"יהוה, when you went out from Seir,
when you marched from the region of Edom,
the earth trembled,
and the heavens opened,
the clouds indeed poured water.
The mountains quaked before יהוה,

16. Hayes, "The Tradition of Zion's Inviolability." 419. cf. Renckens, *The Religion of Israel*. "Corporate worship and various liturgical gatherings to celebrate together their life in God were characteristic of ancient early Israel, both before the establishment of the monarchy (ca 1030 BCE) and the founding of Solomon's Temple in 935 BCE." 195.

the One of Sinai,

before יהוה, the God of Israel.

"In the days of Shamgar son of Anath,

in the days of Jael, caravans ceased

and travelers kept to the byways.

The peasantry prospered in Israel,

they grew fat on plunder,

because you arose, Deborah,

arose as a mother in Israel.

When new gods were chosen,

when war was in the gates.

Was shield or spear to be seen

among forty thousand in Israel?

My heart goes out to the commanders of Israel

who offered themselves willingly among the people.

Bless יהוה.

"Tell of it, you caravaneers who ride on white donkeys,

you who sit on lush carpets

and you who walk by the way.

To the sound of musicians at the watering places,

there they repeat the triumphs of יהוה,

the triumphs of the people of יהוה in Israel.

Then down to the gates marched the people of יהוה.

"Awake, awake, Deborah!

Awake, awake, utter a song!

Arise, Barak, lead away your captives,

O son of Abinoam."

Then down marched the remnant of the noble;

the people of יהוה marched down

for him against the mighty.

From Ephraim they set out into the valley,

following you, Benjamin, with your kin;

from Machir marched down the commanders,

and from Zebulun those who bear the marshal's staff;

the chiefs of Issachar came with Deborah,

and Issachar faithful to Barak;

into the valley they rushed out at his heels.

TRUSTING YHWH

Among the clans of Reuben
there were great searchings of the heart.
Why did you tarry among the sheepfolds?
to hear the piping for the flocks?
Gilead stayed beyond the Jordan;
and Dan, why did he abide with the ships?
Asher sat still at the coast of the sea,
settling down by his landings.
Zebulun is a people that scorned death;
Naphtali too, on the heights of the field.
"The kings came, they fought;
then fought the kings of Canaan,
at Taanach, by the waters of Megiddo;
they got no spoils of silver."
The stars fought from heaven,
from their courses they fought against Sisera.
The torrent Kishon swept them away,
the onrushing torrent, the torrent Kishon.
March on, my soul, with might!
Then loud beat the horses' hoofs
with the galloping, galloping of his steeds.
Curse Meroz, says the angel of יהוה,
curse bitterly its inhabitants,
because they did not come to the help of יהוה,
to the help of יהוה against the mighty.
Most blessed of women is Jael,
the wife of Heber the Kenite,
of tent-dwelling women most blessed.
He asked for water and she gave him milk,
she brought him curds in a lordly bowl.
She put her hand to the tent peg
and her right hand to the workmen's mallet;
she struck Sisera a blow,
she crushed his head,
she shattered and pierced his temple.
He sank, he fell;
where he sank, there he fell dead.

Out of the window she peered,

the mother of Sisera gazed through the lattice:

"Why is his chariot so long in coming?

Why tarry the hoof beats of his chariots?

Her wisest ladies make answer,

indeed, she answers the question herself:

Are they not finding and dividing the spoil?"

A girl or two for every man;

spoil of dyed stuffs for Sisera,

spoil of dyed stuffs embroidered

for my neck as spoil?

So perish all your enemies, O יהוה!

But may your friends be like the sun

as it rises in its might."

The importance of this poem or hymn of praise is striking in its similarity to the Ugaritic language wherein the poet in Judges 5 describes a theophany. In this earliest instance, *the mountains quaked before YHWH, the One of Sinai, before YHWH, the God of Israel* (Judg 5:5). The translation of the verb *quake* assumes the form נָזֹלּוּ (*nazollu*) from the root זָלַל (*zalal, to shiver and shake*). Some scholars interpret the Hebrew in the sense of flowing, liquid matter (as in volcanic magma). The *LXX*, the Syriac *Peshitta*, and the *Targum* all understand the word נָזֹלּוּ (*nazollu*) in this way. Indicative of the theophanic formula is the appearance of *the angel of* יהוה (Judg 5:23) with יהוה personified as the divine warrior defending the ancient clans from their enemies in Canaan.

It is an instructive bit of song for it introduces us into the world of Hebraic poetry–a world which in another thousand years will usher forth in *Sepher Tehillim,* the book of Praises. The theophany described as it is portrayed in Judges 5 is disclosed in this ancient poem dating from the late thirteen-century BCE—not far removed from the events being celebrated. Ancient Israel's first psalm in Judges 5, Deborah's Song, is *"the oldest surviving extended fragment of Hebrew literature."* (REB p. 251).

It is explicitly described as having been sung and it is one of the earliest markers that can be traced to having been laid down at the dawn of the Hebraic traditions. The traditions of ancient Israel refer not only to the sacred texts that have come down to us but also include the life of worship and the liturgies that shaped that worship. Israel's psalms are the best examples we have from the Hebrew scriptures of the shape and the shaping of ancient Israel's worshiping life. In them we have the words Israel spoke in response to the word of יהוה being addressed to them. The origins of several other key markers, one of which is the Zion tradition, is directly connected to the ark narratives. The tradition of the election of Zion by יהוה is, of course, based upon the bringing of the ark to Jerusalem. [17] The connection of the ark tradition with the temple is later called into question by the prophets, particularly Jeremiah.[18]

There are many patterns of thought connected with the ark in the Hebrew scriptures. It was originally designated as the *ark of Elohim* which is the general usage in the books of Samuel. It was considered the place where יהוה was enthroned (Num 10:35–36; I Sam 4:4; II Sam 6:2). With the ark was connected the idea of יהוה as leader of the host. In deuteronomistic thought the ark and the covenant are joined and the "*Ark of the Covenant*" is said to contain the tables of the law. In chronistic thought, the cherubim are for the protection of the law and not for the place where יהוה sits enthroned. In the story of II Sam 6, the ark is brought to Jerusalem and merely placed in a tent. Later the building of the temple and the housing of the ark are combined.

The presence of the ark in Jerusalem meant that יהוה dwelt in the midst of [his] people. Centered around the choice of Jerusalem by יהוה as [his] dwelling place was, very much like the Davidic election tradition, joined to and expanded by pre-Israelite traditions. This is so from the very earliest compositions to the latter ones and brings the book of Psalms to its final resolution and close. The ark represented the *presence* of God at the heart of historic ancient Israel's corporate life and worship. It is in these traditions rather than in the prophetic work of Isaiah, for example, that the origin of the tradition of Zion's inviolability must be found. Memories of the ark of God continued to resonate deeply in the collective consciousness of the psalmists.

> "*The narratives on the youth of Samuel (eleventh century B.C.E.) were written in later times and edited by the Deuteronomistic school, but they include an incidental note on the ark, which bears the mark of authenticity . . . the ark was apparently kept in the temple of Shiloh, in the central mountain range of Ephraim, but there is no indication that it played any significant part in the life of the nation. The narrative merely states: 'The lamp of Elohim had not yet gone out, and Samuel was lying down in the temple of Yahweh, where the ark of Elohim was . . .' (I Sam. 3:3). The text does not suggest that the cultic object was considered as the visible sign of the permanent presence of Yahweh in the shrine. On the contrary, the recital of the vision in which Samuel was called to a prophetic mission clearly implies that the divine manifestation was distinct from the ark. The renaissance of interest in the ark under David was the prelude to a most important development in the Hebraic theology of presence. It contributed to the astounding development of the myth of Zion.*"[19]

17. Hayes, "The Tradition of Zion's Inviolability," 420.

18. Terrien, *The Elusive Presence*, ". . . Jeremiah had so clearly anticipated the annihilation of the temple that he had referred without apparent qualm to the total disappearance of the ark—that ancient palladium of the theologoumenon of glory: '*In those days, says Yahweh, they shall no more say, The ark of the covenant of Yahweh! It shall not come to mind, or be remembered, or missed; it shall not be made again*' (3:16). This oracle shows that the prophet's interpretation of the new mode of presence exploded the confines of an edifice to include the wholly human reality of a new society." 207.

19. Terrien, *The Elusive Presence*, 167.

The concept of God's dwelling in Zion has its origins in, and is based on, the *presence* of the ark of God in the temple in Jerusalem. [20]A variant prophetic tradition made certain distinctions relative to the ark and temple. [21]From several narratives in the Hebrew Scriptures, we know that the ark was closely associated with the *presence* of God. In some 75 psalms dispersed throughout all five books of the Psalter, the *presence* of God in Zion is an essential feature, whether in the prayers of the communal longing to return "home" after the exile, or in the hymns of the community experiencing the *presence* of יהוה in their midst.

The title *Psalms of David* so-called, indicates something of the relationship of David and his line with The Psalter as a communal document; those psalms which are entitled *A Psalm of David,* and appear to suggest Davidic authorship, must be understood with the following caveat: The prepositions in Hebrew are not distinct and may be imprecise. For example, those certain psalms may be understood as meaning *"for, dedicated to, concerning, David"*. Such psalms seem to evoke his persona as the chief representative of the dynasty of David without implying that he himself was the author of each psalm.

There are many psalms that might be assumed as having been authored by David.[22] Such speak too of David as the founder of the temple (2 Sam. 7), even though David did not build it, which marks out the temple as the focal point for the good life and the hope for the future. It is not surprising then that the ark would embody memories of the celebrations and the triumphs of יהוה during the early days of the conquest of Canaan. In Shechem, and likely Bethel and Shiloh as well, the ark conferred its *cultic concreteness* upon both dimensions of the Mosaic covenant: vertical, since it exhibited the bond which united יהוה to Israel; and horizontal, since it cemented the solidarity

20. Wolverton "The Meaning of the Psalms," In *Anglican Theological Review* 47. "Did the psalmists really believe that God actually *dwelt* in Zion? The area could have been a sanctuary (*qodesh* or *miqdash*) for somewhat different reasons—because God was to be met there in connection with his *visitation,* so to speak, or because he kept special watch over it, and not because he actually *dwelt.* One psalmist says: 'Yhwh is in his holy temple; Yhwh's throne is in heaven,' and then goes on to indicate that '[His] eyes see, his eyelids try, the sons of [men]' (Ps 11.4,5). Can it be that God is in both places at once, in heaven *and* at Zion?" 29.

21. Skinner, *Prophecy and Religion: Studies in the Life of Jeremiah* "In effect, Jeremiah seems to say that the temple is not what [men] call it or imagine it to be, but what by their actions they make it. It might have been the place where Yahweh's gracious presence was experienced if they had hallowed his name by lives lived in piety and righteousness. Jeremiah stressed more clearly than Deuteronomy the factor of the invocation of the name [יהוה] in prayer, sacrifice, and other acts of worship. He may have been more aware than the Deuteronomists of the mystery of the ark of the presence which it was believed involves the moral quality of the worshipers." 175.

22. Note: I read the book of Psalms as though it belongs to and reflects David's genius and legacy. In some instances, this may seem to imply authorship; in still others a more complex and nuanced association is intended. I am not suggesting that some, if any of the psalms, were authored by David, only that some were composed in his time. The issues of authorship and the original context of various psalms are questions for historical study and reflection. I take the association of the psalms with David seriously and read those collections as though they were David's or rather are possibly closely associated with him. He was certainly not the sole author, but it's possible he may have been the most prolific.

of the heterogeneous tribes under their shared allegiance. The *ark of Elohim* became known as the ark of the covenant only in the later deuteronomistic traditions, which date from the seventh-century BCE and constituted part of the major reforms instituted at that time during the reigns of Hezekiah and Josiah.

The Deuteronomists are, of course, responsible for the book of Deuteronomy. The other pentateuchal sources reflect the ongoing editorial process of the Yahwistic theologians. In 2 Sam. 6, which is fairly late in the tradition, the ark is first referred to as the *ark of* יהוה. In the editorial composition by the Deuteronomist historian(s) it is clear that the ark of יהוה will be housed in a tent or tabernacle rather than the temple which David longs to erect to the glory of the LORD.[23] The locus of Jerusalem was always understood by Jewish historians, prophets, and psalmists who perceived Zion clearly in theological terms, as Israel's theological home. The theology of Zion is given its clearest expression in the book of Psalms. Jerusalem as a symbol runs like a sacred, golden thread through the entire fabric of Judaism.

> At the center of the thought of Judaism about the land stands Jerusalem. The foundations of the Davidic monarchy were understood in purely sacral terms. Monarchy in the ancient Near east was a sacred and religious institution. A synthesis between Yahwism and the objective realities of the ancient neighborhood resolved the crisis during the age of the Judges, subsequently resulting in David and his kingdom. Prior to the monarchy, Israel was complete as the people of God as a theocracy, Yhwh having been anointed 'the lamp of Israel and the breath of the life of the nation' (Lam. 4:20).[24]

Jerusalem and Zion are clearly closely linked in the Psalter. *I was glad when they said to me, "Let us go to the house of* יהוה*!"* Now our feet are standing within your gates, O Jerusalem. Jerusalem- built as a city that is bound firmly together. (Psalm 122:1–3, NRSV); and, *those who trust in* יהוה *are like Mount Zion, which cannot be moved, but abides forever* (Psalm 125:1, NRSV). cf. (65:1; 76:1,2; 87:1,2; 137:7; 147:12).

Whereas the founding of the monarchy may be viewed as the culminating point of the First Testament, the establishment of the temple and its cultic aspects served as the highpoint of Israel's post-nomadic settled life in Palestine. The meaning and even the memory of the institution of the monarchy in Israel differed dramatically from that of its neighbors. From its seat of power in Jerusalem the bond between יהוה in Israel and the city in which יהוה is worshiped is never as pronounced as elsewhere.

---

23. Hayes, *Understanding the Psalms*, "With the founding of Jerusalem as a royal city and the establishment of the Davidic dynasty, two new and special traditions came into existence, i.e., the election of David and the election of Zion. These two traditions were taken up immediately at the royal court and proclaimed as part of the redemptive *Heilsgeschichte* [salvation history] and royal ideology." 420. Hayes, Idem. "There are many patterns of thought connected with the ark in the OT. It was originally referred to as the *ark of elohim* which is the general usage in the books of Samuel. It was considered the place where Yahweh was enthroned (Num 10: 35–36; 1 Sam 4:4; 2 Sam:2). With the ark was connected the idea of Yahweh as leader of the host."

24. Hayes, *Understanding the Psalms*, 419.

For instance, nowhere in the Hebrew Bible is יהוה ever described as the God of Jerusalem. Such a direct involvement between יהוה their God, and a city made by human hands—as other cities elsewhere in the ancient Near East do commonly associate—is not feasible, in principle, in Israel. This important distinction clearly sets ancient Israel apart from the neighboring monarchies. יהוה will rule over Israel and the kings will be the *anointed ones of the LORD*. They will always and only derive their sovereignty and their legitimacy from יהוה before whom all serve and are subservient. יהוה will not be confined in a house or a city or any sacred space made with human hands.

In the coronation (enthronement) psalms (Pss 2, 45, 93, 95–99, 110) it's been argued that the king is there addressed as a god. But there is no evidence in the Hebrew Bible to support such speculations. [25]On the contrary, many scholars dispute the idea of any divine enthronement festival, and draw attention to the significant connections that exist between these psalms and Third Isaiah. In Isaiah 52:7 the exclamation מלך אלהיך (*your God reigns!*) was the glad news proclaimed to an exiled Israel and provided assurance of a coming deliverance and restoration—not just of exiled Israel but of an exiled planet. Psalm 45:7, where the king appears to be addressed as God, is best rendered: *Your divine throne is for all time and eternity;* and in 45:8, *Therefore has God your God anointed you (NRSV).*

This no more presumes an apotheosis of the king than Israel is thought of as being divinized as a people when she is referred to in a divine utterance from the eighth-century BCE prophet Hosea: *When Israel was a child, I loved him, and out of Egypt I called my chosen/son* (Hosea 11:1, LW). The glory/power of יהוה will be revealed in these sacred spaces, but the power and the glory will never be contained in them or circumscribed by them. In contrast to her neighbors, there is nothing in Israel's history that would suggest any sort of divine kingship having been adopted. [26]

As was noted previously, the *Song of Deborah* in Judges 5 is not only the earliest psalm which attributes decisive activity to יהוה, it is also the oldest extant fragment in the entire Hebrew Bible. So the origins of the Hebrew Bible, it may be said, can be traced to this late Bronze Age song. The story is passed down and centuries later, it extols יהוה

---

25. Vriezen, *The Religion of Ancient Israel.* "Various scholars [S. Hooke, A. R. Johnson, I. Engell and S. Mowinckel] all have argued that not only in Egypt but in Babylon, in Phoenicia and even in Israel, kings were held to be divine beings. They would everywhere observe near enough the same ceremonies that we have come to know so well from the Babylonian festival of the New Year however there is nothing in Israel to suggest that the idea of a divine kingship has been adopted, even though all sorts of parallel elements in the coronation ritual may remind one of Egyptian ceremonial and are in fact borrowed from it. Neither in the case of Phoenicia nor of Babylon is there any demonstrable proof of such a notion. Quite the contrary." 33.

26. Curtis, *Psalms,* "Adherents of the so-called 'myth and ritual' school of thought went so far as to argue, on supposed analogies with beliefs from elsewhere in the ancient Near East, that the Israelite king may have been regarded as divine and that he played the role of God in cultic drama . . . Others without going to such extremes, suggested that the king may have taken part in ritual drama in which he suffered defeat and humiliation at the hands of the representatives of the forces of chaos and evil but was ultimately vindicated and restored by God." 12.

as the delivering agent. Its context is mid-late twelfth century BCE, and lies a little distance from the events celebrated. It is a psalm of thanksgiving and *praise to Yhwh* (י ברכו יהוה) for victory over the Canaanite forces at Megiddo. In Judges 5:11, 13, Israel is called "the people of Yahweh," but יהוה is not a part of the local Canaanite pantheon.

> *Yahweh seems to have been a cultural import to Palestine from the south. This is indicated by the Bible's early theophany poetry (Deut 33:2; Judg 5:4–5; Hab 3:3). According to Exod 17:8, 15–16, a shrine called Throne of Yahweh (following MT) was located in Sinai as one of the station points on the exodus itinerary. A home base for Yahweh in the south also synchronizes with the tradition that this god's particular mountain was situated in the Sinai Peninsula, which stands in sharp contrast to the alternative, "Canaanite" concept of Mount Zaphon in the north (cf. Ps 68:9).*[27]

The Judges 5 poem also highlights the role of יהוה as Divine Warrior who dictates the outcome of the battle by causing an earthquake and sending violent storms (Judg 5:4, 5). Deborah's song elicits the response of all nature in praise of the mighty acts of God. The Song of Deborah exhibits repetitive parallelisms that are reminiscent of fourteenth-century BCE Ugaritic texts. The poem's language is archaic Hebrew and renders the task of translating the text very difficult. Nevertheless, this is precisely what one would expect from the Hebrew Bible's earliest fragment. As was mentioned at the beginning שדי (*shaddai, the god of the mountains*), largely translated the *Almighty* in the *LXX*, appears in the Psalter in Psalms 91 and 68.

In Psalm 91, שדי (*Shaddai*) is indicative of the place of refuge and shelter. The fact that *Shaddai* is included along with the other three divine appellatives, in just one strophe, is singularly notable. Psalm 91 expresses a bedrock confidence in God. Our poet is focused on the character of God's protective refuge of the faithful. To seek refuge in יהוה means one recognizes that nothing is analogous to the God of Israel. Trust is confidence of life in the face of all threats and all three dimensions of the psalmist's being—heart, soul, and mind—participate in this joyous security and the enjoyment of a fullness of life and serenity of spirit, *shalom*.

People who dwell near God, live. People who are far from God, die! The psalmist's concentrated images of refuge seek to repose the sheltering of the soul within the shadow of the divine *presence*. The entirety of ultimate refuge and security resides in God–the Almighty One. Helmer Ringgren connects these refuge images to Israel's worshiping life in the temple. Ancient Israel's experience of

> *the immanence of God in the temple . . . could not be described appropriately otherwise than by using verbs as 'to see' and 'to behold.' This experience filled them with joy and happiness and gratitude. In other words, it strengthened their religious life and was a source of their inspiration.*[28]

27. Nelson, *Historical Roots*, 23

28. Ringgren, *The Faith of the Psalmists*, 19. "The temple served as the spatial representation of the

The *presence* of יהוה reflects very early on the basic and central theological conviction that יהוה acts on behalf of the people of יהוה.

Another early psalm of praise to יהוה was initiated in that crucial hour following the event of the Exodus (15:1–17). Women under the leadership of Miriam sang and danced to an astounding poem accompanied by music, inviting all the people to join them in hymnic praise. The text in Ex 15:20–21 is very explicit that instrumentation was used to accompany the women in song.

> *Israel's history of worship, which reached its climax in the praises of the Psalter, was initiated in that crucial hour at the beginning of the tradition when women, under the leadership of Miriam, sang and danced to music, inviting the people to join them in hymnic praise (cf. The Song of Miriam in Ex 15); cf. The Song of the Sea, a longer poem, influenced by Canaanite literary style and mythical imagery, apparently comes from the period of the tribal confederacy that flourished before the rise of the Davidic monarchy (1200–1000 BCE).[29]*

Dance and song are forms of religious prayer and praise in the Hebrew Bible and there are many references to Israel's singing and dancing before יהוה. Perhaps the most famous instance of celebratory song and dance involves David in a later era (2 Sam. 6), dancing openly and in joyful abandon before יהוה and in the sight of the people! This was considered scandalous by his wife, Saul's daughter Michal, and David was upbraided by her for his unrestrained exuberance. She failed to appreciate the depth of the intimacy in the relationship that existed between David and יהוה.

The Jewish Study Bible [*Tanakh*] says: "*she despised him for it!*" This bond between *the anointed of* יהוה and יהוה was never more evident, never more pronounced, than in the charismatic and gifted person of the young shepherd lad who was to receive Samuel's approbation, *the man after God's own heart* (I Sam 13:14). Luke's account of Paul's sermon in Antioch in Pisidia includes the following quotation: *In his (Samuel's) testimony about him (David) he said, 'I have found David, son of Jesse, to be a man after my (Yhwh) heart, who will carry out all my wishes. Of this man's posterity God has brought to Israel a Savior, Jesus, just as he promised'* (Acts 13:22, 23, NRSV).

It was David who celebrated the entrance of the ark of יהוה into the newly captured royal city of Jerusalem.

> *It has often been suggested that David's decision to bring the ark to Jerusalem in the presence of all the elite warriors of Israel (2 Sam. 6:1) indicates the acuity of his political flair. To be sure, the king probably saw in the cultic object of the ancient tribal confederation a rallying force that was attractive to both northerners and southerners. Beyond its Philistine fiasco, the ark summoned*

---

place of יהוה dwelling amidst the people of God. The liturgical yearly rounds are Israel's way of keeping this reality of the divine presence ever before them. They continually praised יהוה and these poems reflect the core reality of her life before God." 17.

29. Anderson, "The Bible in a Postmodern Age," 36, 37.

to the popular mind the memories of the Holy Warrior in Sinai and Edom as well as the Magnalia Dei in the conquest of Canaan. David's act was probably meant to unite under Yahweh the tribesmen of Israel properly speaking with the brash young heroes of Judah as well as the keepers of the Yahwist tradition in the southern shrine of Hebron. There is no evidence, however, that his move was solely dictated by political opportunism.[30]

It is there and then that the Davidic dynasty is announced to David by the prophet Nathan. This is confirmed subsequently in the entering of יהוה into a solemn oath or covenant with David (2 Sam 7). Here we have the beginning of the *royal theology of Jerusalem* that is to dominate the Psalter. Psalms 2 and 110 are fine examples of this motif.[31]

The event of the Exodus ordeal and subsequent deliverance was celebrated in another unparalleled hymn of praise and thanksgiving. Liberation from Egypt became the core hallmark of the religion of the Hebrews. As a celebration of thanksgiving and gratitude Exodus 15 is unrivaled by any of Israel's later deliverance hymns. Though it was never incorporated into the Psalter, it is used effectively by the writer (s) of the book of Exodus to make the central theological point: God is involved in Israel's history and thereby in her deliverance. The psalm of Moses is written in archaic Hebrew verse and, using parallelism, expresses Israel's trust. Egyptian paintings and reliefs dating to the late second millennium BCE picture horses pulling chariots but not being ridden. But other biblical texts of the eighth-century BCE (Isa 31:1) write of Egyptians traveling on horseback. Regardless, this psalm is a potent hymn marking their deliverance by יהוה and the defeat of the Egyptian pharaoh. This hymn accentuates the fact that Israel's God, Yhwh, acted directly in human history on Israel's behalf. This is the core event in ancient Israel's story.

Exodus 15: 1–18

The Song of Moses

Then Moses and the Israelites sang this song to יהוה
I will sing to יהו, who has triumphed gloriously;
horse and rider are thrown into the sea.

יהוה is my strength and my might,

---

30. Terrien, *The Psalms*, 281.

31. Note: Psalm 110 was later to be understood by Christians as the foreshadow of the victory of the Messiah, the savior-king at the end of the age. It is often applied to Christ in the Christian scriptures, making it the most quoted psalm there. Elsewhere in the Christian scriptures, there are 93 quotations from more than 60 psalms. Among the sayings of Jesus, there are more quotations from the Psalms than any other book of the Hebrew Bible. Jesus last recorded parable includes a summary interpretation taken from Psalm 118:22 (cf. Mark 12:1–12 = Matt 21:36–46 =Luke 20:9–19). Every evidence in the gospels points to Jesus' intense familiarity with the Psalms.

and has become my salvation;

this is my God whom I will praise,

my father's God, whom I will exalt.

יהוה is a mighty warrior;

יהוה is [his] name.

Pharaoh's chariots and his whole army

are cast into the sea;

his elite officers sank in the Sea of Reeds.

The floods covered them;

they sank down into the depths like a stone.

Your right hand O יהוה, glorious in power -

your right hand, O יהוה, shattered our enemies.

In the greatness of your majesty you overthrow your enemies;

you sent out your wrath, and it consumed them like stubble.

At the blast of your nostrils the waters were gathered in a heap;

the deeps congealed in the midst of the sea.

The enemy said, "*I will pursue, I will overtake them,*

I will divide the spoil; my desire shall have its fill of them.

I will draw my sword; my hand shall destroy them."

Then you blew with your wind, the sea covered them;

they sank like lead in the mighty waters.

Who is like you, O יהוה, among the gods?

Who is like you, majestic in holiness,

awesome in splendor, doing wonders?

You stretched out your right hand,

the earth swallowed them up.

In your constant love you led the people whom you redeemed;

you guided them by your strength to your holy dwelling.

The peoples heard and they all trembled;

terror seized the inhabitants of Philistia.

Then the chiefs of Edom were dismayed;

trembling seized the leaders of Moab;

all the inhabitants of Canaan melted away.

Terror and dread fell upon them;

by the might of your arm, they became still as stone

until your people, O יהוה, passed by,

until the people whom you purchased passed by.

You brought them in and planted them especially

on the mountain of your own possession,

the place, O יהוה, that you made your dwelling,

the sanctuary, O יהוה, that your hands have established.

יהוה will reign forever and ever!"

The Song of Moses is accompanied by the Song of the Sea in a later tradition, which served an instructional purpose, and the Blessing of Moses (Deut 32) possesses a prophetic and oracular character. It is rather likely that Israel's earliest poetry was arranged and transmitted orally rather than being the creation of any particular literary composition. It would be another two centuries until the time of Samuel, Saul, and David and the flowering of Israel's psalmic musical poetry. Other traditional hymns of praise likely were sung but no additional compositions are extant to our knowledge. One of the scrolls from the Dead Sea (11QPs a) attributes the composition of over four thousand psalms to David.

> And he [David] wrote psalms: three thousand six hundred; and songs to be sung before the altar over the perpetual offering of every day, for all the days of the year: three hundred and sixty-four; and for the sabbath offerings: fifty-two songs; and for the offering for the beginning of the month, and for all the days of the festivals, and for the day of atonement: thirty songs. And all the songs which he composed were four hundred and forty-six. And songs to be sung over the possessed: four. The total was four thousand and fifty. He composed them all through the spirit of prophecy which had been given to him from before the Most High. [32]

David *was* a prodigious figure and revered well into the second-century CE down to today. The tradition of Davidic authorial compositions was established fairly early on. The objective was to fuse singularly the person of David with the Psalter. This fixed and early tradition suggests the *Davidization* of the book of Psalms thereby conferring a particular special authority to the writings. Even so, the *Five Books of the Psalms*, which provide a certain arrangement and structure to the Psalter is reminiscent of the *Five Books of Moses*. Scribal intentions were most likely intended to attest to a privileged authority and the mantle of certainty of authorship of these two giants in ancient Israel's saga. The legitimization of a Davidic tradition is the subject of some of the oldest historical writings in the Hebrew Bible and consists of the account of David's rise to power (I Sam 16:14; II Sam 5:12) and the throne succession narrative in II Sam 6:28–20:26 and I Kings 1–2. The divine legitimization of the Davidic kingship originated in Jerusalem

---

32. cf. *The Dead Sea Scrolls Translated: The Qumran Texts in English.* 11QPs a, 309.

following the fall of the north (Israel) in 721 BCE, and played a crucial role in ancient Israel's evolving story and lived experience of a learned, experiential trust in יהוה.

> *The psalmist testifies to his intimate trust in Yahweh and expresses confidence (a kind of indirect prayer) that the offenders will be destroyed by Yahweh, from whom they have gone astray. The language is especially appropriate for the king: he is perpetually beside God, who has taken hold of his right hand. God conducts him by the agency of his 'counsel', which is here rather like the personified word and the covenant-graces which assist in guidance. 'Counsel' itself is commonly associated with kings and their political affairs.* [33]

While the exact dates at which time the hymns and prayers now preserved in the Psalter were originally composed cannot be determined with anything like precision, it appears that the great majority of them first surfaced orally. Some of these songs may have come from the poet king himself. Many of these were songs of thanksgiving and were then chanted or sung to instrumental accompaniment before the fall of Jerusalem and during the exile, when in a clearly exilic poem, they are chided and taunted by their captors to *sing us one of the songs of Zion* (cf. Psalm 137).

A thanksgiving hymn to be sung in a foreign land following the loss of Jerusalem and the temple was beyond the ken of a suffering people who never imagined they would ever sing songs of thanks and praise again. Although the Hebrew language does not have a word for *thank*, these psalms, sometimes designated as thanksgiving, or *todah psalms*, capture the essence of Israel's praises offered to יהוה. Claus Westermann contends that since there is no word for *thank* in Hebrew this fact has never been properly evaluated.

The ignoring of this fact can be explained only in that we live so unquestioningly in the rhythm between the poles of thanks and request, of *please* and *thank you;* the thought does not occur to anyone that these concepts are not common to all, have not always been present as a matter of course, do not belong to the presuppositions of social intercourse, nor to those of the contrast between God and humanity. According to the book of Exodus, these very earliest songs of thanksgiving and unbridled joy, gratitude and unitive praise, very soon give way to murmurings, complaints and, ultimately, an outright rebellion against Moses' leadership by the community at Meribah. Harvey Guthrie was the first to observe that

> *when we find passages in the Psalter, as well as the prophetic books, in which Yahweh accuses [his] people of misunderstanding and rebellion, passages which seem to conform in general to a fairly fixed pattern, we find ourselves squarely in the ethos of the faith and institutions of the pre-monarchical tribal confederation.* [34]

---

33. Eaton, *Kingship and the Psalms*, 77.
34. Guthrie, *Israel's Sacred Songs: A Study of Dominant Themes*, 46.

The *ethos* to which Guthrie refers points unmistakably to a pre-exilic date for many of the psalms. Most of them cannot be situated in any particular period, although we do have some glimpses into their era, especially when we view the internal evidence of select psalms. Scholars are reticent to date any of the psalms—beyond their being most likely pre or post-exilic—but we will proceed dangerously and hazard a conjecture on some of them. In Psalms study, conjecture is sometimes all we have as it is drawn from the internal inferences located in the texts themselves.

Certain psalms were most likely composed in the early monarchy (87, 91, 110,); some in the Davidic era (2, 18 which also occurs in 2 Samuel 22). Other psalms included in the early monarchy may be postulated: 23, 25, 40, 51, 56, 132, 144; others during the period of the extended monarchy (9/10, 21, 27, 37, 45, 61, 90, 92, 105, 132, 142). There is more than sufficient support to say that quite a few evidently originated in the northern kingdom (including both the Asaph and Korah collections) and traveled south prior to the fall of Israel in 721 BCE (20, 36, 43, 53 (14), 60, 64, 65, 88, 140); others are obviously postexilic (1, 55, 137, 146–150); still others are early first Temple hymns (15, 19, 31,); others may have their origins in amphictyonic or premonarchical Israel (8, 11, 29, 68,) with Psalm 29 perhaps being the earliest.

That this is the case can be seen clearly in some of the psalms and songs that are situated outside the book of Psalms; for example, Judges 5; Num 23–24; Exodus 15; I Samuel 2 and Habakkuk 3. What we do know is this: though the exact origins of these earliest psalmic traditions are difficult to determine, placing some of them in the pre-monarchical amphictyonic era—the mid-thirteenth to mid eleventh centuries BCE does not seem to be an unwarranted stretch. What is of particular relevance is the wider historical context. Vriezen reminds us that

> *Israel was a very young nation (when contrasted to other nations in the ancient Near East), and at least a thousand years of civilization in Egypt and Babylon had come and gone before she appeared on the scene, that she was almost a thousand years junior to the Phoenician and Canaanite peoples, that she was one of the latest combinations of tribes disgorged by the Syrian-Arabian desert, and that these were still semi-nomadic when Egypt had attained her 18th Dynasty and the high point of civilization in Babylon was already in the remote past. She owed her culture and (in the main, at any rate) her language to one of the junior nations of the Near East, the Canaanites. She herself emerged as a nation between 1230 and 1000 BCE; and her period of greatest prosperity was between 970 and 930 BCE.*[35]

The emergence of Israelite tribes may best be understood when we look at ancient Israel's earliest formative tribal confederation. Here a sacred society of early Israelite clans, which was a social construct of extended families under the leadership of a patriarch, and only later became tribes, or a broader grouping of an amalgamation

---

35. Vriezen, *The Religion of Ancient Israel*, 23, 24.

of clans within a tribal confederation, resulted in the ancient Israelite amphictyony of tribes gathered around a common sanctuary dedicated to the worship of יהוה.

These earliest sanctuaries functioned for about two centuries and were the focal points around which the worshiping life of the early clans of ancient Israel was gathered. Historian John Bright—who represents an earlier historiography—notes how the

> crisis that brought the Israelite tribal league to an end came in the latter part of the eleventh century BCE. It set in motion a chain of events which within less than a century transformed Israel totally and made her one of the ranking powers of the contemporary world . . . we have at our disposal, fortunately, sources that are both exceedingly full and of the highest historical value, much of the material being contemporaneous, or nearly so, with the events described . . . We are far better informed about this period . . . in ancient Israel's history.[36]

Later in the wilderness experience and following their liberation out of bondage in Egypt by the hand of יהוה, Israel as the people of God coalesced around the ark of יהוה, erecting numerous shrines to extol their worship of יהוה. It should be noted that Jerusalem was never part of the amphictyonic institution. Rather, her destiny lay solely with the story of David and was thus linked to the late eleventh century BCE. But Jerusalem plays no part in this early story; in fact, the name occurs nowhere in the Pentateuch. After being captured by David, ca. 1010 BCE, Jerusalem became the royal city *par excellence*. Her sole allegiance was to the king who ruled over the city-state and its inhabitants.[37]

With the bringing of the ark to Jerusalem by David (II Sam 6),[38] an attempt was made to create a religious center for the new nation by connecting the city of David with the old northern cultic object around which earlier tribes had rallied and worshiped. This amphictyonic era served a crucial role in forging ancient Israel's identity. The tribal system had effected a cohesive purpose—one that characterized the liturgical life of the loosely confederated league of the clans of Israel. This stability of the tribal confederation meant that the

> league [amphictyony] survived for nearly two hundred years. This was partly because the emergencies that Israel confronted, being mostly local in character, were such that the informal rally of the clans could deal with them . . . in circumscribing the actions of the clans only in certain well-defined areas while

36. Bright, A *History of Israel*, 184.

37. Hayes, *Understanding the Psalms*, 419.

38. Terrien, *The Psalms*, 77 "The fortress of Jebus (Jerusalem), strategically located in a Canaanite enclave between Israel and Judah for nearly two and a half centuries of Hebraic infiltration in the land of Canaan, finally yielded to the military skill of David and the bravery of his warriors (2 Sam. 5:1ff.). The triumphant king made Jerusalem his capital. This move proved to be a stroke of political genius, for it enabled him to offer a rallying point to both North and South on a neutral ground." 78.

otherwise leaving them their freedom, the tribal organization expressed perfectly the spirit of Yahweh's covenant which had created it.[39]

The origins of ancient Israel, then, are traceable to Late Bronze Age II. This was a relatively peaceful era, unlike what would follow in Iron Ages I and II (conventionally dated as beginning ca. 1200 BCE). Israel's emergence as a nation occurred during a propitious historical moment when there were no great powers vying for domination in the region. Egypt was under coastal attack from the Philistines (Sea Peoples, c. 1175 BCE). Her expansion into Canaan had been seriously blunted; her greatest days were behind her and the Hittite Empire was already in the past. A valid assertion may be made that some of the various collections which comprise the Psalter include early compositions, some of which may be traced from the time of pre-monarchical (amphictyonic) Israel, continuing through the centuries of the monarchy, the fall of Samaria in the north (723–20 BCE), the destruction of Solomon's Temple in Jerusalem (587/86 BCE), the Babylonian exile and the post-exilic period of restoration under the Persians. It is likely that some of these compositions first began to be codified, arranged and edited by a guild of temple scribes during the leadership under Ezra-Nehemiah in the fifth and fourth centuries BCE. Allowing for additional editing and redacting, the book of Praises may well have been received as sacred scripture–certainly no later than 250 BCE as it is included in the *LXX*.

> *The criteria for establishing the Hebrew canon were authorship and antiquity; often the issue narrowed down to the authenticity of books claiming to be part of the canonical era . . . The canon of the Hebrew scriptures has come about on account of two decisions carried out by persons or institutions in a position of authority . . . the coming about of the biblical canon is a triumph of scribal culture in the sense that the scribes succeeded in transforming the written traditions of a professional elite into a national library . . . as a result, the scribal practices of study, memorization, and interpretation became part of the religious habits of a nation. Scrolls were the symbols of Hebrew scribal culture; as the Bible became the symbol of Jewish religion, Judaism assumed traits of the scribal culture. The canonization of the scriptures is the final act in the making of the Hebrew Bible;*[40]

In some of the earliest psalms of the Hebrew Scriptures (e.g. Psalms 11, 18, 29, 68, 78) the most fundamental issues are addressed: the meaning and purpose of human life. For these ancient poets and sages, musicians, composers, and kings, these core convictions concerning human life's endeavors were hammered out over many centuries. The Psalms are life-centered and are not intended to be understood as descriptive poems. Rather they are to be seen as prescriptive liturgies. This means they were not composed as solely personal reflections on a private experience of any individual worshiper. They

39. Bright, *The History of Israel*, 181–182.

40. van der Toorn, *Scribal Culture and the Making of the Hebrew Bible*, 262.

appear more broadly to have served as liturgical guides that shaped and gave focus to the expressions of the whole community of worshipers of יהוה gathered in prayer and praise.

The conclusion that the psalms functioned as corporate liturgies has profound implications for how they are related to the experiences of the community of worship. A span of time of perhaps 800 years may be assigned to Psalm 91, placing its origins either in that period of the early monarchy or, just after it had come to fruition in the eleventh century. Most scholars today see it as a post-exilic hymn of thanksgiving with a divine oracle. I hold with Otto Eissfeldt in classifying it as a song of trust and arguing for an early date—perhaps reflecting the conquest of Jerusalem by David (ca.1010 BCE)—or earlier, and the subordination of *Elyon theology* to that of *Yahwism*.

Eissfeldt's perspective—that more than a few psalms are pre-exilic—represents a fundamental shift and a significant departure from prior views held by most of his contemporaries as well as an earlier era of scholarship–that the psalms were almost entirely post-exilic compositions. We have only come fairly recently to the views of Dahood and of most contemporary scholarship: that either a few, or some, or many psalms are now understood to be pre-exilic poems. Psalm 91, for example, shares an affinity with Numbers 24:16: . . . *the oracle of one who hears the words of God, and knows the knowledge of the Most High (Elyon), who sees the visions of the Almighty (Shaddai), who falls down, but with his eyes uncovered (NRSV);*

> *The patriarchal name Shaddai is characteristically not present in the poetry from the monarchic era. However, Psalm 91 may be an exception! Although Psalm 91's dating must remain uncertain, it does demonstrate an affinity with Num. 24:16 in that 91:1 also places Shaddai in grammatic parallel apposition with Elyon. This raises the interesting prospect that the Psalm (91) may have been strongly influenced by interests stemming from patriarchal or pre-monarchic traditions that were revived in the period of national nostalgia which became prevalent in the late seventh century BCE.* [41]

These oracles in Numbers 24 have been understood by some scholars as referring to examples of David's military prowess and exploits, what would be an obvious example of scribal editing by a Deuteronomist redaction thus pointing to the very early monarchy as a possible historical setting. There was once formally the assertion that the Psalter was the product of more recent literary developments; that most of the psalms were of post-exilic origin and dated to as late as the third and second centuries, well into the Hellenistic Era. Of course this view is no longer viable. The development of the Psalter over the course of a time frame of about a millenium is no longer an altogether uncommonly held assertion.

It is my view that some of the psalms had their beginnings in the distant past where life in a central enclave was authentically Israelite. It is my view as well that a few of the earliest poems in the Psalter likely pre-date David. This enclave of conjoined

---

41. Eissfeldt, *The Old Testament: An Introduction*, 126.

clans and subsequent tribes were simply known as Israel, before the existence of the northern kingdom of Israel. Israel and Judah are frequently referred to in the books of Samuel; taken together, the names commonly designate the people of יהוה as a whole, but this too is problematic. The term "Israel" is ambiguous and has been so for much of Israelite history.[42]

Historically the two sections, north and south, had their deep rivalries and conflicting loyalties dating back to the pre-Davidic era. Only David, with his capture of Jerusalem, was able to meld together the allegiances of both, but only temporarily. Israel and Judah, the United Kingdom, lasted less than a century.

> The two great power blocs, Egypt and Mesopotamia, ruled over everything. Palestine was a plaything of their interests and confrontations. Only in a small breathing space was it possible for David to exist and to win his own area of rule in the space between the two power blocs. But a little later, after the death of Solomon, this structure crumbled away, and from then on the nation of Israel was occupied with world politics only passively, while, for the most part enduring whatever the great powers did to it. Nevertheless, we find this audacious statement about the world rule of Israel's God. We recognize here the basis of the Christian understanding of the world and of history, which Israel had been able to preserve even through the centuries of deepest political impotence.[43]

The old tribal rivalries re-emerged under Solomon who, for all his purported wisdom, lacked the political sagacity and charisma of his father. He failed to appreciate the deep and historic rifts between the two distinct geographical regions. Their sectarian and cultic differences began to surface under the less gifted monarch who misjudged the reaction of the northern tribes with his extravagant and profligate spending on a wide array of building projects. Ironically, it was his construction of the Temple in Jerusalem, which was intended to unite both north and south, that contributed to a disintegration of support as a result of the heavy taxes levied against the larger and more affluent and prosperous north. Upon his death, the fissures that had existed, erupted.

Less than a century after the golden age of a united Israel (ca. 1010–930) the monarchy, upon Solomon's death, was divided between Solomon's equally injudicious successors, Jeroboam and Rehoboam, resulting in two and a half centuries of mutual non-cooperation, competition, and political wrangling. Rehoboam was inexcusably ineffective (2 Chronicles 10) and Jeroboam I, led a counter rebellion. Though more talented and sagacious in his initial handling of Israel's statecraft, Jeroboam was continuously warring (I Kgs 14:19) with the south. *There was warring between Rehoboam and Jeroboam continually* (I Kgs 14:30). Jeroboam I established Israel's first capital in Shechem but the factionalism and warring between north and south characterized

---

42. Note: Rendsburg prefers the use of the term *Israelian* to differentiate the northern tribes and territories from the southern tribe of Judah. There is some merit to his suggestion. cf. Gary. Rendsburg, *Linguistic Evidence for the Northern Origin of Selected Psalms*.

43. Rendtorff, *Canon and Theology*, 58.

both reigns. The age of the relative peace of Solomon's rule had passed and both Israel and Judah were now in for the rough and rugged slog of history. Not until the reign of Omri in the northern kingdom in the early ninth century (ca. 885) BCE was there to be any semblance of political stability in the northern monarchy.

The Omride dynasty did provide Israel with about a century and a half of relative peace and prosperity. The Davidic dynasty with its capital in Jerusalem, faced its own challenges—in addition to continuous border disputes with the larger, stronger and more prosperous north. Judah at this time was essentially a small city-state with sparsely populated towns and villages outside of the immediate area of Jerusalem and scattered about the northern territorial borders and frontier lands. She was relatively poor and lacked the productive power and economic output which the richer northern kingdom enjoyed. Her greatest asset was the temple esplanade in Jerusalem and the traditions developed there would catapult her into the unknown future as Yahweh's people. Her singular extraordinary achievement was in keeping Yahwism alive with the careful and assiduous custodialship of the collections of the psalms over this long period of time.

But Judah too had its own era of peace nearly concurrent with the northern kingdom. Both kingdoms struggled with the gods of Canaan and the polytheistic religions of their neighbors. Followers of יהוה were largely on the fringes of power and culture but it was the *Yahwists* who continued the Sinai tradition of Moses and eventually moved the culture toward the center under Kings Hezekiah and Josiah. Under these kings, they tore down the idols of the high places and renewed their allegiance to יהוה. Yahwism, that is equal to the worship of "*Yahweh alone*," was buttressed by the prophets and the psalmists. This exceedingly brief historical overview provides us with some political context for the emergence of the ancient psalmic traditions and the central role of the worship of יהוה in both north and south over the next two centuries.

There now exists a wealth of evidence to support the view that ancient Israel's traditions, particularly those related to her psalmic liturgies, had a lengthy prehistory that can be tracked with some accuracy. These liturgies demonstrate that the singing of songs in worship with instrumental accompaniment was familiar to ancient Israelite worshipers in pre-exilic times. Such songs would not have been forgotten. It only stands to reason that a certain number of them would have been preserved in the Psalter though hardly in their original form. Today less than half (about seventy) psalms are currently used in the modern synagogue and that number is proportionately higher now than was previously the case. It was to be the early Christian church of the first two centuries of the *Common Era* that would bring the Psalter into liturgical and theological prominence thus wresting its enormous influence from a scattered and disparate Judaism.

The Hebrew Truth

ARCHAEOLOGICAL DISCOVERIES IN THE modern era have brought to light much additional knowledge of the religious poetry of the ancient Near Eastern cultures, particularly Canaanite, Mesopotamian and Egyptian, with whom the Hebrews were in continuous interaction. Research regarding the antiquity of the origins of the Psalms comport well with recent archaeological findings, particularly the excavation of the remains of the ancient Canaanite city of Ugarit. Beginning in 1928 ancient Ugaritic texts and a host of pottery sherds were unearthed at Ras Shamra on the northwestern Syrian coastal plain. Dating from 1450 BCE, these fragments reflect the Canaanite literary culture in Bronze Age II. Ugaritic is an ancient language that shares many linguistic features common to biblical Hebrew. It was to become enormously useful to biblical scholars in studying the Psalms, particularly those psalms that had been resistant to interpretation and understanding due in large part to somewhat corrupted texts (Ps 11). [1]

In 1966 the first volume of a three volume commentary on the Psalms by Mitchell Dahood captured the imagination of scholars. Both Dahood's translation and commentary came under close scrutiny. It was his utilizing of the Ugaritic findings, to open up the text of the Psalms, parts of which had remained very nearly unintelligible, that was to prove controversial. His more vociferous detractors tended to dismiss the implications of his work as being too technical; its conclusions too speculative.

Others insisted he was perhaps a bit too star-crossed in his assumptions, too dependent on the contributions of the Ugaritic findings, too ready to attach an undue influence of Ugaritic on the ancient Hebrew writers and poets. But Dahood, ever the pioneer, had his champions as well. That distinguished scholar in American biblical studies and archeology in the twentieth century, W. F. Albright, reasoned how *Fr. Dahood has contributed mightily to our understanding of the vocabulary of biblical Hebrew poetry. Even if only a third of his new interpretations of the Psalter are correct*

---

1. Morgenstern, "Psalm 11." 221–231. "The text of this little psalm is in rather disturbed condition. The majority of the corruptions must have crept in at a relatively early date, with the result that the versions are of only moderate assistance in the task of reconstructing the original text." 222. Note: Morgenstern's assessment in 1950 was made before the epiphany that is the Dead Sea Scrolls; that is to say, until the findings had become more widely understood and available to scholars in the decades that would follow.

in principle–and I should put the total proportionately higher–he has contributed more than all other scholars together, over the past two thousand years, to the elucidation of the Psalter.[2] This is effusive praise indeed!

Indeed, Dahood's overall contribution to modern Psalms scholarship has been monumental. Most Hebraic scholars today now agree with him that, in the vast preponderance of cases relative to the Psalms, the consonantal text and the Masoretic pointing are in happy agreement.

> *The tendency in recent years [1966] to assign earlier rather than later dates to the composition of the psalms comports with the evidence of the Ras Shamra texts. These show that much of the phraseology in the Psalter was current in Palestine long before the writing prophets, so the criterion of literary dependence becomes much too delicate to be serviceable . . . the inadequate knowledge of biblical poetic idiom and, more importantly, of biblical images and metaphors displayed by the third-century B.C. translation of the LXX, bespeaks a long chronological gap between the original composition of the psalms and their translation into Greek; all of which point to a pre-Exilic date for most of the psalms, and not a few of them (e.g., Pss ii, xvi, xviii, xxix, lx, lxviii, lxxxii, cviii, cx) may well have been composed in the Davidic period.*[3]

There are sufficient examples where the grammatical and lexical details found in the texts at Ras Shamra have yielded to a more coherent translation. Borrowing linguistic traits, this is especially true in the case of some of those psalms that have come down to us with a quite disturbed text thereby making any intelligible translation of the text exceedingly difficult. One of the greatest hindrances to the production of a trustworthy translation is, of course, the fact that none of the earliest Hebrew texts–*the hebraica veritas* as St. Jerome called it–survived.[4] Of course, Jerome translated the Hebrew text into Latin in the early fifth-century, the Vulgate. This marked the end of the supremacy of the Septuagint in the church. Some view this as a disturbing development in the church's history.

About twenty years after the findings at Ugarit—at the mid-point of the twentieth century—a trove of hundreds of fragments from at least five hundred different scrolls was discovered at Khirbet Qumran-the Dead Sea Scrolls. Qumran had been built originally as an Israelite fortress in the eighth century. It had apparently been abandoned until the beginning of the second century BCE when the ancient foundations were used to construct a complex and elaborate settlement. Evidence indicates these structures again were abandoned later in the century after having been damaged by some sort of catastrophe, perhaps an earthquake or a military engagement. Archaeological evidence also confirms extensive fire damage. Although there is no

---

2. Albright quoted in Peter Craigie. Psalms 1–50, vol. 19. *Word Biblical Commentary,* 51.

3. Dahood, *Psalms,* xxx.

4. As quoted in Christoph Barth, *Introduction to the Psalms,* 34.

precise explanation, archaeological data indicate that the complex was abandoned once more. Still later however, the entire site was repaired and reoccupied before the end of the second century BCE. Indeed, much was happening over the course of these two centuries.

These particulars are relevant for our purposes insofar as they may contribute to our understanding of the sort of community that inhabited the settlement from the early second century BCE to the mid-first century CE; a community that preserved the manuscripts and scrolls and produced additional materials which comprise these remarkable findings. The Dead Sea Scrolls have proven to be of incalculable worth for the study of the Hebrew Bible and the book of Psalms in particular.

> *The discovery of other early Hebrew versions of the psalms at Qumran offers further insights into the Septuagint translation. Amongst the Dead Sea Scrolls, over twenty-seven manuscripts of psalms, some of them commentaries rather than translations, many of them fragmentary, almost all in a Hebrew script, were found in eleven caves near the ruins of Qumran; two others were found at Masada and a further two at Nahal Heber and Nahal Seelim. It is now possible to compare variant readings in these scrolls with the Septuagint and the traditionally accepted Hebrew Masoretic Text. The most important discoveries are from Caves 4 and 11, where copies of 120 of the 150 Hebrew psalms have been found, dating from the first and second centuries BCE (Cave 4) and the first century CE (Cave 11).* [5]

In 1947, seven scrolls were found in pottery urns in caves in the Judean Desert. Those scrolls reached antiquities dealers in Bethlehem and after many vicissitudes were finally gathered in Jerusalem and exhibited at the Shrine of the Book in the Israel National Museum. One of the first scrolls to be discovered was a full copy of the book of Isaiah, which provides important evidence for the text of the Bible that was common in Eretz-Israel at the end of the Second Temple period. In time, more and more fragments of scrolls were discovered, some in caves at Nahal Qumran, some at Masada, and some in other locations of the Judean Desert.

One specific area of inquiry that features prominently in the findings has been directly impacted by the results—the poetry of the Hebrew Bible–specifically the book of Psalms. These amazing finds–both at Qumran and Ras Shamra–together have proven to be especially exciting for Psalms lovers. For instance, among some of the richer finds at Ras Shamra [north west Syria] are collections of poetry dating from between the fifteenth and fourteenth centuries, BCE–nearly one half millennium before the earliest of the Hebrew psalms can reasonably be dated.

At Qumran the finding in Cave 11 of a small zigzag scroll containing Psalm 91–which is appended to the end of a series of non-canonical apocryphal psalms—bears the simple title, *David's*, an early attestation to the influence David played in the

---

5. Gillingham, *Poems and Psalms of the Hebrew Bible,* 9.

collections of the Psalter. There is no inscription or title heading to Psalm 91 in either the *MT* or our English Bible versions. The *LXX* bears the title, *Praise Song. David.* Whatever the relative dates of the individual psalms, the scrolls from Cave 11 clearly show that *Books IV (Pss 90–106)* and *V (107–150)* were edited relatively late and probably were the last to be assimilated as individual collections into the Book of Praises. The poems of Books IV and V are predominately songs of thanksgiving and praise.

The discoveries at both sites have essentially transformed much of our previous knowledge concerning the Hebrew language and its relatedness to the other languages and religions of the neighboring cultures in the ancient Near East. These fantastic discoveries have revolutionized biblical studies and continue to shed light on our understanding of the Hebrew Psalms. Amid the hundreds of scrolls at Qumran are twenty-seven manuscripts of psalms. Some of these are ancient commentaries rather than translations, many of them are fragmentary, and almost all of them are written in Hebrew script. Copies of the Hebrew psalms were found, dating from the first and second centuries BCE -(Cave 4) and the first century CE (Cave 11).

Over this span of at least two centuries, clearly there existed a scribal community (Essenes?) with its own tradition of gathering, copying, editing, and arranging the texts. Scholars believe the earliest of these scrolls were copied around 150 BCE whereas the latest ones were written in the early—mid first century CE before the destruction of the Second Temple (70 CE). The scrolls fall into several categories: biblical scrolls, scrolls of "interpretations," which are a kind of ancient *Midrash* (homiletic commentary, often including stories) on the books of the prophets, scrolls containing writings that express the beliefs and customs of the people of Qumran, and others. The official publication of the scrolls and fragments of scrolls is the forty-volume series, *Discoveries in the Judean Desert.* In the past few decades many studies have been published pertaining to the Dead Sea Scrolls, the identity of the members of the Qumran sect, their way of life and views, the relation between them and rabbinical literature, their relationship to earliest Christianity, and so on.

The biblical scrolls discovered in the caves of Qumran, include fragments of every book of the Hebrew Bible except the book of Esther. Scrolls featuring fragments from Deuteronomy, Isaiah, and the Psalms are particularly plentiful. Regarding the Psalms, 120 of the 150 psalms are represented in part or in whole in the scrolls. Why scholars in that period may have dealt with these particular books more than with the other books of the Bible is not known. Perhaps in some future finds, more will be revealed. Regarding the text, there are some differences between the various scrolls of a given book and also between the scrolls and the Masoretic text (which is best represented, for example, in the *Aleppo Codex*)[6] In some of these the spelling is very

---

6. An early tenth-century CE Hebrew codex (a bound book) created in Tiberius on the Sea of Galilee, the center of Masoretic activity at the turn of the first millennium and in which the book of Psalms follows straight on after Chronicles, and Psalm 1. It is written in the same prose style as 2 Chronicles 36. One of its significances is in its suggestion that poetic (such as psalmody) and prosaic genres existed alongside one another very early on.

full. Extra Hebrew letters, such as *alephs, vavs,* and *hehs* are added to words in the codex to indicate their pronunciation. Sometimes the texts differ from that of the *MT* in a number of words or even in full sentences.

Comparison of the text to that of the *MT* shows that in the thousand years that passed between them, extensive textual work was done in order to determine the precise wording and spelling of the Bible's vocabulary. The results demonstrate a consistency and a remarkably high degree of correspondence and agreement.

The Masoretes rejected the versions of the Bible that differed from the *MT* such as those which are reflected in ancient translations and the Samaritan version of the Torah. The accepted version was scrupulously preserved by means of a special apparatus of Masoretic annotations which was created for that purpose. Vocalization and cantillation marks were inserted to preserve the precise pronunciation tradition. This has resulted in significant shifts in attitudes and understanding of the Psalms. The implications for the study of the biblical language, given its relationship to neighboring cultures and the sharing of common linguistic roots, place Israel squarely within the family of Northwest semitic languages. These *"linguistic similarities"* provide us with a window through which to view the Hebrew language in the wider context of the family of ancient semitic languages. [7]

The *Aleppo Codex,* tenth-century CE (ca. 930) belongs to a large family of Masoretic documents and contains vocalization, cantillation marks, and Masoretic annotations. This codex (which was severely damaged in Syria following Israel's independence in 1947) represents the text of the Bible that was the product of the Masoretes of Tiberius, the best representative of which is the *Aleppo Codex* itself. One of the best known codices and closely related in time is *MS Leningrad (MS Saint Petersburg,* in the Russian National Library, St. Petersburg. This is a complete codex of the Bible which was written in Egypt in 1008 CE by Shmuel Ben Ya'aqov and has been preserved intact to this day. The vocalization and cantillation marks are very similar to those of the *Aleppo Codex.* A codex is a book with bound pages and is written on both sides. Consequently, scholars used this codex to reconstruct the lost parts. This codex is preferred by contemporary scholars because it is a complete Bible. The *Aleppo Codex* is characterized by superior scholarship and is the most revered copy of the Hebrew Bible. It survived intact for more than a millennium (930–1947) and is considered the *textus receptus* of the Hebrew scriptures. It contains the version that was considered the most authoritative copy and reliable text of the Bible in first millennium CE Judaism.

Most editions of the Bible are based on *MS Leningrad,* early eleventh century CE, the best known for being the text for the latest editions of *Biblia Hebraica* (2004 CE) and the *JPS Bible (Jewish Publication Society),* with English translation. Other very valuable codices closely related to the *Aleppo Codex* are: *MS British Museum Or. 4445,* which contains the Five Books of Moses and is earlier than the *Aleppo Codex; MS*

---

7. cf. van der Toorn, *Scribal Culture,* 37f.

Cairo of the prophets (the former and latter) which is attributed at the end to Moshe Ben Asher, the father of the *Masorete* of the *Aleppo Codex;* two codices of which only a few pages remain have been identified by the scholars of the *Masora* as being *very close to the Aleppo Codex.* The most ancient books of this type were written in the ninth and tenth centuries CE; that is to say, a thousand years after the time of the Dead Sea Scrolls. No other codices have survived from that long intervening period except for a few Geniza fragments that might have been written in the eighth century CE.

Over generations, the Bible was copied in hundreds if not thousands of manuscripts. These manuscripts differ from one another in many details: the date and place of their writing, the form of the script, the plené or defective spelling of words, the vocalization system, details of vocalization and cantillation marks and so on. Some old manuscripts have been judged by scholars of the Masora as being *manuscripts very close to the Aleppo Codex.* These are generally manuscripts from the tenth and eleventh centuries CE which were written in the East. The system of vocalization and cantillation marks is very similar to that of the *Aleppo Codex* and the plené conform to a large extent to the Masoretic annotations and spelling.

The two sites at Ras Shamra and Qumran with their amazing finds, initiated a tidal wave of excitement, discovery and subsequent research that would first engulf and finally, sweep along in its wake the quiet, settled world of biblical and theological studies. This archaeological tsunami crested then broke upon the shores of Jewish rabbinical schools and Christian seminaries and secular graduate programs in the 1960's and 70's. Its effect caused seismic shifts that reverberated along religious and theological fault lines. Even as we continue to unravel the mysteries of the Dead Sea scrolls, the twenty-first century universe of biblical and theological studies still reverberates with the rumblings of those first temblors of a previous generation. Very simply, these discoveries and findings have reconfigured the landscape of nearly all that passes for serious psalmic scholarship today.

One is required–in the light of these sometimes inconvenient data—to take seriously a whole range of incontrovertible and sometimes annoying facts. The struggle today over the nature of biblical and revelatory "authority" is frequently characterized as a battle between biblical minimalists and maximalists. This is the direct result of the ongoing dispute over the relevance of archaeological findings and the dating (a very fluid enterprise) of manuscripts, codices and pottery sherds and their particular and specific application when assaying the accuracy and historicity in interpreting the meaning of the biblical text. The archaeological excavations and their findings must be treated with great care when ascertaining the degree of relevance to the biblical materials.

Exhibiting a wide range of activity around these writings, and taking into account that they were obviously treasured as sacred, approaching these texts today requires an openness to them and an awe and respect in contemplating their unique significance. They invite further inquiry into what seems to be a firmly fixed tradition, at least in their use and consideration of the songs and hymns of praises. Not of little significance is the fact that it is now possible to compare variant readings in these scrolls with the *LXX* and the traditionally accepted *MT*.[8] Various linguistic evidence and findings demonstrate how much of the phraseology in the Psalter was already current in Palestine, long before the writing prophets. The criterion of literary dependence, however, is much too delicate to serve as a dependable or reliable point of reference.

Kings, priests and prophets, but above all, unknown poets and composers, contributed their unique gifts throughout this process. Of the Psalms, unlike any other book of the Hebrew scriptures, it must be asserted that all Israel, the people of God from generation to generation, took part in its composition over a very long period of time. Westermann concludes:

> *Only at the very end were they fixed in written form and included in the collection. They were first prayed, sung, and spoken by many extremely different kinds of people. Only later, at the point where these many voices were gathered in worship, did they finally receive the form that is normative for all and accessible to all. This process of liturgical shaping took many generations.*[9]

Each of the psalms has an extensive prehistory that goes back to the deepest recesses of Israel's conscious memory of psalmody. This is part of what is referred to as *sacred memory* and it has become part of Israel's precious gift to the world. It is not beyond plausibility to surmise that one or more of the psalms, which later found their way into the final collections may have been composed by some of Israel's greatest prophets: Jeremiah, Isaiah, and Habakkuk come to mind. That some may also have been composed by women ought not be ruled out of hand (e.g. Deborah, Miriam, Hannah and Huldah). The *superscriptions* that appear in the first line of the text in 116 of the 150 psalms continue to hold interest captive particularly by their attributions–among others—of authorship, all of which continue to raise questions among scholars. These are usually brief titles conveying various bits of information about the compositions that follow. In the ancient Near East, it was uncommon for an author to sign his or her name.[10] The later scribal tradition draws a parallel with Moses: *Moses*

8. cf. James A. Sanders, *The Psalms Scroll of Qumran Cave, 11*. cf. Alastair G. Hunter, *An Introduction to the Psalms*. "The original suggestions in relation to the significance of this material [Dead Sea Scrolls] were made by James A. Sanders (1967). Sanders faced considerable opposition to his theories; it is pleasing now to see that they have been strongly supported, if not completely vindicated. Whatever our conclusions about the Dead Sea Psalms material, one thing is certain: that the urge to form significant groups around either theological or liturgical themes is well developed. There is . . . no reason to doubt that similar processes were natural to the editors, composers, collectors, and users of psalms in the mainstream temple. Thus the Qumran material, far from being the eccentric work of an isolated sect, can be seen as part of a firmly established tradition. Perhaps the thesis . . . that those who founded Qumran were part of, or closely related to a Jerusalem sect, helps us to understand the closeness of the relationship between the authorities in the temple and the sectaries by the Dead Sea, at least in their use of the Psalms." 28–29

9. Westermann, *The Psalms: Structure, Content and Message*, 162.

10. van der Toorn, *Scribal Culture*, "*Pseudonymity* is the strategy of an author who wishes to

gave the five books of the Torah to Israel, and corresponding to them, David gave the five books of the Psalms to Israel (Mid. Ps 1:2). [11]The exact meaning of much of the information in the psalms' superscriptions are unknown to us today. Indeed, their meaning and what it is they depicted had been largely lost by the time of the translation of the *LXX*, third century BCE.

> *At issue is the time of composition and the authenticity of the information. Critical scholars pay little attention to the titles, assuming that they are later midrashic additions. They point to the variations in the headings between the MT and the LXX. It is true that the headings in the LXX vary both in content and number . . . The study of the headings in the LXX reveals to what extent the superscriptions create problems in the study of the psalms.*[12]

Some of them were even written in a language other than Hebrew and captions refer to an assortment of psalm types: *mizmor, miktam, maskil,* and *shir.* Still others address the purpose or the historical setting of the poem. For example, the specific collection of the *Songs of Ascents,* sometimes designated the *Pilgrim Psalter* (Psalms 120–134) appears to echo the pilgrimage of worshipers ascending up to Jerusalem–or other shrines erected to the worship of יהוה for the annual festivals. Still others refer to a music leader or choirmaster and suggest a purely vocal setting; still others appear to offer specific instructions that may allude to certain rituals.

The superscriptions illustrate that the psalms are musical compositions and are intended to be sung. Various instruments, unrecognizable today, were apparently selected for use in the accompaniment of the performance of the song: the *gittith, nehiloth, sheminith, alamoth,* and *mahalath.* Suffice it to say that many references in the superscriptions to the songs themselves invoke a variety of meanings that remain unclear to us today. There can be no doubt that the Psalms are rooted in the deep past—in ancient Israel's sacrificial worship, rites and liturgies. The ancient poetry of the Bible is language with a purpose and Hebrew poetry, above all else, is the discourse of the heart. The language of this "poetry of the heart" is the very stuff of the psalms. [13]

---

optimize the chances of a favorable reception of his work. It is to be distinguished from attributed authorship. *Pseudepigraphy* is the doing of the author; attributed authorship is the work of the editor. If the editor attributes it to a presumed author, it is to explain rather than to gain its reception by the public . . . traditional collections attributed to famous kings are Psalms and Proverbs. By the evidence of these books themselves, the attributions to David and Solomon are in fact simplifications . . . at the time the various collections originated, the Davidic authorship was not a doctrine yet. David was believed to have written a number of psalms, but other famous men of the past . . . were credited with religious poetry as well . . . from the Hellenistic period onward the name 'David' was the standard designation of the entire Psalter. Such was David's reputation as pious king, skilled musician, and organizer of the temple liturgy, that he absorbed paternity of all the Psalms. "36–37.

11. Braude, The *Midrash on the Psalms,* 111.

12. VanGemeren, Psalm 131:2, 45. Note: Another attempt to reconcile the discrepancies is to treat the titles as colophons (notes at the end of the psalms). But this explanation, too, is unsatisfactory.

13. cf. Elliott Rabin, *Understanding the Hebrew Bible: A Readers Guide.*

Nowhere is this poetry more richly textured than in the psalms of confidence. As a specific form-critical genre[14] these psalms constitute a depth of theological erudition that is compact, yet expansive; concise, yet with a precision of meaning that is seamlessly conveyed through the subtlest form. The frequently inaccessible, restrictive and endlessly qualifying and formidable language of systematic theology needs the poetic medium for much of its expanse and expression. According to Sebastian Moore, an English Benedictine, it's almost as though these ancient poets would have us understand that *God behaves in the psalms in ways [He] is not permitted to behave in systematic theology.* [15]

But the uniqueness of the poetry, with its powers of allusion and alliteration, assonance and onomatopoeic features profiled in Hebrew poetry, convey the rich texture of the oft times hidden and mysterious truths that theology seeks to elucidate. Poetry is that form which can best illustrate our need for balance in the weighted world of formal theological and philosophical constructions. Israel in its poetry associated itself with יהוה the holy hidden One who is both far off and near at hand; the immanent and simultaneously transcendent holy, hidden Being; the communicative, revelatory One of the heart.

> *Over a century ago, Rudolf Otto described the human perception of the mysterium tremendum atque fascinans which produces the sense of what he called 'the numinous.' Derived from the Latin numen, such a term corresponds more or less to the Gk. daimon. It generally refers to the spiritual powers, not necessarily personified, which are ascribed to natural objects of exceptional significance, especially to those endowed with forces of a benevolent or of a destructive nature which [man], in order to survive, needs either to enlist or to tame."*[16]

That this divine *presence* was openly acknowledged by Israel is in itself an amazing thing. The fact that YHWH was engaged actively in the drama of Israel's history and her recognition of this fact, lies at the heart of the story of her redemption and salvation. The poetic discourses during the turbulent eighth century BCE, the time of the prophets Amos, Hosea, Micah and First Isaiah, include some of the greatest compositions in the Psalter (e.g. 4, 19, 27, 31, 90) and the collections of Asaph and Korah.

Some of these poems either pre-date or are coextensive with those prophets, particularly with First Isaiah who, during this epic century in Israel's history, represented theological thinking at its keenest. The psalmists mirrored both the uniqueness,

---

14. Note: In the early 20th century, Herman Gunkel first began classifying each psalm according to literary type and identified five major types of psalms: Hymns or Songs, Thanksgivings, Communal and Individual Laments/Complaints and Prayers. Certain other 'sub-types,' with a somewhat narrower focus, were also classified. Some of these are: Royal, Zion, Pilgrimage, Wisdom, and Trust/Confidence. *Form criticism* refers to these "attempts to identify and then classify the various types (*Gattungen*) of literature found in the biblical text in order to help place the texts within the lives of the people [*Sitz im Leben*] who preserved and handed them on and in order to aid in interpreting the texts." cf. Nancy deClaisse-Walford, *Reading from the Beginning: The Shaping of the Psalter,* 20.

15. Quoted in Kathleen Norris, *The Cloister Walk,* 39.

16. Terrien, "The Numinous, the Sacred, and the Holy in Scripture," 99.

universality and exceptionalism of the Hebraic *theology of presence*. The eighth-century BCE was to witness the emergence of the internal controversy over the ascendancy of Yahwism. With the cataclysmic destruction of the northern kingdom of Israel at the hands of the Assyrians, late eighth-century, it is now believed that many of these northern traditions found their way south to Judah. An earlier northern prophetic tradition in the ninth century BCE featuring the Yahwists Elijah and Elisha of the books of the Kings, already had been at work during this time of political, religious and social upheaval. These two northern prophets were active in their harsh condemnation of the Israelite monarchy for its rejection of יהוה and its endlessly idolatrous predilections and practices. These early prophets demanded a return to the core belief of YHWH alone.

There is an undeniable autobiographical stamp to the spiritual terrain in the ongoing formation of the Psalter. However, a deeper knowledge and understanding of biblical poetic idiom and of biblical images and metaphors had been generally inadequate—until recently. This is best illustrated by the translation of the *Septuagint* that bears faithful witness to the long chronological gap existing between the Hebraic psalms and the subsequent translation into Greek—about 800 years. Also instructive in showing the method of the composition of psalms are the books of Chronicles. The Chronicles were compiled not long before the fifth-century BCE by the Levitical singers of the Second Temple. The Chroniclers themselves pay especial attention to the rituals, liturgy and music of the pre-exilic period. Examples abound throughout showing an editorial instrument of combining and adding northern songs to the Psalms.

> Stories such as those in 2 Chronicles 30 and Jer. 41:4–5 could easily serve as the context for the authorship of many of the northern psalms with their Zion-based theology. Even Psalm 78, whose purpose is to argue that Zion and the Davidic dynasty are now replacing Shiloh, could fit into this scheme. Note that Shiloh is specifically mentioned in Jer. 41:5 . . . it is probable that most of the northern psalms date from before 721 B.C.E., but this is by no means certain. It is possible for any or many of them to date from after 721 B.C.E. It is still conceivable that still other chapters in the book of Psalms await a determination of northern origin. . . . there are 36 poems in the book of Psalms wherein linguistic evidence points very clearly to northern provenance.[17]

One such post-exilic example is found in I Chronicles 16 where we have a psalm, said to have been sung at the consecration of the temple, which is compiled wholly out of Psalms 96, 105, and 106, none of which bears a superscription. It is frequently referred to as a poem composed certainly no later than 400 BCE, in honor of the Davidic covenant and is sometimes entitled David's *Psalm of Thanksgiving.*

---

17. Gary Rendsberg, "Linguistic Evidence for the Northern Origin of Selected Psalms," 103, 104.

TRUSTING YHWH

I Chronicles 16: 8–36

O give thanks to יהוה , call on his name,
make known his deeds among the peoples.
Sing to him, sing praises to him,
tell of all his marvelous works.
Glory in his holy name;
let the hearts of those who seek יהוה rejoice.

Seek יהוה and his strength,
seek his presence continually.
Remember the wonderful works he has done,
his miracles, and the judgments he uttered,
O offspring of his servant Israel,
children of Jacob, his chosen ones.
He is יהוה our God;
his judgments are in all the earth.

Remember his covenant forever,
the word that he commanded, for a thousand generations,
the covenant that he made with Abraham,
his sworn promise to Isaac, which he confirmed to Jacob as a statute,
to Israel as an everlasting covenant, saying,
*"To you I will give the land of Canaan as your portion
for an inheritance."*

When they were few in number, of little account,
and strangers in the land, wandering from
nation to nation, from one kingdom to another people,
he allowed no one to oppress them;
he rebuked kings on their account, saying,
"Do not touch my anointed ones;
do my prophets no harm."   Psalm 105

Sing to יהוה, all the earth.
Tell of his salvation from day to day.
Declare his glory among the nations,
his marvelous works among all the peoples,

88

For great is יהוה, and greatly
to be praised; to be revered above all gods.

For all the gods of the peoples are idols, but it is יהוה
who made the heavens, Honor and majesty
are before him; strength and joy are in his place.
Ascribe to יהוה, O families of the peoples,
ascribe to יהוה glory and strength.

Ascribe to יהוה the glory due his name;
bring an offering, and come before him.
Worship יהוה in holy splendor;
tremble before him, all the earth. The world
is firmly established; it shall never be moved.
Let the heavens be glad, and let the earth rejoice,
and let them say among the nations,
" יהוה *is king!*"

Let the sea roar, and all that fills it;
let the field exult, and everything in it.
Then shall the trees of the forest sing for joy
before יהוה, for he comes to judge the earth.   Psalm 96
O give thanks to יהוה, for he is good;
for his unfailing love endures forever;
Say also: *"Save us, O God of our salvation,*
and gather and rescue us from among the nations,
that we may give thanks to your holy name,
and glory in your praise.
Blessed be יהוה, *the God of Israel,*
from eternity to eternity."   Psalm 106:1, 47, 48

This Davidic hymn of praise from Chronicles provides us with an example of how the psalms were used in the post-exilic temple. The books of the Chronicles were completed shortly before 400 BCE and it is believed that the inclusion of the three psalms which comprise this psalm, is the editorial work of the Levites, the priests who were the custodians of the temple worship. All Israel is the focus of this exhortation as they had so recently returned from their exile in Babylon. The whole community gathered in Jerusalem to offer sacrifices and to seek יהוה, just as the patriarchs did in the distant past. They are urged to tell out the wonders of יהוה in their deliverance once again. A special feature of the Chronicler's work is the appeal to the people of the North to recognize the centrality of יהוה; to come and be welcomed into the ritual and worshiping life of the temple in Jerusalem. This psalm is also an example of how other psalms from the book of Praises were being used in worship in the post-exilic era and too, how the burden of its message was concentrated on the praise of יהוה and the glory of that Name. The poem closes out Book IV and is concluded with the doxology: *Blessed be יהוה, the God of Israel, from eternity to eternity!* This shaping of liturgical nuance and usage is prevalent and conforms to the theology of the writers of the Chronicles.

Another and perhaps clearer example of changes in tone by a later revision corresponding to changing needs or situations can be illustrated by Psalms 9 and 10. These two psalms originally constituted one psalm, an alphabetic acrostic of 44 verses, two verses to each letter of the 22 letters of the Hebrew alphabet. The original psalm can be identified by its acrostic formula which is preserved in Psalm 9:1–18 and 10:15–18. In place of the original form, intervening verses have been inserted or substituted while others, not acrostic, are completely different in tone.

A final example: In Psalm 144, the author has stitched together a series of verses from other psalms; verses 1–2 = 18:2; verse 3 = 8:4–5; verse 4 = 39:5; verses 9–10 = 18:49–50. In still other cases it is impossible to clearly distinguish the individual components from each other to say that one set of verses is earlier than another. Such are examples of the degree of editing certain psalms underwent and which took place over a period of time. It was only over the course of the ensuing centuries that the Psalter would eventually arrive at something like a final form, culminating in a fixed Hebrew canon at a time during the late first to early second century CE.

The *Septuagint* represents a still further development of the Davidic tradition. Here additional psalms were ascribed to David as well, although this is clearly unwarranted since these superscriptions were absent in earlier Hebrew texts. The final form we have today is the result of the confluence of those various collections which survived the compilation and editing process. Having passed through the crucible of history and the severe trials, tribulations and conflagrations that Israel was to encounter, endure, and somehow survive, it is nothing short of remarkable that the final form of the book of Psalms has come down to us today in its present state. The assiduous care and painstaking preservation of these texts is a bold witness to the enduring faith of ancient Israel. Despite appearances to the contrary, their steadfast trust testifies mightily to the conviction that יהוה is sovereign over everything. For ancient Israel, יהוה is the God who is active in human history!

> We encounter here again the unity of religion and politics so characteristic of Israel. The political history could not be examined simply for its own sake, because God was active in it. But it can now be seen from this examination of history that the activity of God does not consist merely of [his] helping [his] people. To the contrary! The downfall of the people is itself God's activity; it is

[his] judgment on the people who failed to live up to the covenant obligations.
The election of Israel is thus in no way a guarantee of security; rather, it signifies
the highest responsibility, and it includes the awesome possibility that [he] holds
[his] people to account. This consciousness was kept alive in Israel especially by
certain individuals who had a decisive voice in the picture of the period of the
Kings: the prophets. They had proclaimed the judgment of God time after time,
but they had also shown Israel the way into the future after the catastrophe. [18]

The fall of Jerusalem in 587/586 BCE,[19] even more than being a military, religious,
and political catastrophe, ushered in an era of theological crisis that has remained
virtually unchanged for 2600 years. It is altogether remarkable that Israel's downfall
did not in fact mean the end of her religion. The catastrophe did not bring the history
of Israel's religion to a close. Such an historic parenthesis, with its obliteration of the
three core social, political and religious institutions central to the life and identity of
its people—land, temple and monarchy—required a fundamental reassessment and
revision.

Compositions and collections, editing and compiling, all played a central part
of the community's liturgical function in their worshiping life in God. The liturgists
and musicians who composed many of these particular psalms lived between the amphictyonic era and the Persian restoration–roughly 900 years.[20] Claus Westermann
underscores this point:

the Psalms did not first originate as literature usually originates among us. They
arose out of the worship of Israel . . . they were not first written and then sung,
but vice versa: They were first sung and prayed for a long time– perhaps for
a very long time—before they were written down. And those who wrote them
down were not the same people who composed them; instead they were the ones
who collected them. The process of collecting and writing down the Psalms was
in itself a very important and significant step, but it was a step which came some-
what late in their development. [21]

This understanding of the process presumes a long, rich, and varied life of the
Psalms in oral tradition. The Psalter is characterized by the two basic counter poles of
lament and praise. On this point we are on solid ground. In between these two poles,

18. Rendtorff, *Canon and Theology*, 38.

19. Renckens, *The Religion of Israel*. "It is, very simply, altogether remarkable that Israel's downfall
[587 BCE] did not in fact, mean the end of her religion. The catastrophe did not in any sense bring
the history of Israel's religion to a close. It is more true to say that Israel's religious history really began
at this point." 223.

20. Gillingham, *Psalms through the Centuries*. "It seems fairly certain that many psalms were
composed in the pre exilic period–psalms for the king to use in the Temple (2, 72, 89, 110 and 132),
psalms which ratified the conviction that God would protect the city of Zion from invasion (46, 48),
and psalms which would be used in times of national distress (74, 77, 79, 80, 82). Other psalms with
archaic language and Canaanite motifs are probably early: these include Psalms 29 and 68." 5.

21. Westermann, *The Living Psalms*, 12.

ancient word-smiths conveyed an uncanny sense of, and an unassailable confidence in, יהוה their God. Westermann continues:

> *Praise and lament are the two basic melodic sounds which, like quiet echoes, accompany God's actions on this long arc of history. The polarity of praise and lament is different from the well-known polarity of petition and thanksgiving in our modern prayers. The ellipse which circles about the two foci of lament and praise is both more extensive and more precise in its course than that around petition and thanksgiving.* [22]

To read and study the book of Praises is to be led inexorably toward the praise of יהוה as Israel's final word. Doxology may be the beginning word but praise is the final word. This is so theologically because in praise, more than any other human act, יהוה is seen and declared to be God in all fullness and glory. It is so eschatologically because the last word is the confession and praise of God by the whole cosmos (Psalms 146—150). Praise more than any other human activity involves the expression of complete devotion to God. In the extravagant exaltation of the transcendent LORD, praise requires a particular sort of liturgical cadence and rhythm. In ancient Israel all praise of יהוה is eschatological.

A larger and longed-for fulfillment of the promises made to them by יהוה is never far from the poets' minds. The psalmists were liturgists, lyricists, musicians and, yes, theologians. The performance and participation of the worshipers in liturgical actions and settings ought not be presumed facile. These hymns and songs, prayers and praises were at the heart of their communal celebrations. These actions, as described are *not simply ideological constructs designed to mask sociological realities or statistical word fields for the lexically inclined. The psalmists were masters of word and image, and their poetry reflects the mosaic of Israel's faith.*[23]

Their mastery of the language served a common purpose in that it was possible to stir the community toward the actions of prayer and praise of יהוה . Only in this manner could the community's response to the glory of יהוה be actualized in its worshiping and liturgical life. Israel was acutely aware of the importance of language in telling the story of the dramatic acts of יהוה on their behalf in human history.

This historical accent lay at the core of communal praise and recital. This is essentially Israel's theology of the recital of God's gracious acts in her history.

> *The recital of the Psalms make two foundational theological claims . . . God is good, gives gifts, and rescues in response to need. On the other, the ones who suffer must repent and they will be healed. The two affirmations together propose a world of moral symmetry which is canonical and non-negotiable. Those who*

---

22. Westermann, *Praise and Lament in the Psalms*, 37.

23. Brown, *Seeing the Psalms: A Theology of Metaphor*, 15.

do not share this moral symmetry are not given voice in these Psalms (Pss. 78, 105, 106, 136).[24]

It is also her core confession of faith. Praising יהוה is ever at the heart of ancient Israel's life and existence. *Praise is practically equivalent to Israel's concept of faith. The starting-point for theology, as discourse about God, is not the intellectual question: 'What can we say about God?', 'What sense does it make to speak of God?' Much more does theology begin by speaking to God and . . . reflection on God develops from speaking to [Him].* [25]

In this respect for the psalmists, any theology of the Psalms must first begin with the character of יהוה and second, with Israel's intimate partnership with יהוה in covenant. Consistently and persistently, the psalms bear unmistakable witness throughout that any and all theological discourse is rooted in the actual, lived relationship between Israel and יהוה. What is always in question is existence in relation to יהוה and the quest for God in the hopelessness of existence pushed to its limits. Theology is always rooted in the real, existential life experience of encountering יהוה in all life's situations. It grows first, therefore, not from thought, but from life.[26] The Hebrew accent on life and life-affirming values is a key theme throughout the Psalter. For the poets of the ancient way, true life, *shalom,* simply cannot be experienced without knowledge of and obedience before יהוה.

Psalm 31 is a marvelous prayer to יהוה for assistance in daily living in which the people of God petition and express complete confidence which results in a final song of thanksgiving. It is a prayer for God's assistance in which petition, complaint, and trust coalesce in a marvelous concluding song of thanksgiving for the help that has been received.

Psalm 31

To the choirmaster. A psalm of David

In יהוה do I take refuge. Let me never be abased,

but in your justice, set me at large.

Incline your ear to me and speedily save me.

Be for me a rock of refuge,

a stronghold to deliver me.

For you are my crag and my strong fortress;

For your Name's sake, lead me and guide me.

---

24. Brueggemann, *Abiding Astonishment: Psalms, Modernity, and the Making of History* 48, 49.

25. Westermann, *The Living Psalms,* 143.

26. Westermann, *A Thousand Years and a Day,* 134.

Trusting YHWH

Deliver me out of the snare they have set for me
for you, יהוה , are my place of refuge.
Into your hands I commit my spirit.
You have redeemed me, O יהוה , faithful God.

O God of truth, you detest those
who worship false and empty gods.
But as for me, I will trust in יהוה.
I will rejoice in your steadfast love and constancy.
For you are full aware of all my afflictions,
and take notice of my adversities; you have
not given me over to my enemies,
but rather have set my feet in a broad place.

Be gracious to me, O יהוה , for I am sore distressed;
my eyes are wasted away with tears,
my soul and my heart are vexed with grief.
For my life is spent with sorrow
and my years with sighing;
my strength fails because I am in misery
and my bones disintegrate.

In the face of all my foes
I am a reproach;
I am an object of derision to my acquaintances;
even my friends are afraid of me!
Those who see me in the street
avoid me like the plague;
I am like one who is dead—out of mind;
I have become like a broken pitcher.

I hear the whispering of many
and I am surrounded by fear;
they scheme together against me,
they are plotting to take my life.
But יהוה—I rest fully in your care;
I will say, "You *are my God*."
My times are in your hand,

deliver me out of the hands of my oppressors.

Let your face shine upon me.

In your steadfast love, save me.

Let me not be put to shame for I call on you.

Shame the evil doers! Let them go to Sheol!

Let their lying lips be stilled;

Let them be silenced in the grave,

for they speak insolently against the just,

with full-throated arrogance and contempt.

How great is your goodness, יהוה,

that you keep those who stand in awe of you,

you have accomplished wonders to those who trust in you,

in the sight of all!

You hide them in the covert of your presence

from all human plots.

You hold them safe within your shelter

from disputative tongues.

Blessed is יהוה who has wondrously shown me

such a steadfast love

when I was beset as a fortified city under siege.

I had said in my anxiety, "*I am far removed from your sight,*"

But you heard my alarm

as I cried out to you for help.

Love יהוה, all you saints;

יהוה preserves the faithful—

but views the haughty with scorn.

Be strong, and let your heart take courage,

all you who hope in יהוה.

There is a moral and theological symmetry to these poetic reflections which, throughout the articulation of their beliefs and core convictions, undergird the centrality of יהוה and the divine *presence* in the midst of human life. Psalm 31 states that nowhere is יהוה considered to be anything less than completely invested in humankind. This consciousness of the experience of being sheltered and protected is not a reference to the temple's area of asylum and refuge as such. Rather, the determining factor is always trust in יהוה alone, who gives to the lonely and repeatedly oppressed, security and victory over a dangerous isolation.

The mighty acts of Israel's deliverance form the essence of the story of her re-demption. This story is part of a long history that stretches back to the *Exodus* and is relived anew in each successive generation. It also adds to that story by relating the circumstances of God's victory as experienced in their own time. The history of redemption inspires God's people to praise, proclaim, and hope. In Psalm 71:14–16, the poet writes: *I will hope continually, and I will praise you* יהוה *yet more and more. My mouth will tell of your righteous acts, of your deeds of salvation all day long, though their number is past my knowledge. I will come praising the mighty deeds of* יהוה *God, I will praise your righteousness, yours alone* (NRSV). The acts of deliverance reveal the goodness and blessing of יהוה to [his] people.

The redeemed of יהוה experience no want for their great God satisfies them com-pletely–materially and spiritually. יהוה establishes a victorious kingship so that the people of God may bear witness to the sovereignty, lordship, and love which יהוה has demonstrated on their behalf. The upward cry for salvation is constant. *Save us, O Yhwh our God, and gather us from among the nations, so that we may give thanks to your holy name and glory in your praise* (106:47, LW). "יהוה, *save!*" is the most com-mon prayer of the poets.

Actual deliverance is promised by יהוה to the godly, meaning those whose ways are now in alignment with the way of יהוה. יהוה is righteous and true and just and delivers those who concern themselves with the exacting standards of justice and righteousness. יהוה favors [his] beloved–those who aspire to live an accurate life in keeping with the demands of the covenant. With loving protection as a form of re-demption, *shalom* is the gift of יהוה that proves itself precisely in the face of acute attacks and threats. *In its own religious world shalom is a comprehensive term for a condition of life, a quality of experience, a state of being. A person has shalom when life is whole, when one is experiencing the wholeness that makes life complete. It is the health and well-being of living in all its levels.*[27]

All Israel is the object of the fidelity, love and grace of יהוה who is the subject of the Psalter's continuing dialog and conversation. The Psalter underscores these phenomena through the fullness of its very different texts. These compositions are full of surprising reversals, unexpected twists, and exchanges. And yet each is inter-woven with one another throughout the various collections. It is in these collections of psalms that we may hear the voice of Israel; and through it, the voice of God. *These voices must be distinguished and each received for what it is; but it is wrong to separate them, and to try to hear one without the other. For by the very fact that they are both heard together, they bear witness to the presence of God amongst [men], and of [man] with God.*[28]

The references to Job (the silence of God) and Ecclesiastes (the indifference of God) are representative of some of the *non-establishment* voices in the Hebrew canon.

27. Mays, *Preaching and Teaching the Psalms*, 11.
28. Lohfink, *In the Shadow of Your Wings*, 8.

But these voices of Israel in the laments of the Psalter are on display having made their appeals to God without so much as a divine response to their desperate pleadings (cf. Psalm 88). It is Walter Brueggemann's contention that

> *important elements of the experience of the Israelite community are excluded from this canon, just as the modern scientific reconstruction of the history of ancient Israel excludes some experiences. This establishment recital has no room in it for those who do not share in this persuasive and adequate drama of guilt and grace (just as the scientific account has no place in it for those who do not share in its story of power).*[29]

But these voices must not be separated for each is a part of the overall witness of ancient Israel. They bear witness to the incomparability of יהוה when contrasted to the worship of other gods and, ultimately, to the exclusion and, finally, the actual declaration of their extinction, the death, or the non-being of all other gods (Ps 82) in the face of the awesome reality of the One God of All.[30]Israel's one, true God of All is יהוה. In the words of Rolf Knierim,

> *Psalm 82 depicts a trial in heaven, the moment in which the transition happens from polytheism to monotheism, on the ground that the God of Israel (the one who is meant in the Psalm) condemns the gods to death because they have judged unjustly, shown partiality to the wicked, and failed to protect the weak, fatherless, afflicted, destitute, and needy . . . he is to rise and judge all the nations.*[31]

29. Brueggemann, *Abiding Astonishment.* His criticism may be directed toward the interpretative inclinations of the "Biblical Theology Movement" of the past century, which "tended to give the establishment recital such weight that other voices were largely unnoticed. Such . . . did not force those other voices out of the literature of the Bible." 49.

30. Sanders, *The Monotheizing Process: Its Origin and Development.* "Along with the gradual development of a protocanon of recitals of God's involvement with Israel there also developed the concept of there being One God of All. Monotheism, like canons, did not start full-blown by the decree of a king or central government. It developed out of the necessity early on to unify the ancient tribes that made up the early Israelite coalition of groups that in various ways replaced the Canaanites in the Palestinian area. 25.

31. Knierim, "*On the Interpretation of the Old Testament by the Church,*" 55–77. Note: I am not at all sure that Knierim is correct here. I see the transition from polytheism to henotheism to monotheism as a process taking place over a long period of time. Israel was not a monotheistic people throughout at least much of the pre-exilic period. To understand the transition to have occurred so abruptly is a radical departure from understanding it as an evolving process. But if he is correct this would place Ps 82, a northern Asaphite psalm, sometime in the 7th BCE during the "Yahweh alone" reform under Josiah. This would account for the abruptness of the occurrence he advocates. The reforms instituted by Josiah–the "boy king—wrought profound changes in Judah at the time and the ascendancy of יהוה would be a reflection of the Deuteronomistic historians who favored the Sinai theology tradition wherein Moses instituted a monotheistic belief in יהוה even though the weakness in this view offers no accounting for Israel's continuous dabbling in Canaanite polytheism and their panoply of fertility cults. The Yahwism of the psalms reflects what appears to be a constant struggle to extinguish the beliefs and practices of any worship other than fidelity to Yahweh alone as the One God of All. This marks Israel's journey from henotheism to a monotheistic faith. It is this interior way of יהוה which is preserved in Sepher Tellihim.

Psalm 82 details how יהוה, in all authority and incomparability, has decreed from the council of heaven that all other gods have been judged and consigned to death! In contrast to the polytheistic gods of Canaan, the poet acknowledges that he had a false understanding about the *elohim* (gods) and their relationship to יהוה. He admits to holding a syncretistic view of the deities when he wrote: *I had thought: "You are gods, sons of Elyon, all of you."* But now, with the confidence of a prophet, he announces the result of God's judgment: *'Nevertheless, you shall all die like mortals, and you shall fall, all of you, like any human'.* (82:6 NRSV).

The poet has, in effect, been converted from a henotheistic to a monotheistic belief in the One God of All. The effect is not simply to marginalize other gods but to render all other gods extinct. They have no actual *being*. In reality, and using this imagery as a literary device to establish absolute sovereignty, there is no divine assembly consisting of a cohort of foreign deities. The poet asserts that unlike the surrounding cultures with their primary deities, Baal and El, יהוה has no other gods with whom to contend because יהוה alone is supreme. Here in Psalm 82, a peak text, the poet experiences a drastic transformation of thought and belief: יהוה is the One God of All!

Psalm 82

A psalm of Asaph

God has taken command in the divine assembly,
and in the midst of the gods holds judgment:
How long will you judge unjustly and
show partiality to the corrupt?

Give justice to the weak and the orphan;
maintain the right of the lowly and the destitute.
Defend the lowly and the needy;
deliver them from the hand of the oppressor."
They have neither knowledge nor understanding,
they walk around in darkness; all the
foundations of the earth are shaken.
I had thought, *"You are all gods, all of you—*
children of Elyon (the Most High);
nevertheless, all of you shall die like any mortal,
and fall like any earthly ruler."
Rise up, O God, and bring justice to the earth,
for you rule; all the nations belong to you!

The divine assembly is an image used by this Elohistic poet to underscore the exclusive uniqueness and the utter predominance of Israel's God who is all! This incomparability of יהוה is framed in Israel's response to the henotheistic claims of her neighbors and many Israelites concerning the worship of יהוה among the other gods of Canaan. To say then, that these gods are of no consequence to יהוה is not accurate. Belief in false gods militates against the true worship of יהוה, the worship that is due only to the God of Israel who is the One God of All. This is idolatry and it will not be tolerated by יהוה. The *gods of the Most High* are dismissed and the basis of their sentence of death is due to their refusal to do justice on behalf of the poor and disenfranchised. In other words, the *gods* of the divine council have forfeited their authority to preside over humankind! This description of the heavenly council by the poet is perhaps a rejoinder to those in Israel who were tempted to believe in יהוה above all other gods.

The movement toward יהוה *alone* is a persistent and constant theme throughout the Psalms.[32] It is these two voices of lament and praise that are heard continually throughout the Psalms. These are interwoven by the poets into a tapestry of conversations that range to and fro between Israel's faithfulness and unfaithfulness toward יהוה; between the voice of the fidelity of יהוה both in word and deed toward Israel, and Israel's response in words and deeds to יהוה.[33] The Psalter represents these conversations as they played out over a period of nearly a millennium and there are no other phenomena like them in the Hebrew Scriptures. This fact alone gives the Psalter its unique pride of place within the biblical canon.

---

32. Crenshaw, *Defending God*, ". . . the author of Psalm 82 deconstructs the notion of a host of deities comprised in a heavenly assembly, analogous to royal courts below. An utter failure to protect the rights of marginalized citizens, to ensure social and ethical justice, has convinced the psalmist that the divine assembly has forfeited its claim on terrestrial devotees. In the psalmist's view, a single deity remains, one who judges the divine assembly and condemns it to moral status. On this remaining god's integrity and commitment to justice the psalmist rests all hope for rectitude among humans." 45.

33 cf. R. B. Y. Scott, *The Psalms as Christian Praise*, 64.

The Incomparability of YHWH

THE INCOMPARABILITY OF יהוה is a recurring theme throughout the Psalter and is frequently reinforced, for example, by the imagery of *rock and refuge*. The writers of the psalms often use rock and refuge imagery to refer to the trustworthiness and confidence they place in יהוה who is the One who is utterly, completely and eternally reliable. This recurring theme of refuge is, in essence, a filter through which the Psalter in its entirety may be viewed theologically and serves as one of its broadest meta-phorical contours. Specifically, *rock and refuge* psalms are oftentimes paired together; for instance, Psalm 18 (*The LORD is my rock, my fortress, and my deliverer, my God, my rock in whom I take refuge* 18:2) and Psalm 19 (*O LORD, my rock and my refuge* 19:15 REB).

Psalm 92, one of our three psalms uses the rock and refuge imagery as well. *Show that יהוה is trustworthy and upright; he is my rock, and there is no unrighteousness in him* (92:35 REB). Linguistic and stylistic evidence suggest that Psalm 18 may be one of the earlier psalms in the Psalter, dating most likely from the mid to late-eleventh century BCE. It is also practically identical to the poem in 2 Samuel 22, which is probably from an older source than the psalm, though it is not clear if the writer of the psalm (David?) copied it in part or in whole from 2 Samuel or if both were copied from an anonymous but earlier common source.

Psalm 18 certainly places us deep in ancient Israel's past and possibly pre-dates the monarchy. It most likely has a northern origination and close attention must be paid to its theophanic description (vv. 7–15).[1] The immediate question for us is one of God's capacity to contain chaos and restore or maintain order, all under the aegis of our perceived capacities for faithfulness and trusting confidence, never a small order for anyone's life. This idea of the incomparability of יהוה when placed in the direct light of comparison to other gods, is unique to those psalmists who share a perspective on the monarchy that is often at variance and frequently in conflict with the prophetic

---

1. Franken, *The Mystical Communion with JHWH in the Book of Psalms*. "Verses 17 and 18 show us the connection with what actually happened. To be drawn out of many waters and to be delivered from haters is the same fact. The theophany is the psalmist's faithful interpretation of the meaning of events in which he usually was successful." 76

tradition. יהוה is the proven deliverer who gives Israel her identity. It is only in יהוה that Israel exists at all; she lives and moves and has her very being in יהוה.[2]

This is Israel's dictum and it is Israel's Creed. Israel believed in, and Israel prayed to יהוה. When Israel borrowed literary forms and cultic practices from its Canaanite neighbors, it did not merely imitate them. It is essential to focus on what is distinctive in Israel's worship. These borrowed forms were transformed and the practices of their worshiping life were converted. Such "borrowing" was common in the ancient literary world.

In contrast to her neighbors, ancient Israel extolled יהוה not only as the God of Israel but as *God Most High.* עליון (*Elyon*) will not tolerate the refusal of the gods to act benevolently on behalf of the poor. יהוה is a just God and will do justice! The people of God had entered into an eternal covenant with יהוה, who is the only God and who took that covenant absolutely seriously.[3] At its heart this is a covenant that is concerned with matters of justice, holiness and faithfulness. יהוה is the God Who is in love with Israel and it is an awesome love! Psalm 82, then, is a critically important psalm wherein the God of Israel puts the other gods on trial.

> In Canaanite mythology it was the high god El who convened the council of the gods. In Ps 82:1, it is Israel's God who has displaced El and who convenes what turns out to be anything but a routine meeting. In extraordinary fashion, Israel's God proceeds to put the other gods on trial . . . Psalm 82 represents God's desire for and enactment of retribution against unjust gods. [4]

The event in Israel's life that marks יהוה as incomparable is the act of deliverance in history—in human time. יהוה heeds Israel's cry to be delivered from their bondage and servitude in Egypt. יהוה acts justly on their behalf in history and their deliverance from the hands of an oppressive pharaoh marks יהוה as the redeeming God. There are no rivals. This is the witness of the poet of Psalm 82. God is concerned fundamentally with matters of justice for the powerless, the weak and the dispossessed. God's demand for uncompromising justice in human affairs is rooted in the very character and nature of the one true Sovereign—יהוה. The protection of these lesser ones is the

2. Labuschagne, *The Incomparability of Yahweh in the Old Testament.* ". . . the idea of Yahweh's incomparability is very closely linked with [His] uniqueness, and these expressions denoting Yahweh's incomparability were at an early stage in Israel's history considered to be confessions of [His] uniqueness" 14.

3. Kraus, Psalms *A Continental Commentary:* Vol 2 (Psalms 60–150) 157–158. cf. Broyles, Psalms, New *International Biblical Commentary* "It makes sense that the book of Psalms should reflect this conflict between Yahwists and worshipers of other gods, so prevalent in the prophets. In several places, the OT is reticent to acknowledge explicitly other so called gods and instead employs wordplays or euphemisms . . . the fundamental issue of the psalm is probably not the private issue of false accusation but the corporate issue, to what deity should people appeal?" 53.

4. McCann, *A Theological Introduction to the Book of Psalms.*122. cf. Knierim, "Old Testament Form," pp. 55–77. Note: Some scholars (McCann) have called Psalm 82 the most important text in the Hebrew bible because the line of demarcation is formidably drawn between polytheism and henotheism, and a strict monotheistic belief in יהוה.

decisive criterion for the justification and the legitimization of the universal Lordship of God, monotheistically! What we have here is not a concept that monotheism is a proof of truth as such, but that it *depends* on a proof of truth; the truth of universally inclusive justice for which the specific criterion is the deity's protection of the poor.

יהוה is incomparable. יהוה *alone* is the one true God! Scholars are not alone in an assessment of the divine qualities of יהוה. Throughout the entirety of the Hebrew Bible, there is a basic connection between this incomparability and the fact that יהוה is the God who acts in human history on behalf of the weak, the oppressed, and the powerless. This was the fundamental reality of the Hebrews situation in Egypt before their incomparable God acted decisively on their behalf. This is precisely what יהוה is demanding with these interventions in history. It is the ancient Hebrew tradition that insists that love of justice resides in the heart of יהוה. James Crenshaw adds that

> . . . the author of Psalm 82 deconstruct(s) the notion of a host of deities comprised in a heavenly assembly, analogous to royal courts below. An utter failure to protect the rights of marginalized citizens, to ensure social and ethical justice, has convinced the psalmist that the divine assembly has forfeited its claim on terrestrial devotees. In the psalmist's view a single deity remains, one who judges the divine assembly and condemns it to moral status. On this remaining god's integrity and commitment to justice the psalmist rests all hope for rectitude among humans.[5]

Irrespective of this universal emphasis and its increasing centrality to Israel's self-understanding, theological discourse did not begin with extolling יהוה as the Creator. True, יהוה is before, behind, and beyond the whole created order. The Psalter contains magnificent songs and hymns of creation to the Creator, such as Psalms 8, 19 and 104, showing that Israel had a creation story like the other ancient peoples. But Israel's theology did not begin with creation. The invocation to worship is based solely on the call of the people of God out of servitude, slavery, and bondage. Israel's worship was not grounded in a creation faith because this was not their primary collective experience. It is their root experience of deliverance from slavery to liberation and promise which forms the basis of the sacred story.

It is the event of "exodus" that is enshrined in the collective memory of the psalmists; that continues to bear witness to Israel's growing confidence in the incomparability, fidelity and trustworthiness of יהוה. Where this trust in יהוה is overtly the theme of an individual psalm, then that psalm fits the genre we call the psalms of confidence or song of trust.[6] Yet ancient Israel did have reason to praise יהוה for the superintendence of the earth and the universe–what little the poets knew of its seeming infinity. All creation serves at the word of יהוה, the Commander in Chief, in

---

5. Crenshaw, *Defending God*, 45.

6. Gillingham, *The Poems and Psalms of the Hebrew Bible*. 225. cf. Hossfeld and Zenger, Psalms 2 in *Hermeneia* ". . . the psalms of trust have their *Sitz im Leben* in times of anxiety, and as prayers against fear and despair they are texts of hope–not the expression of false self-assurance and 'certainty of salvation.'" 433.

gaining victory to redeem [his] people. *God rides the ancient skies above, and thunders with a mighty voice* (68:33 REB). The taming of chaos, the ordering and governance of creation, and the centrality of humankind in God's act of creation, is affirmed by the poet of Psalm 8. *When I look up at your heavens, the work of your fingers, at the moon and the stars you have set in place, what is a frail mortal, that you should be mindful of [him], a human being, that you should take notice of [him]?* (Ps 8:4,5 REB).

Similarly, the poet of Israel's greatest creation hymn, Psalm 19, declares: *The heavens proclaim the glory/power of God, and the firmament shows forth the work of God's hands. Day unto day takes up the story and night unto night the message. No speech, no word, no voice is heard yet their span extends through all the earth, their words to the ends of the earth* (19: 2–5, LW). The resplendence of God's mighty act of creation and all nature's witness to the might and power of יהוה is a central theme of these creation hymns. This conviction may be translated into today's terms in the following manner. All creation is the act of God's word and is under the control and power of יהוה. This is a profound statement of faith, given our continually unfolding discoveries and increased knowledge of the immensity of *the vast expanse of inter-stellar space, galaxies, suns, the planets in their courses, and this fragile earth our island home* (The Episcopal Book of Common Prayer, Eucharistic Prayer C, 370).

An array of cosmic phenomena such as asteroids and anti-matter, black holes and supernovas, quarks and the wondrous quirks in this unfolding, expanding universe/multiverse all are subject to the Creator's will and purpose; geological and meteorological phenomena on earth–earthquakes and tsunamis, volcanic eruptions and magma floes, fires and floods, all nature is subject to יהוה. Chaos erupts and disrupts human life but the God of the created order will prevail, even after billions of suns are turned to stone. The eternal promise declares that one day there will be peace across the great uncharted void of space and time.

The effects of modern human life and activity on this one, small and delicate planet increasingly raises questions about our stewardship of the earth's natural God given resources. The subsequent moral decisions we make collectively through our enactment of and participation in a wide swath of public policies will have lasting consequences. This is, I believe, the paramount theological question of our time: How ought the creature honor the creation and in so doing glorify the Creator? This is our constant challenge and it is the challenge of all humanity not to love the creature more than the Creator. The boundaries of our habitation are ordered of יהוה for the good of all humankind. As a race we violate these sacred boundaries to our own peril. To fail to take seriously the responsibility of humanity in the created order is to risk ignoring our God-given mandate to exercise dominion and to be faithful stewards of the delicate order and balance of this magnificent planet.

To people of faith ancient Israel's theological world-view may be discerned throughout the Psalms. Theirs is not really that different from ours. It consists of the following propositions: יהוה is the Creator of all that is; יהוה superintends the whole created order; the call and deliverance of the people of יהוה and their subsequent election into the eternal covenant; the assiduous care and providence afforded the people of God throughout its long history; the mighty, saving deeds of יהוה recounted in Israel's salvation story; the promise of a universal redemption of the whole world–all are enshrined within the events and circumstances of human history–a history whose sphere of reality is the sphere of God's activity and purposes in the world. יהוה promises to be an attentive and sojourning *presence* in the life of the people of God and that promise extends to us today.

Between *the world of hurt and the God of faithfulness* (Brueggemann), Israel's legacy of trusting יהוה was shaped and articulated from one generation to the next. The single common thread that runs throughout the entire corpus is confidence and trust in the power of יהוה as demonstrated in the acts of deliverance, protection, and salvation. The blessings of godliness and spiritual enlightenment are open to all who seek יהוה as the highest good in life. יהוה is the *One God of All*. This is the monotheistic assertion of the Yahwists. [7]

Over the course of time, that is, over many, many centuries, the psalmists described the mighty deeds and works of יהוה in their own historical moment. The mythopoetic language of the psalms ought not to surprise because Israel used the literary heritage of her neighbors to great advantage to demonstrate the superiority, uniqueness, and incomparability of יהוה who is the God of the heavens, the seas, the depths, the earth, and the entirety of the cosmos.

The extent of the sovereignty of יהוה over the world stresses the incomparability and the superiority of יהוה when contrasted with all other gods. Ultimately, יהוה renders all other gods extinct! Throughout its history Israel was constantly contesting and combating the influence of the gods of Canaan. The encroachment of the Baal fertility traditions of the ancient Near East continued to be an enticing allurement. In Israel's story it is the God who makes a way out of no-way, a people out of no-people, a blessing out of no-blessing, who is greatly to be praised! יהוה is enthroned upon the praises of Israel and Israel is for all time the people of יהוה.

For our three psalms, we say that the genre of Psalm 91 is an individual song of trust with a divine oracle.

> *The psalm is intended for instruction and exhortation and is designed to challenge and strengthen the faith of those who trust in Yahweh. Thus Ps 91 is an enduring encouragement of faith, which asks us to respond to its affirmations. The case for faith is not put in the language of argument; it declares the reality. We are challenged to ground our endeavors in trust in Yahweh, a trust which will not fail, and which leads us along a way where we will see more and more of the saving work of God until finally our knowledge will be complete.* [8]

7. cf. Sanders, *The Psalms Scroll.*

8. Tate, Psalms 51–100, Vol 20. *Word Bible Commentary.* 459. cf. Futato, *Interpreting the Psalms.* "While the songs of confidence have no unifying structural shape several characteristics nonetheless

Psalm 91 is closely connected to what comes before it, Psalm 90, and after it, Psalm 92. In thought, context and language these three psalms taken as a triad, open *Book IV* (90–106) and belong together. In terms of *form criticism*, the method is not very helpful in determining a specific genre of the psalms of trust. Each of our psalms begins with the blessedness of those who find a dwelling place in יהוה. In conjunction, and in the face of the stark reality of the human condition, Psalm 91 embraces boldly the promises of divine protection and refuge, concluding with an oracle wherein יהוה has the last and final word. The reference to taking refuge under God's wings occurs elsewhere and outside of the Psalter only in Ruth 2:12: *May יהוה reward you for your mercy, and may you have a full reward from יהוה, the God of Israel, under whose wings you have come for refuge!* The concept appears in similar expressions in Pss 17:8; 36:8; 57:2; 61:5; and 63:8. According to Otto Eissfeldt, strict lines of demarcation of the various "types" (*gattungen*) as stressed in the form critical motifs may be problematic when subscribed to uncritically.

> *Ps. xci may perhaps be described as a 'psalm of conversion' which attests how a pious man who was formerly devoted to אל שדי עליון (El Shaddai, Elyon) has now turned to יהוה and is confirmed by a priest of יהוה in the certainty that he is indeed under the latter's protection. The same may be true of Ps. Cxxi (another psalm of trust) for here there speaks one who after a vain search in other cults has now found full satisfaction with יהוה, and receives a friendly welcome from the priest of יהוה to whom he has declared his allegiance. If this is correct, then it becomes especially clear wit h these two psalms how uncertain is their allocation to particular 'types' and how indistinct is the borderline between 'cultic' and 'spiritual' songs.[9]*

The *LXX* also adds the heading *"Praise. A Song of David"* to Psalm 91, although as previously noted, the superscription's authenticity is doubtful and is not present in the earlier texts. In Psalm 92 the godly respond to the extravagant promises in praise and trust. Each of these three psalms directly implies an open invitation to anyone seeking after יהוה. Psalm 90 describes God as *our refuge/dwelling place* (REB); Psalm 91 affirms יהוה as *my refuge and my bulwark, Elohay (my God) in whom I trust* (91:2, LW).

As far as Psalm 92 is concerned there is reason for thanksgiving to יהוה and the praise of *Elyon* because no other help is needed: *It is good to give thanks to יהוה; to sing praises to your name, O Elyon (Most High). I will declare your benevolence every*

---

hold this category together. As the name indicates, the distinguishing characteristic of this category is their unwavering confidence or trust in God's ability and willingness to deliver from adverse circumstances." 161.

9. Eissfeldt, *Introduction to the Old Testament* 123. "...if Ps. xci and Ps. cxxi are really 'psalms of conversion', then they obviously belong in the temple since it is here that a transfer of allegiance to Yahweh was effected. But what we have here is the experience of individuals which is used to give a consolatory warning to others." 126

morning, and your faithfulness every night (vv.1–2 REB). Psalm 92 brings the triad of psalms to a crescendo emphasizing the very nature of יהוה. *Declare the uprightness of* יהוה; יהוה *is my rock; there is no unrighteousness in [him]* (v. 15, NRSV). Everything is brought low before the rock of deliverance prompting Martin Luther's remark that

> *the Psalter originated from below. It rises with a crescendo and cadence that overwhelms the forces of darkness and death. Other books [referring to those in the biblical canon] have much ado about the works of the saints; but say very little about their words. The Psalter is a gem in this respect ... [I]t relates not only the works of the saints, but also their words, how they spoke with God and how they prayed.* [10]

Psalm 91 functions as a sort of antidote to corrupted beliefs and describes the fearlessness that the one who trusts in יהוה may come to possess. In the Babylonian Talmud, this psalm is referred to as *the song against evil occurrences* and *the song against plagues*. Contrasts are also drawn against those who trust in magic and astrology, sorcery and witch-craft. In ancient Israel these were all strictly forbidden, although they were practiced. The primary purpose of Psalm 91 is not to issue guarantees against catastrophes and random misfortune. Rather it is to promote Yahwism—faith in יהוה *alone*—as opposed to the various syncretistic practices which were prevalent, not only throughout the religions of the ancient Near East, but in Israel as well.

The allurement of the gods of Canaan remained a constant enticement to Israel. In the Psalter we may listen to the way of Israel's poets speaking in the *presence* of the Holy One. It is the troubled conscience of Israel that is brought into the *presence* of יהוה in worship in the sanctuary. In the laments and confessions, the complaints and pleadings, we are able to listen to the cries of those who are afflicted by a sense of guilt.

> Many *of the psalms of individual lament presuppose that sickness and other ills are the direct consequence of divine judgment following on sin, even in advertent sin (e.g. Ps 90:7 8). In some of these hymns a morally rational world-view, in which virtue is always rewarded and wickedness always punished, is maintained in defiance of experience.*[11]

The key to understanding Psalm 91 as a psalm of trust lies in interpreting its imagery. The dominant image describing the obligation of the suppliant is that of seeking and taking *refuge* in יהוה (vv. 1–2, 9, cf. v. 4). This seems to be not an abstract metaphor but a concrete symbol for trust in God that derives from the temple and the

10. E. Theodore Bachman, (ed) *Luther's Works, "Preface to the Psalter"* vol, 35. [56]. Note: Luther's Commentary on the Psalms is one of the pearls in all Christian commentary. He elucidates each psalm with a passion for the interior life of the heart of each poet. Luther's German Psalter served as a towering bulwark of erudition in introducing the sacred text of the Holy Scriptures to the German people and in so doing, virtually assured the broad acceptance of the work of the Reformation among the peasantry. The development and subsequent direction the Protestant Reformation was to take in Germany may be attributed largely to this monumentally impressive theological document.

11. Blenkinsopp, *Wisdom and Law in the Old Testament,* 43.

cherubim wings outstretched over the ark of the covenant. We have noted previously how the psalmists frequently use *rock* and *refuge* imagery together in referring to the trust, faith, and confidence they place in God. More than anywhere else in the Hebrew scriptures, these psalms reflect the human side of the reality of Israel's life lived in the *presence* of יהוה The faith of Israel reflects a larger world-view that, in the words of Konrad Schaefer,

> *depicts reality, both actual and distorted, with a broad panorama of images. In the conception of a world of interconnected parts, human behavior has repercussions in the cosmic order. The unsteady moral climate reverberates in the collapse of the world's foundations.*[12]

The protection of יהוה in Psalm 91 is further spelled out by images of a hiding place (v. 1), a shade from the burning sun (v.,4), a military fortress (vv. 1–2), a mother bird protecting her brood (v. 4a), military defenses (v. 4b), and the ministrations of angels (vv. 11–12). The images depicting threat derive from a hunt, the fowler's snare (v. 3a), disease, the lethal pestilence (v.3b), disasters (v. 10a), the plagues (v. 6), battle (an enveloping shield) and a covert refuge, which protects against the arrow that flies by day (vv. 4–5), and deadly animals—the cub and viper, lion and serpent (v. 13). In a series of richly textured metaphors, יהוה is described variously by the psalmists: *fortress, bulwark, rock, crag, safety, strength, haven, stronghold, shield, defender, rescuer, protector, deliverer, shelter,* and *strong tower.* These are all words that bear on the idea of יהוה as מחסי (*machasa, sheltering refuge*).

The term *word-field* or *semantic field* refers to a particular word cluster that shares a common meaning or sense. The imagery of *refuge* is exceedingly rich and connotes both a literal and symbolic *gravitas*. In terms of conducting an insightful and illuminating analysis of a particular semantic field recurrent throughout the Psalter, this particular metaphor of refuge is a promising foundation upon which a meaningful attempt at constructing a theology of the Psalms might be erected. Jerome Creach states how within the Psalter,

> *a universe of terms has grown together to communicate the common idea of dependence on Yahweh over against other sources of protection . . . it seems clear that the Psalter contains a 'refuge piety', in which dependence upon Yahweh is the supreme virtue and this virtue is communicated with a multitude of terms.*[13]

---

12. Schaefer, Psalms, *Berit Olam,* 78.

13. Creach, *The Destiny of the Righteous in the Psalms,* 90. "In Psalm 92 the godly respond to the extravagant promises in praise and trust. All three [psalms] directly imply an open invitation to anyone seeking after God. Psalm 90 describes God (Adonai) as *"our dwelling place,";* Psalm 91, affirms the Lord (Yahweh) as *'my refuge and my bulwark, my God in whom I will trust'* (91:2). As far as Psalm 92 is concerned, there is reason for thanksgiving and praise because no other help is needed: *'It is good to give thanks to Yahweh; sing praises to your name, O Elyon. I will declare your benevolence every morning, and your faithfulness every night'* (vv.1–2). Psalm 92 brings the triad to a convincing crescendo: *'Declare the uprightness of Yahweh; Yahweh is my rock; there is no unrighteousness in [him]'* (v. 15)." 97.

This refuge imagery can be traced as it weaves its way through our three psalms. The variety of evocative images allow Psalm 91 to be used for any situation of threat. But it may well be that these 150 psalms in the canonical collection were chosen precisely because they were not so tied to any specific historical situation as to inhibit their appropriation and application in any day and age.

> We should keep in mind the transcending intention that moves beyond the earthly realm of this life in those psalms in the OT in which life in the presence of Yhwh produced a very complex concept of life, and in which death, away from God's presence, in Sheol, produced an equally complex concept of death. If we do, the shift in meaning with its tendency to announce the fulfillment of the original meaning, becomes more easily understood. Nevertheless, it is not legitimate to displace the kerygma [the core proclamation] that is proper to the OT with a proclamation that it has been fulfilled, especially since the disputes with Judaism are long past and the method of arguing from 'the Scripture' which was then possible is no longer relevant today.[14]

Seybold, who sees these three psalms as linked inextricably, comments: *It is not for nothing that the psalmist, after a straightforward opening calling on the name of YHWH, relates what is worrying him, and blurts out what has frightened him.* [15] Of the fourteen or so psalms of trust in the Psalter, nearly all fall within the genre of the laments or psalms of complaint. The individual laments or complaints have rightly been called *the backbone of the Psalter* for they are the commonest type of psalm. Almost one-half of the psalms belong to this genre. Nearly all the psalms of individual lament contain expressions of trust and confidence that they will be heard; thus they already contain within them that which suggests trust and praise. But the psalms of trust, as an individual classification, represent certain psalms which are brighter in tone and are more effusive in their confidence in the protective and custodial care of יהוה throughout life. Most but not all songs of trust have a lament motif, but nearly all psalms of lament do have a statement of trust. Bernhard Anderson is right to caution that

> the line between the lament and the song of trust often cannot be drawn sharply . . . Psalm 139, which we tentatively classify as a lament, sounds like a psalm of trust in the inescapable God who knows us better than we know ourselves and from whom there is no escape, whether in the depths of Sheol or the farthest reaches of the universe.[16]

14. Kraus, *Theology of the Psalms*, 198, 199.

15. Seybold, *Introducing the Psalms*, 64.

16. Bernhard Anderson, *Out of the Depths*. 178.

cf. Mowinckel. *The Psalms in Israel's Worship*. "The tone of the protective psalms are brighter than that of the psalms of lamentation. Above all, the confidence and assurance of getting help is more prominent in them. In some of them especially in those which according to their form are individual—it is altogether predominant. Such have been called 'psalms of confidence.'" 220.

The psalms of lament or complaint were composed specifically for such times when life was not well-ordered, but rather disoriented. The laments typically articulate the variegated struggles of human life. The tone of the confidence psalms is brighter than that of the psalms of laments. Above all, especially in Psalm 91, the confidence and assurance of getting help is more prominent; in some -especially in those which according to their form are individual—it is an altogether predominant indicator. Such have been called the psalms of confidence. While some scholars see the songs of confidence as a development of the expressions of trust that often brings a lament to conclusion, others associate the songs of confidence more with the songs of thanksgiving. One may, therefore, call Psalm 91 a psalm of trust *sui generis*. It is, most of all, its metaphorical clarity that is so instructive and comforting to the life of the faithful who live life in the pursuit of יהוה [17]

Psalm 91*

* The heading or superscription of Psalm 91, first as it appears in one of the Qumran scrolls, Cave 11, and then the third century BCE Septuagint (LXX). Note that the Masoretic Text (MT) and most English Translations and Versions (ESV) supply no superscription. Scholarship, tradition, and most modern translations follow the MT.

David's. [11QPs11] // Praise song. David's. [LXX] // Untitled [MT; ESV]

The one who dwells in the secret place of (the Most High) *Elyon*,
and who passes the night within the shadow of (the God of Heaven) *Shaddai*, speaks:
"I will say to יהוה, ' You are my refuge and my bulwark,
You are (my God) Elohay in whom I put my trust'."

Surely יהוה is the One who will rescue you from the snare of the fowler,
and deliver from the lethal arrows that rain down ruinous destruction.
[יהוה] will cover you beneath a feathering cloak,
and will conceal you in a covert refuge.

The constancy of יהוה will be both enveloping shield and sheltering barricade;
You will fear nothing—neither the terrors abroad in the night,
nor the arrow that flies by day;
neither the plague that stalks in the dark,
nor the scourge that wreaks havoc at high noon.

---

17. cf. Tozer, *The Pursuit of God.*

A thousand may fall on your left side, myriad thousands at your right;

but you yourself will remain unscathed.

Make no mistake! You will see it all—

gazing intently with your eyes wide open.

You will witness what becomes of the wickedly corrupt—rotting corpses all.

Because you are the one who has made יהוה *"my refuge,"*

and *Elyon, "my haven of fastness,"*

No disaster shall overtake you;

no calamity shall approach your dwelling.

יהוה will command angels to guard you're going out and coming in;

gentle aides will lift you up in their hands,

so you do not lose your footing and stumble on a stone.

You will stand astride the cub and viper;

you will trample under foot both lion and serpent.

[יהוה speaks] *"Hear this: I will rescue the one who yearns after me;*

I will be a bulwark of safety;

I will lift you to a high place because you have acknowledged my Name.

To the one who cries for me, I will answer; when in dire straits,

I will be with you and raise you to a place of honor; I will save.

I will fill your days full with contentment;

and demonstrate my saving power for a lifetime."

The striking images of Psalm 91 that are used in the poet's confession boldly adjudicate the sole claim of יהוה to act in the defense of those who seek after יהוה. The poet's judicious use of metaphor and simile might lead the reader to imagine the endangered faithful בצל שדי יתלונן (*dwelling in the shadow of Shaddai*), suggesting an eaglet taking refuge in a high and inaccessible aerie, there nestled beneath the באבר תוי סך (*sheltering wings*) of its mother. The theme of refuge in Psalm 91 is notably characterized by this feminine metaphor, which is also familiar to the prophet in First Isaiah. Also, in Psalm 91:4, the Hebrew noun סֹחֵרָה (*sokherah, shield*), is a *hapax legomenon* meaning it occurs *only* here in the Hebrew Bible and is understood to refer to a surrounding enclosure or a rounded and encompassing shield.

This protective imagery is intended to be synonymous with the outstretched pinions with which יהוה completely circumscribes those who are pursued and hounded by their foes. They are rich metaphors. The protected one is surrounded by יהוה whose sheltering is omnipresent. It is from within this place of refuge that the poet speaks these words of confidence. The feminine image of יהוה as a mother bird spreading her wings and surrounding her little ones in protection and safety occurs elsewhere in the Hebrew Bible (Isaiah 40:31, *but those who wait upon* יהוה *shall renew their strength, they shall mount up with wings like eagles, they shall run and not be weary, they shall walk and not faint, NRSV*); but it is especially poignant in this psalm. יהוה is an ever *constant help* and *presence* to the afflicted and the helpless; יהוה spreads the protective shield of a feathering cloak over those who flee to יהוה for refuge. This verse and this psalm contain some of the most tender and intimate language in the whole Bible.

The feminine symbol of protection is redolent of the cherubim in the temple with their wings outstretched over the ark of the covenant. The relevance of the poet of Psalm 91 lies in his facing off against the many perils to faith. He deserves special attention on account of his exquisite poetical gifts. The durability of his faith is matched by the forcefulness of his language. Bold and tender illustrations are set over against each other in striking contrast (vv.11 f., 13); again, the poet continually changes the object on which his thoughts dwell, speaking now of יהוה (vv. 3, 11 f.), now of humans (vv. 5 f., 7 f., 13)—one object sometimes directly merging into another (vv. 4, 9 f.). All this imparts to the whole psalm a lively inner rhythm and gives us an inkling of the active interest which the poet himself takes in what he has got to say about trust in יהוה. The appeal of the psalm lies partly in the simplicity and beauty of its poetry, strengthened by the serene confidence which it exudes. But even more notable is the genius of the poet which is evident in the extraordinary promises of a trusting relationship with יהוה.

In Psalm 91 we are in the company of a certified spiritual warrior. To express this inner, intimate relationship in simple language is not an easy task. This psalm could easily have degenerated into a monotonous repetition of metaphorical flourishes. On the other hand, the poet avoids this by virtue of his expressions of profundity. In a distinct fashion this quality emerges in the beauty of the poetry, which transforms the metaphors into authentic spiritual expressions. Even when יהוה has resolved to deal with Israel in all the varied changes and chances of her common life, and in ways other than those of which ancient Israel may have anticipated the venture of faith to take, Israel may still choose to dwell in the *presence* of divine protection and guidance. The bending of the arc of the will toward יהוה becomes the constant desire and deepest longing of the individual suppliant for whom the sole meaning and purpose of life is to dwell within the *shadow of Shaddai*.

No other psalm in the entire Psalter confronts us with such a wide range of threats that inhabit the spiritual domain as does Psalm 91. It is in the face of these multiple current and structural threats to one's life that one may pray oneself into the hope, indeed, into the confidence and trust that proves so buoyant to the soul seeking reassurance and certitude. One may learn to calibrate the search for this vitality of life and salvation and redemption for these are promises that adhere to the one who finds protection and is gifted with *shalom* (fullness of life) in trusting יהוה. Comprising nearly half of the entire Psalter (when one includes the communal or corporate laments), the psalms of lament or complaint occur most frequently in *Books I (Pss 3–41), II (Pss 42–72),* and *III (Pss 73–89).*[18] They may be either the plaintive appeals of an individual's pleas to יהוה for assistance, or the corporate cries and intentions on behalf of the larger community.[19]

Brueggemann draws this important distinction: *The term [lament] is distinct from lamentation, which is a dirge over a death or over a city and people. The lament is really a complaint, a cry to the Lord to be delivered from some distress. It can be either individual or collective.* [20] As was mentioned at the beginning שדי (*shaddai, the god of the mountains),* usually translated the *Almighty* in the *LXX,* appears in the Psalter in Psalms 91 and 68. In Psalm 91, *Shaddai* is specifically indicative of the place of refuge and shelter. The fact that *Shaddai* is included along with the other three divine names, in just one strophe, is singularly notable. Psalm 91 expresses a bedrock confidence in יהוה. Our poet is focused on the character of God's protective refuge of the faithful. To seek refuge in יהוה means one recognizes that nothing is analogous to the God of Israel.

Trust entails a confidence of life in the face of all threats and all three dimensions of the psalmist's being -heart, soul, and mind–participate in this joyous security and the enjoyment of a fullness of life *(shalom)* and serenity of spirit. People who dwell near God, live. People who are far from God, die! The psalmist's concentrated images of refuge seek to repose the sheltering of the soul within the shadow of the divine *presence.* The entirety of ultimate refuge and intimate security resides in God—the Almighty One! Helmer Ringgren connects these refuge images to Israel's worshiping life in the temple.

> *Ancient Israel's experience of the immanence of God in the temple . . . could not be described appropriately otherwise than by using verbs as 'to see' and 'to behold.' This experience filled them with joy and happiness and gratitude. In other words, it strengthened their religious life and was a source of their inspiration.*[21]

---

18. cf. Gillingham, *Psalms through the Centuries.* "Although Gunkel classifies psalms of confidence as a specific form, it is better to apportion such psalms more according to their moods. Certainly no particular cultic occasion may be determined: the psalm serves to meet the moods and various suppliants in various situations of need. This is thus a good example of a category where form critical analysis is a limited tool, and where reference to the life centeredness of a psalm is particularly apt." 225.

19. Hossfeld and Zenger, *Psalms 2* (Hermeneia): 429. cf. Jean-Pierre Prevost, *A Short Dictionary of the Psalms,* "The LXX translates the verb בטח ('*batach*' as '*elpizein*' to hope) rather than '*pistuein*' (to believe). The Hebrew indicates more the interior, subjective disposition of trustingness felt toward a person, rather than the objective response of one's intelligence or will to the contents of revelation." 69.

20. Brueggemann, *The Psalms and the Life of Faith,* 68.

21. Ringgren, *The Faith of the Psalmists.* "The temple served as the spatial representation of the place of יהוה dwelling amidst the people of God. The liturgical yearly rounds are Israel's way of keeping this reality of the divine *presence* [italics mine] ever before them. They continually praised יהוה and these poems reflect the core reality of her life before God." 17.

Psalm 91 is a virtual compendium of encouragement in faith. The Mosaic connections between Psalms 90, 91 and 92, taking into account the absence of a superscription in Psalm 91, undoubtedly contributed to the combining of Psalms 90 and 91 into a single psalm in certain of the earlier manuscripts. That the superscription attributes Psalm 90 to Moses suggests an older, mature and elegiac author who has witnessed and experienced the bitter disappointments and frustrations of human life. Traditionally attributed to *Moses, the Man of God,* it is sometimes conjectured this is because Moses was the only human being recorded in the Hebrew scriptures to have had the courage to confront יהוה in the wilderness and *"convince"* יהוה to *change [his] mind!* At any rate, the superscription attributing the psalm to Moses is understood to be an honorific recognition of ancient Israel's hero. To wit, the psalm is not authored by Moses.

All in all, the related combination of the three psalms—when taken together—is supported in no less than six Hebrew manuscripts, all dating from the earliest centuries of the Common Era. Clearly the triad is intended to be read and understood as a single literary unit which emphasizes the core themes of shelter and refuge. Security and protection are afforded the person of faith throughout life.

These convictions lie at the core of the psalms of trust and this triad is the linchpin of the entire genre. A lovely example of a psalm of complaint that is also infused with a resolution of trust is Psalm 130. The complaint is real and it is deeply felt, initially, emanating as a cry of the heart. There is pain and desperation in the opening voice. But there are also clear overtones of acceptance and patience and the optative mood of the psalm is one of confidence and hope. This poetry is a passionate prayer of the heart by this poet of the *Pilgrim Psalter.*

Psalm 130

A Song of Ascents

Out of the depths I cry to you, O יהוה.

Adonai, hear my cry! Let your ears be attentive

to my voice, my pleadings!

O יהוה, if you kept an account of all our sins,

O Lord, who could survive?

But with you is found forgiveness:

for this we revere you.

I wait for יהוה, my soul waits, and in your

word I hope; my soul waits for יהוה

more than sentinels who watch for the morning,

more than sentinels who watch for the morning.

O Israel, hope in יהוה!

For with יהי there is steadfast love,

and there is great power to redeem.

It is יהוה who will redeem Israel from all its sin.

With certain psalms like this one, one can almost track word for word the way the poet constructs the petition. There is a humility and a willingness to admit wrong-doing, although none in particular is specifically mentioned in this psalm—merely acknowledging that wrongdoing may be contemplated even if it cannot be named. This is a person whose desire is to have a clean heart, a clear conscience. Some see in it a trust in God's forgiveness and the eager expectation that it will soon be granted. I rather think the plea of the poet is for God to hear [her] prayer! There is manifold trust which under-girds the language of prayer and a clear recognition that יהי is utterly capable in addressing the cry of her supplications—note the plural! But when will the response of יהי come? One gets the distinct impression that this poet has prayed prayers like this before. She is in familiar territory. This prayer cries out with the recognition that it has been, or many others like it have been prayed before. She knows that she can hope and trust in the word of יהי and in the assurance of steadfast love.

Then there is the beautifully expressed patience, confidence and an emphasized willingness to wait all night long if necessary for יהי to respond. The psalm concludes with the poet acknowledging Israel, the broader community of the faithful, which is the ground of the confidence being expressed. The prayer is anchored in the reality of the faith and steadfastness of the community. A statement of certitude concludes the poem, which is really a prayer requiring the attention of יהי. The promise of redemption is stated, and ends the prayer, matter—of—factly. One cannot read this poem-prayer and remain convinced that יהי would have neglected to answer her cry! This personal complaint is a lament which involves some serious praying. But its horizon is broadened to include Israel in redemption as well. So it is both individual and corporate. This personal and communal accent is true of many of the laments and also of the songs of trust.

Embedded within the lament formula in both the individual and communal psalms of complaint are richly textured metaphorical images that aspire to an intimate relationship of trust in God. When identifying the laments, the reader watches for the use of a whole host of metaphors: *my rock, my crag, my shade, my refuge, my fortress, my stronghold, my shield, my horn of salvation, my deliverer,* and *my bulwark.* These metaphorical recitals are indicative of the psalmists' keen interest in conveying that sense of reliability, incomparability, the trustworthiness of יהי and the deeds and actions commensurate with the persons who place a whole-soul trust in the sufficiency of יהי. The themes of protection and security are grounded in the proven faithfulness of יהוה. This psalm breathes joy for here is a profoundly God-centered person. This poet knows to whom she is addressing her complaint and precisely what it is she is praying about!

This is the reality that infuses the poet's entire being. Here is a believer who hangs onto יהוה, come what may! When speaking of God as refuge our psalmist in Psalm 91 imagines God as a fortress or as a tower of defense. The righteous' declarations of seeking refuge in God are metaphorical expressions of dependence on the incomparable God. Therefore, this language in Psalm 130 is closely related to words that communicate the notion of having confidence in and reliance upon the incomparability of יהוה. While the language of refuge is drawn from the images of escape and hiding, an active trust communicates the inner sense of security in, and the thirsting, unquenchable desire for, God.[22] This intimacy of expression is reminiscent of language frequently attributed to David. Psalm 91 for instance, could be one composed by David (although I doubt it) as it has its own very long history. And while any attempt at dating individual psalms is usually frustrated, this psalm seems to suggest a composition with origins likely in the early monarchy.

> While the exact dates at which the hymns and prayers now preserved in the Psalter were originally composed cannot be determined, it clearly appears that the great majority of them, like the proverbs and hymnic poems later collected . . . surfaced orally and were chanted or even sung before the fall of Jerusalem. Some of them have come perhaps from David himself. For example, the psalms of Korah (Psalms 84–85; 87–88) may well have originated at the ancient sanctuary of Dan, near the ravines and headwaters in the foothills of Mount Hermon.[23]

In short, the psalm is a kind of microcosm of all the refuge language of the Psalter. The theme of refuge is ineluctably ubiquitous throughout the Psalter. Although the Hebrew poets do not necessarily confess a glorious life that awaits us beyond the grave, their focus is clearly on the Lord's refuge in this life. They are full aware of those things that can assault and hurt the soul.

It is not surprising then that Psalm 91 is one of the psalms appointed for the Daily Office of Compline. Here Psalm 91 and Psalm 4 function together to focus the heart on the protection afforded the faithful one as night falls. Nightfall was a fearsome reality to the ancients. It was believed that demonic evil stalked about in the dark and people resorted to superstitious practices–the wearing of inscriptions, amulets, pendants, and the like (some have been discovered in archaeological digs). Upon retiring for the evening, following a day of busyness and activity, Psalm 4, another

---

22. Anderson, *The Bible in a Postmodern Age*, "It is only in the context of the here and now that the psalmist finds consolation. For the psalmist, as for many modern people, death is the final limitation; accordingly, as in the case of Job, the answers to the pressing questions of human life must be found now. Like a deer that pines for fresh water, they 'thirst for God' (Ps.42:1) with the whole being, and they seek the satisfaction of that thirst in this life." 74.

23. Terrien, *The Psalms*, 53.

psalm of trust, serves as a reminder that we all need to be on guard against forces not benign, that do not have our best interests at heart; that we all require protection from things which can assault and hurt the soul.

Kathleen Norris writes:

> The Compline Psalms 4 and 91, remind us that we all need protection from forces beyond our control, even as they reassure us that protection is ours. The night will come with its great equalizers, sleep and death. It will pass over us, and bring us forth again into light.[24]

Psalm 4 begins with an outright and unqualified declaration of confidence: *God is my Vindicator!*[25] It is a perfect example of a song of trust and it complements the extravagant use of metaphors of Psalm 91.[26]

Psalm 4

To the leader: with stringed instruments
A Psalm of David

When I cry out, answer me! You are my God–my vindicator.

Defend my righteous cause for it is just. I was in a tight spot, hemmed

in, with no room to maneuver; yet you provided space for me to move;

O יהוה, how gracious of you—to take notice of me in the past, and in days to come.

You there—self-important ones–who garner for yourselves rank and privilege

as though it is your birthright; how long will you hold my personal integrity in contempt?

How long will you continue to pursue slander and falsehood against me?

How long until you cease consorting with the vain, empty idols of your own delusions?

Reckon on this fact: יהוה will extend merciful compassion on all who

are faithful and loyal devotees; יהוה always hears my cry when I am

in distress; gracious and generous are the ways of faithfulness.

24. Norris, *The Cloister Walk*, 38.

25. Curtis, *Ancient Psalms and Modern Worship*. This psalmist "has even greater cause for happiness. The psalmist's sleep is undisturbed . . .this peaceful sleep would contrast with those of v. 4 who lie awake pondering their lot. But the *peace* is not simply that of the undisturbed night. It is that sense that all will be well, and all manner of things will be well: the *shalom* which comes from complete trust in God." 8, 9.

26. Terrien, *The Psalms*, "Other psalmists have ardently desired to 'see' the face of Yhwh (Pss 17.15; 27.8), but the poet of Psalm 4 asks only for the reflection of the divine light. Any legitimate theology of Presence endorses the integrity of the mystery without renouncing any of its benefactions. Calvin underlined his final reaction to Psalm 4 by saying that its author 'finds total repose in God, and draws from it his pleasure and satisfaction." 101.

Ponder this in your heart as you lie upon your bed:

Do not risk coming up short. Do not miss the mark. Live an accurate life.

Beware of darkness; examine your conscience; shed the tears of remorse.

Then bring forth legitimate sacrifices that are acceptable, and presented

with motives arising out of a contrite heart. Entrust your life to יהוה alone!

Many of you whine, saying: *"O that we might see better times. יהוה,*

the lamp of your presence has gone dark; you have hidden your face from us!"

But I will say this at the end of the day: יהוה has planted a deep joy in

my heart, surpassing those who celebrate amid their abundant harvests of grain

and wine and oil. Fools—they think it the work of their own hands.

Even now, I am completely at peace. Sleep will come at once;

I dwell in the *presence* of יהוה;

it is only here that I sleep in safety.

The poet's meditation reveals a long experience of sustained, rightful piety. It does not hide a last-minute conversion. This poet is a person of faith, tried and true, confirmed by the word "pious" in the sense of devoted and trusting, not naive or pietistic. The psalm is not a complaint in the usual sense, but it is a prayer of unwavering confidence in יהוה. [27]The poet of Psalm 4 is content on dwelling in the *presence* of יהוה. There is nothing more that he desires and so his prayer is rooted in the conviction that the annoying idolaters will not win out in the end. His confidence in יהוה is absolute and it completely motivates what he has got to say about his God. [28]

His insights, too, into the spiritual world are considerable: [29]Reckon *on this fact,* and *ponder this in your heart . . . Beware of darkness . . . Do not miss the mark . . . Live an accurate life . . . Entrust your life to* יהוה *alone! . . . The lamp of the presence of* יהוה *has gone dark for the idolater.* But the poet is living in the complete peace he experiences; of the many blessings he has received from יהוה over the course of a lifetime: room to maneuver, space to move, merciful compassion, examination of conscience, and finally, יהוה *has planted a deep joy in my heart.*[30] This encouragement in faith anchors

---

27. Terrien, *The Psalms*, 101.

28. Rogerson, Psalms 1–50 *Cambridge Bible Commentary*, Psalm 4 ". . . suggests a special relationship founded on the loving faithfulness that exists between God and [his] servant, and this is the very basis of the psalmist's confidence." 27.

29. Westermann, *The Living Psalms* ". . . the speaker no longer complains about the enemies; rather, he seeks to bring about a change in their behaviour, to prevail on them to consider what they are doing. This is something that occurs only rarely, almost never, in fact, in psalms of lament. It is a consequence of that change from lament to trust which is determinative for this psalm. The confident trust in God which fills the speaker also affects his attitude towards his opponents." 125.

30. Kraus, *Theology of Psalms*. ". . . we should emphasize that this consciousness of being protected is provided not by the temple's area of asylum and protection as such; the determining factor is trust

his life in all things. There is a tender sublimity to this psalm which is probably why it is appointed as a psalm at nightfall. Physical and spiritual refreshment, safe-keeping, and room to maneuver—all are the promised benefits of this absolute trust.[31]

Psalms 90, 91 and 92 share similarly predominant themes and content. In the light of this fact the longing for refuge and abiding confidence in the near, capable and tender care of יהוה is obvious in these three psalms. When taken together, the three are inter-related thematically and theologically. The case for faith is not made in the language of argumentation. Together, these three psalms declare the limits and boundaries of human life and these are intended for instruction and exhortation. They are designed to challenge and strengthen the faith of those who trust in יהוה *alone*. The psalmist's recognition of human limitations is reflected in the resounding affirmations of the confidence and trust that comes to the one who chooses to dwell within *the shadow of Shaddai*. Here the language of trust and confidence in יהוה eclipses all other declarations in the Psalter.

The movement from lament to praise in Psalms 90, 91, and 92 is palpable and reinforces the centrality of יהוה and the role this fundamental affirmation played in the life of the ancient people of God. Although these songs come to us from a great distance in time the inward quality of their conversing with their God bears such a powerful witness to their faith and trust. In not a few of them, we have the strange quality of insistent prayer; prayer that is deeply intimate and straightforward in its appeals, in lament, and in praise. Learning how to pray, desiring to become a learned prayer, saturates the psalm.

> Breaking down a perceived distance and the creation of a sense of nearness and presence is a major function of prayer. The Psalms are of great importance in the recognition of distantness, which results from various kinds of stress and distress, and in the closing of that gap, which threatens spiritual health and even life itself. The very recitation of psalms . . . serves to diminish distance and enhance nearness and presence.[32]

The ancient poets betray an amazing knowledge of their own hearts. In pleading mercy, they do not deceive themselves, appeal to extenuating circumstances, minimize their offenses, or revel in excessive introspection. All their griefs and woes and despairs are lifted up into the *presence* of the Holy One. Their hurts and sorrows, sadness and shame—all may be raised to יהוה in prayer. This is exactly how Jesus taught his disciples to pray. It is moving to see how these psalms of trust rarely end

---

in Yahweh . . . who gives to the lonely and repeatedly oppressed person security and victory over his dangerous isolation . . . [shalom] is the gift of God that proves itself also in, and precisely in, the face of acute attacks and threats. Dwelling securely is not a sacral, self-evident thing but a gift of the God of Israel." 150.

31. Levine, *Sing unto God a New Song*. ". . . the desirable spiritual path is similarly portrayed as a wide one." 158.

32. Tate," The Interpretation of the Psalms," 369.

on the self-centered note—unlike many of the broader individual psalms of lament. They bring into the horizon of their concerns the afflictions and needs of the whole worshiping community. The community as a whole is the particular focus of the loving care of יהוה. Through it all there remains a tactile resilience which is anchored in prayerful confidence and a learned trust in יהוה that is practiced again and again over time. Roland Murphy observes how scattered throughout the Psalms

> are formulas of trust, such as "You are my God" (31:14; 22:10; 25:5; 44:4). This attitude is the basis of any prayer. Such trust could emerge from Israel's historical experience or personal experience. The theme has created the narrow classification for the psalms of trust, but 'trust' permeates the entire Psalter. Be alert to the vocabulary of trust–words like 'refuge,' 'fortress,' 'shield,' 'rock,' 'deliverance,' and 'shadow'. Personal notes of praise, love, and trust are sounded, even in the midst of all the self-centeredness that characterizes lament. ' Taking refuge,' either as a noun or verb, occurs in the psalms thirty-seven times (out of fifty-eight in the entire Bible!); two-fifths of all the occurrences of בטח (batach, ' trust,' as a verb or noun) are in the Psalter (about fifty times). The implication is not simply that the psalmist has nowhere to turn (which may be true), but that it is only on the Lord that one can rely with certainty. Notes of complaint and lament do not have the last word; motifs of intimacy with God sweep the reader into a complete relationship.[33]

The faith of the poets of Israel is a lived faith in the living God. The credo of the Psalter which is the poets' confession of faith, finds expression throughout the entire book, celebrating and avowing יהוה as the origin of all life.[34] יהוה is the source; indeed, יהוה is *the God of my life* (42.8) who will *show me the path of life; in your presence is fullness of joy; at your place of honor are unimagined glories for evermore* (16:11, LW). There is a core confession of faith that is expressed in the prayers throughout the Hebrew Scriptures. This faith is compressed in Ps 36:9: *For with you [יהוה] is the fountain of life, and in your light we see light.* This is life itself; its origin, its source, its sustenance, its light. In Kraus's cryptic statement:

> Life is not some power that proceeds from itself or is grounded in itself. Those who offer their prayers in the Psalms know that they are 'absolutely dependent' on Yahweh. All life comes from [Him]. The place where Yahweh is present is designated as the 'source of life'.[35]

33. Murphy, *The Gift of the Psalms*, 51.

34. Goldingay, "*Psalm 4: Ambiguity and Resolution*," 161–72. "The addressees are not merely personal assailants or people who attack the suppliant in YHWH's name, but people who are unfaithful to YHWH. It is against their delusions about YHWH and other gods that the psalm puts the real facts about YHWH's listening, from which they are hiding." 165.

35. Kraus, *Theology of the Psalms*, 163. cf. Crollius, "DeReK in the Psalms," *Biblical Theology Bulletin*. 43. "The poet who conceived this psalm was the heir of a tradition that had for generations transmuted faith (*fiducia*) into a credo (*fides*) and vice versa, belief into utmost confidence. His conversion had incorporated this belief in his mortal but conscious flesh. Different from his mystical vision, the pantheism of another age fused within the Great Whole the aspirations of the human self. He adored a

Psalm 91 is one of the most precious and audacious of all the psalms for many reasons, not the least of which is its bold refuge and protection imagery. Confidence and trust, hope and glory, all rest on the salvation of Israel whose existence rests in the hands of יהוה. There is an intimacy and an immediacy to the poet's pursuit of God. As the promises unfold in response to the dangers and threats enumerated, the fullness and depth of redemption unfolds: *With long life will I satisfy him, and show him my salvation.* (91:16, NRSV). The psalmist knows יהוה intimately and knows *he is not bereft because he trusts completely in God; in what [He] has been and what [He] is, his Protector, the Upholder and the Restorer of his honor, the One who lifts him out of his humiliation to a sense of dignity and a consciousness of worth. He speaks from religious experience.*[36]

The words that describe יהוה as *salvation, deliverer,* and *helper* usually refer to military or judicial intervention; terms that describe יהוה as *refuge* and the *object of trust* do not. Goldingay observes that when Israel fails to be pure of heart, it cannot complain if יהוה ceases to be good to it. Yet at the same time, the commitment of יהוה to Israel was made to Israel as Israel actually was; it was not based on Israel's purity of heart. The further implication is that when Israel fails to be pure of heart, יהוה cannot simply abandon her as if the relationship was a contract rather than a covenant.[37] Such trust in יהוה as refuge is not, as Jerome Creach emphasizes, some

> passive 'hiding away' but a declaration of faith that claims the past action of Yahweh and expects Yahweh to intervene on behalf of [his] people again in the future. This is an example of the 'thematic unity' between Psalms 90, 91, and 92. The overriding sense of Yahweh as 'refuge' is communicated by the combination of refuge words with terms describing Yahweh as savior.[38]

Israel's God, the One God of All, is the God of salvation. Because of its judicious use of potent metaphors for deliverance and its promise of refuge as a haven for the trusting suppliant, I am not alone in situating Psalm 91 within the genre of the psalms of trust (with a divine oracle), a sub-set of the genre of the psalms of lament. Songs of trust illustrate powerfully Israel's willingness to be utterly vulnerable to the ways of the world, outwardly, while remaining fully open before the call and will of יהוה inwardly. *Purity of heart is to will one thing, the love of God* (Kierkegaard) over and against all

---

deity whose transcendence was not absorbed by a compassionate immanence. Yahweh the Passionate is also the *El* of cosmic parameter, who at last will reign on the earth as in the heavens." 181.

36. Leslie, *The Psalms: Interpreted in the Light of Hebrew Life and Worship*, 347.

37. Goldingay, Psalms 2 in *Baker Commentary on the Old Testament*, 238.

38. Creach, *Yahweh as Refuge and the Editing of the Hebrew Psalter*, 95. cf. Bonhoeffer, *Psalms*, "It is grace to know God's commands. They release us from self-made plans and conflicts. They make our steps certain and our way joyful." 31, 32. cf. Kirkpatrick, *The Psalms*: ". . . 'save' is the constant prayer, 'salvation' the constant desire of the Psalmists. The Hebrew words thus rendered denote primarily enlargement, liberation from a state of confinement and distress, power to move freely and at will, and so deliverance generally. Such deliverance comes from [Yahweh] alone: it is largely sought as the proof of [His] favour." 16.

other concerns. The inner disposition is to cohere with the outward action and word. The eternal covenant implies not simply unswerving obedience and a single-minded devotion to the will of יהוה. It requires a trusting and surrendering heart. These matters of the heart are characteristic particularly of Psalm 91, but also of each of the psalms of trust and confidence. The yearnings and desires of the human heart are what matter most to יהוה.

Surprisingly the psalms do not give precedence to one disposition of the heart over another. More important is the inner journey of making one's way to God. As long as the psalmists' hearts are not *turned back* (Ps 44:18) or *set on perverseness* (Ps 101:4), they *wait for the Lord* (27:14) and pray, *Teach me your way,* יהוה, *that I may walk in your truth* (Ps 86:11). Whether God puts *gladness* (Ps 4:7), *troubles* (Ps 25:17), or *tumult* (Ps 38:8) in the heart, whether the heart is *broken* (Ps 69:20), *blameless* (Ps 119:80), *steadfast* (Ps 108:1), or *pierced* (Ps 109:22), all these are, or can be, *highways to Zion* (Ps 84:5). Spread throughout the Psalter are numerous references to the meaning of Israel's trust and confidence. They underscore the meaning of life as it is lived in the *presence* of יהוה.

> The *[righteous] enjoy success and fruitfulness even in old age . . . this statement continues the prominent idea of Pss 90:10 and 91:16 and is perhaps part of the motivation for the placement of these three psalms; each psalm deals with the brevity of human existence and the reward of extended life and security for those who recognize YHWH as the only source of refuge.*[39]

These are statements of hope primarily where the thought is of trust and refuge in God. They therefore agree in describing as decisive that aspect of hope which involves the moment of personal surrender. In these *psalms of the heart* there is little mention of such evil inclinations for those oriented to God. There is, rather, the underlying and resolute conviction that the pathway to God lies within. The pursuit of יהוה is an interior pursuit. Wholeness comes as יהוה instructs the heart to know, reorienting understanding as needed. The psalmists become confident and trustful when it comes to matters of the heart; they choose to follow the way that leads to God. *When the law of their God is in their hearts, their steps do not slip* (Ps 37:31); *I delight to do your will, O my God; your law I love from the depths of my being* (Ps 40:8 NRSV). The ancient poets have come to know, understand, and value what is required of them–in the heart and what is the requisite disposition for living one's life in the *presence* of the holy within the refuge of יהוה. Walter Brueggemann writes movingly of the psalms of trust and confidence:

---

39. Creach, *The Destiny of the Righteous in the Psalms*, 97. cf. Weiser, *The Psalms*. "The true aim of the whole psalm [91] which stands out prominently right from the beginning, is to demonstrate that this living relationship with God has the quality of actuality which the [man] who trusts in God will be able to experience in [his] own person in all the afflictions and perils of life as the saving, protecting, strengthening power of God." 606.

These psalms are some of the best known and best loved, for they offer a faith and a life that has come to a joyous trusting resolution. The speaker of these poems cannot imagine a situation that would cause doubt or trouble enough to jeopardize the trust. The relationship has been tested severely, and Yahweh has shown himself to be profoundly reliable and powerful. That is to be celebrated.[40]

The faithful person turns to prayer and also witnesses to the good way, where there is awe of God, turning from sin, stillness and meditation, worship that finds and holds on to God, and above all, trusts absolutely.

In such trust the psalmist concludes, confident that יהוה will fill the heart again with rejoicing, and make [his] peace known in every danger. This is a powerful affirmation of life lived in relationship with יהוה. The faith of Israel is always being worked out and articulated on a continuum of trust in יהוה in every situation. It expresses itself in the anguished cries for help by the one who feels abandoned by יהוה or even betrayed by יהוה. It is in the joyous shouts of praise that those who have experienced the LORD'S grace and goodness come to know that יהוה is Lord of all.

Israel's sorrows, however, continued to mount and raised questions concerning the ability of יהוה to care for them. The neighboring nations were all too aware of this and often taunted Israel with the sarcastic question, *where is your God?* Hence the psalmists affirmed the importance of life as a witness to the One God of All. Life is important! Schleiermacher, in one of his selected sermons, emphasizes how each individual in Israel was an important and essential reflection of God's glory. The place of God's people as a witness to the justice and fidelity of יהוה explains the emphasis on the present and the urgency and immediacy of the expressions of trust in יהוה now!

These psalms wrestle with the problems of human existence within the context of this life. The psalmists are not satisfied with the notion that the imbalances of life will somehow be corrected in another form of existence beyond human experience. They believe that God's dealings with human beings take place in this earthly sphere.[41]

Lacking the theological horizon of the Second Testament, they concentrate on the problems of life here and now with a fierce and passionate intensity. They represent what Zenger calls *"realized theodicy"*; they affirm God by surrendering the last word to God. The incomparability of יהוה is dear to the heart of the faithful poet who abandons all and, in that abandonment, trusts explicitly in this reality: יהוה is the One God of All. In the poets' horizon of trust, יהוה is the only deity that is needed.

---

40. Brueggemann, *Abiding Astonishment*, 163.

41. Anderson, *The Bible in a Postmodern Age*, 74.

Northern Songs

KNOWING WHAT WE KNOW now, it only makes sense that the book of Psalms should reflect the conflict between the Yahwists and those who either worshiped other deities or who knew their God as אלהים (*elohim*). Each of these three psalms, Psalms 90, 91, and 92, represents fundamentally a call to Yahwism. They implore us to respond to their astounding affirmations. Although the preference for the divine name יהוה is dominant throughout the Psalter, there is one notable exception. This is illustrated by what is commonly referred to as the *Elohistic Psalter*.

At the beginning of *Book II* (Psalm 42) and continuing through Psalm 83 in *Book III*, the accumulation of evidence strongly suggests that editors compiled material from the earlier collections of other psalms in which there was a deliberate and frequent revision of the usages of the divine name יהוה, to אלהים (*elohim*)—although the use of יהוה is not completely absent, the general distribution and selection of the divine names and approbations correspond positively to the psalms in this group and, in most cases, point to a dating in the eighth century BCE. Specific references to Judah, Zion, and David seem to support this supposition and the shift in usage away from יהוה to *Elohim* suggests the particularity of the editorial format of the Elohistic Psalter—but it does not necessarily support the idea of the initial pattern of the poetry.

The *Elohistic Psalter* includes all of the *Asaph* group (50, 73–83) and part of the *Korah* group (42–49). Both collections are considered to be of northern provenance and represent an earlier stage in composition from those of the post-exilic era. In this early stage it seems likely that a variety of smaller collections were brought together to form a larger one. Certain psalms of northern origin, for instance, would prove useful in the south and would have been edited and compiled by those in the northern sanctuaries before the fall of Samaria in 721 BCE, and psalms which were composed and used by northerners who had remained loyal to the worship of יהוה in the temple in Jerusalem.

These two sorts of psalms originated prior to the beginning of the Assyrian campaign in 731 BCE. Some of them are considered to be of relative antiquity. Their usage may be traced back to some of the earliest liturgies conducted by the household of faith assembled for worship around the amphictyonic shrines. Both the *Korah* and *Asaph* collections are northern compositions, dating from *at least* the eighth-century

BCE. The internal data point directly to this historical phenomenon of the Israel of the north and take us back even farther into the distant past of her life and identity. When the Psalter is viewed through this lens our understanding of these northern poems deepens and our perspective is sharpened. The entire book of Psalms, then, serves as a compendium of "snap-shots" of ancient Israel's developing and vibrant faith. This dynamic is at work throughout to illumine the entire Psalter.

The *Elohistic Psalter* provides us with one of the more dramatic insights into Israel's journey toward Yahwism and her monotheistic faith. These *psalms of the north* can be recognized foremost by their clear references to particular geographical locations and names (e.g. Mount Horeb and Tabor); other geographical features of the north by their specific references to Jacob, the God of Jacob, the Shepherd of Israel, the God of Joseph, and to יהוה as the warrior god, יהוה צבאות (*Yhwh Sabbaot*).

Additionally, certain unique forms in the language of the Hebrew text exhibit a distinctly northern dialect. If one finds a striking number of words or grammatical forms that are characteristic of northern dialect (e.g. Psalm 36 and the use of the form *bal* as a negative particle), one may reasonably conclude that the text is of northern origin. One psalm which is neither in the Korah or Asaph collections, or in the Elohistic Psalter, but is a good example of a northern song, is Psalm 36. It is an individual prayer for help and the poet nevertheless praises God. This act of trust underscores the character of God and anticipates the protection and care of God.

Psalm 36

To the Leader. Of David, the servant of the LORD

Sin speaks to the sinners
in the depths of their hearts;
there is no fear of God
before their eyes.

They flatter themselves in their own eyes;
they have no knowledge of their own guilt.
In their mouths are mischief and deceit
and all wisdom and good has ceased.
They plot mischief and the defeat of goodness
as they lie in their beds.
They are set on wicked ways,
they persist in doing what is evil.

O יהוה, your steadfast constancy reaches to the heavens,

your truth to the skies.

Your justice is like God's mountains,

and your judgments are like the great deep.

To mortals and animals, you give protection.

O יהוה how precious is your love.

My God, all people may take refuge

in the shadow of your wings.

They feast on the abundance of your house;

they drink from the river of your delights.

For with you is the fountain of life

and in your light we see light.

Continue your steadfast love to those who know you,

and your deliverance to the upright of heart!

Do not let the foot of the arrogant crush me

nor the hand of the wicked cast me aside.

See how the evildoers lie prostrate!

They are altogether flung down, unable to arise.

Psalm 36, which stands outside the Elohistic Psalter, serves as an example of a northern song with vestiges of an indelible northern dialect. Although much of this evidence is of a technical nature and a matter of details of the Hebrew language, the consideration of internal evidence will impress any serious student of the Psalter. The significance of these northern songs lies in their influence on the subsequent results of the editorial process. Note in this psalm the occurrence of both divine names. What remains of these northern songs is a specific and identifiable feature of an Elohist theology which emphasizes the transcendence and salvation of the God (אלהים) of Israel, although in this example the personal Name of יהוה stresses both the immanence and the universality of divine care: *O יהוה, how precious is your love. My God (אלהי) all people may take refuge in the shadow of your wings.*

Each of these northern psalms, whatever their specific geographic origin, would have come south through Jerusalem and been subjected to the editorial sway of the southern group. We believe these northern psalms were appropriated centuries later by post-exilic editors of the Second Temple period. It is fascinating how the final editorial revision of the book of Praises reinforces the role these northern songs played in influencing ancient Israel's theological, liturgical and worshiping life.[1]

1. Rendsburg, *Linguistic Evidence for the Northern Origin of Selected Psalms*. "The following poems evince a sufficient concentration of northern grammatical and lexical features to merit the

It is the emphasis on the transcendent, for example, that is the feature of theophanic activity around the sanctuaries in the worship of God that represents a variety of amphictyonic settings. Yahwistic theology tends to stress the immanence of God and focuses on the centrality of the worshiping space of the Jerusalem temple. Appreciation and a recognition of these kinds of distinctions are admittedly simplistic but there are several distinguishing features to be highlighted. Here we will let Jerome Creach summarize:

> It has long been recognized that Psalms 42–83, Book II plus the collection of Asaph psalms at the beginning of Book III [Psalms 73–83], contain the label Elohim for God more than four times as often as the personal name יהוה ('LORD'). Moreover, Psalm 14 occurs with slight changes again as Psalm 53, and three of the lines of Psalm 14 that contain Yahweh, when reproduced in Psalm 53, have Elohim instead of Yahweh.[2]

It remains a continuing feature that within the psalms in the *Elohistic Psalter*, the poets lay great stress on one's absolute trust and confidence in God. In these psalms the accent is more often than not on the God of salvation and the growth in faith of the poets.

> 'Salvation' signifies the whole process of redemption extending to vindication and the enjoyment of covenantal privileges. The Lord alone will save, because he is faithful and able. The Lord is faithful in giving his love (hesed) and rewards, and he is also able in that he is 'strong' as a 'rock' and a 'fortress' lit., 'high place'; The psalmist's confidence lies ultimately in the Lord. Resting in God requires waiting and patience. Even while he has many reasons to fear, the psalmist's faith rises to a new height in believing the promise of God that the righteous 'will never be shaken.' Yhwh is entirely capable of defending the poets from any threat, any danger, any foe. In contrast to his great confidence in the Lord, the psalmist has little faith in the kingdom of humanity. Humanity in opposition to the Lord is destructive, selfish, and deceitful. Yet faith in the Lord overcomes the strongest opposition.[3]

The data suggest to many scholars that Psalms 42–83 were once a separate collection and that the editors manipulated the appellatives for God to create this unity. The theory is not without its flaws, not the least of which is an explanation of why an editor would have such an editorial interest. Nevertheless, assuming that the theory is correct, there is much to suggest that when the *Elohistic Psalter* was incorporated into the book of Praises it was altered to create the current "book" structure we know

---

conclusion that they originated in northern Israel: Psalms 9–10, 16, 29, 36, 45, 53, 58, 74, 116, 132, 133, 140, 141. In addition, the collections of poems ascribed to Korah (Psalms 42–49, 84—85, 87–88) and to Asaph (Psalms 50, 73—83) show a similar concentration of northern traits, enough to justify their inclusion in this study." 112.

2. Creach, *The Destiny of the Righteous in the Psalms*, 161.

3. VanGemeren, *Ibid*, 484.

now. It is also of note that the name יהוה appears in higher frequency in the last three psalms in Book II (five times in Ps. 69; two times in Ps. 70; four times in Ps. 71; *Elohim* (אלהים) appears ten times, three times, and ten times respectively). All of this speaks to the particular kind of editorial activity that occurred fairly late in the story of the Psalms. It is accurate to state that each of these northern songs was funneled through the community of post-exilic Jerusalem and the traditions and conditions that arose following the completion of the second temple (ca. 518 BCE).

The experiences of the transcendence and immanence of God as the foci of emphases and theological orientation, run like a fissure through Israel's long history. It is commonly asserted that the Yahwist tradition predates the Elohistic tradition by at least a century and a half and is rooted in ancient Israel's earliest traditions. It is the Yahwist's theological perspective and orientation that characterize the Psalter as a whole. These are all possible clues for what lies behind the intentional replacement of the name יהוה with אלהים (*elohim*) throughout the Elohistic Psalter. Peter Craigie enlists this note of caution: *Although the existence of an Elohistic Psalter can be postulated with a reasonable degree of certainty, what cannot be determined with any conviction is whether or not there were other earlier 'collections of collections'.*[4]

In the absence of any firm evidence to the contrary, it may be assumed that the final stage of compiling the various collections which make up the Psalter were brought together by the assimilation of a variety of largely anonymous editors. These would have assembled various collections and other psalms not included initially in any collection. It is difficult, if not impossible, to know precisely at what time the book of Psalms was stabilized into the form we now have. On the instability of the final stages, Klaus Seybold appeals to the view that, *while in content and order the central core of the Psalms already existed in Qumran at that time, neither the final selection nor the final order of the texts, particularly of the texts in the last third of the Psalter, had been determined.*[5]

The views of authorship of individual psalms and collections based on the superscriptions must be viewed tentatively at best. The titles or superscriptions do *not* date from the origins of the individual psalms and clusters of psalms. Rather, they are dated to a time when they were being gathered, collected, and arranged. Of the 150 psalms in the Psalter, 116 have titles and these are incorporated within the text of the various modern editions of the Bible; they are translated and stand at the outset of these psalms in most modern English versions of the Bible. The superscriptions represent the work of the editors of the early collections. Westermann reminds that

> *this is the universal conviction of scholarship today, that even though many of the details about such superscriptions and notations remain obscure, the important point to be affirmed is this: all psalms lived in the worshiping community for a long time–usually for a very long time–without any superscriptions ...*

4. Craigie, *Psalms 1–50*, 29, 30.
5. Seybold, *Introducing the Psalms*, 79.

conclusions can be drawn from the superscriptions only concerning the time of their compilation and the understanding people had of the Psalms at that particular stage. [6]

Although the dating of these superscriptions cannot be determined with any precision, it is now widely accepted that they most likely originated in the post-exilic period and were appropriated into the final stages of the process compiling the Psalter by the second century BC in the Hellenistic era. Brevard Childs has argued convincingly that the thirteen superscriptions that make historical references to David are the sole product of exegetical activity and are not a reflection of any independent historical tradition.[7] Many of these titles appear in the *LXX*, though much of their meaning was apparently not even understood by those translators in the third century BCE.

Some scholars, however, rather believe this to be indicative of their antiquity. Suffice to say that the meanings of the superscriptions remain lost to us today. The intention of these titles apparently was to provide several types of information: specific musical arrangements and tunes, liturgical directives, a designation of a particular type of composition (e.g. *mizmor,* 57 psalms; *miktam,* 6 psalms; *maskil,* 13 psalms; and *shir,* 30 psalms), and historical context (13 psalms), with presumed authorship—116 psalms with superscriptions, or titles, in all.

Given this evidence the traditional attribution of Davidic authorship to nearly half of the Psalms can no longer be supported, particularly when contrasted with the corresponding internal evidence in the text. The data support the view that the superscriptions are later additions. The "historical" assertions which form the basis for conferring the authorship of 73 psalms to David are no longer sustainable. What can be postulated, however, is that some of the *first Davidic Collection* (Psalms 3–41), and parts of the second (Psalms 51–72), the *Prayers of David,* may perhaps be attributed to David, given their close connections to the "succession narrative" in 2 Samuel and 1 Kings 1, 2. David remains none the less the initiator of the psalm genre and the organizer of Israelite liturgy. So he can be called the principal author of the Psalter, that is, the most notable and the most eminent. But it is unfortunately impossible to know approximately how many or which psalms have the poet king as their author. [8]

Since the original purpose and intention of the superscriptions remain largely unknown further conclusions may be contemplated. Some conclusions postulated are that some of the psalms, particularly those in *Book II, may* be attributed to David's hand; that some psalms in *Book III may* emanate from an ancient Davidic school;

---

6. Westermann, *The Psalms: Structure, Content, and Message,* 19, 20.

7. Childs, "Psalm Titles and Midrashic Exegesis." 137–50.

8. A. A. Anderson, Psalms I New *Century Bible.* ". . . there is no reason to doubt that David actually composed certain psalms and songs, but it is well-nigh impossible to say which of them, if any, were preserved in the Psalter. Many scholars regard the historical notes as based on 'speculative exegesis of disconnected details' in a midrashic style and a number of Psalms bearing the phrase 'of David' seem to be later than the reign of David, or the speaker is a descendant of David." 44.

that each of the compositions has a very long history, from origins to final inclusion; that different sorts of people over a very long period of time are responsible for and representative of authorship; that what emerges from the final corpus is a theological perspective on the divine-human encounter that is explicitly and uniquely Hebrew. What appears most likely is this: in its final form, that is, the gathered collections comprising the five books, the Psalter reflects an intentional *"Davidization"* of many of the compositions.

> The story of David testifies at once to the grandeur and the misery of the warrior king. The Court Diary which is now embedded in the Second Book of Samuel does not conceal the contradictions and conflicts which wrenched the character of this extraordinary man. Shepherd and musician, David was physically brave and aesthetically sensitive. Guerrilla leader, he elicited uncommon loyalties but he would on occasion deal treacherously with his most devoted servants. Astute diplomat, he reconciled factions, secured alliances, and conquered an empire, but he did not foresee the deleterious effects of military conquest and colonial expansion. Consummate politician, he served the nation more than himself and he was ridiculously weak with his own family. At once magnanimous and cruel, he resorted to murder for raison d'etat or if driven by erotic passion, but he also preserved a keen sense of social justice. Above all, he exhibited in his own life the ambiguities of religion. The purity of David's faith assumed a quality of elegance which has often gone unnoticed in modern times.[9]

This had the effect of conferring honorific significance and recognition on Israel's greatest king, thereby enshrining in her collective memory that one shining century that witnessed the historic apex of Israel's national ascendancy under the united monarchy.

The story of David is one of intrigue and the mystery of a complex personality.[10] The united monarchy marked an era of fleeting grandeur (1000—930 BCE) that would soon be eclipsed by a divided monarchy in the last third of the tenth-century. None of this assessment, however, diminishes in the slightest the luster and vibrancy of the Psalter. It continues to engage us as revelation, inspiration, and authoritative witness. Spiritually and poetically the Psalter as a whole remains the greatest hymn book ever composed. It has been the inspiration, the model, and the source of the great hymn writers of all the ages down to today. It represents the very heart of the Hebraic *theology of presence* and has contributed liberally to the highest thought in Christian worship and liturgy for two millennia.

---

9. Terrien, *The Psalms*, 367. Note: The authenticity of the tradition associating David with the founding of psalmody in Israel has merited increasing scholarly support in recent years. Davidic authorship of at least some of the psalms in the so-called Davidic collection cannot be completely or summarily dismissed. cf. Nahum M. Sarna, "Studies in Biblical Interpretation" *The Psalms Superscriptions and the Guilds,* 335–36.

10. Terrien, *The Psalms*, 230.

It simply is impossible to conceive of the *First Testament* or the *Second Testament* for that matter, without the book of Psalms. The Yahwists, who were the successors to the pre-exilic traditions of Sinai (poets, authors, composers and the like), interacted within a framework of a brilliant vitality that is reflected in the exilic and postexilic prophets and sages. They began to confer upon Hebraic faith its unique quality of inwardness and breadth, which was subsequently to save Yahwism from its threatened obsolescence of temporal and territorial hegemony. Exiled in 587 from Jerusalem, the myth of the inviolability of Zion was shattered once and for all and the earthly rule of the Davidic house was gone. These Yahwistic poets purposed to live within the proximity of the eternal, abiding *presence* of יהוה beyond the space time continuum of temple, land, and nation. They became *the theologians of the interior quest* who were no longer satisfied simply with either the former institutions or mere intimations of the ultimate.[11]

Their priestly counterparts were the custodians of temple worship. But unlike them the Yahwists did not make the mistake of reducing the ultimate to the proximate. Thereby they invite us to make a candid appraisal of how the promises of God are evidenced in our interior and personal reality; to bring our own flagging spirits and wounded feelings of disappointment before God. [12] We do so because, after all, it is יהוה who is the only one who can resolve our dilemma, whether by changing the circumstances or by changing our understanding and redirecting our expectations. As a result of these sorts of encounters, Israel's relationship with God was enhanced not diminished. No longer were they restricted to the sacred space of the temple or hemmed in by a political structure. Israel's experience of the *presence* of יהוה survived the destruction of the temple, the demise of the monarchy, and the annihilation of her national life.

> Faced with such a cataclysmic void in their sacred space, hallowed history, and personal lives, these poets resorted to the interior life. As a result, these were the poets who became the theologians of the ear, and not the eye. They sang the name 'Yhwh' while anticipating the nearness of the presence. It was this confluence of judgment and grace by which these theologians and word-smiths dared to approximate the mysteries of the effulgence of glory! [13]

11. Terrien, *The Psalms*. "The startling character of the psalmist's discovery lay in his glimpse of a new theology of *presence*: no longer *elusive* as it now seemed to be, it would someday surround him and hold him forever. The menace of 'Life's profound disorder, Ephemerality,' had already retreated from his horizon." 319.

12. 183 Hossfeld and Zenger, "Psalms 2." "There is in the Psalms no quick and easy resignation to suffering . . . in the deepest hopelessness God alone remains the one addressed . . . to do battle against God for God." 47.

13. Terrien, *The Psalms*. "Poets of the interior quest, they were never satisfied with mere intimations of the ultimate, but they never committed the clerical sin of reducing the ultimate to the proximate. Having faced the void in history and in their personal lives, they knew the absence of God even within the temple esplanade and festivities. The inwardness of their spirituality, bred by the temple, rendered the temple superfluous." 279. Note: The Hebrew word is כבוד (kabod) or glory/power.

This sole worship of יהוה came into direct conflict with the henotheistic and polytheistic theologies that remained prevalent throughout ancient Israel's life and ongoing history. The contagion to Yahwism ranged far and wide for centuries and surfaced repeatedly throughout the Hebrew Scriptures. In several places, the Hebrew bible is reluctant if not reticent, to acknowledge explicitly other so-called gods, rather employing wordplays or euphemisms. There are frequent references to those who have either chosen other gods in concert with יהוי, or those who have rejected יהוה completely to follow after other gods. This is, of course, the sin of idolatry. The polytheists knew that the special godhead they addressed and worshiped in a special case, was the only one or the only aspect of the godly world that they needed. Franken reckons that

> in fact this is not a tendency towards monotheism, but the human need to exalt the
> human relation with the godhead in order to find the highest degree of connection.
> It is not the result of, nor does it result in any form of theoretical monotheistic
> tendencies. This is what has struck the psalmists, who adhere to [Yhwh] alone.[14]

The adherence to a strict monotheism resided in the Yahwist's insistence that only יהוה is worthy of worship and praise; that only יהוי is the One God of all the earth! The Psalter is the primary witness document to this uniquely extraordinary phenomenon of "Yhwh alone." Its adherents were committed to the belief in the incomparability of "Yahweh alone." Such was this profound conviction and personal witness to the *presence* of יהוי in the midst of the worshiping community.

The pure joy of worshiping יהוי in the temple is highlighted in our next psalm. Psalm 84 is a song of Zion and is usually described as a hymn which expresses devotion to the temple in Jerusalem. Although Zion appears only once in the psalm (84:8b) it reflects a longing for festival worship and probably describes the pilgrimage of worshipers to the autumnal festival—the Feast of Tabernacles. The fierce longing for an enduring and eternal dwelling place of יהוי is certainly in the poet's horizon of personal interest and reflects his passion for the things of God. In this respect it is related to Psalms 23, 91, and 92. In its climax and at its core this song calls "happy" those people who have anchored their lives in יהוי who is the source of their hope and strength. In the opening theme, enthusiastic joy in יהוי and unshakable trust are reflected in the first strophe (84:2–5). Joy and trust are the gifts of the love of יהוי and point to an inner strength that empowers the poet to withstand all obstacles and overcome all impediments.

This psalm is one from the Korah collection (Pss 42–49; 84–88) and is most likely an early northern song originating in the sanctuary of Dan from possibly the late tenth-century to the early ninth-century BCE. Its concerns are, of course, shaped by the historical circumstances of the geo-political realities of the Northern kingdom of Israel. Within this scenario, Psalm 84 is thought by some scholars to be the earliest of all the songs of Korah reflecting a shift toward the more general term *elohim* in

---

14. Franken, *The Mystical Communion with JHWH in the Book of Psalms*, 57.

reference to יהו. The occurrence of *Zion* in 84:8b is most likely an addition to adapt the psalm to Zion usage after the fall of the Northern kingdom in 721 BCE.

Psalm 84

To the leader: according to The Gittith.
Of the Korahites. A Psalm.

How lovely is your dwelling place O יהוה Sabaʾoth (Lord of Hosts)!
My soul longs, indeed it faints for the courts of יהוה;
my heart and my flesh sing for joy to the living God.
Even the sparrow finds a home, and the swallow a nest for herself,
where she may lay her little ones, at your altars, O יהוה Sabaʾoth.
My king and my God.

Happy are those who dwell in your house,
ever singing your praise.
Happy are those whose strength is in you,
whose hearts are set on the pilgrims' way.

Journeying through the valley of Baca,
they make it a place of springs;
the early rain also covers it with pools.
They go from strength to strength;
the God of gods will be seen in Zion.

O יהוה Sabaʾoth, hear my prayer;
Give ear, O God of Jacob!
Behold our shield, O God;
gaze on the face of your anointed.
For one day in your courts is better than
a thousand elsewhere. I would rather be a doorkeeper
in the house of my God than live in the tents of the faithless.

For יהוה God is both sun and shield;
lavishing on us favor and honor.
No good thing does יהוה withhold
from those who walk with integrity.

O יהוה Sabaʾoth, happy are all who put their trust in you.

The language of these verses emphasizes a passionate delight for the temple and the *presence* of יהוה. Pilgrimages and festivals are almost universal features of religious life and are concerned with the physical and sensory aspects of religious faith. This psalm even intensifies this by describing those whose hearts are filled with longing for the living God. They bear within themselves a life force that is completely inexhaustible and tireless as they journey on from strength to strength. The same is true of those whose trust in יהוה is absolute and unqualified. *Those who hope in יהוה will continually renew their strength; they grow wings like eagles. They run and are not weary; they walk and are not faint* (Isaiah 40:31, REB).

The theocentricity of this psalm is only intensified and gives it *a massively eschatological perspective* (Zenger). It implies a kind of spiritual transformation that enables the worshipers to make their way through the aridity of those times in life when their only cry is for the waters of spiritual refreshment that comes from יהוה alone. Through the psalms we too may become more aware of how it is that we are pilgrims journeying on through life toward the goal of Zion!

Psalm 84 is a brilliant light within the Hebrew Scriptures. Its text formulates the *nevertheless* of hope. Even though it was first and foremost the language of the pilgrims going up to Zion, the message of this psalm is eternally valid. We who are *"the people of the Way"* (Acts 9:2) often find it difficult not to be overwhelmed by our personal grief and sadness, our surging waves of resignation and multiple sorrows. Here in the Psalms is where the poor in spirit find consolation and joy. The text of this psalm was put to music by Johannes Brahms in his *German Requiem* in the affective anthem, *"How Lovely is thy Dwelling Place."* In the perfected state of the faithful righteous, in which they even now, after death, find their home in the heavenly dwelling, now are at rest from their labors.

What Elie Wiesel says of the Hasidim applies to those who live in this way from the strength of יהוה, and those who, on the way, are *equipped with mysterious strengths, [they] wander the earth, warm it and change it, now, somehow, mightily empowered to transform doubt and care into enthusiasm, into the praise of life.*[15]

---

15. Quoted in Hossfeld-Zenger, "Psalms 2." 358.

Existential Quandary

THE OVERALL THEME OF Psalm 90 is the eternity of God and temporal human limitations. Few psalms are more eloquent with respect to the topic of human beings lacking divine blessing as is this psalm. Here the eternity of God is juxtaposed to the judgment—or the wrath—that consigns all humanity to death. *All our days are surely passing away in your anger, and we finish our years as a sigh* (v.9). Book IV commences with Psalm 90 and concludes with a sweep of Israel's salvation history (105–106).

As a communal lament Psalm 90 affirms that the eternal God and creator of the world has ever been Israel's protector.[1] But God also allows humankind, which is as transient as grass, to age, wither, and die. In the wrath at human sin God disciplines and corrects the covenant community. Our brief lives are now characterized by suffering and adversity; they come to an end in weakness and dissolution. The community asks for wisdom, the restoration of God's favor, a fresh revelation of divine power, and a blessing upon human labor and endeavor.

The brevity and frustrations of human life tend to wear us all down. The human condition is characterized by the unconditional and inevitable barrier of death which brings an abrupt and final end to human existence. In this sense the psalm reflects ancient Israel's own age of anxiety. Here hope and despair are intermingled in an unforgettable prayer that beseeches יהוה to turn and bless the suffering community of all humanity by drawing near in the divine *presence*. Facing national catastrophe, the people turn again to Moses in Psalm 90. Not only this psalm but all of *Book IV* is dominated by the *Man of God*. In the preceding Psalter's *Books, I–III*, Moses is mentioned only once (Ps 77:21).

However, in *Book IV* he is mentioned seven times (Ps. 90:1; 99:6; 103:7; 105:26; 106:16, 23, 32). Nancy deClaisse-Walford suggests that the meaning of this prominence of Moses in Book IV lies in the fact that Psalm 90 *marks a turning point in the Psalter, a turn away from looking back to the days of King David and a turn toward looking forward to the reign of God as king over Israel once again, just as during the time of the wilderness wandering.*[2] Only in this manner may the southern kingdom of Judah hope to avert a

---

1. Koch, "Is there a Doctrine of Retribution in the Old Testament?" 137. cf. Bowker, "Psalm XC." *Vetus Testamentum,* 17 (31–41).

2. deClaisse-Walford, *Reading from the Beginning: The Shaping of the Hebrew Psalter.* 104. cf. Kruger, "Psalm 90 und die Verganglichkeit des Menschen," *Biblica* (1994) 91–119.

similar fate like that which had befallen the northern kingdom of Israel. In the Psalter, life in יהוה is invested with the highest value and importance. In certain of the psalms that came from the north in the early to mid-eighth century BCE (Pss 60, 68, 74, and 78) the tone of Yahwistic pleading is discernible in the *Elohistic Psalter.*

Viewed against the backdrop of the warnings of the contemporary prophets (Hosea, Amos, Micah and Isaiah), it is remarkable how the story of ancient Israel can be tracked within the psalmic text itself.

> *Each psalm has a long and extensive prehistory. Only at the very end was it fixed in written form and included in the collection. It was first prayed, sung, and spoken by many extremely different kinds of people. Only later, at the point where these many voices were gathered in worship, did it receive the form that is normative for all and accessible to all. This process of liturgical shaping of the Psalms took many generations.*[3]

In what is a conscientious effort to recapture the letter and spirit of Moses as the revered founder of Israel's institutions, Psalm 90 represents a nostalgic return to the past as the source of all good things. W. F. Albright, who always writes persuasively of Israel's life and history, interprets the effects the events of the eighth century had on tiny Judah to the south: *No longer was there facile optimism about Israel's future. As the Northern Kingdom and most of its neighbors had fallen, so would Judah unless it abandoned its evil modern ways, its sophisticated adaptations of foreign culture.*[4] The psalms in *Book IV* bypass the glory days of the Davidic kingdom.

In the larger scheme, *Book IV* marks a significant shift away from the trappings of earthly royalty common to *Books I-III* toward the primacy of God's glory and safety in יהוה. Throughout *Book III* the people of יהוה have lived through the horrors of exile. The key to the shift from the Davidic monarchy to Yahwistic theocracy in Psalm 90, reorients the focus of the Psalter to the importance of the Mosaic covenant at Sinai and יהוה as almighty sovereign in response to the failure of the Davidic covenant (Psalm 89). Hardly any attention is given to the past deeds of David the hero. Any hope for the survival of the Judean monarchy and the temple is sealed under such conditions in which each new successive reign is to be instructed in the way of יהוה under the prevailing historical circumstances.

> *The key to the shift from the Davidic monarchy to Yahwistic theocracy is Ps 90, which shifts the focus of the Psalter to the importance of the Mosaic covenant and YHWH as king in response to the apparent failure of the Davidic covenant.*[5]

The Moses hymn (Psalm 90) is a discourse on human existence: its frailty, mortality, and transience. The prayer, simply put, is a direct appeal for blessing and divine

---

3. Westermann, *The Living Psalms*, 16.
4. Albright, *The Biblical Period from Abraham to Ezra*, 83.
5. Wallace, *The Narrative Effect of Book IV of the Hebrew Psalter*, 15.

favor despite all human failing to the contrary.[6] It is not so much an appeal to the glory days of the past as it is an appeal for the *presence* of יהוה amid the harsh realities of the present. Beneath the language of deep time lies a resilience and reservoir of trust in the face of what appears to be the insurmountable limitations on humankind's mortality.

Psalm 90

Prayer—Of Moses, the man of God

Adonai, you have been our dwelling place in all generations.
Before the mountains were born,
or the earth and the cosmos were brought forth,
even from eternity to eternity, you are God.

You turn humankind back into the dust, and say:
"*Back to what you once were, mortals.*"
To your eyes a thousand years are but a single day,
and yesterday, now over and gone, is but a watch in the night.
You sweep humanity away; all of you but a dream,
like grass that sprouts and flowers in the morning,
yet it withers and dries; and before dusk it is gone.

We too are consumed by your anger;
we are terrified by your fury;
having summoned up our sins, everything is made
manifest in the light of your countenance;
so it is that all our days dwindle before your wrath;
we bring our years to an end like a sigh.

Our lifetime is so brief—seventy years,
or if we are strong, perhaps eighty—
but they only add up to boisterous anxiety and stormy troubles;
so abrupt are they gone with the wind, and we with them.

---

6. Brueggemann, *The Message of the Psalms*. "There may be a wistfulness, even chagrin, but Psalm 90 is not a meditation on futility and death, as much as the power of God in the face of human reality" 112. cf. Rendtorff, *God's History*. In Psalm 90, "confidence in the unalterable faithfulness of God constitutes the ground on which all the rest stands, and it is deeply anchored in the past, back to the time of creation or even before the beginning of the world. God stands with [his] faithful at the beginning, before all other occurrences. But this psalm knows also that the disorders of life do not come by chance." 61.

Who is it who has felt the full force of your anger?

Your wrath is as great as the fear that is due you.

Teach us to be mindful of the brevity of our days,

that we may gain hearts full of wisdom.

O יהוה—how long until you turn your face toward us?

We beg you to have compassion on your servant (Israel)!

Satisfy us in the morning with your steadfast love,

so that we may sing and be happy all our days;

make our future as bright as our past was dismal,

for we remember those years when you were correcting us.

Let your servants show forth your wonders;

O, let our children see your glorious power.

יהוה, our God! Look favorably upon us; prosper our handiwork—

O, we implore you—make the work of our hands succeed.

The fact that the later addition of the superscription ascribes this psalm to Moses, the man of God, expresses something of the high esteem in which the mighty *lawgiver* was held and the reverence and deference shown him. Moses is most certainly not the author of this psalm but rather he is the recipient of this honorific title. One could only think, then, of the interjection of the words of this psalm as having been spoken by the nation's greatest son. The reason for this ascription may perhaps be found in the fact that the psalm shows reminiscences of the history of creation and the story of the fall and the curse of humanity as well as the wilderness song and the blessing of Moses (Deut. 32 and 33). Psalm 90 is often given the classifications of a wisdom psalm or a communal lament even though it does not give any impression that it was occasioned by a specific national catastrophe so much as it is the makings of a human catastrophe. Marvin Tate may be right when he makes the plausible suggestion that Psalm 90

> belongs to the category of learned philosophy-that is, a literary composition contributed to the Psalter by sages and designed for the purposes of personal piety and devotion. Psalms of learned philosophy, or those believed to have been composed by the sages of ancient Israel are relatively few. The genre is usually identified as Wisdom Psalms and consists of an appeal to the wisdom tradition of ancient Israel in her attempts to reconcile the rewards of the devout and blameless and the commensurate recompense of the wicked and unfaithful who have not followed Torah and therefore are reproached and denounced as 'faithless.' [7]

Whatever its genre the psalm establishes the long view perspective that before all, and from all eternity, there is God: *Lord [Adonai], You have been our dwelling place*

7. Tate, "The Interpretation of the Psalms," 475.

throughout all generations. Before the mountains were brought forth, or even before the earth and the cosmos were born, from eternity to eternity, you are God (90:1,2 NRSV). In Hebrew it is rendered literally, *and you gave birth to the earth and world.* The verbal form in the Hebrew text pictures the Creator giving birth to the world in orderly and non-chaotic manner. In the *LXX* and some other ancient witnesses, the text assumes a (passive) verbal form. In this case the earth becomes the subject of the verb and the verb is understood as third feminine singular rather than second masculine singular. Mortals are as mere *grass* and are (*swept away like a dream,* 90:5; cf. 102:3–11).

Death therefore is the ultimate boundary. When human beings are cut off from the holiness and grandeur of God, humans die. The psalmists faced the issue of human mortality squarely and with a sobering reality. The ancient Israelites accepted the fact of death. But especially when it was tragic and when it came by violence or treachery or disease, they saw in death something requiring divine attention. That Israel required the attention of יהוה—and even demanded it—is a persistent hallmark to a stubbornly insistent faith.[8]

The Hebrew reads, *from eternity to eternity you are God.* Instead of אֵל (*el,* God) the *LXX* reads אַל (*al, not*) and joins the negative particle to the following verse, making the verb תָּשֵׁב (*tashev, to be swept away as a flood*) a jussive. In this case 90:3 reads as a prayer: *do not sweep us away, please no, not back to a low place.* However, taking תָּשֵׁב (*tashev*) as a jussive is problematic in light of the following form, וַתֹּאמֶר (*vatomer, and you said/say*).

In this context the shortened prefix form indicates what is typical of the world. The Hebrew word דַּכָּא (*dakka'*) carries the basic sense of being *crushed or ground, decimated* as in *grind into dust.* Elsewhere it refers to those who are *crushed in spirit or contrite of heart.* Psalm 34:18 reads, יהוה *is near to the brokenhearted, and saves the crushed in spirit.* And in Isaiah 57:15; For *thus says the high and lofty one who inhabits eternity, whose name is Holy: I dwell in the high and holy place, and also with those who are contrite and humble in spirit, to revive the spirit of the humble, and to revive the heart of the contrite* (NRSV).

If one accepts this nuance, then verse 3 is making the unmistakable observation that God is leading humankind to repentance. The verb שׁוּב (*shuv, to return*), which appears twice in this verse, is sometimes used of the term repentance. But the following context laments humankind's mortality and the brevity of life, so it is doubtful that 90:3 should be understood so positively. It is more likely that דַּכָּא (*dakka'*) which here refers to *crushed, decimated matter* is like the dust of death that fills the grave. In this case one may hear an echo of the grim reminder in Genesis 3. *By the sweat of your brow you will now eat food until you return to the ground, for out of the earth you were taken; for you*

8. Crenshaw, *Defending God,* "Many modern theists seem ignorant of the rich tradition of protest within the Bible itself. Honest wrestling with the uncertainties of the ancients links believers over millennia at the existential level." 111.

are of the dust, and you will be returned to the dust (3:19 NRSV). In this manner, the poet pleads with God, *please, no; do not reduce us to the dust of death!* (90:3).

It is commonly asserted that the Hebrew Bible in general and the Psalms in particular, say little about life beyond the grave. This assertion can be challenged. True, in the Hebrew bible there are only a few passages which speak of life beyond death, and none at all of any immortality of the soul, which, of course, is not a Hebrew idea at all, but rather a Greek one. The first passage is Isaiah 26:19, where the Israelite dead are called forth to rise from the dust and live. *Your dead shall live, their corpses shall rise. O dwellers in the dust, awake and sing for joy!* This passage is probably early third century BCE, during the time of the rivalries of the Ptolemies and the Seleucids in Palestine.

The other is Daniel 12:2 in the first half of the second-century BCE where we read of a partial general resurrection. *Many of those who sleep in the dust of the earth shall awake, some to everlasting life, and some to shame and everlasting contempt* (NRSV). The question is also raised in Job 14:14 (*If mortals die, will they live again?*), but the poet turns away from it as being too much to hope for. The idea is scouted as being ridiculous in Ecclesiastes (3:18–21 NRSV) *The fate of humans and the fate of animals is the same; as one dies so does the other. They all have the same breath, and humans have no advantage over the animals, for all is vanity. All go to one place; all are from the dust, and all are turned to dust again.* Still others may appeal to Ezekiel's vision of the valley of the dry bones and the prophecy concerning the whole house of Israel. *Therefore, prophesy to them and say, "Thus says* יהוה *your God: I am going to open your graves, and bring you up from your graves, O my people, and I will bring you back to the land of Israel"* (Ez 37 NRSV).

True, there is no specific reference to a resurrection to eternal life found in the Psalms. Christians assume this simply was not within the purview of the Hebrews' knowledge; that only the full revelation of the Christ has made known this mystery to us. But there are always exceptions and logic alone dictates that one not succumb to the law of excluded middle. Are there possible exceptions to this limited understanding of an afterlife in the Psalms? Are there not faint glimmerings of a longed for deliverance from death, from the power of Sheol? What do we have in Psalms 16, 49, 56 and 73— the beginnings of a formative belief in the resurrection of the dead in the ancient Hebrew tradition? May not this hope be gleaned from these texts?

Unquestionably there is the fuller development of a doctrine of the afterlife that unfolds in the later post-exilic theologies of Job and Third Isaiah and the apocalyptic writings of Daniel offer emergent revelation concerning יום ליהוה (*the day of the LORD*) and the recapitulation of the whole creation by God's new and regenerative acts of power and exalted glory. Even a resurrected body is contemplated! The significance this had for late post exilic Jews is reflected in some of their later writings (e.g. 2 Maccabees 7).[9] Christians, of course, come to this discussion of a resurrection of the body to eternal life with something quite completely different in mind.

9. cf. Snaith, *The Distinctive Ideas of the Old Testament,* 89, 90.

The resurrection of Jesus as the Christ of God is the core conviction and belief of the Christian faith. Accordingly, resurrection stands as the antidote to human sin and the actual effects and consequences of humanity's over-reaching sense of its own autonomy, inflated self-importance, and innate *concupiscence*. This is the language that is front and center in Psalm 90. We humans are transient beings. Our very natures are in conflict with God's eternal values. What it is we long for is a spiritual life. As one contemporary puts it: *We are spiritual beings in search of human experiences!* Psalm 90 is not simply about the transitoriness of human life and an unavoidable and ignoble death. It is a didactic on human nature. We turn now to a theology of human nature. *Concupiscence* is a classic theological term of Latin derivation and it is attributed to Augustine of Hippo in the early fifth-century CE. A counter movement under Pelagius–by all accounts a stellar Christian—had adopted certain views on human sin that were to be rejected by the church councils.[10]

Although a large part of Augustine's doctrine of human sin as *concupiscence* was not formally adopted in the church's subsequent creeds and councils, it greatly influenced Martin Luther and the Protestant reformers a thousand years later. *Concupiscence* is most familiar to us from its usage in the King James (Authorized) version of the Bible. It occurs in Romans 7:8, Colossians 3:5, I Thessalonians 4:5 and James 1:13–15 and is commonly interpreted as *wrongful desire* or *willful wrongness* from the Greek (Ἐπιθυμίαν) or *covetous desire.*

Although it refers to humankind's innate predisposition toward wrongful desire—which is denoted by Augustine as having a primarily sexual connotation—this by no means exhausts the broader meaning of the term. It is not fundamentally about pan-sexual desire. Rather it includes *all* that proceeds from the desires of the human heart and will and represents our baser inclinations toward that which God would not have us do or be. It's used in the *LXX* by way of connecting the theme to the Ten Commandments, specifically, *thou shalt not covet* (Deut. 5; Ex 20).

10. Note: Although the case could be made that it had some adherents, the council of Carthage in the early 5th century (419 CE) condemned the teachings of Pelagius. A closer examination of the views of Pelagius, so suddenly become famous, brought to light the fact that it contained the fundamental ideas which the Church afterwards condemned as "Pelagianism." In it Pelagius denied the primitive state in paradise and original sin (cf. P.L., XXX, 678, *"Insaniunt, qui de Adam per traducem asserunt ad nos venire peccatum»*), insisted on the naturalness of concupiscence and the death of the body, and ascribed the actual existence and universality of sin to the bad example which Adam set by his first sin. Pelagius's ideas were chiefly rooted in the old, pagan philosophy, especially in the popular system of the Stoics, rather than in the teaching that was subsequently promulgated by the church. Pelagius believed that human sin was not compulsory whereas the church had decided that human sin is the result of an inherently sinful nature traceable to humanity's parents, Adam and Eve, thereby infecting all humanity. In this view, death is not "natural" but rather it is an invasive corruption of the human race. Human death was never God's intention for humanity at creation. This view was to dominate Augustine's understanding, the legacy of which became the church's position on "original sin." Such a doctrinal position is still an open theological issue today. That there is an implicit connection between human sin and death is amplified by Paul in Romans 5.

In the Protestant Reformation, Martin Luther referred to it as humanity's innate desire for autonomy (*the human heart is hopelessly curved inward toward the self*). Luther's understanding interprets what it is that lies at the root of humankind's rebellion against God's sacred order of creation. Human *desire*, self-will and an inveterate conniving to be like God poisons all people and infects everything. Paul in Romans 5 articulates the Christian understanding of sin as resulting in the invasion of death into the created order–absolute death, physically and spiritually—as the consequence of human transgression.

The result is separation from God. The poet of Psalm 90 places human sin in the context of God's wrath: *For all our days pass away under your wrath; our years come to an end like a sigh (v. 9, NRSV)*. The wrath of God is a theological fact that takes into account humanity's sin as rebellion against God and is set in the wider domain resulting in humanity's limits—the stark and hard reality of death. But Psalm 90

> *does not mean we are faced with an arbitrary God who may not like us or who turns our life into absurdity by cutting short our days. It does mean that the one who is the ground of our being has created for us lives that manifest love and righteousness, that continue the good purposes for which God has brought the universe into being; that the universal failure so to live places our lives under the limitation and judgment of death.*[11]

Eternity is not the extinction of time; it is the creative unity of all time and cycles of time, of all past and all future time. Eternity is eternal life. It is not eternal death. The eternity of יהוה is juxtaposed to the judgment (*wrath*) that consigns all humanity to death. *All our days are surely passing away in your wrath, and we finish our years as a sigh* (v.9). Yet there remains the perspective that is anchored in confidence and hope. Taken together our three psalms form to buttress a triad of trust: the perspective on mortality (90), the promise of protection (91), and the paean to eternal praise (92). These three psalms function together as a unit and are interwoven in theme and structure. They serve to support the response to the situation raised by the poet in Psalm 89, which begins as a hymn of praise to יהוה. *I will sing of the constant love of Yhwh, forever; with my mouth I will confess your faithfulness to all generations. I will declare how your constant love is established forever; for your fidelity is as firm as the heavens* (89:1,2 NRSV).

The shift and new focus of the psalm then hinges on verses 38 and 39: *But now you have spurned and rejected [him]; you are full of rebellion against your anointed and have renounced the covenant with your servant; you have defiled [his] crown in the dust* (NRSV).[12] The fundamental idea on which the entirety of Psalm 90 is constructed is

---

11. Miller, *Interpreting the Psalms*, 119. "There is no moment in all our time that we have not been in God's hands. God is the one in whom we live and move and have our being and in whom we can ask the question about our life in the face of death." 127.

12. *The Jewish Study Bible* puts it: "Yet you have rejected, spurned, and become enraged at Your anointed. You have repudiated the covenant with Your servant; You have dragged his dignity in the dust" Ps 89: 39–40.

put at the head in order to indicate its theme, thereby stressing the viewpoint which guides the poet as he develops his thoughts. This is nothing less than the human longing for the eternal while experiencing the limitations of the temporal.

The statement *Lord, you have been our refuge from one generation to another* is formally a retrospect. By virtue of the psalmist's trust in God it embraces the whole of Israel's ancient traditions. It is, however, by no means intended to convey the thought that God has now ceased to be the refuge of [his] people. On the contrary, the backward look upon all past generations who have continually lifted up their eyes to יהוה as the fixed point in the flux of history will find confirmation in Yhwh. The individual suppliant knows this for it has been learned in the hard school of sin's deleterious and tragic effects.[13] Human sin and the rejection of the conditions of the covenant have inevitably consequences for Israel. No longer are the kings seen as the anointed of יהוה. There is a radical disjunction between the anointed leadership and the integrity of that leadership in the eyes of יהוה. The people of יהוה now stand in severe contradiction to the sworn covenant with David. The totality of the sentence of death in the face of the choices human beings make has repercussions that are not limited to human mortality. In his commentary James Mays notes how this psalm attributes all human demise in death to God's anger toward humanity's rebellion.

> *Death is the final and ultimate 'no' that cancels any pretension to autonomy from the human side. The mortal is returned to the dust (dakka'), which elsewhere means 'contrition,' a probably double entendre in the psalm. The psalm . . . does not leave misery and death meaningless. In seeing human finitude under the sign of God's wrath, the psalm stands with Genesis 3 and Romans 1–2.*[14]

The role and the rule of the Messiah's defeat of sin's curse will actualize in the world what will become the ultimate reality of the entirety of creation. *By this radical conception of death [the death of death]*, writes Karl Barth, *the autonomy of the power of the resurrection is guaranteed as independent of the life which is on this side of the line of death. The void brought into being by the death of Christ is filled with the new life which is the power of the Resurrection.*[15] In terms of the resurrection of Jesus, resurrection is not so much a miracle as much as it is an enduring relationship. The best way to speak about the Resurrection is not to say, *"Jesus rose from the dead"*–as if it is a self-generated miracle in defiance of all natural law–but to say, *"Jesus was raised from the dead"* (as

13. cf. Romans 1 is Paul's articulation of the nature of human limitation in the face of divine judgment.

14. Mays, Psalms, *Interpretation* Series, 291. cf. In *Christ and Adam: Man and Humanity in Romans 5*, Karl Barth emphasizes how "death is an objective and alien power that is now exercising its lordship over [man]. Death, like sin, is an intruder into human life; in the original scheme for [man's] world it had no place at all. When sin broke into the world (Rom 5:12), death found the way by which it would claim all [men]. That is what happens when as a result of [his] sin [man] is condemned. Death is not so much God's direct reaction against [man's] sin; it is rather God's abandoning of the [men] who have abandoned [Him]." 53.

15. Karl Barth, *The Epistle to the Romans,* 194, 195. cf. Weaver, "From Paul to Augustine: Romans 5:12 in Early Christian Exegesis." 187–206.

many early Christian texts state unequivocally!) and which implies directly that Jesus was *acted upon by God* in space and time. The Eternal and Exalted Christ is now revealed as the blueprint, the promise, the pledge, the guarantee of what is always happening everywhere, all summed up in one person so we can see it in personified and human form. The exaltation and the glorification of the Christ breaks death's grip on life and, in so doing, cancels out completely sin's disastrous curse on the human race! Death is an intrusion into God's world and the resolution of this altogether foreign reality is the final act of the obedience of the Messiah!

Now, if we can understand that Jesus is the human archetype, the stand-in for everybody and everything, we will get that much closer to the heart of the Christian gospel message. This is precisely why Jesus nearly always referred to himself as *"the Son of Man."* His resurrection is not so much a miracle that we can argue about, philosophize about, believe, or disbelieve, but rather it is an invitation to look more deeply at what is always actually happening in the life process itself. Jesus, or any member of the "Body of Christ," cannot really die because all are now participating in something that is eternal—the Cosmic Christ who comes forth from God—and who comes *to* us and who is *for* us.[16]

In the Hebrew scriptures, David's kingship is that agency through which the rule of יהוה is extended from heaven to earth and divine dominion over cosmic chaos includes attention to the details of historical disorder. Just as sun and moon are in the heavens, so David's line will be the enduring witness on earth to the reign of יהוה. The defeat, humiliation, dejection, and even death (89: 45, *You [Yhwh] have cut short the days of his youth; you [Yhwh] have covered him with rejection, with shame, REB*) of the anointed of יהוה constitute a breach in and a rejection of that covenant. Divine wrath prevails and the steadfast love and righteousness of יהוה are called into question. If the earthly correspondent to the heavenly rule is vanquished and vanishes, then what of the heavenly rule? This is the enigma for which Psalm 89 seems to offer us no resolution.

> *The answers are essentially: Yahweh is king; Yahweh has been our refuge in the past, long before the monarchy existed, and will be our refuge now that the monarchy is gone; blessed are those who trust in Yahweh. This book [Book IV] begins and ends with Moses, who led Israel before there was a monarchy. Ps. 90 asks the 'How long?' question that was raised in Ps. 89:47, but the question is raised in a fresh way, not in the context of the lost monarchy but in the context of Israel's sin.*[17]

From there the poet's hymn in Psalm 89 degenerates into a bitter complaint concerning the rejection of the Davidic Covenant. It is exactly the opposite of Psalm 18 and contradicts the promises of Psalm 2. It sets forth an unbearable and inscrutable mystery. The Messiah will suffer the wrath of both father and God, the rock of his salvation. The chosen one is now the rejected one. The reversal is the plot of the psalm and the problem for which it sees no resolution. In its long course, it elaborates more

16. Rohr, *A Meditation on Transformation: Dying into Life.*

17. Holladay, *The Psalms through Three Thousand Years,* 78.

fully than anywhere else the correspondence and coherence between the sovereignty of God and the person of the Messiah.

The key theological fact of that relationship is the burden of its dilemma. This carefully drawn parallel between the kingship of God and that of David assumes that the latter is integral to the former. The consciousness of standing together with יהוה in the same long living tradition of faith is precisely what strengthens the poet's resolve to trust in יהוה.

> *If the poetic medium of Psalms is an instrument for reconstructing time and space and the order of history and society in the light of faith, the optative mood of the prayers and the celebratory note of some of the songs of thanksgiving lead at points to a strikingly utopian vision. Though the psalms, that is, are uttered out of the real dangers and fears and doubts of a historical or existential here and now, they also sometimes project, like the last lines of Psalm 90, an image of what life must be like sheltered by God from the wasting winds of mischance, when human performance and divine expectation are in perfect accord.*[18]

The worshiping community of ancient Israel found firm support in the faith of its ancestors. It shares this together as the people of God even though it candidly faces the disturbing truth about the transitoriness of human life. Without having one's feet firmly planted on the ground of trust in God, one would hardly be able, in view of the hopeless predicament of humanity, to adopt the course that follows and plea for God's mercy. This existential pathos of Psalm 90 virtually drips throughout and sets the stage for the bold declarations of Psalm 91. The storyline in Psalms 90 and 91—at the beginning of *Book IV (Pss 90–106)*—refocuses the reader's attention away from the harsh realities of the exile and the failure of the Davidic covenant (Ps 89), to the Mosaic perspective on human mortality and limits.

Only then may the renewed promise and blessing of יהוה be realized by the faithful (Ps 91) and the gracious compassion and the readily available deliverance of יהוה promised in Psalm 92 be fulfilled. The reader is moved continually from the direct petition for deliverance from the judgment of יהוה in 90:13 to the supplication of blessing from יהוה at the end of the psalm; and, finally, to a summation of the actualized experience of that blessing in Psalm 91. These allusions prepare the reader, not for the return of the Davidic monarchy, but for a theocentric recognition of יהוה as the true exalted king over the people whom the reader will encounter in Psalms 93–100. Here, as well as in Psalm 121, which is another song of trust, the vow of trust precedes the promise of blessing. *I lift up my eyes to the hills–from where will my help come? My help comes from Yhwh, who made heaven and earth* (121:1, 2, NRSV).

While Psalm 121 brings together the assurance of God's protection and blessing in particularly poetic ways, its meaning was further amplified for the pilgrims reciting it on their way to Jerusalem because of the numerous allusions that are made to other

---

18. Alter, *The Art of Biblical Poetry,* 129.

passages of scripture describing God's steadfast love, ability to safeguard, and assurance that there is no need to fear. Who among us contemporary Christians cannot empathize with our forebears in faith? This psalm is the prayer of persons of faith entrusting their fear and anxiety about the frailty and vulnerability of human existence to the care of God from whom life comes and to whom life returns. The meaning of the superscription may refer to an ascending style of poetic construction of the Hebrew language or more likely, it refers to the ascent of those on pilgrimage while passing through the mountainous terrain surrounding Jerusalem. This journey could be fraught with danger as brigands and outlaws laid in wait for the pilgrims. This psalm is one of simple and unabashed trust and confidence in God's providential care and help. It is the broad metaphorical contour for the individual's journey throughout life.

Psalm 121

A Song of Ascents

I will look up, lifting my eyes to the hills—
from where is my help to come?
My help shall come from יהוה who is
Creator of heaven and earth.

My God will never allow my foot to slip;
The One who guards me never slumbers nor sleeps!
יהוה is your keeper; יהוה is your shade at your right hand;

The blazing sun will not scorch you by day;
nor the grip of the moon's nightly terrors assail you.

יהוה will guard you from all evil; יהוה keeps your life.
יהוה will guard everything about you;
In all your comings and goings, יהוה will favor you;
This is so, both now and for evermore.

D. H. Lawrence mocks this little psalm in his poem, *The Hills*. He writes: *I lift up my eyes unto the hills, and there they are, but no strength comes from them to me. Only from darkness and ceasing to see strength comes.* But his mockery can't rob the ancient hills of their mystery. He may say of them, *"there they are,"* but he can't stop there. He must go on in his poem, which then plunges directly into the darksome abyss and more mystery. Sleep. Death. Poets have long recognized that sleep is not only the source of dreams, but is emblematic of death. Or John Donne's Holy Sonnet #10, where he calls *"rest and sleep"* the pictures of death. . . . . *To die, to sleep; The* connection is perhaps most famously made familiar to us by Shakespeare in Hamlet's soliloquy, *"To be or not to be. . . ."* (Act III, Scene 1).

But the perspective of Psalm 121 is supremely important precisely because it offers concrete evidence for how blessing is to be understood—not only in the psalm but also throughout the First Testament. Blessing is only accounted for by God! God's eternity in Psalm 90 is described eloquently in the language of deep *time*. These words come to us from the farthest past yet speak to our present era. In the sweep and scope of the eternal, to *see things from a broad perspective, . . . the perspective of eternity, means that things are put in proportion, and begin to lose their power to disturb and control us. We let God's gift of seeing reality in terms of eternity control all that we do whether it is praying, arguing, sleeping.*[19]

Hope is not in the first instance a situation of ambivalence toward the future, a wish or the indication of a goal that one awaits with tension. It is above all, and the *Septuagint* emphasizes this very strongly, a situation of surrender and trust. The translators of the *LXX* did not make any real distinction between the two Hebrew words for refuge and trust, חסה (*chasa*) and בטח (*batach*)',[20] translating them instead with the Greek words, ἐλπίς (*elpis*) and πεποιθότας (*pepoithotas*). But the common themes of hope, trust and refuge are clearly present and discernible in both psalms. The costliness of exile, the transitoriness of humanity and the refuge of יהוה, all bring these Psalms together. They are presented in two very different genres of composition. Psalm 90 may be designated as a communal lament with hymn and credo, whereas Psalm 91 is an individual song of trust with a concluding divine oracle which uses the language of salvation (91:14–16); Psalm 121 is a poem of simple trust which is intended to serve as a metaphor for the earthly pilgrimage of life.

This is what the Moses hymn asserts: *from eternity to eternity,* that is, *from form to form* and *world to world*, God *is*. Before all, and from all eternity; *Before the mountains were brought forth, or even before the earth and the cosmos were born, from eternity to eternity, you are God* (90:2, NRSV). Even the mountains, most permanent and immovable of all things on earth, are born and shall die. God, who *was* before their birth, *will* be after their death. Mortals are as mere grass and are swept away *like a dream* (90:5; cf. 102:3–11). God's measure of time is not our measure. *For a thousand years in your sight are but as yesterday when it is passed* (90:4, NRSV). Divine measurements are always and ever beyond all human calculation and all human knowing.

---

19. Rogerson, *The Psalms in Daily Life*, 22.

20. Creach, *The Destiny of the Righteous in the Psalms*, 32. "'*Batach*' is important because of its close relationship with '*chasa*' 'as well as the frequency of its occurrence in the Psalter (52 times). Although '*batach*' can mean simply '*believe*', in most cases the word has the connotation of inner security and trust." 32.

Fulcrum of Mercy

THE TRIAD OF PSALMS that opens *Book IV* functions as the *fulcrum of the Psalter*. It is sometimes referred to as the Psalms' *editorial center*. Psalm 92 serves as a kind of benediction to all three psalms: *The righteous flourish like the palm tree, and grow like a cedar in Lebanon. They are planted in the house of* יהוה; *and flourish in the courts of our God. In old age they still produce fruit; they are always green and full of sap, showing that* יהוה *is upright;* יהוה *is my rock, and there is no unrighteousness in him* (Psalm 92:12–15, REB).

The group of psalms that follow (93–100) is united by genre and motif. יהוה affirms rule over the earth. יהוה reigns, clothed with majesty; יהוה is robed in majesty and is armed with strength (93:1). Here two dominate features stand out: the closeness to God of the person addressed, and the strength of the promises of protection by יהוה to the person. The promises of God are poured out with warmth and abundance and the psalmist feels safe, whatever happens, knowing that he is under God's gracious protection. Trusting in God, he is patiently at rest. His anxiety is removed for he knows that God grants *shalom*, which in the words of Nahum Sarna is *deliverance, freedom, and the possibility of life opening up into a width and breadth that is rich and full.*[1] The promise of *shalom* is the gift of יהוה!

Psalm 91 continues the motif of יהוה as refuge, *because you have made Yahweh, who is your refuge, even Elyon your place of dwelling;* Psalm 92 also serves as a bridge from the 'refuge' psalms (90 and 91) to the 'Yahweh is king' psalms that begin with Psalm 93: יהוה is Israel's rock (92:15) and refuge, and at the same time YHWH is *'on high'* forever (92:8). *It is good to give thanks to* יהוה, *to sing praises to your name, Elyon.* Psalm 89 brings to an end any flowering of Davidic messianic hope and prepares the reader for what follows in Pss. 90–92. The question of *"How long?"* is allowed to hang suspended until יהוה speaks the word of hope. The eternity of יהוה is juxtaposed to that of human life and its ultimate limitations. Humanity's limit of mortality and its existential angst, which are the fundamental boundaries and the reality of all human life, are only overcome by the word of יהוה. That word is from eternity to eternity. It is the final word on humanity's dilemma and it is the word of hope.

---

1. Sarna, *Songs of the Heart: An Introduction to the Book of Psalms,* 120.

The Israelite view of after-life is characterized by the shadowy Sheol existence which was largely negative. It was only in the late post-Exilic period that a different idea of life after death was gradually formulated. Had the author of this Psalm believed that the after-life provided for a final judgment of God, he would have found little difficulty in explaining the prosperity of the wicked and that misfortune of the righteous. Therefore, it seems that he also must have shared in the common Sheol belief. On the other hand, it may represent a tentative venture to go beyond the then current beliefs, although the result would be a glimpse rather than a firm faith. If this was the case, then it is understandable why the Psalmist remained content that God was his portion forever without giving a more definite shape to his hope.[2]

If Psalm 91 was used in connection with any of these liturgies, as appears to be the case, its function may well have been to spell out further protection against the myriad afflictions that befall the faithful. The true aim of Psalm 91, then, stands out prominently right from the beginning. It is to demonstrate that this living relationship with God has the quality of actuality and the person who trusts in God will be able to experience now, and in their own person, *shalom*. In all the afflictions and perils of life the saving, protecting, strengthening power of God will sustain the pilgrims on their journey of faith. Only someone who in times of severe stress and danger trusted יהוה and was rescued could possibly have uttered such bold and challenging instruction.

Our three psalms are unflinching. Without hesitation or doubt, these poets affirm that it is יהוה who comes to the aid of those who dwell in the sheltering arms of God. Just as Israel was protected in her wilderness journey to Zion, so will those who love יהוה be protected in their journey through life. The recipient, then, does not just accept passively the blessing received from יהוה but embraces it boldly and with a trusting heart. Psalm 91 is unique in its description of this boldness that the one who trusts in יהוה may possess. This is in contrast to those who put their trust in such things as magical amulets, superstition, other gods and the like. Here is an example from Christian history:

The Psalms had become so central in the lives of common Christians in the West, that, by the time of the translation of the Bible into the English language by John Wyclif in 1382, they had penetrated into folk belief. Thus, the opening verse of Psalms 91–'He who dwells in the shelter of the Most High, in the care of the God of heaven'–was a favorite inscription for a protective amulet.[3]

2. A. A. Anderson, *Psalms* II, New Century Bible. 535.

3. Holladay, *The Psalms through Three Thousand Years*, 184. cf. Seybold, *Introducing the Psalms*. The various usages of Psalm 91 and its myriad applications: amulets, necklaces, rings, and other jewelry were not uncommon in ancient Israel. "Even the Biblical Psalms were not immune to being drawn into the ideas and practices of magic. There are signs that Ps. 91, or parts of it, was used at a very early stage for the deterring of demons. A small fragmentary scroll found at Qumran (11QPsAp) contained, alongside apocryphal texts, Ps. 91. Use as a charm is likely." 213.

It is the singular purpose of Psalm 91 to encourage and promote confidence in and true obedience to יהוה whose *presence* is assured to the trusting heart. The early hymnists, composers, instrumentalists, and poets of the rescue and refuge Psalms, like 46 and 91, for example, while extolling the nearness of God in Zion, understood that the *presence* of יהוה was not made manifest only to be limited to Zion, or Sinai, or Jerusalem, or even to the Temple alone. These psalms rather seek to offer, not explanations, but meaning. Concepts explain; images in poetry provide meaning. Many aspects of human life such as undeserved suffering or the mystery of grace are inexplicable. Their capacity to plumb the depths of human experience assists us in finding meaning in the present without living our lives in dread of the future. The elusive *presence* of יהוה ranged far and wide, extending over the whole earth and to peoples everywhere. It is this conviction that stirred the hearts of the early poets to face the risks anywhere and welcome the future anytime.

Psalm 92 is predominately a hymn of praise, though the praise is firmly rooted in a rescue from danger: *My eyes have seen the downfall of my enemies; my ears have heard the doom of evil assailants* (92:10,11, REB). It is linked to Psalm 91 by the title *Most High (elyon)* and points forward to the enthronement psalms (93, 96–99) by portraying יהוה defeating the wicked from on high: *For your enemies, O יהוה, for your enemies shall perish; all who do evil shall be scattered* (92:9, NRSV). The extended reflection in Psalm 90 has profound implications for reading the king's confession of mortality in Psalm 89:47–48. *Remember how short my time is–for what vanity you have created all mortals! Who can live and never see death? Who can escape the power of Sheol?* (REB). Indeed, it appears to be more than accidental when Psalm 89 speaks of God's wrath and anger being directed against his anointed. Now it is the righteous, God's servants, who must chafe and suffer under the stringent requirement of their moral constraints.[4]

In Psalm 90, Moses' prayer for God's mercy is based on the fact that Israel's repeated recalcitrance and disobedience has made her situation increasingly untenable because her life is entangled and enmeshed in the very life of יהוה. As a consequence of the covenant's demands she now stands naked before the holiness of God's *wrath and anger* and is fully exposed to these mortal restraints. This prayer seems to answer a prayer for the king who, as an individual, has experienced God's wrath because of his moral limitations. Based on this pairing of Psalms 90 and 91 and the way the theme of mortality plays out in them, it seems likely that the king is to be understood as a representative or a symbol of Israel in its suffering. When looking further at these

---

4. cf. Thomas Kruger, "Psalm 90 und die Verganglichkeit des Menschen," *Biblica* 75. Note: Kruger does not believe the psalm [90] is an explicit meditation on the frailty of human life. Rather, he suggests that because of the language used, the psalm reflects the poet attempting to make sense of the period of exile. The psalmist is acknowledging the desperate situation for humanity and is attempting to understand how humanity can once again experience the blessings which are only provided by יהוה. Israel in her debasement, in her loss, knew this to be true–that only יהוה could heal, restore, and redeem a lost people; that her plight could only be restored by a saving act of יהוה.

two psalms and others in close proximity, there seems little doubt that it is the heroic figure of David who has become not only a symbol of the monarchy but also a symbol for Israel as a nation under the sovereignty of Yhwh. David now bears the sins and the shame of the nation. It is David who models for us as well the inner attitude of the human heart in the face of human sin. Psalm 51, entitled a *Prayer of David*, addresses what is the appropriate response of human beings to the reality of sin. *I have sinned against* יהוה, declares David in II Samuel 12:13. *Have mercy on me, O God, in your goodness, in your great mercy wipe away all my sin; wash me clean of my guilt, and purify me from my sin* (Ps 51: 2, NRSV). This psalm at its heart is an openly honest acknowledgment of the hard reality of sin and the fact of its unavoidable and permanent effects. Sin and its tawdry aftermath must never be minimized, but it can be forgiven. This is David's hope and confidence just as it is ours. The punishment for sin exacts the terrible toll it takes on our own relationship with the holy One. It is this causality that infects our lives and reduces to naught our own schemes and plans rising out of our human hearts. In this manner as well, Psalm 90 lays particular stress on the apparent hopelessness and uselessness of human endeavor with the waning desire/belief that

> with God's blessing, there is something solid, lasting, and well-founded in human endeavor. Each of our lives is fleeting–and the greatness of the poem of Psalm 90 is that it never loses hold of this painful truth, even in the hopeful piety of the conclusion–but the works we perform, out of a proper awareness of our vulnerable mortality, can have substance [and] are our human measure of continuity and renewal from one generation to the next . . .[5]

There is something unique in this psalm, a rise and fall of praise and lament, of consideration and prayer, of melancholy and hope. If we want to grasp its meaning, we must follow it, word by word, feeling what the poet has felt, trying to see what he has seen, looking at our own life through his vision, as it is interpreted though his mighty words. These words come to us from the farthest past, yet they speak to our present existential situation and to every future. Later generations in Israel expressed their feeling for the incomparable power of this psalm by attributing it to Moses, whom they called "the man of God." Here the reality of the transitoriness and brevity of life lays siege to all our best laid plans. The poet of Psalm 90 insinuates that our perception and recognition of the reality of human sin is severely limited due to the fact that we can never on our own fully realize the fundamental relationship that exists between sin and mortality. *For we are consumed by your anger; by your wrath we are overwhelmed. You have set our iniquities before you, our secret sins in the light of your countenance* (90:7, 8 NRSV).

Because we all tend to live for the moment, our vision is nearly always blighted. We are largely unaware of the opposition that maintains between the divine and the human will. The widespread failure of the divine reality to produce an impression

5. Alter, *The Psalms: A Commentary*, 129.

upon us is surely the poet's aim. We are not even aware of God's wrath and thus we show no fear of God. From the human side of the linguistic equation, we use the words anger and wrath as though they were emotional declarations rather than, in point of fact, the theological predicament they represent. We can only speak anthropomorphically about the "wrath of God." This is the reality of the human condition and the existential dilemma it represents.

To make his words bring home to us the importance of the fact of יהוה, and to impress that reality upon our minds, the poet sees human sin and the pessimistic valuation of life as linked together. Drawing the ultimate conclusion from that attitude of mind, and carrying it so far that it leads to the complete negation of life, the poet executes with ruthless honesty the self-condemnation that sin exacts. The inner impossibility of such an attitude toward life is self-evident. But this is precisely the point to which we all must be brought if we are to become aware of the despair which such an attitude of mind entails. However, although sin is the harsh assessment of the human situation, thank God it is not the final word.

To pay attention to the eternal reality is in some sense to transcend evanescent life. This perspective on eternity is thus able to impart to human life lasting purpose and value. There is no other way to a genuine faith than the one which continually compels us to acknowledge the harsh reality and the awful and costly implications of sin to a humanity gone astray. The sincerity to abandon all hope in our own strength and cast ourselves wholly upon God's mercy marks the beginning of our journey into a living faith and a resilient trust. The way of ancient Israel's journey of faith was paved with mercy. It was certainly David's way, and it is our way today. That we continue to live under this mercy is all grace!

Just as the Moses hymn declares in its opening, *Lord, our dwelling place in all generations*, so does Psalm 91 begin with an existential and cosmic certitude: *The one who dwells in the secret place of Elyon, passing the night within the shadow of Shaddai speaks: 'I will say of יהוה, you are my refuge and my bulwark, Elohay (my God) in whom I put my trust'(LW)*. Alexander Ryrie has noted how Psalm 92 closes a Mosaic introduction to *Book IV* and thus builds on and confirms that the promises of Psalm 91 are not empty. In 91:14, יהוה states, *I will protect those who know my name*. Psalm 92 makes clear immediately at the outset that the psalmist knows יהוה by name.[6]

The primary purpose of Psalm 92 then, is to provide an answer to the problem of the deliverance of the suffering righteous from the apparent triumphal escapades of the faithless. The deliverance of the righteous out of the clutches of evil and destruction is a prevalent theme of protection; of the salvation of the poets throughout the Psalter. In this way the recasting and reshaping of Israel's faith-salvation stories are an important motif equally relevant for people of faith today. Although faith must be grounded in certain tenets that do not disappear when challenged, faith is never a static adherence to the past. Rather, it responds to new circumstances by applying

6. Ryrie, *Deliver Us from Evil: Reading the Psalms as Poetry*, 93.

adhered to beliefs in new and fresh ways. As *Books IV* and *V* of the Psalter make clear, exile, with the loss of the land, temple, and the Davidic monarchy, did not nullify these concrete expressions of faith. But it required a different view of them than Israel had before the trauma of 587 BCE. For Christians, this restatement of faith should seem quite familiar. After all, the church has participated directly in the fresh appropriations of traditional beliefs. The monarchy that was lost in the Babylonian defeat was recast as a future hope. So the church found fulfillment of that hope in Jesus of Nazareth as the risen Christ of faith. In other words, the Christian faith is the direct heir of this shift in thinking and its formulations in the early Christian scriptures are, for Christians, retrospectively apparent in the continuing hope that appears in *Books IV* and *V*. Karl Barth maintains that the Christian church

> is *the new Israel of God. In contrast with the Gospel of Jesus Christ, there is thrust upon our attention–Israel, the Church, the world of religion as it appears in history, and, we hasten to add, Israel in its purest, truest, and most powerful aspect. We are not here concerned with some . . .form of religion, but with the ideal and perfect Church . . . the Church confronts the Gospel as the last human possibility confronts the impossible possibility of God. The abyss which is here disclosed is like to none other.*[7]

For all their power to speak with emotional immediacy to seekers down through the centuries the Psalms remain rooted in an ancient Near Eastern world that straddles Late Bronze Age II and Early Iron Age I. We today are so far removed—culturally, linguistically, historically, religiously—that at first glance these affirmations of the ancient faith may appear utterly, strangely naive. This is not to be wondered at in view of the great distance that separates us from them and their world. Indeed, we are looking over thirty-three centuries into the past, sifting through the encrustation of traditions that have been edited repeatedly over the intervening era. In certain respects, the Psalms remain quite alien and inaccessible to modern people who frequently may be put off by the pleas and pleadings of the poets, particularly in the psalms of lament or complaint. The laments and complaints of the Psalms often serve as an affront to modern ears and this reaction may even be heard expressed in today's church!

> When we want to 'feel good about ourselves' (which I have actually heard seriously proposed as the purpose of worship), when we've gone to the trouble to 'get a life,' current slang suggesting that life is a commodity, how can we say, with the psalmist, 'I am poor and needy' (Ps 40:17) or 'my life is but a breath' (Ps. 39:5)? It all seems so damned negative, even if it's true.[8]

While it is true there is a great deal in the Psalter that remains difficult and obscure for us there are yet a sufficiently high number of these poems and hymns that

---

7. Karl Barth, *The Epistle to the Romans.* 332.

8. Norris, *The Psalms with Commentary*, 103.

remain intimate, timeless. It is the psalms of trust where their *sitz im leben* in times of anxiety is more fully framed. As prayers against fear and despair, they are texts of hope, not the expressions of false self-assurance and certainty of salvation.

The thoughts of the poet take up the theme of trust in God, the keynote of Psalms 90–92. The ancients knew instinctively that exercising trust is hard work. For this reason, it would be a mistake to presume these psalms are permeated with the spirit of utter hopelessness. The poets do not indicate how they conceive of that hope in practice. But the confidence with which they direct their petitions to יהוה in the face of the futility of human affairs implies that, in view of the transitoriness of life, they seek and find permanent support in יהוה. It is precisely the limits of mortality which are placed upon humanity that are ordained by God. These limits become the gateway to our eventual redemption. God only desires for us what is best for us.

It is this transitoriness that becomes the point at which the poet realizes that it is יהוה who shows him the way to the true understanding and meaning of life. As a unity of prayer, poetry, and song, each of these psalms belong to a world which is no longer our world. We will never fully understand or decipher much of that world; it is foreign and so removed from us by distance, ethos, and time. Although their remoteness from us may be daunting, these obstacles are not completely insurmountable. It is all the more amazing that despite their distance *from* us, they can still speak directly *to* us without explanation or equivocation. They can be repeated by us again and again for the Psalms are words *from* worship, they are mostly the words *of* worship, and they are the particular words to be used *in* worship. For thousands of years and up to the diversity of our modern world, these particular songs of the heart have been able to lead people into the heart of true religion—the actual practice of communion with God in God's *presence*.

> *Preserving as it does a selection of [at least] 700 years of psalmody, such an anthology is bound to reflect a wide diversity of styles and attitudes. This diversity helps to explain why the Psalms are the only book of spirituality that has remained common to the entire spectrum of Jewry and Christendom, from Hassidic rabbis and Mt. Athos monks to American Quakers and the Salvation Army . . . the Psalms constitute far more than a manual of devotion . . . They produce fields of force which maintain on the one hand the tension and ease of an equilibrium between emotional contemplation within the confines of cultic space, and ethical passion for the world outside, on the other. Such an equilibrium led the psalmists to transcend racial and ritual particularity in spite of the fact that the shelter of a shrine, the enjoyment of a closed brotherhood, and the delights of liturgical aesthetics might have led them to indulge in a socially irresponsible pietism.[9]*

The form-critical method that is used in accessing the Psalms first came into prominence during the past century and existed largely for the purpose of ordering

9. Terrien, *The Psalms,* 278, 279.

the Psalter for research and study. It produced significant results in pursuit of the critical understanding of the origins, development, and formation of the Psalter. Today, Psalms studies are in a state of flux, but there is an increased emphasis on their literary content and the shaping of the collection itself; there seems to be a renewed focus on the role they play in the edification of faith development and spiritual formation and maturity.

In the face of human anxieties and the existential struggle for wholeness of being, the laments emerged from many and various stages of Israel's liturgical and historical life settings. These are the same human struggles that have played out over the centuries. Although the exact setting, type, and genre of the individual psalms will always remain largely unknown to us, what still speaks to us today is their sheer force when we directly confront the truth of their declarations. In a very real sense then, the psalms of trust challenge us with the will to believe; to the acknowledgment that יהוה is worthy of our uncompromising trust and confidence; that in יהוה is incomparable blessing and in whom rests our eternal surety. What יהוה desires for us is, ultimately, unimaginable!

The point is that within the range of the lament forms they have always sought to serve a higher purpose. The faithful will not be disappointed by the power inherent in these poems; to seek after truth and find trust and confidence in God has its own rewards.[10] What the poets demonstrate is that the psalmists of ancient Israel were committed to a profound level of trust in יהוה confident that this trusting faith would be rewarded by the *presence* of יהוה in the midst of life. Our access to their message and meaning can reveal to us spiritual insights that may only be gleaned from a distance. John Goldingay underscores how each of the psalms has its own uniqueness, validity, and relevance for our time and can be heard anew in every age. They possess this quality of timelessness which resonates with contemporary seekers. It is fundamentally accurate to say that the Psalter is, by far, the Bible's most introspective book.

> *Faithfulness needs to be a matter of the heart and thus the actions of the hands, not merely a matter of our words, for it is the heart that generates schemes against other people. Likewise, the heart needs to be the locus of trust within us, otherwise we become embittered. These are demanding expectations, and the pressures of life may mean that we come to the end of our hearts' resources; but even this need not be catastrophic, because when our hearts come to an end, God is still its place of refuge.*[11]

The psalms probe the interior landscape of the human heart and can rightly be called *Theo-poetry*,[12] because they continue to speak not about some partial aspect of life, but about faith in God as the foundation and meaning of all life. And at the heart

10. Eaton, *Kingship and the Psalms*, 72.
11. Goldingay, *Psalms 2*. 418.
12. cf. Cas J. A. Vos, *Theopoetry of the Psalms*.

of the matter there is always יהוה! To live in the proximity of the divine *presence is* all that is needed.

The faith and the trust of the ancient poets are acknowledged in the earliest centuries of the Christian church in its struggles to come to terms with and to harmonize the practice of prayer with the understanding of a wise and sovereign God. The Christian view of prayer acknowledges the affinities between the church's practice and prayer as a general religious phenomenon. It learned from the Hebrew Psalms (and especially from the Lord's Prayer) how to transcend sorcery, magic and fatalism.[13] The God who created humankind with free will is also sovereign over the supra-spiritual world and the natural order. This confidence, even in our contemporary world, connects us to our ancient spiritual ancestors in faith. With them and with the guidance of their life experiences in trusting this particular God, we too may possess an attitude of the heart–when facing human life in all its complexity–which is one of trusting faithfulness. The ancient poets of the Psalms surrender to the divine will and model this for us.

Psalm 91 as an individual poem of trust, comes to us from a particular cultural, historical, and religious milieu. Yet its capacity to connect with us at the level of our own soul's struggles can be profoundly stirring and heartening. Time and distance may be transcended by prayer and meditation in trusting יהוה in every conflict and struggle of life. This is particularly true of the psalms of trust for there is something else at work in the interface between the reader and the poet. The faithful person turns to prayer and also witnesses to the good way where there is awe of God, turning from sin, stillness and meditation, and worship that finds and holds onto God. In such trust the psalmist concludes, confident that יהוה will fill the heart again with rejoicing and make peace known in the midst of danger. These actions are then rooted within the willing and compliant hearts of the faithful.

The Psalter demonstrates a directness in speaking to God which we in the modern era largely have lost. Its prevailing climate is not that of a moderate, pious sameness, but a contrast of intensity–of hot and cold; the lament that vibrates with pathos, exchanges with a charged and jubilant praise. Behind the quiet words of trust one can still hear the raging of the powers with which this trust is confronted. There is a realism about the Psalms that should resonate with a generation which, with considerable justification, accuses the church of turning a blind eye to the actualities of human life and failing to reconcile the actual discrepancies between human experience and an active faith. Roland Murphy notes, *The Psalter comes face to face with human experience and does not shrink from verbalizing it and relating it to a kaleidoscope of divine truth. Anyone who is repelled by the idea of complaining to God should rethink the meaning of faith, which is not stoicism.*[14]

---

13. Pelikan, *The Christian Tradition*, 39, 40.
14. Murphy, "The Faith of the Psalmist," 231.

The measure by which we may find the blatancy of the laments embarrassing is the measure by which we each must judge our own openness to life. Psalm 73 keeps surfacing because, for example, it functions as an accurate barometer of human experience. Psalm 73 is an account of faith under fire.

> "... the reperception, resignification, and redescription of faith voiced in Psalm 73 are accomplished through the reality of solidarity, presence, and communion ... Clearly the culmination of Psalm 73 presents faith now prepared for the lyrical self-abandonment of praise. This one psalm is a powerful paradigm for Israel's often-enacted journey from obedience through trouble to praise. The speaker has traversed, as Israel regularly traverses, the path from obedience to praise, by way of protest, candor and communion.[15]

Its movement is from lament to confidence. In this manner it speaks to our contemporary needs.[16] Whatever a person's lot, he or she can read a group of psalms and be reinvigorated in order to continue the quest to find a route to God. In our seeking and searching, יהוה is nearer us than we are to ourselves. Because the Psalms are first and foremost theological poetry, there are many things about how that poetry functioned in ancient cultures that we simply cannot access today. In a beautifully written essay, Beth Tanner writes:

> ... part of this new theological landscape is to admit where our knowledge is less than we would hope. Chances are we will never recover how the Psalms were used in the cult, and if that is true, then we can certainly know even less about how the poetry formed the society as a whole and the faith and worship life of individuals. We must be willing to say there are things that we do not understand about the interaction of this poetry and our ancient ancestors, and there are also parts of the Psalms where meaning is as elusive as a puff of smoke.[17]

To be sure, each of the ancient poets had their own individual perspectives to draw upon and sought to articulate their personal experiences of trust and confidence

15. Brueggemann, "Bounded by Obedience and Praise," 71.

16. Broyles, *Psalms*. "This psalm [73] is a favorite for many because it rings so true to our feelings and experience. Many of us have felt disappointed in God. When we feel life has treated us unfairly, we often betray our belief in the sovereignty of God by blaming and abandoning [him]! The psalm confesses what we are afraid to admit, and so helps us to be honest before God about life's temptations and our readiness to sell out. The psalm's first half is largely negative (vv.1–14) and the second half largely positive (vv. 15–28). Marking this pivot is the beginning of direct address to God ("your children," v.15). Key words (particularly evident in the Hb. Text) help to mark the sections and development of the psalm. This psalm is particularly about the heart (vv.1,7,13,21,26)." 299.

17. Tanner, "Rethinking the Enterprise," in *Soundings in the Theology of Psalms*, 144. Note: Actually, what is significant for the psalm's structure is the change from lament to a declaration of confidence. Compare Psalm 4 and hence Psalm 73 which may be designated as a psalm of trust. But in contrast to Psalm 23, the avowal of trust motif is here not expanded to form an entire psalm. The point is rather that the progression from lament to the declaration of confidence is pictured exclusively in terms of the contrast between the godless and the faithful. This contrast governs the whole psalm and takes in fact the form of a meditation–the psalmist reflects on the contrast.

in יהוה. The psalms of confidence are only found within the laments of the Psalter. They are unique to its corpus. If the thanksgiving is connected to the lament, in that it speaks of an earlier deliverance, the psalm of confidence is an even more intrinsic part of the lament because it speaks of trust in spite of all appearances–a confidence within the present uncertainties for those who are caught in the nexus between faith and experience. In Psalm 91 the poet's close, intimate bond with יהוה is spelled out in striking images affirming his existence and is grounded in the grace of יהוה. Only from יהוה comes *the cup of salvation* (116.13). The poet understands his destiny: all that makes up life is completely in the hands of יהוה to give and to shape. The gift is יהוה. None other is needed. The common basis of all the psalms is a constant, total and exclusive trust in the God of Israel. [18]

The Psalter is a kind of constellation of praise, prayer, and pedagogy or instruction (Torah), the fundamental elements of religion in which authentic faith comes to expression. Religion is essentially the praise *of* God, prayer *to* God and the practice of a life of trust and obedience *before* God. [19] Psalm 91 remains relevant to seekers and inquirers in every age. Only someone who in time of danger had trusted God, and was rescued, could have uttered such bold and challenging instruction. Together with Psalm 46, Psalm 91 comprises the most impressive witness in the Psalter to the strength that springs from trust in יהוה alone. When the soul is the still center of the individual suppliant, there is the soul at rest.

> In *the midst of it all the psalmist finds a stillness toward God. Before the almighty Lord, his soul is a still centre. And the meaning of this silence of the spirit is trust–profound and decisive acknowledgment that power belongs to God, and in [Him] alone is salvation; [He] is faithful, and the source of all true hope. Perhaps it is on the way toward this stillness that wavering people are counseled to 'pour out' their heart before God. As they lay all their fears and doubts at [His] feet, they too will be granted that stillness which is the best prayer for the mighty deeds of the Saviour.*[20]

Dwelling in the hiding-place of God is meant to express the safety and peace of mind that come from a sense of protection against persecution; staying overnight in the shadow of the Almighty expresses that feeling of being out of danger for someone else keeps watch. This latter picture derives from the ancient custom of the right to hospitality accorded to the guest, sojourning in the shadow of the hospitable house, and entrusted to the protection of the host.

In this connection the poet intentionally uses the ancient divine names, עליון and שדי (*Most High* and *Almighty*). Originating in the pre-Israelite phase of religion and conferred upon יהוה in the First Testament, these names are intended to impress,

18. Tate, "The Interpretation of the Psalms," 459.

19. Mays, Psalms: *Interpretation,* 3.

20. Eaton, *The Psalms: A Historical and Spiritual Commentary,* 234.

by their venerable sound, the transcendent power of God. It is quite impossible to compare the protection which יהוה is able to grant with what others may look for in other patron gods or in other places of refuge. The singular comprehensiveness and depth of the trust placed in this God of the Patriarchs is based on the fact that the supreme God, whose name one dares utter only with awe and trembling, is precisely the One whom the individual may call *my God*, as if God existed for her/his sake alone. Thus the God fearing person is being lifted out of [her] desultory environment by a personal confession of trust in יהוה. This personal confession presumes a particular stance toward life which recognizes that what is involved in trusting יהוה is a *"long obedience in the same direction."* Psalm 85, an Elohistic composition, is a communal prayer and lament for deliverance by God.

Psalm 85

To the leader. Of Korah. A psalm

יהוה, once you were favorable to your land
and restored the fortunes of Jacob,
you forgave the guilt of your people
and pardoned all their sins.

You averted all your wrath
and turned away from your hot rage.
Restore us again, O God our helper!
Put an end to your indignation toward us.

Will your anger burn hot against us forever?
Will your anger never cease?
Will you not revive our lives again
so that your people may rejoice in you?

Show us your constant love, O יהוה
and give us your saving help again.
Let me hear what God, יהוה will speak,
a voice that speaks of peace and friendship,
peace to the faithful, to those who turn to God in their hearts;

Salvation is near at hand for those who fear God,
that the glory of God may dwell in our land.
Constant love and mercy will meet;

justice and peace will kiss each other.

Faithfulness shall spring forth from the earth
and justice will look down from the sky.
יהוה will give what is good
and the whole earth will yield its increase,
Justice will go before her
and peace shall follow in her train.

This psalm exudes promise and fulfillment. For the poet of Psalm 85, life is now reoriented in a new relationship imparting to one's whole existence a special character. *Salvation is near at hand for those who fear God, that the glory of God may dwell in our land* (85:9, REB). Here are deep wells of faith and confidence that issue forth from the poet's confidence in God's capacity to deliver salvation. Without hesitation or doubt the psalmist declares that God comes to the aid of those who choose to dwell within the sheltering arms of יהוה. Just as Israel was protected in her wilderness journey to Zion, so will those who love יהוה be protected and accompanied in their journey through life.

Each of these challenges so common to human life and experience is articulated with a no-holds barred approach to the more crushing realities of human life. When one surrenders and submits to the divine will one may experience the blessing of יהוה in strangely disguised forms: serenity, not necessarily success; security, not necessarily prosperity; safety, not necessarily comfort. The One upon whom we are called to rely in the midst of the gritty and untidy messiness of life promises to be our intimate, watchful companion on the immense journey. The promises of יהוה to ancient Israel, to dwell with them, abide with them, and share their life, are staggering in their implications. Very simply, dwelling in the *presence* of יהוה is the highest good.

> *The [righteous] enjoy success and fruitfulness even in old age . . . this statement [v.15] showing that Yhwh is upright; Yhwh is my rock, and there is no unrighteousness in [him] continues the prominent idea of Pss 90:10 and 91:16 and is perhaps part of the motivation for the placement of these three psalms; each psalm deals with the brevity of human existence and the reward of extended life and security for those who recognize YHWH as the only source of refuge.*[21]

The trusting souls who place their lives in the hands of יהוה and surrender their wills to the divine will, plea mercy in the midst of a heartlessly merciless world. The essence of the faith of Israel is reflected throughout the various psalms collections. This faith tradition still has the power to reveal to twenty first century seekers that which remains common to us all; our most difficult conflicts; our deepest aspirations and longings; our shared human experience of the stinging lash of loss, pain and grief; our fears and abandonment, sorrows and yes, our sadness. But all these very human

---

21. Creach, *The Destiny of the Righteous in the Psalms*, 95. Eaton, *The Kingship and the Psalms*, 234.

situations are clearly in the horizon of the poet of Psalm 85 who is not untouched by the feelings of our infirmities but rather is captured by an awareness that sorrow and sadness, pain and grief and loss will not have the final word. Indeed, his focus is on God. *Where there is genuine struggle over truth that does not result in war, God's salvation is on its way. When the passion of steadfast love is kindled, yet fidelity is not forgotten. God's salvation is on its way. When people fight for justice without leaving mercy in the dust, God's salvation is on its way.*[22]

> *If Psalm 90 and the Psalter as a whole are intended in part to respond to the crisis of exile and the failure of the Davidic covenant, then Psalm 90:1 is a particularly pertinent and powerful affirmation. God is really the only place that counts. The land is not indispensable, the temple is not indispensable, [the monarchy is not indispensable], because God is our dwelling place. In short, God is the only necessity for the life of God's people and the life of the world.*[23]

The poets invite the person who longs to dwell in God's *presence* to take refuge in יהוה and receive promised protection from all danger. Here is a God unlike any other. The common basis of each of the psalms of confidence is a constant, total and exclusive trust in the only God we need. This trust is particularly pronounced in Psalm 91. *Because you have made יהוה your refuge, and elyon (Most High) your dwelling place, no evil shall befall you, no scourge come near your tent* (91:9, 10 Dahood).

The totality of blessing for the person of faith is vouchsafed in this promised intimacy amid the persistence of a nurturing companionship throughout life. The divine *presence* is always elusive and it lies at the heart of the psalm's sphere of reality. All this imparts to the whole psalm a lively inner rhythm and gives us an inkling of the active interest which the poet himself takes in what he has got to say about trust in יהוה. Indeed, this is the crux of biblical faith. The life of faith, such as it is, is life lived on the border of the holy.[24] It is life beyond the parameters of presumed safety, comfort and ease. It is life lived on the liminal boundary of the far frontier. It is life lived on the edge of glory. Living on the boundary is to be self-forgetful, trusting, and open to the experience of יהוה as [he] moves us toward wholeness. Artur Weiser describes how a genuine faith in יהוה

> *reaches its ultimate soaring height, leaving behind in its bold flight every doubt which a sober and realistic valuation of the situation might raise. What, humanly speaking, is quite improbable and indeed almost impossible, is within the reach of faith; this is the divine miracle. Such a faith sees only the God who saves; all else sinks into oblivion.*[25]

---

22. Hossfeld and Zenger, *A Commentary on Psalms 51–100*, 367.

23. McCann Jr., *Psalm 73*, 156.

24. Countryman, *Living on the Border of the Holy*, 78.

25. Weiser, *The Psalms*, 119.

Practiced obedience is a very tough slog for us because faith by its very nature seems to require the impossible. Yet a practiced faith can and does inspire and build confidence in trusting God. This realization is the beginning of our maturity in the life of faith. It is by this enlargement of faith that our psalmist encourages his readers. What is remarkable about ancient Israel's psalmic traditions is the stubborn maintenance of that most ubiquitous Hebrew conviction: trust and confidence in יהוה. In the middle of chaos, suffering, and under the sentence of death, life is chosen.

This is the theme of Psalm 76, a song of Zion, where God 's actions display all might and power and crush all resistance. It is first and foremost a song of salvation and deliverance. This theme of salvation is particularly prevalent, and poignant in the Elohistic Psalter. For if it was indeed a liturgy hymn of eighth-century BCE Israel of the north, before the Assyrian disaster of 721 BCE, then its identity of Judah at the outset is a *closing image of the composition, with YHWH as the 'guardian lion' from and on Zion.*[26]

Psalm 76

To the leader. Do Not Destroy. A psalm of Asaph. A song

In Judah God is known;
In Israel God's name is great.
You set up your abode in Salem (Jerusalem),
your place of dwelling in Zion.

It was there you broke the flashing arrows,
the shield, the sword, the weapons of war.
You, יהוה, are glorious,
more resplendent than the everlasting mountains.
Stouthearted warriors were stripped of their booty;
they slept the sleep of death–none was able to lift a hand.

At your rebuke, O God of Jacob,
both horse and rider lay stunned.
But you alone are awesome!
Who shall stand before you when your anger is roused?

From the heavens you uttered your judgment;
the earth in terror was stilled
when God arose to judge

26. Hossfeld-Zenger, "Psalms 2," 271.

to save all the inhabitants of the earth.

Human wrath will serve only to praise you;

those who survive it rejoice in you.

Make vows to יהוה your God, and fulfill them.

Let all pay tribute to the one who strikes fear,

who cuts off the spirit of princes,

who strikes terror in the rulers of the earth.

Psalm 76 is focused on God's abode and place of powerful activity, which the poets know as Zion. The destruction of the weapons of war is associated with the divine activity from Zion. The weapons of war are are then matched by rendering the elite warriors powerless before the judgment of God. It is in this psalm of Asaph where we witness the act of divine judgment against oppression and injustice and all is tempered by God's constant, uninterrupted love and compassion.

In the Hebrew scriptures, God's wrath is a dimension of God's righteousness and justice that is directed against the faithless and the evildoers. But even God's judgement and correction are always tempered by God's love and compassion. *For a brief moment I abandoned you, but with great compassion I will gather you. In overflowing wrath for a moment I hid my face from you, but with everlasting love I will have compassion on you, says* יהוה, *your Redeemer* (Isaiah 54:7, 8, REB). The entire community is exhorted to praise the God of Israel who does what the poem has declared so vividly. Obediently, the poet makes his personal vow to God and pays the willing tribute of his heart in thanksgiving for the goodness of salvation that has been procured on his behalf. Such are the benefits of a sustained obedience wherein all the saving benefits may accrue to the faithful. It is this experience of God that we need; for which our souls long.

> To say 'God is good' can be a routine statement. Such a statement of 'orientation' can be one made in untested, rather unthinking and shallow faith. But in this context it is more than routine. The conviction is one that has been sharply tested by what the suppliant can see going on in the community. Here it is uttered as a statement of 'renewed orientation' after an experience of 'disorientation' such as the one the psalm will recount, and it thus gains a new depth. With spiritual bravery, the Midrash goes as far as to count the afflictions of which the psalm speaks as themselves gifts of God's goodness. They are good because they contribute to the purifying of the heart.[27]

In these psalms we are invited to participate in this ancient model of obedience: its substance, its formation, and its practice. Like our spiritual ancestors we seek to trust God in the midst of suffering in order to find the strength not to be overwhelmed

27. Goldingay, "The Dynamic Cycle of Praise and Prayer and Psalms," 401.

by our grief. We seek to trust God in order to find, if not answers, then at least some comfort and strength in enduring our suffering with faith. When it comes to the Christian epistles, suffering is openly embraced as a necessary corrollary to the life of obedience and faithfulness. For instance, the difference between St. Paul's understanding of faith, writes Johannes Weiss,

> and the religion of Abraham and Judaism is that Paul no longer awaits the ful-fillment of further outstanding prophecies, but proceeds upon completed facts; therefore, he distinguishes between the concept of faith and that of hope; he turns backward and relates himself essentially to the past and the present.[28]

It is in this tension of a practiced and long obedience in response to the demands of faith that one grows and matures in confidence and trust. The compensations of obedience are a constant theme of the Elohist psalmists. No rewards are greater than those which come from doing the will of God. We find a way out of no-way. That way is the way of trusting faith and joyful obedience to the call of יהוה in the midst of our lives. Like the psalmists, we seek to trust God in order to find the courage to stand up against those who would crush us—in every generation. All these—strength, comfort, courage—have been considered valid reasons to seek hard after God.[29] Some of the sharpest accusations against God occur in the praise of God. It is praise that clings fast to God and continues to seek after God at a time when everything seems to speak against God. Suffering, injustice and oppression are the culprits of the poets as well for *there is in the Psalms no quick and easy resignation to suffering . . . in the deepest hopelessness God alone remains the one addressed to do battle against God for God.*[30]

It is no incidental fact then, that in Psalm 91, *the last word belongs to Yahweh, and the last word is caring protection. It is the ground for confidence that the last word is not spoken by us, but to us.*[31] As Bonhoeffer avers in an Advent homily, *it is a grace to know God's commands. They release us from self-made plans and conflicts. They make our steps certain and our way joyful.* Bonhoeffer lays a fundamental stress on the grace that seems to grasp the poets' resilient convictions. Throughout the Psalter our poets lay claim boldly to the eternal promises of יהוה and never let go! They balance their lives, indeed their entire existence is utterly dependent on this fulcrum of mercy that they have found, experienced in their daily lives, and then submitted to trusting all their ways to יהוה.

---

28. Weiss, *Earliest Christianity,* Vol. II, 425.

29. Pleins, *The Psalms,* 43. cf. Sarna, *Songs of the Heart,* 90.

30. Hossfeld and Zenger, "Psalms 2," 11. cf. Bonhoeffer, *Psalms: The Prayer Book of the Bible.*

31. Brueggemann, *The Message of the Psalms,* 127.

Counter-Witness and Ambiguity

PART OF THE INTENDED legacy of this ancient poetry-prayer-praise-hymn book is that it is to be prayed, not simply read; meditated on, not merely sung. The Psalter is certainly central to the discipline of the monastic communities. It remains at the liturgical heart of the daily rounds of the offices based on the breviaries; and so, the Psalter is continually to be *ruminated on and interiorized*. The Psalms do what all good poetry does: they address the heart of the matter—the hungering, aching, longing and oft times broken heart. The children of God may experience a kind of living death amid the alienation and vexations of life in God's world. This poet in our next psalm, pours out his soul in his appeal to יהוה to hear and assist.

How my soul is so filled with troubles, and my life draws near to Sheol. I am counted among those who go down to the Pit; I am like those who have no help, like the forgotten among the dead, like the fallen that lie in the grave, like those whom you [Yhwh] have forgotten, lost and cut off from your care (Ps 88:3–5 REB).

Suffering in life for the ancient Hebrews, may be described metaphorically as a struggle over death in the midst of life. *The cords of death entangled me; the torrents of destruction overwhelmed me. The cords of the grave coiled around me; the snares of death gripped me* (18:4–5 REB). Notice the verbs, *entangled, overwhelmed, coiled,* and *gripped*; such are the pictures and descriptions of the full blown despair and despondency of an anxiety ridden soul in turmoil. It is nowhere described more graphically than in these cries of desolation and isolation, depression and despair. The genius of the various psalms of lament is that amid the cries of anguish and the feelings of rejection, confidence in יהוה is still affirmed. When a poem of lament openly despairs of the absence of יהוה, there is yet purpose. [1]

For instance, who can meditate on Psalm 88, the achingly saddest psalm in the entire Psalter and the most desolating of all the laments and not be deeply moved? It is *extremely enigmatic and darkly uttered* (Eusebius). Its first word is יהוה, the name God gave specifically for invocation, and its last word is *darkness*. Here the poet's

---

1. Futato, *Interpreting the Psalms: An Exegetical Handbook.* "While the songs of confidence have no unifying structural shape, several characteristics nonetheless hold this category together. As the name indicates, the distinguishing characteristic of this category is their unwavering confidence or trust in God's ability and willingness to deliver from adverse circumstances." 161.

confidence in the efficacy of prayer is severely tested. It emerges rather weakly out of a poem saturated with thoughts of abandonment, affliction and darkest despair.

> But I, O יהוה, *cry out to you; in the morning my prayer comes before you. But why do you cast me out,* יהוה*? Why do you hide your presence from me? I am miserable and have been close to death since my youth; I suffer your terrors and I live in desperation. Your anger sweeps over me and your assaults threaten my destruction* (88:13–16 LW).

The Korahite collection consists of songs originating in the north and these are particularly bound up in expressions of God as refuge and salvation. Indeed, this psalm begins: O יהוה *God of my salvation, at night I cry out in your presence, let my prayer come into your presence, turn your ear to my cry* (88:1, 2 NRSV). It is believed that this psalm, Psalm 88, originated in the early eighth century BCE near the ancient sanctuary of Dan in the far north of Israel. This psalm may have gone through numerous iterations over many centuries, as the multiple superscriptions seem to imply. The poet of this psalm is in particular anguish and we might suggest in the 21st century view of things, a severe depression or psychosis. It is essential to recognize from the outset that Psalm 88

> is a carefully composed, highly poetic text, usually interpreted as a 'psalm in sickness' or as the 'desperate prayer of someone deathly ill,' or as the lament of someone mortally ill, with a strongly reflexive impact, its Sitz im Leben the banality of the sickbed. To understand the psalm correctly one must therefore be aware . . . of the situation of seriously ill persons at that time, and the religious attitude the society of the period expected of those deathly ill [2]

That it was collected and included in the psalmic materials bears an essential witness to the raw honesty and integrity of the broader text. In this psalm there is no apparent resolution to the issue of human pain and suffering. All appears lost. The poet is isolated, alone and wishes for death. Worst of all, יהוה is not responding. The poet begins his lament with the formula of trust. He appeals to the *presence* of Yhwh: "*turn your ear to my cry!*" This is most assuredly the view from this poet's sickbed and it is painful to read his complaint and to feel his isolation.

Psalm 88

> *A Song. A Psalm of the Korahites.*
> *To the leader: according to Mahalath Leannoth.*
> *A maskil. Of Heman the Ezrahite*

> O יהוה God of my salvation
> at night I cry out in your presence,

---

2. Hossfeld-Zenger, "Psalms 2," 391.

TRUSTING YHWH

let my prayer come into your presence
turn your ear to my cry.

For my soul is filled with troubles,
my life is on the brink of the grave.
I am reckoned as among those who go down to the Pit;

Despairing, I have reached the end of my tether,
like those who are alone in the grave,
like the dead who lie in their graves,
like those whom you remember no more,
cut off, as they are, from your hand.

You have laid me in the regions of the tomb,
in places that are dark, in the depths.
Your anger lies heavy upon me,
I have gone under, overwhelmed by your waves.
You have stripped me of all my companions;
you have made me a thing of contempt to them.

I am in prison and cannot escape;
my eyes grow dim, sunken with grief.
O יהוה, every day I call out to you;
I spread out my hands to you.
Do you work your wonders for the dead?
Do the shadows rise up to praise you?
Does your saving help extend to the land of forgetfulness;
your fidelity in the place of nothingness?
Will your wonders be known in the dark
or your mercy in the land of oblivion?

As for me, O יהוה, I cry to you for help;
in the morning my cry comes before you.
O יהוה, why have you cast me out?
Why do you hide me from your presence?
I am wretched, close to death; since my youth
I have borne your terrors; I am desperate.

Your anger has swept over me;

your dread assaults have destroyed me utterly.

They surround me like a flood all day long;

from all sides they press in on me.

You have caused friend and neighbor to abhor me;

now my only companion is darkness.

Out of this bleakest and most agonizing description of human travail and distress, Psalm 88 offers to us truthful counter-witness about God's hiddenness, ambiguity, and negativity to Israel's core testimony about what is generally believed to be true of God over time. This ambiguity lies at the core of Israel's lament tradition:

> *God is the God of covenant, doxology, and presence. It takes a strong faith in God to keep talking to God, to keep up the dialog when one's orientation is disrupted and shattered and we are in despair. The confession of trust is so powerful in the lament that it reinforces this promise of the enduring faithfulness of Yhwh. In the midst of the suffering and the enemies, the psalmist asserts the whole basis of offering up the lament in the first place: God hears, cares, and acts. This is faith that knows what it is talking about. It is rather easy to profess trust in God when all is well. It is much more difficult and very painful to do so when the going gets tough and one finds oneself in the pit of disorientation.*[3]

Psalm 88 encapsulates an immense tradition of faith and experience and at once sets the suffering and the cry to heaven in the context of a relationship, a mutual knowledge that is stronger than any affliction.[4] It is in the lonely cries of the night of alienation and anxiety that the human soul may still cry out to God. To maintain the conversation in the bleakest of times may be the strongest witness we have to faith. This is certainly one of the rawest accounts of the anxiety of a despairing faith. It is rooted in the experience of that sense of complete and utter abandonment. The depths of despair are often endured most acutely by those who have at one time or another, tasted the goodness of God and the closeness of communion with God. When the *presence* of יהוה is absent, all life is at risk.

> *The psalmist is not saying that trust in God will allow one to easily escape terrible situations. What the psalmist is trying to do is to enable the worshiper to*

---

3. Dombrowski Hopkins, *Journey Through the Psalms*, 87.

4. Kirkpatrick, *The Book of Psalms*, writes: "The saddest psalm in the whole Psalter is a pathetic cry of hopeless despair . . . the last word is darkness." 189. cf. Brueggemann calls the psalm "an embarrassment to conventional faith." cf. Eaton, *Psalms: A Historical and Spiritual Commentary* "The psalm gives a voice to all who are in the depths of suffering, without light, unable to express hope, almost at the end of their strength. It leads them to direct their supplication—or it directs it for them–again and again to the Lord, the only Saviour. It is a voice also for those who, in loving sympathy, would pray on behalf of any in such extremity of suffering." 315.

remember God's active presence . . . when dangers threaten. To say that God is our refuge is to say more than God is our way of escape.[5]

This experience of adversity and disorientation is directed fundamentally to theocentric concerns, which are distinct from what we might call existential concern. It is this quest for authentic human engagement with the *elusive presence* of יהוה that makes the Psalter a truly holy book. Kathleen Norris, zeroing in like a laser on this fundamental characteristic of this psalm, describes how this

> *situation of human life before God is also what makes us squirm . . . for it plunges us into the world of the biblical imagination, which is not straightforward, quantifiable, logical, or particularly efficient. It is a narrative and poetic world, both simple and complex. It is ancient and new, both metaphorically and psychologically sophisticated, emotionally direct.*[6]

It is a truth to say that none of us can pray aright the psalms of complaint without first shedding our own self absorption and egocentricity. Our self-consciousness will be an impediment to taking on a new awareness between the awesome fears that shrink us and the unimaginable capacity for love that enlarges us; between the need for vigilance in the face of danger and the trust, beyond measure, that allows us to sleep the sleep of angels. A psalm of complaint, Psalm 88, written from the depths of an unrelenting despondency, can actually school us in the disciplines of prayer. Bonhoeffer, beyond peer in his teaching on prayer, provides us with an existential context for the soul that may find itself adrift in a sea of misery like so much flotsam bobbing about—aimlessly—in an angry ocean of meaningless and absurd suffering.

> *For if we are to pray these ancient psalms anyway like right, we must first ask how we can understand the Psalms as God's Word, and then we shall be able to pray them. It does not depend, therefore, on whether the Psalms express adequately that which we feel at a given moment in our heart. If we are to pray aright, perhaps it is quite necessary that we pray contrary to our own heart. Not what we want to pray is important, but what God wants us to pray.*[7]

The Psalms then are a sort of anthology of richest mean. The entire *book of books* serves to collect and catalog a whole host of human responses to the acts of God and to the words of God. Remember that there were vast stretches of time that

---

5. A. A. Anderson, Psalms 2, *New Century Bible*, suggests that the poet is like "one whose life is drawing near Sheol [and] is separated from God, although theoretically this separation is not yet absolute. There remains the possibility that God might decide to deliver the unfortunate [man] who is, for the time being, *like* the dead who can no more expect help from God, or who are cut off from God's hand. It may be true to say that Yahweh's power extended also to Sheol, but for some reason or other [he] did not wish to interfere with the existence of those in the underworld. This negative attitude may have been emphasized in order to break down the popular cult of the dead and necromancy." 626.

6. Norris, *The Psalms with Commentary*.

7. Bonhoeffer, *Psalms*.

passed when יהוה was not speaking at all! Revelation presumes a recipient or recipients who are being addressed by the word of יהוה ; when God is silent is a far more common reality than when God is disclosing or revealing aspects of truth that call forth a response on the part of the hearer. These are primarily the words of response and must be understood in this light. They inaugurate in the reader a disposition that, having heard the revelatory word, the hearer is persuaded to be open to seeking after the divine *presence.* The guiding initiation of revelation is, more often than not, an action that is presented directly to the human heart. Humans are always the subjects for the revealing of truth and how this truth will capture and then move the heart to respond in wonder and awe. But these peak experiences of a transcendent supra-reality, in the total scope of things, are exceedingly rare—although the Bible is full of them.

Indeed the Bible, and the book of Psalms in particular, are a compendium of revelation and revelatory occurrences that confront the reader full in the face. It is in this human phenomenon that persons are called upon to respond to the written and the spoken word, where true religion is made, or becomes, alive. This is why we refer to the scriptures as sacred, holy, or the word of the Lord. For by them, that is, in these particular words, the truth of God and God's world are made manifest. This is why the Bible is so important. It can transport us into the world of God—a world which is unlike any other.

> *The guiding counsel of God seems to me to be simply the divine Presence communicating itself direct to the pure in heart. [He] who is aware of this Presence acts in the changing situations of [his] life differently from[him] who does not perceive this Presence. The Presence acts as counsel: God counsels by making known that [He] is present. [He] has led [his] son out of darkness into the light, and now [he] can walk in the light. [He] is not relieved of taking and directing [his] own steps.*[8]

An individual psalm then, is never merely the isolated, anguished lament proceeding from the heart of one lonely poet–although Psalm 88 may be a possible exception. It is always preceded by something that proceeds from God. It is in these particular words and images that faith is born. What our psalmist desires is a life of intimate communion with God in the here and now, and the desire that can be echoed by all who repeat the psalm today. Many who use the words of the psalms as prayer will also envision that communion as continuing after the death of the earthly body. These anguished cries and ecstatic utterances are addressed to יהוה, and yet this *talking to* יהוה can, and frequently does, change abruptly over into *talking about* יהוה.

When יהוה prevails the people of God rejoice in their deliverance, even when that hoped for deliverance appears to be impossibly hopeless. This is a theological axiom of the book of Praises. Faith for the psalmist is not always quiet confidence. It may take

---

8. Buber, *Right and Wrong,* 46.

the form of a fury that rages against יהוה amid an anxiety that shudders in the divine *presence*; in an anguish that interrogates and cross-examines God.[9] *But I, O יהוה, cry out to you; in the morning my prayer rises before you. O יהוה, why do you cast me off? Why do you hide your face from me? Wretched and near death from my youth onward, I suffer your terrors; I am desperate (88: 13–15, LW).*

Because the book of Psalms is the whole book of a peoples' response to God's deeds and God's words, it must be understood in this light. When we encounter the world of the Psalter there is really nothing else quite like it anywhere in the Hebrew Bible. [10]The spiritual topography of these poems places us in uncharted territory. Here we engage compositions that are complex in their construction, compiled in varied collections that are both foreign and familiar. We are moved with the core conviction that human witness and daily experience demand a voice—our voice; that it be expressed with tears and shouts of praise and wonderment, joy and fury, rage and prayer, and stillness. The invitation is more explicitly extended to the godly ones who are in the land—the inheritors of the word of promise.

The psalmists' accounts of their experiences of the enduring, abiding fidelity of יהוה are an integral part of the conversation. These relationships are based upon the fidelity of יהוה and are a constituent part of what Westermann describes as *the charged exchange between God and [man] . . .consequently, the psalms cannot be fully comprehended by any of our modern terms. They are prayers and hymns at the same time, but they do not correspond exactly either to our hymns or to our prayers.*[11] These hymns and prayers are the basis of ancient Israel's faith, belief and theology. As stated before, they are first and foremost life-centered.

The poetry of the Hebrew Bible is always a response to life. In these responses of the poets there are no quick and easy resignations to suffering, grief, and loss. In their experiences of hopelessness and despair, God alone remains the one being addressed. It is within the crucible of lived experience that theological language needs the poetic medium for much of its expression. Poetry's powers of allusion remind us of the more hidden and mysterious truths which theology seeks to express. For instance, the variety of ways in which the experience of the *presence* or the perceived absence of יהוה are expressed, is more than equaled by the variety of moods and characteristics with which the silence before יהוה is invested. The God of Israel stands in a lively and vibrant personal relationship with the one who prays. That is the unequivocal accent of the Psalms. יהוה is the personal, knowable, communicative and faithful God.

---

9. Buber, *Idem.*

10. Westermann, *A Thousand Years and a Day.* ". . . the psalms belong to a world which is no longer our world, and we will never fully understand or appreciate much of that world . . . because of their remoteness they speak from that distance a language which possesses validity for every age and which can be heard anew in every age. The Psalms are inexhaustible." 11.

11. Westermann, *The Living Psalms*, 264.

The faithful person turns to prayer and also witnesses to the good way, where there is awe of God, turning from sin, stillness and meditation, worship that finds and holds to God, and above all, trusts in [him]. In such trust the psalmist concludes, confident that the Lord in [his] own time will fill the heart again with rejoicing, and make [his] peace known in every danger.[12]

The poets of יהוה—which is really to say, all Israel—are fully engaged in this conversational dialog that represents the human side of the holy encounter. The world of יהוה draws the Yahwistic theologians into an orbit of holiness and divine speech. This is especially noteworthy when considered alongside the fact that in ancient Israel, communal awareness generally prevailed over personal individuality. There is a discernible frankness, a counter-intuitive acceptance regarding the way of יהוה, even while there is an awareness and a willing admission of human sin. In an honest and open attentiveness to human frailty, despair and hope are always mixed in an alloy that is all together fully human. The conscientious reader of the Psalter will soon learn to grow and embrace these attitudes, which are not to be polarized.

Throughout the Psalms there is always this open acknowledgment of the reality of the *presence*—the holy nearness of יהוה; the poets are never reticent about human weakness and sinfulness, which can even be used as a motive to move יהוה to action. יהוה is the God of all that is holy. It is the theology of the poets toward which the people of יהוה are continually being drawn. The holy place is none other than the dwelling place of God; it is where יהוה tabernacles among [his] people. John Rogerson confirms that this special relationship is founded on the loving faithfulness that exists between God and [his] servant. This is the very basis of the psalmist's confidence. This is so because as the distinct people of יהוה they are being called to reject all hypocrisy and are encouraged to grow in devotion to all that is true. Faithful humility, hopeful patience, love, integrity and right-mindedness—these are the accents most characteristic of Hebraic spirituality. [13]

The symbols of the divine *presence*—especially the metaphor *fountain of life*—are closely drawn throughout the Psalter. Nothing in all of God's world is deemed more important than this promise of the everlasting nearness of יהוה to [his] people. This Hebraic *theology of presence* is fundamental, not only in the Hebrew scriptures, but it assumes paramount importance throughout the Psalter. At its root the whole idea of the *presence* of יהוה is represented by the Hebrew noun לפניך (*lepanim*, face/s), which is the face of יהוה, turned toward us in kindness, love, and grace.

Biblical Hebrew did not apparently possess an abstract word meaning 'presence.' The expression 'the face of Yahweh' or 'the face of Elohim' was sometimes specifically used to designate the innermost being of God, inaccessible even to a man like Moses, but the word panim, 'face' was ordinarily used metaphorically

---

12. Eaton, "Psalm 4," 72.
13. Rogerson, "Psalms 1–50," 27.

*in composite prepositions to designate a sense of immediate proximity. More of-
ten than not, the storytellers merely said that God 'appeared,' literally, showed
[himself']* [14]

It is this nearness of the *presence* of יהוה that is Israel's greatest consolation and
joy. This is true throughout her long and arduous history and it is this theme of the
intimacy, the nearness of יהוה that is ubiquitous throughout the Psalter. When one is
rightly aligned with the *presence* of יהוה there is no room for ambiguity. The experience
of the people of the holy is always enjoined in the relationship that exists between יהוה
and the people of יהוה. That experience nearly always turns out to be conversational.
In its laments and supplications, amid fear and awe, the Psalms constitute far more
than a manual of devotion. Like the poetic discourses of the prophetic tradition, they
represent theological thinking at its keenest. They mirror both the uniqueness and the
universality of the Hebraic *theology of presence.* That is to say, in the psalms the voice
of Israel is heard and through Israel's voice we hear the voice of God. These voices
must be distinguished and each received for what they are; but it is wrong to separate
them, and to try to hear the one without the other. For by the very fact that they are
both heard together, they bear witness to the *presence* of God amongst humanity, and
of the inviting word to humans to reside daily in and with God. The rewards of living
daily in the *presence* of God are of inestimable worth![15]

What ancient Israel feared most was that the voice of יהוה would go silent; that
יהוה would turn away; that the holy and attentive gaze would be averted; that the
divine *presence* would be withdrawn. So that the lonely poet cries out in desperation,
יהוה, *hear my prayer and let my cry for help come to you. Do not hide your face from
me when I am in dire straits* (Ps. 102:1, 2, LW). But the God who creates and acts is
also the God who may choose to remain silent and refuse to act when God's corrupt
people face defeat and the temple is reduced to ashes. God's silence informs the silence
of human trust. The perceived act of יהוה absenting [himself] remained Israel's persistent anxiety and her severest dread: *Has God's steadfast love ceased forever? Are God's
promises at an end for all time? Has God forgotten to be gracious? Has God's anger shut
up [his] compassion? I say, 'It is my grief that the right hand of Elyon (the Most High)
has changed'.* (77:8–10, NRSV).

In her praising and in her sinning, in her drawing nigh in refuge and in her
churlish rebellion, this was ancient Israel's predicament: the prospect of the abandonment by יהוה of the covenant people lies at the heart of Israel's angst. This fear of
the Lord is, paradoxically, the foundation of life, the key to joy in life and long and
happy days. But it is not a guarantee that life will be always easy, devoid of difficulties
that seem to mar so much of human existence.[16] So it is with the work of theological

14. Terrien, "Towards a New Theology of Presence," 65.

15. Jinkins, *In the House of the Lord,* 45. cf. Terrien, "Towards a New Theology of Presence," 78.

16. Craigie, Psalms 1–50, *Word Bible Commentary,* 145.

method in interpreting the ancient texts and the formation of a living faith. A living theology possesses vitality and always takes its stand on the boundary between the old and oft times austere systematic theology and the new, enlivened theology. It must continually be reformulated. If a person's whole intellect is to be brought into the sanctuary of God, then living on the boundary between the old and the new is imperative. But humanity's sin and willfulness will not be tolerated. To imagine that one is the master of [his] own destiny is in essence to reject this transitory life. Such a stance is ultimately based on a rejection of God and the divine will; that is, on human mismanagement, on sin.

Where the antipathy between God and humankind comes to light in this way, there sin is always manifestly operative. Human beings will always hide from themselves the shocking fact that by their very natures they are opposed to the will of God; they will never reach that point on their own where they are capable of apprehending the innermost depths of human nature. Whatever may be tried to hide one's self from one's self, God will always *set it in the secret light of [his] countenance.* In the *presence* of God, where demands for obedience are made known, the psalmists come to understand that it is the basic attitude of human beings to seek to assert their own will.

Not only are our particular secret faults revealed, but all is revealed, in its true nature, as humanity's falling short of the mark. All of us are created for glory, but sin mars our vision of what it is God has purposed for us. One stands before God subject to an awesome reckoning. Measured against the will of the divine Judge, the inward shallowness and futility of human life is now laid pitifully bare. No longer is this some mysterious fact which humanity seeks in vain to explain; rather it is the result of a singularly wrong and misguided orientation toward human life and to its divine purposes. In having an all too familiar connection with human guilt and sin, humanity dare not gaze too deeply into the soul lest the ultimate reality of rebellion be exposed in the light of the countenance of יהוה.

Trust in God is not something more or less played out in life's back room or in the wider sphere of *religion.* Knowledge of God and communion with God are at the very heart of life or they are nowhere. It is a learned grace, then, to practice the discipline of being attentive to the call of the holy in the midst of life. William Countryman states how

> attentiveness always requires patience, a hopeful willingness to wait while the
> HOLY reveals itself, even if that seems to take far longer than we should wish. It
> calls for love—the love of the TRANSCENDENT draws us onward, an answer-
> ing love of our own wills from within, and a love for the neighbors who share this
> adventure with us. [17]

---

17. Countryman, *Living on the Border of the Holy,* 27. cf. Craigie, Psalms 1–50, *Word Bible Commentary,* 145.

For the poet of Psalm 91, the heart of religion is the acknowledgment that one's life is lived under the rightful sovereignty of God. Confidence in the mercy and trustworthiness of יהוה is among life's most audacious values. Rolf Rendtorff sees the meaning of God's faithfulness as rooted in creation; that there has never been a time when God was anything but faithful in word and deed. This fidelity is the very character of God. It is who God is! God's faithfulness, God's constancy (חסה *hesed*) exists from the beginning of the world and it will continue until the end of all things. It is the ground and measure of all things.[18]

Given the fact of God's faithfulness, human beings come to learn over the course of a lifetime, that terrible tragedy and God's power/glory are allowed to commingle, neither negating the other. It is in this conjunction of human tragedy with the divine *presence* that trust is born, faith is renewed, and confidence is restored. A broken heart may indeed be mended; but there is no inoculation against its being broken. A broken heart is always nearest יהוה; and yet a mature and learned faith bears witness to the goodness of יהוה even when the powers of hell are in full rage against the servant of יהוה. Bad things do happen to the people of יהוה and it is in the crucible of suffering and pain, loss and grief, that the awful nearness and *presence* of יהוה may be experienced most acutely from the human side of the equation.

Over and again throughout the Psalter, one common theme may be discerned, particularly within the individual laments. The spiritually crushed may find restoration, but the forces that wield oppression are only held at bay, not crushed. When the psalms are willingly and fully engaged they can serve to dispel the naiveté of that faith which does not contain within it the strength to stand against stiff trials and the onslaught of evil. *In a proper universe, good deeds receive their just rewards and wicked conduct is promptly punished. Such is the unreal world that persons of deep religious convictions have painted for millennia. The survival of that vision of a just world order has come only at enormous expense.*[19] Our willingness to enter more fully into an engagement with the dynamic patterns of faith expressed in the various psalmic laments will depend in large part on how we understand our own relationship to the nearness of יהוה as expressed in the Psalter.

The Psalms are of essential importance in the recognition of that distantness, which results from various kinds of stress and distress and in the closing of the gap which threatens spiritual health and even life itself. The simple recitation of various psalms may serve to diminish that distance and enhance vitality, nearness and *presence*. While it may seem to us *platitudinous to underscore the sense of the Lord's presence to the psalmist, the generation that lived through the 'God is dead' movement needs to come to terms with Israel's understanding of the divine presence. Life lived in the presence*

18. Rendtorff, *God's History*, 60.

19. Crenshaw, *The Psalms: An Introduction*, 93. cf. Harkness, *The Providence of God*, "Christian redemption centers in a dual fact—first, that evil exists, and second, that God is not content to leave us in it." 81.

of Yhwh is the only life worth living.[20] This is the consistent witness of the poets of the Psalter and it is particularly accentuated in those psalms designated as the psalms of trust and confidence. Trust and confidence in the grace, care and near *presence* of יהוה are unqualified and absolute. In those psalms that speak of the poet's thirst for God, there is a spiritual resilience and an acknowledgment that only יהוה can assuage that thirst which emanates out of the depths of the soul. In this psalm, the term *my soul* is repeated thrice. This thirst is for the things which make for friendship with God and Psalm 63, *a Psalm of David*, illustrates this theme beautifully.

Psalm 63

A Psalm of David when he was in the Wilderness of Judah

O God, you are my God, for you I long;
for you my soul is thirsting.
My body pines for you
like a dry, weary land without water.

So I gaze on you in the sanctuary
to see your strength and your glory.
For your loving-kindness is better than life,
my lips will speak your praise.
So I will bless you all my life,
in your name I will lift up my hands.

My soul shall be filled as with a banquet,
my mouth shall praise you with joy.
On my bed I remember you.
On you I muse through the night
for you have been my help;
in the shadow of your wings I rejoice.

My soul clings to you;
your right hand holds me fast.
Those who seek to destroy my life
shall go down to the depths of the earth.
They shall be put into the power of the sword
and left as the prey of the jackals.

20. Murphy, "The Faith of the Psalmist," 231.

But the king shall rejoice in God;

(all who swear by God shall be blessed,)

for the mouth of liars shall be silenced.

Grail Translation

This psalm begins with language that could only point to a lament, but the affirmative testimonials in vv. 4, 5, 6, 8 and 9 speak clearly to the point: this is a psalm of trust *par excellence*.[21] It functions as a prayer to God, to the *God of my life*, expressing both assurance and a soulful commitment to living a life of nearness to God. The scribal authorities who added the historical note to the superscription obviously took it for granted that David was the speaker.[22] Some scholars think of this poem as written by a suppliant who is a king taking refuge in the temple where he spends the night (v 7) in prayer in the sanctuary for deliverance from his tormentors. It may well be a kingly prayer, for this is clearly a person of prayer who expresses a powerful and longing desire for the nearness of the *presence* of God.

The powerful metaphorical language of thirst in an arid land with no water and a fatigue brought on by lack of water, all speak to the poet's thirst for God as an exhausted wanderer in the midst of life. It is in the sanctuary where the poet's desire is to experience the strength and glory of God alone. It is to be near the *presence* of God where this thirst may finally be slaked. It is the love which is better than life and the shelter of *the shadow of your wings* which confront the reader with this witness to the fullness of a life lived in God in the here and now. In the words of Zenger this poem's accent is about a *contentment-achieving soul*.

Our capacity to identify with these songs and their statements of profound confidence—and to begin to see them functioning in the personal dimensions of our own lives—can strengthen our resolve to experience the sheltering grace and abiding *presence* of God. The notion of a wideness in God's mercy and opening up with space

21. McCann, Jr. *The Book of Psalms*, "Psalm 63 has been used from earliest Christian times as a morning psalm. Given its widespread use and its eloquent and powerful expression of faith in God, it is not surprising that it has been a favorite of persons as varied in time and place as John Chrysostom, Thomas a' Kempis, and Theodore Beza, who, in keeping with v.6, regularly recited the psalm at night. This history of use is testimony to the adaptability of the psalms and their ability to transcend the circumstances of their origin and to be perennially available to express the praises, prayers, and piety of the people of God" 929. Cf. Prothero, *The Psalms in Human Life*, 77, 141.

22. Wilson, *The Editing of the Hebrew Psalter*. "While linking the psalm with the event in 2 Samuel 15–16 may offer some insight into the internal mind-set of David at the time, that is more helpful for understanding the Absalom narrative than for interpreting the psalm. The psalm stands on its own strength, and indeed, the attempt to spell out the specifics of the setting behind the distress of the psalmist and to identify the enemy precisely as Absalom often has the unfortunate effect of so fixing the historical reference that the reader is distanced even further from the psalm and hindered from appropriating its insights for personal application. If this is merely a psalm describing David's response to personal circumstance centuries—even millennia—ago, why ought I assume that this psalm can influence the way I respond today to my own situations of distress? It may well be that the 150 psalms in the canonical collection were chosen (for the most part) precisely *because* they were not so tied to specific historical situations as to inhibit their appropriation and application in any day and age." 128.

to maneuver is portrayed by the psalmists particularly within the genre of the psalms of trust. More fundamentally, the composers of these psalms were confronted with the task of expressing in poetic form a paradox at the heart of biblical religion: the universalistic belief is in the One God of All who is the LORD of all the earth. This is the God who has chosen—as the medium of [His] relations with humanity—the particularity of a covenant with a particular people. This paradox had a major geographical corollary. The psalms, it is now believed, came to be used in and around the temple cult in Jerusalem. But how was the Israelite to imagine the capital city of a tiny nation-state, first conquered by David for strategic and political reasons, as the *city of our God*, the God who was master over all the nations of the world? The One God of All?

There is a veiled reference which alludes to a spectacular military defeat that was inflicted on an alliance that, at some point in the distant past, had threatened to invade Israel from the sea. Ancient Israel was not a sea-faring culture. They saw the seas and the great deep as dark and foreboding. The language used in the Psalter and in Isaiah to describe what appears to be some sort of naval threat (Ps 48, and Is 23, and the reference to Tarshish), shows how vividly the Korahite poet located Jerusalem in historical time and space. In this hymn of Zion the poetic perception of the routing of a sea-borne foe serves as a reenactment of the ultimate triumph at the Reed Sea.

Facts of geography--the mountainous eminence of Jerusalem over against the watery expanses of the Mediterranean--are turned into a symbolic pairing that depicts concretely the dominion of יהוה over all the earth and the power of the divine *presence* within human history. The spatial imagery of the poem takes us from Jerusalem to the far reaches of the known world. The glory and the strength of Zion is the subject of this psalm. The poet or a designated and representative figure instructs the community to make a solemn procession around Zion, to behold its grandeur and its greatness. All the people are to respond in the praise and adoration of the God who calls Zion and all its surroundings, invincible. The people of God are called to see its greatness as a pointer to God, who dwells there and who guides and leads them, as a particular people, throughout all generations. God rules them and will protect them.

Psalm 48

A Song. A Psalm of the Korahites

Great is יהוה and greatly to be praised
in the city of our God.
his holy mountain, beautiful in elevation,
is the joy of all the earth, Mount Zion,
in the far north, the city of the great King.
within its citadels God has shown

himself a sure defense.

Then the kings assembled,
they came on together.
as soon as they saw it,
they were astounded;
they were in panic, they took to flight;
trembling took hold of them there,
pains as of a woman in labor, as when an east
wind shatters the ships of Tarshish.

As we have heard, so have we seen
in the city of יהוה of hosts,
in the city of our God, which
God establishes forever.

We ponder your steadfast love, O God,
in the midst of your temple.
Your name, O God, like your praise
reaches to the ends of the earth.

Your right hand is filled with victory.
let Mount Zion be glad, let the
towns of Judah rejoice because
of your judgments.

Walk about Zion, go all around it,
count its ramparts; go through
its citadels, that you may tell the next generation
that this is our God, our God
forever and ever.
He will be our God forever.

*To contemporary readers, the claims made about Jerusalem are likely to seem
highly exaggerated or perhaps even extremely parochial and dangerously wrong.
To assert that Jerusalem is the indisputable and indestructible capital of the world
was probably as inflammatory in ancient times as it would be today. Besides, we
know that Jerusalem was not indestructible; hostile kings and their forces were
not put to flight by the very sight of Jerusalem. Indeed, the city was destroyed
in 587 BCE by the Babylonians and again in 70 CE by the Romans. Was the*

psalmist simply mistaken? Was his or her perception blurred by an overly zealous nationalism? Was the psalmist a political propagandist? So one might cynically conclude. But before dismissing the psalmist as a naïve optimist or a misguided patriot or a clever politician, we must remember that the details of Psalm 48 are as much metaphorical as geopolitical. What Psalm 48 embodies is 'poetic form used to reshape the world in the light of belief.' In this case, Jerusalem, a seemingly ordinary place, has become the eye of faith 'the city of the great King' (v.2), a powerful symbol; of God's reign in all places (vv. 2, 10) and in all times (vv. 8, 14). In effect, the psalmist has created in poetic form an alternative worldview, a new reality that for the faithful becomes the deepest and most profound reality of all: God rules the world, now and forever! Psalm 48 articulates the faith that no power on earth or the passing of any amount of time can ultimately thwart the just and righteous purposes of a steadfastly loving God. [23]

The temporal indications unite the present with the relatively distant past and the Moses victory as well as with the indefinite future generation; *this is our God, our God forever and ever. God will be our guide forever* (48:14, NRSV). To the people of God, the towering ramparts of the fortress-city had become the nexus for all future time and space. This protective shield of יהוה over Jerusalem is also descriptive of one of the benefits that accrues to those who seek to enter more fully into the path of life, which is ever the path יהוה traverses with the faithful. This psalm is in recognition of the benefits of the covenant promised to them by the ever gracious God, יהוה of heaven and earth.

> *. . . the phrase 'path of life' can hardly be understood in any other sense than as a life lived in communion with God which will be carried on even after death; in other words, as the consummation of salvation, the future form of which is at present still hidden from the poet. But God [himself] will remove the veil from that mystery, and only then will the psalmist be able to share in the perfect fullness of joy in God's presence . . . the raptures which God's hand holds in readiness for [him] last for ever. It is in such a joyful affirmation of God's life-giving might that the power of the biblical faith is to be found, a faith which far surpasses the other religions because it enables [man] by virtue of [his] faith to adopt a positive outlook on the total reality of life including death.* [24]

While the precise historical reference is probably unrecoverable, Jerusalem is still treated as dwelling in historical time and space. Protection is therefore granted in such a way, Carroll Stuhlmeuller writes, so that *each trial strengthens and purifies God's servants. This idea is at the root of the sapiential [wisdom] books . . . God's servant will find himself or herself at peace . . . sensing God's presence, arriving at eternal glory.*[25] The everlasting covenant will ultimately yield to an eternal weight of glory beyond all measure.

23. McCann, *The New Interpreter's Bible,* Vol. IV. 873.

24. Weiser, *The Psalms,* 178.

25. Stuhlmueller, *Psalms 2,* 74. "The author of Ps 16 belongs to that group of God's creatures,

Edge of Glory

IN THE PSALMS THERE is a demonstrative and a unitive connection between the *presence* of יהוה and the *glory/power* of God. The idea of the *glory* (כבוד *kabod*) of God is illustrated by the account of the divine *presence* that Moses encountered on Mount Sinai:

> *Then Moses said to Yhwh, 'Show me, I pray, your glory. And Yhwh said, 'You cannot see my face; but it shall be that, while my glory passes by, I will hide you in the cleft of the rock; I will cover you with my outstretched hand, until my glory passes by: and I will then remove from your face my hand, and you shall see my hind parts; but my face shall not be seen (Ex 33:18–23 NRSV).*

The *glory/power* of the *presence* of God affects one's whole being and way of life as one lives in the joy of God's love, mercy, grace, and forgiveness. Psalm 73 touches on this hope for the glory that extends beyond life to that future fullness of life when God will take care of all our needs.

> *The "glory" (kabod, v.24) of God is [his] blessed presence, which Moses experienced on Mount Sinai (Ex 33:18–23; 34:6–7, 29–35). But hope extends beyond this life to the future, when God will take care of all [his] children's needs. The joy of fellowship with God as experienced in [his] protection and guidance is so intense that the psalmist bursts out a rhetorical question (v.25). The clear answer is that there is no one but God, his Sustainer in heaven, with whom he longingly desires to fellowship even while in the flesh; therefore, he is more prepared to face his present existence with all of its problems. He is prepared to grow older and experience failing health and even adversity because God is his' strength,' 'portion' (v.26), and 'refuge'" (v.28).[1]*

But in the meanwhile, and in the painful and sorrowful experiences of human life, our needs do not always seem to be met to our own satisfaction. The fundamental idea at the root of the term כבוד (*kabod, glory*) is one characterized by *weight* or

---

endowed with gracious temperament, sincere heart and intuitive perception; these cannot but suffer more than the rest of us. The suffering, however, does not spread gloom, for it springs from an exquisite peace and leads in the final words of Ps 16 to the *fullness of joy, at thy right hand pleasures evermore* . . . We note a special association of Ps 16 with Isa 57:1–19 which also deals with . . . the entry of devout Israelites into peace." Ibid., 115, 116.

1. VanGemeren, *Psalms*, 566, 567.

heaviness, or the Latin, *gravitas*.[2] It conveys the idea of something that is a profoundly substantive phenomenon; a manifestation of consummate dignity, preeminence and majesty. These are also the features of theophany referred to earlier. Throughout the psalter (כבוד, *kabod)* has at least four uses and these may be distinguished as follows: First, in Psalm 49, it is used to describe the wealth and material possessions that seem to give *glory/power* or distinction to a person; in this instance, it is used negatively: *those who trust in their wealth and boast of the abundance of their riches? Surely, no ransom can avail for the price of one's life, for there is no price one can give to God for it . . . mere mortals cannot bask in their own glory (כבוד, kabod); they are all alike—like the animals they will all pass into the grave* (Ps 49: 6, 12 REB).

The second use distinguishes the dignity, splendor and honor of the human person. Psalm 8 describes this *glory/power* (כבוד) and the exaltation of the human creature. The glory and dignity of human beings are set in the context of creation's parameters and boundaries. Irenaeus of Lyons wrote that *the glory of God is the human person fully alive.* And Calvin added: *The chief end of [man] is to glorify God and to enjoy [him] forever.* Psalm 8 characterizes the dimensions of the human being and appropriates our place in the immensity of a vast cosmos. Humankind is given a divine identity and a God-given meaning and purpose to our place within the structure of the universe/ multiverse. We are intended to exercise God-given dominion toward the ends of life and human fulfillment on this planet. We are called to be agents and stewards of all that has been entrusted to us. That is the true nature of the כבוד *(kabod, glory/power)* bequeathed humanity at creation—a summons to the stewardship of creation!

Third, the Hebraic tradition sets forth clearly what is conferred upon Hebrew faith–its quality of both inwardness and breadth. We live in the proximity of God and are called to reflect the effulgence of the Creator's כבוד *(glory/power)*, both inwardly and outwardly, through the work of our hands. This psalm is a call to live life under the scrutiny and the sovereignty of יהוה. We are to bring honor to יהוה and reflect the image of divinity implanted within us at creation. Psalm 8 clearly recounts the work and the language of creation in Genesis 1. This justly celebrated psalm is a luminous instance of how poetic structure was made to yield a picture of the world that eloquently integrated underlying elements of Israelite belief.

The poem might be described as a kind of summarizing paraphrase of the account of creation in Genesis, more or less following the same order of things created and stressing, as does Genesis 1, humanity's God-given dominion over the created world. The difference in form, however, between the two texts is crucial, and instructive. Genesis 1, being narrative, reports creation as a sequence of acts indeed, as a kind of regulated procession moving from the dividing of light and darkness and the making of heaven,

2. Buber, *Right and Wrong*. "*Kabod,* whose root meaning is the radiation of the inner 'weight' of a person, belongs to the earthly side of death. When I have lived my life, says our Psalmist to God, I shall die in *kabod,* in the fulfillment of my existence. In my death the coils of death will not embrace me, but thy hand will grasp me. 'For', as is said in another Psalm related in kind to this one, the sixteenth [Ps 16], *'Thou wilt not leave my soul to Sheol'.*" 48.

earth, and sea to God's rest on the seventh day after the creation of the animal kingdom and humankind. It is all forward movement from origins through time to the fulfillment of humans as the crown and glory of all creation. Psalm 8 assumes as a background this narrative process, but takes it up after its completion, and, like many lyric poems, it is the complex realization of one moment of perception: the speaker looking around at the created world and marveling at it, and humanity's place in it.

> . . . but with even a grudging suspension of disbelief we can see how the poem's [Psalm 8] finely regulated sequencing of images and actions is a strong translation of the monotheistic belief in a world-embracing God Who chooses a place, and takes sides, in the large sweep of history. The personal and penitential psalms, in any case, are the ones that continue to speak most unambiguously to a wide range of readers, even with all the transformations that the faith of Jews and Christians has undergone since biblical times.[3]

The nature and being that is humankind's identity have profound implications for understanding the identity of the Creator. In the Christian scriptures' Epistle to the Hebrews, chapter 2, the author's use of Psalm 8 portrays Jesus as the supreme representative of all humanity. He is the authentic human being whose life and suffering are not incompatible with his glory and honor–so our human suffering is not incompatible with our sharing in God's glory. *It was fitting that apart from God, for whom and through whom all things exist, in bringing all children to glory, should make the pioneer of our salvation perfect through sufferings* (Heb. 2:10 NRSV).

Psalm 8

A Psalm of David

O יהוה, our Sovereign, how majestic
is your name in all the earth!

You have set your glory above the heavens.
Out of the mouth of babes and infants
you have founded a bulwark because of your foes,
to silence the enemy and the avenger.

When I look at your heavens, the work of your fingers,
the moon and the stars that you have established;
what are human beings that you are mindful of them,
mere mortals that you care for them?

---

3. Alter, *The Book of Psalms: A Translation with Commentary*, 121.
cf. H. Richard Niebuhr, *Radical Monotheism and Western Culture*, 13–15.

You have made them a little lower than gods
and crowned them with glory and honor.

You have given them dominion over the work of your hands;
you have put all things under their feet,
all sheep and oxen, and also the beasts of the field,
the birds of the air, and the fish of the sea,
whatever passes along the paths of the sea.

O יהוה, our Sovereign, how majestic
is your Name in all the earth!

The structure of Psalm 8 iterates that human glory and dominion are *derivative*. Structurally and theologically, human dominion is bounded and limited by God's sovereign majesty. To focus on the boundaries of Psalm 8 without an awareness of the center is escapist; human beings do have a central role in the created order. However, the greater danger is that we focus on the center without an awareness of the boundaries and over-shoot these fixed parameters and proscriptions. *To put human dominion at the center of things without the context of God's sovereignty is positively dangerous. When the exercise of human dominion ceases to be derivative, when it becomes unbounded, then dominion is in danger of becoming disaster.*[4]

This psalm gives us the extreme example of envelope structure—the repetition in a refrain of the first line as in the last. It is a common ending device in many bodies of poetry and is used frequently in the Psalms' biblical verse. The appropriateness of a refrain for our poem is clear enough. A perfect circle is closed: the majesty of God, affirmed at the beginning, is restated verbatim at the end, but with the same sense through the intervening eight lines of what it means for the name of יהוה our Sovereign to be majestic throughout the earth. The Hebrew says specifically *all* the earth, thus framing the whole poem with two symmetrical *alls*, and that monosyllable, a mere grammatical particle, becomes the chief thematic key-word of the psalm. The dominion of יהוה over *all*, heaven and earth, angels and humankind, and creatures of the field, and air and sea, subjects *all* at the feet of humanity's assignment of god-like dominion over and stewardship of earth's created order, riches, and resources.

Historically this is the core conviction of the ancient Hebrews' world-view. Creation is the work of יהוה first and last. The giftedness of humankind as the crown of creation is an awesome responsibility that is borne solely by the whole human race.

O Yhwh our God, how great is your name in all the earth! You have set your glory above the heavens; When I look up at your heavens, the work of your fingers, at the moon and the stars that you have arranged; what are human

---

4. McCann, "Righteous, Justice, Peace," 58, 59.

beings that you should pay us mind, mere mortals that you should even care for us? Yet you have made us a little less than the divine beings, and have crowned us with glory and honor; you gave us power over the work of your hands, and have placed everything under our care (Ps 8:1,3–6 REB).

A little less than the divine beings suggests strongly that we are people who, created and fashioned in the image and likeness of God, are bound for glory; that that is our eternal destiny.

And now, fourth, and most important of all: כבוד (*kabod*) describes the forms in which יהוה reveals both the signs and the personification of the divine *presence.* Any specific discernment of the *presence* of יהוה—within and encompassing all glory/power—cannot be determined in space and time. It will not be confined to any particular location or in any definable reality. It is a trans-reality of the divine phenomena's numinous *presence.* Any particular location, any one space including the temple sanctuary in Zion cannot contain כבוד (*kabod*). Not even in Jerusalem, the city of David.

Two psalms will serve here as fine examples. Psalm 11, which we considered earlier, states very clearly: *Yhwh is in [his] holy temple! ⁵Yahweh's throne is in the heavens! Yahweh's eyes behold and scrutinize with a searing gaze all humankind . . . For Yhwh is righteous; Yhwh loves righteous deeds; only those of an upright heart shall behold Yahweh's glory/power* (Ps 11:4, 7, LW). Psalm 11 pictures יהוה as assaying all the affairs of humankind and promising that only the *upright heart* shall see the glory of יהוה.

> He [the poet of Ps 11] begins by affirming that Yahweh is firmly established in the temple. This is the basis for seeking refuge there. Then he suddenly declares that God's throne is in heaven. Could it be that a later 'editor' of the text has added this phrase in order to ensure that no one gets the impression that Yahweh's presence is limited to the temple in Zion? This would certainly reflect a later view in Israel and a quite understandable concern on the part of a later reader. Perhaps this offers a clue that as this psalm moved to its present canonical state it came to be seen in a broader and more 'spiritual' light. It affirms the spiritual care of Yahweh for the trusting righteous rather than reflecting an institutional cultic setting which required Yahweh's presence in the temple.⁶

Israel's destiny is to learn how life is to be lived on the edge of glory כבוד (*kabod*). In Psalm 29, one of the earliest psalms, the ancient poet describes an early theophany: Psalm 29 finds the *glory/power* of יהוה reflected in the fury of the thunderstorm. Psalm 29 illustrates the awesome power of יהוה in theophanic imagery. It was to be Israel's

---

5. Craigie, *The Destiny of the Righteous in the Psalms,* "The Lord is in his holy temple," symbolizing [His] presence amongst people, but [His] '*throne is in the heavens*', signifying transcendence and might greater than that of any enemy. It is the double recognition that gives the psalmist confidence; God is both immanent, and therefore present with him in his crisis, but also transcendent, and therefore in control of the apparent chaos of that crisis." 133.

6. Bellinger, *Reading and Studying the Book of Praises,* 97.

destiny to learn how life is lived on the edge of glory כבוד (*kabod*). There is a hard edge to ancient Israel's learned experience of יהוה

In terms of Israel's experience of כבוד Psalm 8 finds it in the way the cosmos reflects the assertion of the authority of יהוה over against all resistant powers, and asserts the dignity and *godlikeness* of human beings. The poet of Psalm 29 describes in numinous language the revelation of the *glory/power* of יהוה at work in nature. What he is picturing in theophanic images is the creative power and might of God's work that commands the attention of all creation. The glory of יהוה is to be ascribed by the amazed poet. The climactic end result is all of creation's unitive cry, *Glory!*

Psalm 29

A Psalm of David

Ascribe to יהוה, O heavenly beings,
ascribe to יהוה glory and strength.
Ascribe to יהוה the glory of [his] name;
worship יהוה in holy splendor.

The voice of יהוה is over the waters;
the God of glory thunders, יהוה over mighty waters.
The voice of יהוה is powerful;
the voice of יהוה is full of majesty.

The voice of יהוה breaks the cedars;
יהוה breaks the cedars of Lebanon.
יהוה makes Lebanon skip like a calf
and Sirion like a young wild ox.

The voice of יהוה flashes forth flames of fire.
The voice of יהוה shakes the wilderness;
יהוה shakes the wilderness of Kadesh

The voice of יהוה causes the oaks to whirl,
and strips the forest bare;
and in the temple all cry "Glory!"

יהוה sits enthroned over the flood;
יהוה sits enthroned as ruler forever.
May יהוה give strength to the people!

May יהוה bless the people with peace.

Nineteen times יהוה is addressed in this most ancient psalm. The task of this poet is to call attention to the overwhelming *presence* of God as dominant over everything in creation. This fearful theophany is considered one of the oldest in the Psalter–as is this psalm. Indeed, there is a rich psalmic tradition of poets crying out to יהוה in desperation, with a sense of divine abandonment that יהוה is either inattentive to their cries or unable to hear them. This too is a hallmark of the Hebraic understanding of the divine *presence* of יהוה in the midst of the people who cry out most for the saving word of hope and salvation. None of this comes easily to our psalmists. Their pleadings and supplications make manifest the acute perception of their communal struggle to understand; and in their understanding, to accept, beyond their own comprehension, that the reality of the divine *presence* is beyond dispute.

It is here where faith in God's protection, which is expressed so elegantly in Psalm 91, is both present and proleptic. In reaching forward to the hope–the time of God's ultimate conquest of chaos and evil, suffering and death— it projects an eschatological reality back into the heart of the origins of Israel's ancient story. We will call this an eschatological retrograde!

> *The psalmist is now aware of being close to God even when it does not look (or feel) like it. Further, the psalmist is aware of a commitment to coming near to Yhwh to worship and seek Yhwh's help rather than moving away from Yhwh to approach other deities or to look to other resources so as to fix things for oneself . . . Being near Yhwh means making my Lord Yhwh my refuge, the one who is committed to being the place of safety where I hide and thus find that deliverance. It is not that the psalmist is now satisfied with a spiritual nearness to God and therefore can live with people's attacks. The psalm's duality is present-future, not inner-outer or earthly-heavenly. The psalmist is now once more convinced that God comes through for people and does act to put down wrongdoers[7]*

It is a theological maxim of the Psalter, and it is the witness of the Hebrew scriptures, that chaos and evil are presently being restrained; that all is under the watchful eye of the Creator. The total defeat of chaos, evil and death will be effected at the end of human history. In the meanwhile, יהוה dominates the whole created order and controls the chaos–this in spite of an abundance of evidence to the contrary. Our own experience of chaos and disorder in human life would tell a different story. This is an affirmation which cries out in the dark of humanity's experience of natural disasters where the view can sometimes be that things in the world of nature appear to be coming unhinged from the moorings of more orderly patterns.

The God of biblical faith, as has often been noted, is not only the God of the cosmos alone but also the God of history. These convictions are held in tension and reflect what is for us the very tough slog of faith! A good many psalms, including those

---

7. Goldingay, "Repetition and Variation in the Psalms," 416, 417.

referring explicitly to the Judean king and classified as *royal psalms,* are responses to the most urgent pressures of the historical moment, whether they are pleas to יהוה to save the king and people–in space and time—or on the occasion of a national crisis or as celebrations of recent or remembered military victories.

Poems of this sort abound in the pre-monotheistic world, where every nation was presumed to have its own particular god of battles whose intercession was solicited in time of military need. The development of Hebrew monotheism, *Yahwism,* has taken centuries and later accountings of the problem of suffering, evil, and the essential nature of the goodness of the God of Israel were read back into the earliest traditions. One of these traditions was *wisdom,* understood unambiguously as the ability of humankind to shape reality by virtue of their experiences and insight and, in so doing, gain mastery of life. But this too, failed to prove itself against a more complicated theological ethos—a more complex wrestling with the fact of evil and the human futility at ordering the world. This is God's domain.

Whatever Israel's wisdom tradition knew of the world, it knew that in any confrontation between humankind and any of life's great misfortunes, only God is competent to deal with it. The world has no contribution of its own to make. For the Hebrews the world was not a battleground between God and any of the evils found in it. There was no split in the world. From all parts of it–except for the underworld–there arose praise, and all its parts and opportunities were, in their turn, once again the objects of enthusiastic praise. It is a world that is thoroughly worthy of trust, and the understanding of humankind in these teachings was a non-tragic one. Even if life was subject to many different limitations, these were nevertheless not imposed by fate, but could always be accepted.

That is a remarkable paragraph! What a view of the world it is. Of course, the price which Israel had to pay for this refusal to split the world dualistically, to regard it, instead, as a good creation, open, in each of its movements, towards God, might appear to be a high price to pay. Israel was now forced to understand all the disruptive misfortunes as being statutes or decrees of יהוה. What is implied is a phenomenology of humankind in which human beings are tied to an environment in which they find themselves both subject and object, active and passive. Without this environment to which a person is turned, and which is turned toward the person, any assessment of what it means to be a human being simply is not possible in Israel. Israel only knew a related person, related to other persons, to its environment and, not least, to יהוה their God.

This self-testifying understanding of creation is understood solely in terms as a contribution to the phenomenology of the human being and of the surrounding world. The wisdom tradition is, perhaps, Israel's last final word on the subject. It is the Christian understanding that chaos and evil, suffering and death have been defeated by the power of Christ's cross and resurrection. Another way of putting this dilemma of all humanity is that we are caught in the crossfire of the battles that still rage, but now we are called to live within this new stratagem of reality. It is clearly the witness of the Christian

Scriptures that Jesus is the knowledge that true power belongs to God alone. The distinctive mark of God's power is demonstrated in Jesus who, in his chosen weakness and powerlessness, lays aside and surrenders all power in abject humility, obedience and death! This paradox lies at the heart of the mystery of the Incarnation.[8]

> *At the heart of the Christian faith in Jesus is the knowledge that true power belongs only to God. The distinctive mark of God's power [glory] is service and self-giving . . . If there is a Christian solution to the problem of suffering, therefore, it lies in such an understanding of the power of God.* [9]

The insinuation of the word כבוד (*kabod*)) into the Psalms is not always readily appreciated. One of the more natural interpretations refers to the ark of God as the symbol of the כבוד (*glory*) of יהוה. For the psalmists, *glory/power* is chiefly the possession and characteristic of יהוה. It is given by יהוה to the people of God or to anything which is connected with the *presence* of יהוה. In Isaiah 60:7, יהוה promises to *glorify the house of my glory.* The meaning of the text is clear: יהוה will impart to this sacred space something of the beauty and majesty which is the prerogative of יהוה alone. *Glory* is one of the qualities which is distinctive of יהוה. Isaiah, in one of his earliest utterances, uses it to describe this self-manifestation in judgment to bring to futility the pride and vainglory of humankind. The term glory may manifest a fearsome trans-reality for it speaks to the numinous quality that is inherent in divine revelation. The poet is humbled before the majesty of Yhwh.

> *Enter into the rock, and hide in the dust from the terror of Yhwh, and from the glory of Yhwh's majesty. Enter the caves of the rocks and the holes of the ground, from the terror of Yhwh and from the glory of Yhwh's majesty, when Yhwh rises to terrify the earth; to enter the caverns of the rocks and the clefts in the crags, from the terror of Yhwh, and from the glory of Yhwh's majesty, when Yhwh rises to strike terror in the earth* (Isaiah 2:10, 19, 21, NRSV).

In view of the parallel between *power/glory* in Psalm 78:61, where the poet writes, *God abandoned [his] dwelling at Shiloh, the tent where [he] dwelt among mortals, and delivered [his] power to the captivity, [his] glory to the hand of the foe,* it is better perhaps to interpret כבוד (*glory)* as connoting the visceral affectation of divine *power.* The psalmist means that יהוה surrenders divine power so as to be temporarily obscured; in the wilderness, יהוה embraces humility on account of the people's sin. *When the people tested the Most High God (El Elyon) and rebelled against Elyon (Most High) . . . then God abandoned the dwelling place at Shiloh, the tent of dwelling among mere mortals, and delivered the divine power to captivity, [his] glory into the hand of their enemies* (Ps 78:56, 61, REB).

---

8. cf. Paul's Letter to the Philippians: ". . . Christ Jesus, who, though he was in the form of God, did not regard equality with God as something to be exploited, but emptied himself, taking the form of a slave, being born in human likeness. And being found in human form, he humbled himself and became obedient to the point of death–even death on a cross" Phil. 2:6 REB.

9. McGill, *Suffering: A Test of Theological Method,* 63.

In 1 Samuel 4:21 this loss of the ark to the Philistines marked Israel's loss of the glory that gave her distinction from and preeminence over her neighbors. *The glory/power has departed from Israel, for the ark of God has been captured.* It was only after the captured ark of the covenant wreaked mayhem among its Philistine captors that it was relinquished to its proper home! Only God is sovereign over all creation including the created order of humanity. In stories recounted by Israel's neighbors, their divine beings struggled endlessly to assert authority over such primordial entities. The psalmists urge the divine beings of their contemporary and competing cultures to recognize the God of Israel's authority because יהוה has no such difficulties. יהוה speaks and the word that sounds forth hushes all malevolent forces. And all creation cries "*Glory!*" (Ps. 29:9).

The language of the Psalter is not just descriptive and metaphorical. It is also proscriptive and literal in conveying the sense of a cosmic hush at the sound of the voice of יהוה; at the manifestation of *glory/power*.

> *The search for God arises from the psalmist's past experience of fellowship and enjoyment of God's goodness. The psalmist changes metaphors from that of the desert to that of a prophetic vision. He has had a vision of God's beneficence: holiness (in the sanctuary), 'power' ('oz), and 'glory' (kabod). Even as Isaiah had a vision of God's holiness and glory (Isa 6:1–3), so the psalmist confesses that he has had a glimpse of the beatific vision. The God he worships is the Great King, who promised to be present among his people in 'the sanctuary.' The symbol of the presence of the glorious and powerful King was the ark of the covenant (1Sa 4:21; Pss 78:61; 132:8;)*[10]

The Psalms, by its diverse language, asserts throughout that it is יהוה who reigns over the cosmos; that there was a specific moment—in time—when יהוה asserted authority over the dynamic powers who resisted that sovereignty and took a seat on the throne of all worlds. Psalm 29 asserts that there was such a moment and that it had permanent consequences; that Yahweh's assertion of authority would last forever. This is the effect of the shout in Psalm 29, where all cry, כבוד (*Glory*)! That the *glory/power* of יהוה is revealed in extraordinary phenomena, which the psalm describes, is reminiscent of the prophet Isaiah. *God's glory is the actualized manifestation of the divine presence. God's power overwhelms all other occurrences and the poet bears witness to this fact of divine sovereignty* (Zenger).

This is evidently clear from Isaiah's inaugural vision: *In the year that King Uzziah died, I saw Yhwh, sitting on a throne high and lifted up, and the hem of [his] robe filled the whole temple. Seraphs were in attendance above [him]; each had six wings: with two they covered their faces, and with two they covered their feet, and with two they flew. And one called aloud to another saying: 'Holy, holy, holy is Yhwh of hosts; the whole earth is full of Yhwh's glory!* (Isaiah 6: 1–3, NRSV). Unquestionably the *glory/power*

---

10. VanGemeren, *Psalms*, 489.

of יהוה is here regarded as something that can be perceived and apprehended. Isaiah leaves no stone unturned in attempting to awaken the senses of the hearers of his proclamation. *Then the pivots on the thresholds shook at the voices of those who called, and the whole house filled with smoke. And I said: 'Woe is me! I am lost, for I am a man of unclean lips, and I live among a people of unclean lips; yet my eyes have seen the King of glory, Yhwh of hosts'!* (Isaiah 6: 4–5, NRSV).

This much is clear from Isaiah's account of his great inaugural vision. The prophet sees the glory of the enthroned יהוה with skirts filling the temple. There is no clear indication of what it was that Isaiah saw or how he recognized that it was יהוה, but his vision and the experience of it, was obviously self-authenticating. The attendant seraphim in addition to the solemn *Trisagion, Holy, Holy, Holy* declare that *the whole earth is full of Yhwh's glory.* Unquestionably the glory of יהוה is here regarded as something perceptible, something, a part of which at least, Isaiah witnesses. The glory as such has no ethical significance except in so far as it is the method of manifestation of one who is undoubtedly an ethical being. The phraseology suggests that the skirts which fill the temple and the glory which fills the whole earth refers to the phenomena of fire and smoke. Some think that the smoke is caused by the billowing clouds of incense that would fill the temple in connection with the sacrificial observances. But in view of Isaiah's horror at these occurrences, this interpretation is questionable. Another more probable interpretation connects the visual smoke and shaking of the foundations with the phenomena of a great storm, or more likely, an earthquake.

Not much has been written–surprisingly, concerning the great earthquake that is said to have occurred in the year of Uzziah's death (ca 742 BCE). It is referred to specifically in Zech. 14: 5, 6: *and you shall flee from the earthquake in the days of King Uzziah of Judah. Then Yhwh, my God, will come, and all the saints with [him].* It seems plausible that Isaiah's reference to darkness and light, images of the fire and smoke and the shaking of the pillars of the temple, have their origins in the phenomena attendant upon an earthquake. This earthquake by which the prophecy of Amos may be dated, we assume, is recording the same historical event: *These are the words of Amos, who was among the shepherds of Tekoa, which he saw concerning Israel in the days of King Uzziah of Judah and in the days of King Jeroboam son of Joash of Israel, two years before the earthquake. (Amos 1:1,2, NRSV).*

If the cloud and fire are being used metaphorically to describe a particular geological occurrence in the eighth century BCE by which the כבוד (*glory/power*) of יהוה is made manifest to Isaiah, then we are in the presence of what would be a historically verifiable event and possibly related to Isaiah's experience of the immanent *glory/power* of God. Such an extraordinary description of כבוד (*glory*) partly reveals and partly conceals the *presence* of יהוה by which, through, and in part, by means of, these physical phenomena. Isaiah is rendered vividly conscious of the awe-filled *presence* of יהוה. This call of Israel's great prophet is thereafter effected throughout his long ministry in deeply troublesome times. We moderns seldom stop to consider what was so prescient to the ancients—that God remains fully active in the events of human history. We tend to function almost solely off the scientific grid. We have our meteorological explanations of cause and effect for earthquakes, tsunamis, volcanoes, hurricanes, typhoons, tornadoes, fire and flood.

The witness of the Hebrew scriptures offers another explanation: the glory (כבוד *kabod*) of יהוה will be revealed in extraordinary physical phenomena, as described above, as well as in the still small voice of calm. God still speaks today! יהוה is ever active in the midst of human life—if we have ears to hear and eyes to see. Nothing has changed and yet everything has changed. Revelation, as a way of apprehending the knowledge of יהוה, is woven into the fabric of human history. יהוה is the LORD of all history and every human story, be it the individual history of each individual life or the history of the rise and fall of nations and empires. Such glory and power are not limited by human actions, events and consequences in history. They lie at the heart and center of the human drama. A *theology of glory* is replicated over and over and is communicated unambiguously throughout the Psalms. It represents Israel's own sense of history—the final decrees and declarations toward a people who are related directly to הוה in covenant. The trajectory and the arc of Israel's history bends toward an *eternal weight of glory*.

Spirit and Power

IN THE LITERATURE OF ancient Israel, the spirit of God is generally conceived as an impersonal but divine force, deriving from its primary significance of *breath* or *wind*, the two principal derivatives of life-force and power. In Genesis 1 the spirit is present at creation. As the creative power of יהוה, the spirit is closely associated with the divine word: *By the word of יהוה were the heavens made, and all their host by the breath of his mouth* (Ps 33:6, NRSV). It is also the mode of God's activity towards [his] people, so that we read of the *spirit of judgment* (Is 4:4), and the *spirit of salvation* (Is 26:18, *LXX*). As a divinely sent energy, the spirit possesses the heroes whom יהוה raises up to be the deliverers of the community of Israel from oppression at the hands of her enemies. It is the spirit of יהוה that *took possession of Gideon* (Judg 6:34), enabling him to rally the tribes to deliver Israel; further, *and the spirit of יהוה came upon Jephthah* (Judg 11:29) as he began his victorious march against the Ammonites; finally, Samson is endowed with incredible strength to rend a lion: *and the spirit of יהוה rushed upon him;* and to smite the Philistines: *then the spirit of יהוה rushed upon him* (Judg 14:6, 19).

In the First Testament spirit is nearly always associated with power. But not only with merely temporary and temporal, sudden accessions of physical strength or courage in battle. Leaders and rulers may also come to possess a more permanent endowment of the spirit, giving them the qualities of wisdom and judgment which their offices and assignments may require. The spirit which was in Moses is imparted also to the seventy elders of Israel, manifesting its presence in their case in the form of prophesying. *So יהוה said to Moses . . . I will come down and talk with you there; and I will take some of the spirit that is on you, and put it on them; and they shall bear the burden of the people along with you so that you will not bear it all by yourself* (Num 11:16,17 REB). Joshua possesses this spirit, either, according to Num 27:18, before he is commissioned by Moses as his successor through the sign of the laying-on of his hand, or, in the version of the story given in Dt 34:9, as a consequence of that token of spiritual kinship, or identification, with his spirit-possessed predecessor; and lastly, after Samuel had anointed David, *the spirit of יהוה came mightily upon David [and remained upon him] from that day forward* (1 Sam 16:13, LW).

The distinctive characteristic of Isaiah's reference to the *shoot out of the stock of Jesse* is that the s*pirit of יהוה shall rest upon him* as the divine energy which will cause him to exhibit all the attributes of the ideal ruler (Is 11:2). Most especially, the spirit is the prophetic energy which enables people to become the recipients and the bearers of the interpretation of divine revelation. Balaam and Saul are inspired by its power to prophesy (Num 24:2; I Sam 10:6ff.); Elisha, as Elijah's successor in the prophetic ministry, receives a double portion of the spirit which comes upon him (2 Kgs 2:15); the prophet Isaiah is described as *the spirit-bearing man who is mad* (Hosea 9:7 *LXX*); it is by יהוה and [his] spirit that the prophet is sent (Isaiah. 48:16); through the entering in of the spirit a prophet may receive–without any intermediary—the direct revelation of God (Ez 2:2); in the power of the spirit he may be caught away from one place to another (1 Kgs 18:12); and, as in the case of Elijah and Elisha, powerful deeds may include even the raising of the dead back to life (2 Kgs 2:14–15)!

In relation to prophetic inspiration, the idea of the spirit is closely aligned with that of the *hand of* יהוה (Kgs 18:46). Its operation is also present in other modes of apprehending divine revelation, such as non-prophetical forms of divination and the interpretation of dreams (Gen 41:38). It is also the spirit of wisdom, understanding and knowledge by which the artist Bezalel is enabled to reproduce the heavenly pattern in the construction and furnishing of the tabernacle (Ex 31:3–11); and it is the spirit that is the source of David's inspiration as a poet: *The spirit of Yhwh speaks through me, his word is upon my tongue* (2 Sam 23:2, REB).

One instance of the spirit's possession of an individual is especially important for his office as a prophet and as the fulfiller of the divine purposes of redemption through suffering. The righteous servant of יהוה is one upon whom יהוה has imparted this spirit. *Here is my servant, whom I uphold, my chosen, in whom my soul delights; I have put my spirit upon him* (Is 42:1 NRSV). The spirit inspiring the utterances of the prophets is the means whereby God's ethical requirements and judgments upon Israel are made known to the covenant people. *They angered* יהוה *at the waters of Meribah . . . for they made his spirit bitter, and he spoke words that were rash* (Ps 106:33, NRSV); it is the power through which the sovereign authority and pastoral care of יהוה is rendered efficacious in the life of the nation.

The spirit is actively involved throughout the Psalter and is something more than simply an impersonal and divine energy. As the *holy Spirit* it is the mode of God's self-manifestation and is virtually identical with the *presence* and the glory, or, specifically, the *messenger or herald* of יהוה (Ps 51:11); *Where can I go from your spirit? Or where can I flee from your presence?* (139:7). The prophet Haggai writes: *Work, for I am with you, says* יהוה *of hosts, according to the promise that I made you when you were brought out of Egypt. My spirit dwells among you; do not fear* (Hag. 2:5, NRSV). And the spirit is said to have been *set in the midst of Israel* (Is 63:11); but by Israel's rebellious conduct, it is the spirit who is *grieved, or wounded* (Is 63:10).

For the faithful, however, and this is particularly true in the *LXX*, the spirit is portrayed as a guide and leader; *Teach me to do your will, for you are my God. Let your good spirit lead me on a level path* (*LXX*, Ps 143:10). The spirit's activity is an integral part of the covenant relationship between יהוה and the people. It is not at all surprising that the thought of a renewal of this activity is closely bound up with Israel's eschatological hope and, in particular, with the expectation and the anticipation of a new Covenant. The faithful remnant, according to Isaiah, will be cleansed of moral defilement by *the spirit of judgment and the spirit of burning* (Is 4:4 NRSV). In the future age of blessedness, the spirit will *be poured upon us from on high,* bringing about the era of judgment and righteousness *until a spirit from on high is poured out on us, and the wilderness becomes a fruitful field* (Is 32:15–16, NRSV). In those days God will pour the spirit upon the seed of Jacob as the servant of יהוה (Is 44:3, 5). This outpouring of the spirit will be directly connected with devotion to the Name of יהוה so that one will *write on his hand, 'Unto יהוה'.*

In Luke's writings, we have the close association between the outpouring of the spirit and salvation by the name (now the exalted name of Jesus as Messiah), which is a marked feature of the thought of his gospel and the book of the Acts of the Apostles in the Christian scriptures. There is no explicit mention of the spirit in Jeremiah's pronouncement of the new Covenant though it is probably implied in the anticipation of a new law which will be written on the flesh of human hearts. *The days are surely coming, says Yhwh, when I will fulfill the promise I made to the house of Israel, and the house of Judah. In those days and at that time I will cause a righteous Branch to spring up for David; and he shall execute justice and righteousness in the land* (Jer. 33:14–16, NRSV). The similar prophecies of Ezekiel state: *I will put my spirit within you, and you shall live, and I will place you on your own soil; then you shall know that I am יהוה. I have spoken and I will act* (Ez 37:14, NRSV).

Here it is expressed in the strongest terms possible that the hope in the age of the New Covenant involves the entire community of Israel; all may participate in the spirit as the life-principle of a nation which will truly know יהוה. This expectation is reaffirmed in *Jubilees (1:21–25),* and as late as about 320 CE, Rabbi Acha cites Isaiah 32:15; 61:11, and Lam 3:49f. indicating that the bestowal of the spirit of God is to be a primary characteristic of the age of final redemption. In the prophecy of Joel: *it shall come to pass afterward, that I will pour out my spirit upon all flesh; and your sons and your daughters shall prophesy, your old men shall dream dreams, your young men shall see visions* (2:28 NRSV).

This bestowal of the spirit is conceived in terms of a universal outpouring of the prophetic gift. However it may be envisaged, it is associated with cleansing from ethical defilement and remission of sins, a thought which is also prominent in the many passages of the Hebrew bible in which the action of the spirit is portrayed by the imagery of cleansing, healing and life-giving water, particularly the *water of pardon* flowing from the ideal temple of Ezekiel's vision (Ez 47:3). All Israel will be possessed by the spirit in the days of the renewed Covenant; but it is to be associated in a special measure with the community's leadership. Isaiah's ideal ruler is to possess the fullest endowment of the spirit. *The spirit of Yhwh shall rest on him, the spirit of wisdom and understanding, the spirit of counsel and might, the spirit of knowledge and the fear of Yhwh. And his delight shall be in the fear of Yhwh* (Is 11:1–3 NRSV), and the Messianic hope is of one who will be anointed with the inward unction of the spirit of God.

This hope of a spirit-possessed Messiah is most explicitly stated in certain post-canonical writings (cf. *Enoch, Psalms of Solomon*). It is, however, important to notice that in Second Isaiah's figure of the Servant (Is 42:1–6) the ideas of spirit-possession and covenant relationship are already united in the person of an individual redeemer–*thus says* יהוה, *the Redeemer of Israel and his Holy One, to one deeply despised, abhorred by the nations, the slave of rulers, Kings shall see and stand up, princes, and they shall prostrate themselves, because of* יהוה, *who is faithful, the Holy One of Israel, who has chosen you* (Is 49:7f. NRSV).

It is also clear, both from later Jewish literature and the Second Testament, that the notion of a spirit possessed Messiah was sometimes closely associated with the eschatological hope of a universal outpouring of the spirit as in Isaiah: *The spirit of* יהוה *is upon me, because* יהוה *has anointed me;* יהוה *has sent me to bring good news to the oppressed, to bind up the broken-hearted, to proclaim liberty to the captives, and release to the prisoners* (Is 61:1, NRSV). Again, in Isaiah, this eschatological reference is made to the Name of Yhwh. *I am Yhwh, that is my Name; my glory I give to no other, nor my praise to idols. See, the former things have come to pass, and new things I now declare; before they spring forth, I will tell you of them* (Is 42:8,9 NRSV).

The Messiah at his coming is expected to be the agent of יהוה in the general bestowal of the spirit in the age of fulfillment. *Here is my servant, whom I uphold, my chosen, in whom my soul delights; I have put my spirit upon him; he will bring forth justice to the nations* (Is 42:1 NRSV). Luke's gospel follows the Hebrew Testament in its conception of the nature of the divine spirit. In Luke's writings the spirit is still, generally speaking, impersonal; it is the mode of God's activity in dealing with humanity and the power in which God is active in Jesus among the people. It is in terms of the First Testament's view of the spirit, and as the historical fulfillment of the hopes which associated the Messiah with the spirit and the outpouring of the spirit of prophecy with the last days and the new Covenant, that St. Luke interprets these events. [1]Indeed, the Holy Spirit is the central theme and purpose of the two books attributed to Luke and forms one of the bases for the later development of the Christian doctrine of the holy Trinity. [2]We will be looking at this connection more closely in the pages just ahead.

---

1. Authorship of the Gospel according to Luke and the Acts of the Apostles are attributed to Luke, the Evangelist. The Lucan corpus is the largest of the "New Testament" and provides us with one of the strongest witnesses to the person and role of the Holy Spirit's presence with and in Jesus, and in the early apostolic church's life and bears witness to the newly emergent community's faith in the salvation brought by Jesus, the Christ of God.

2. Conzlemann, *Commentary on Luke.* He refers to the Gospel of Luke as *"The Gospel of the Holy Spirit."*

The connecting thread which runs through both parts of Luke's work is the theme of the operation of the Spirit of God. Jesus declared in citing Isaiah, *The Spirit of the Lord is upon me, because he has anointed me to preach the gospel to the poor: he has sent me to proclaim release to the captives, and recovering of sight to the blind, to set at liberty them that are bruised, to proclaim the acceptable year of the Lord* (Luke 4:18–19 NRSV). Peter tells the Pentecost crowd that this Jesus who was crucified and slain, *God has raised up . . . . being therefore by the right hand of God exalted, and having received of the Father the promise of the Holy Spirit, he has poured forth this which you have seen and heard* (Acts 2:32–33 REB).

Through the death and exaltation of the Messiah, the spirit which operated in Jesus has come to be imparted to his followers; to be the bond of union between them and himself and the power by which the divine sovereignty into which he has entered is made effective through the preaching of the gospel in the spirit's power and under its guidance and aegis. Although the activity of the divine spirit is the essential theme of his writings, Luke has little to say concerning the nature of that spirit (apart from being vitally invested in the person and work of Jesus) that is not already found in the Hebrew Testament.

In its correlation between the role of the Messiah and the *presence* of the spirit in the Hebrew Scriptures, particularly those in the *messianic psalms,* the church would vindicate the monotheism that had been at issue in its conflicts with Judaism. It came to terms with the concept of the *logos* over which it had been in dispute with paganism. The doctrine believed, taught, and confessed by the church catholic of the second and third centuries led to the formulation of the doctrine of the *Trinity* in the fourth century. In this dogma Christianity drew the line that separated it from pagan supernaturalism and it reaffirmed its character as the *Faith of Salvation* that rested upon the foundation of the apostles and prophets. Initially, the first Christians were Jews and in their new found faith they connected a continuity with the old. They remembered how their Lord had said that his purpose was to fulfill the law and the prophets, not to abolish them. To these earliest first-century CE Christians, the law and the prophets *were* the sacred scriptures.

In this manner the period before 70 CE and the sacking of Jerusalem and the destruction of the second temple by the Romans, witnessed these tensions within Jewish thought. This was widely reflected in the beginnings of Christian theology. For instance, the party headed by James shared significant analogies with Palestinian Judaism. The so-called *missionary party*, which came to be identified with Paul, as well as the Christian apologists of the second century, reflected distinct affinities with the Jewish thought of the Hellenistic diaspora. It was in this milieu of burgeoning attempts to clarify their understanding of the message of the gospel that occupied the attention of the early Christian communities.

The extent and scope of this *continuity question* erupted into a controversy between Peter and Paul (Acts 6–7) and continued to challenge the church well into the third century. At issue was the basic question: *What is new about the new covenant?* The conflict that arose between Hellenistic Jews and Hellenistic Jewish-Christians was the question of the continuity of Christianity with Judaism. The differences between the way the question was addressed in the first century church (Acts 15) and the way it was addressed by Paul in Galatians suggests the manner in which the church faced this dilemma. After 70 CE this internal conflict continued to mark the relationship between Christian and Jewish thought everywhere. The relation of Christian doctrine to Jewish and pagan thought is a subject worthy of investigation for its own sake.

> *The very legitimacy of the development of Christian dogma has been challenged on the grounds of its supposed Hellenization of the primitive message; the contrast between Greek and Hebrew ways of thought has been used to explain the distinctiveness of Christian doctrine. These are only modern versions of an ancient debate.*[3]

It is to this critically important theological articulation of Christianity that we now turn. In the Hebrew tradition, and also according to the Christians scriptures, the model for understanding the power of God lay in the one who creates and sustains the whole created order. We Christians must always be wary of any prevailing tendency toward all forms of supersessionism when it comes to encountering and interpreting divine revelation in the ancient Hebrew texts. *Supersessionism* is known today as an old idea: Christianity's alleged superiority over against the witness of Judaism. This assumption by many Christians seems to flow very naturally, and it is still widely assumed that Christianity's "superiority" has supplanted Judaism as the divinely chosen religion. This view, common as it is in today's church, does not adequately or accurately reflect the larger issue of Christianity's dependence upon the Septuagint in the formation of its gospel of Jesus as the Messiah of God. Supersessionism remains an illegitimate claim. Brevard Childs comments:

> *Christianity can make no legitimate theological claim to be superior to Judaism, or that the New Testament is of a higher moral quality than the Old Testament. Human blindness and sin envelop the one as much as the other. Rather, the claim being made is that the divine reality made known in Jesus Christ stands as judge of both religions. This assertion means that Judaism through God's mercy has indeed grasped divine truth in Torah, even when failing to recognize therein the truthful manifestation of God in Jesus Christ. Conversely, Christianity, which seeks to lay claim on divine truth in the name of Christ, repeatedly fails to grasp the very reality which it confesses to name. In a word, two millennia of history have demonstrated that Jews have often been seized by the divine reality testified in its Scriptures, but without recognizing its true name, whereas Christians have evoked the name, but frequently failed to understand the reality itself . . . For the Christian church the continuing paradox of its faith lies in its encounter through*

3. Pelikan, *The Christian Tradition*, 12.

the Jewish Scriptures with the selfsame divine presence which it confesses to have
found in the face of Jesus Christ.[4]

The fundamental importance of this perspective on divine power from the Christian point of view, lies in its openness toward the ongoing development of a theological and biblical understanding that takes seriously the revelatory accounts of both the Hebrew and the Christian traditions. In the Psalter there lies a nascent awareness of the essential character of the life giving and life-loving יהוה. The nature of the reality of this God whom Christians have come to call Lord and Christ, is not some sort of philosophical construction, either in the Psalms or in the Christian writings. It is a relational orientation, implying an existential transaction that takes place between the worshiper and the one being worshiped. It is implicit within the context of liturgy and worship that both the word and the action must bear unitive witness to the true nature of the One and Only God of All.

The all-important work of theological formation is first encountered and finally envisaged and Christians alike contributed to this work. We Christians are so easily given to this attitude of superiority in interpreting our Christian Testament texts as representing the fulfillment of all the promises to Israel, in Christ, that all too often the sacred text of the First Testament is virtually ignored in the church. This practical agnosticism has dogged the church for a very long time. Had *Marcion* had his way in the second-century CE, the Christian church would have jettisoned the Hebrew Bible completely since, as Marcion and the Jewish synagogue establishment believed, the Hebrew scriptures did not prophesy the coming of Jesus; that is, that in Jesus of Nazareth, the Christ, Messiah had not come.

> *For that reason it cannot be said that in its decision to include the Jewish*
> *Scriptures in the Christian Bible, the orthodox church adequately responded to*
> *Marcion's challenge. It did so only in part. It was not until the late eighteenth*
> *century and its general acceptance in the nineteenth century that the Christo-*
> *logical veneer was stripped away, and Israel's Scriptures began to be understood*
> *historically and developmentally in their ancient contexts. The new scholarly*
> *conclusions that resulted were, however, no less of a challenge to some tradi-*
> *tional Jewish ways of interpreting the Bible than they were to inherited Christian*
> *modes of interpretation. That has reopened the question as to the religious and*
> *theological significance of this shared scriptural canon today . . .*[5]

The struggle, therefore, over the authority of the Hebrew scriptures and the question of the continuity between Judaism and Christianity's scriptures represented the earliest form of the search for a tradition that has ever recurred throughout Christian history.[6]

4. Childs, "Toward Recovering Theological Exegesis," 128.

5. Sanders, *The Monotheizing Process*, 65.

6. Pelikan, *The Christian Tradition*, 14.

Very early on, the Christian church sought to appropriate the scriptures as their own, by combing through them for references to the Messiah. Most frequently cited were those references in the Psalms that spoke of the enthronement of the king (Psalms 2, 45, and 110) which was made to apply to the exaltation of Christ in the resurrection of Jesus, whereby the church appropriated to Christ the status of cosmic lordship. Already in the Second Testament, Psalm 110 was a favorite proof text for this claim: *Yahweh says to my lord (the king), 'Sit at my right hand (the place of honor) until I make your enemies your footstool.' Yahweh sends out from Zion your mighty scepter. Rule in the midst of your enemies'"* (Ps 110:1, NRSV). The scepter is to be understood as the symbol whereby God gives to the king the authority to rule over all foes. And in Psalm 45, *Your throne, O God, endures for ever and ever. Your royal scepter is a scepter of equity* (Ps 45:6 NRSV). The church's own express understanding of the meaning of the Messiah found its roots in the Hebrew psalms and, more specifically, in very select psalms (e.g. Psalms 2, 45, and 110). Here Psalm 110, a royal psalm, is particularly apt. It is the most quoted psalm in the Christian scriptures and was taken up by the early Christian church as a reference to the exaltation of the Christ.

Psalm 110

Of David. A Psalm.

This is the revelation of יהוה to my Master:
> *"Sit at my right hand;*
> *I will put your enemies*
> *under your feet."*

יהוה will send out from Zion
your scepter of power;
Rule in the midst of your foes.
Your people will offer themselves willingly
on that day when you lead your forces
on the holy mountains.

From the womb before the dawn,
the dew of your youth will come to you.
יהוה has sworn an oath and will not change his mind,
> *"You are a priest forever*
> *according to the order of Melchizedek."*

The Master is at your right hand;

he will shatter rulers on the day of his wrath,

He will judge all the nations,

filling them with corpses;

heads will be shattered far and wide.

He shall drink from the stream by the path,

and will stand with head held high.

In ancient Israel, this poem would speak of the assurance of victory for God's priest-king whereby יהוה asserts the authority of ruling power and confers the priestly office upon the king. The poem is ancient and attests to the role of יהוה in bequeathing authority to the selected monarch, who is to rule over the people of God with justice and equity. Originally the poem probably had something to do with certain rights and privileges granted the individual king at his enthronement in Jerusalem. But the symbol of the scepter of power, which is given by יהוה, bespeaks divine authority over all foes and enemies. The defeat of Israel's enemies is really the victory of יהוה and is celebrated by the very ancient figure of Melchizedek, the King of Salem, who is called *"priest of God Most High"* in the pre-Israelite era (Gen 14:17–20). This poem, Psalm 110, is central to ancient Israel's understanding of the role of יהוה in history. All enemies will one day be subjected to divine authority: *Sit on my right; I will put your enemies beneath your feet.* History is purposeful and is moving toward the consummation of all things. In this manner the early Christian church invested this psalm with the reference to Christ's exaltation and dominion over all enemies.

These texts were interpreted so convincingly by the Christian church in the first-century CE and forward that even some Jews were constrained to admit that the Messiah was to suffer, though not that he was to be crucified (*cf. Trypho in his Dialogue with Justin*). In these and other ways the Christian church commandeered the whole Hebrew bible very early on and Judaism was put increasingly on the defensive. In these and other ways, the church took possession of the LXX scriptures—or at least of those portions that were susceptible to Christian interpretation.

On the basis of such convictions, it was possible to read the "Old Testament" as a Christian book and to see *"the words of Christ"* not only in such passages as Psalm 22, as seemed explicitly warranted by the "Christian Testament", but also in many of the other psalms as well. [7] The issue of the continuity of the new faith of Christianity with the old faith, Judaism, reached its apex in the doctrine of the holy Trinity. For in it the church thought it able to vindicate the monotheism that had been at issue in its struggles and conflicts with Judaism in the earlier centuries. The statement of doctrine issued at Nicaea drew the line that separated Christianity from both pagan supernaturalism and Jewish monotheism. Christianity was to be the religion of divine

---

7. Sanders, *The Qumran Psalms Scroll*, 65.

revelation that issued forth in salvation; where creation and redemption flowered into a unitary whole; where the Messiah came and completed the work of the redemption of the whole world.

An appropriately and carefully measured understanding of the theological category of divine revelation serves as an antidote to any arrogance of attitude and supposed superiority. Rather it ought to foster a measured humility. It is possible—and necessary—to maintain the integrity of the Jewish religious tradition with its own sacred texts without denigrating its antecedents. This begins with a right approximation and understanding of the true nature of the power of the One God. Christianity minimizes its own Jewish roots to its peril. It is a generalized axiom to assert with Augustine, that the Second Testament is in the First, concealed; the First Testament is in the Second, revealed. Both tradents are inherently complementary to the other. Without a recognition and an appreciation for the role of the spirit's power, which is made manifest throughout the Hebrew Bible and the Psalms, there is no way the fourth-century Christian church would have rejected the heresy of Arius and adopted the theological stance of Athanasius.

This wrestling with a new understanding of the power of God as revealed in Jesus was the task of the whole church represented by its bishops. The doctrine of the holy Trinity would never have been formulated *had there not been a need in the community to address it!* In the fourth-century, the church struggled with its own understanding of the role of the spirit's presence and power in their midst. It had been a long road from that first-century CE Pentecost in Jerusalem to the Council of Nicaea in 325 CE. Fundamental distinctions had to be ironed out and it is to this theological resolution that we now turn for this example from the Church's own history. After all, it was only the very character and divine nature of this One God—as believed by both Jews and Christians—that was at stake.

The Nicene Wedge

AN HISTORICAL EXAMPLE OF the process of this understanding of the nature of divine revelation of the One and Only God of All, may be illustrated with a brief consideration of the core Christian doctrine of the holy Trinity. The basic context of all Christian theology is first and foremost rooted in the doctrine of the Trinity. [1]It is Christian dogma's attempt to clarify what is to be believed, accepted, and taught about the true nature of the One God of All, the Almighty, who reveals and self discloses the nature and the essence of the divine being in the person of Jesus of Nazareth. We now look more closely at the early Church's affirmation of a Christian doctrine of God and the meaning of what it was that was finally articulated at Nicaea.

What happened at Nicaea, an ancient city in Bithynia northwest of Constantinople in 325 CE, was to have both profound implications and permanent effects for the future of the Christian church. It is difficult for us contemporary Christians to appreciate fully what was at stake in the early fourth-century. A titanic struggle was being waged over the formulation of a Trinitarian doctrine causing those earliest theologians to read back into the earlier texts of both the Hebrew and the Christian Scriptures their understanding of the nature of the power of God and specifically that which resides in Christ and the intrinsic relationship of the power/glory that exists between the Father and the Son. What emerged was the basic consensus that force *is no attribute of God* (*Epistle to Diognetus*).

This is the core principle of Trinitarian theology. The *divinity of God* does not consist in God's ability to push things around, to make or break, to dominate and control. The Christian doctrine of the holy Trinity is foremost about God's essential use of power. God's essential use of power is restraint! God sends, seeks, invites, calls, and persuades but, most of all, God loves. This is certainly true of the understanding of יהוה in the Hebrew scriptures and is particularly evidenced throughout the Psalms. Divine glory/power in the Psalms is always connected to the covenant relationship between the people of יהוה and יהוה. The theophanic activity as it occurs in select psalms has as its purview the demonstration of divine glory and power for the benefit of the human witness and creation, all of which is under the authority of יהוה.

---

1. Wolfhart Pannenburg, in a lecture given at the University of Chicago, 03.07.2001, is reported as saying: "The Trinitarian doctrine of the Christian church is the higher mathematics of theology."

In understanding something of the development of the Christian doctrine of the Trinity, it is helpful to be familiar with its historical and cultural antecedents. The early Christian community's doctrines did not emerge solely from within some particular historical vacuum nor was the infant church untrammeled by the events and circumstances of history. The Christian movement began first as the *Jesus movement* in a predominantly Hebraic culture and a community that searched the Hebrew scriptures diligently for evidence of that testament's prophetic references and witness to the coming Messiah, the Anointed One of God. The movement also was conceived as the resurrection community and gathered its formation during a time when it was met with open hostility and severe persecution. Its formation and subsequent development were forged on the anvil of dissenting views that arose almost immediately as the various Christian communities sought to order their lives and coalesce around certain core beliefs that would mark its distinctive orthodox values. The basic interpretation of the meaning of the central Christian proclamation is rooted in the event of the Christ.

This was no easy undertaking and it was not accomplished without myriad stresses to its common life and purpose. Indeed, the dominant cultural phalanx that was a rampant Imperial Roman polytheism expressed openly a protracted hostility to the fledgling movement that was safeguarded during its vulnerable infancy by the Holy Spirit. This is no less true of the subsequent growth period of the church as it passed through several periods of persecution and hardship over three centuries. The notion of the holy Trinity may have been first birthed in the midst of the celebrated cultural norms and practices prevalent in classical Rome. For instance, the pantheon of Mithras, the Unconquerable Sun and its two torch bearers, *Cautes*, sunrise, and *Cautopates*, sunset, bore the symbol of a three branch pine tree forming a *Mithraic trinity*. [2]*Mithraism,* an ancient Persian religion that worshiped Mithras, the god of light and truth and the opponent of darkness and evil, survived and thrived in Cappadocia in the eastern region of the Empire until at least 300 CE. Such dominate cultural and religious symbols of the godhead were prevalent and the early church's primitive Trinitarian formulations had to contend with these competing icons and images.

In particular, around the latter third of the third century, Cappadocian theologians struggled mightily to express the meaning and discern the implications of a doctrine of the Trinity. What is the inner relationship between the Father, the Son and the Holy Spirit of God? The doctrine is nowhere stated explicitly in the Christian scriptures but rather was deduced particularly later on in the fourth-century CE. It has been claimed by some that a formal statement can be drawn legitimately and inferentially from the scriptures of the Second Testament–however none of the patristic theologians ever sought to wrest from the Christian scriptures *proof* of the Trinity within the Christian texts. On the contrary, the doctrine not only was not based *on the*

---

2. cf. "*Triplicity* is a symbol of godhead, and it means that god is the origin of all life," wrote the ancient Greek author, Plutarch, speaking of the pagan god, Osiris (quoted in J.N.D. Kelly) *Early Christian Creeds*, 253.

Bible, it was formulated apart *from* the Bible. This fact may trouble some Christians who cannot accept those realities of doctrinal formulations that were to become the hallmark of the faith apart from any biblical witness at the time of its origination. For instance, R. P. C. Hanson notes how it is that

> *two of the Cappadocians, Basil and Gregory of Nazianzus, admit silently that the Scriptural evidence for the Spirit as a distinct hypostasis within the Godhead is inadequate. Basil in his De Spiritu tries to take refuge in a most unsatisfactory doctrine of secret unscriptural tradition on the subject. Gregory, though he tacitly rejects Basil's device, in effect appeals to the experience and practice of the Church to supplement Scripture at this point.*"[3]

The Nicene Creed as we know it today is essentially the *Creed of Nicaea/Constantinople*. This example of early Christian creedal formulation illustrates the ongoing process that took place within the Christian church to articulate its own assessment of the primacy of *both* the witness of the Scriptures and the apostolic traditions of which the sacred scriptures were the inheritor. The church's further development of what would become fundamental Christian dogma, shaped and projected its self-understanding of the essence of the Christian gospel into an alien and pagan world. That the church's dogmatic pronouncements would come to dominate the surrounding culture so completely, and that it would accomplish this mission in less than four centuries following the event of Jesus Christ, is undeniably astonishing and remarkable. The true δόξῃ (*LXX, glory*) of God is now made manifest in the person of Jesus who did not come to us in billowing clouds of glory but rather as a human infant in abject humility, helplessness and fragility, the vulnerability of the Incarnation.

The basic premise of the Trinitarian controversy that erupted between Arius and Athanasius centered on this inner relationship between Jesus the son and God the father in the nature, the manifestation and the use of divine power in the person of Jesus. Arius insisted that God was One, undivided, eternal, unbegotten, unmade and absolutely transcendent; that Christ was not one with God but that there was a *then* in eons past when Christ, or the Son, was not; that he had been, at some point in time, in eons past, "created by God."

Arius sought to isolate the being of God as the One Eternal Father by whom all things and all beings were made. This included the Christ or the Son of God and the Holy Spirit too. What Athanasius and the other Trinitarian theologians came to understand and recognize was the very essence of divinity: the absolute freedom of God and the revelation of divine generosity, or love.

Athanasius and the majority who carried the day situated the being and the essence of the divinity of the godhead in totality, inclusive of the persons of the Son and the Holy Spirit. That there being, in substance, is the union of absolute love and the defining characteristic of God. It is the totality of self-giving which proceeds from

---

3. Hanson, *Studies in Christian Antiquity,* 245.

the relationship inherent between the Father and the Son. In place of a self-contained and absolute power, and in place of a self-sufficient and divine autonomy, which was Arius's contention, the Nicene theologians came to understand the nature and the being of God in terms of the richness of the reality that each person of the Godhead contributes and communicates to the other. It is this absolute freedom in the self-giving of the Christian godhead that defines the Triune God of the Nicene Creed.

The aloof and isolated deity of Arius, whose being is alleged to be *static,* and by whom many modern atheists (and Unitarians) seem to be persistently haunted, bears no resemblance to the Trinitarian God. It is this One and Only God who's very being is best expressed in form as an inner communion. It was this essential idea that lay at the heart of the controversy and which the fourth-century CE Cappadocian patriarchs, primarily Cyril and the two Gregory's, strove mightily to impress upon their fellow bishops, especially those who represented some of the western provinces of the empire who gathered at the invitation of the emperor Constantine in the Nicaea conclave.

That *God and Jesus and the Spirit are One* is the particular "wedge" that served to differentiate the critical distinctions inherent within the affirmed doctrine of the Trinitarian godhead at Nicaea. This differentiation would be clarified and ratified later at church councils in Constantinople, Ephesus, and Chalcedon over the next century and a half. The future implications for the Christian church, that is, what was wrought at Nicaea, can scarcely be exaggerated 1800 years onward.

Herein lies the exposure of the *Arian myth of the fixity of God.* It was not simply deemed to be unsustainable by Athanasius. Rather it was judged erroneous, and finally, heretical. The Cappadocian settlement of the fourth-century CE Trinitarian controversy reflected the thought of the pre-Nicene Christian communities wherein the faithful had worshiped God the Father, as revealed in the person of Jesus Christ, and under the aegis of the Holy Spirit without any suspicion that this God might not be simply and absolutely the One God of All in all fullness. The essence of their faith was that this God into whose life they had been graciously drawn, was indeed the God of Jesus and the psalmists. In this manner, the church preserved the Oneness of God and the monotheism which had been a bone of contention between Christianity and Judaism.

> The use of 'Spirit' for the divine in Christ was most prominent in those early Christian writings which still showed marks of the Jewish origins of Christianity; at the same time even these writings also echoed the Trinitarian language of the church. The conflict with Stoicism seems to have been a significant force in inhibiting the unreflective use of 'Spirit' as a term for the divine in Christ, even, in fact, as a term for God. The distinction between 'according to the flesh' and 'according to the Spirit' in Romans 1:3–4 was originally a way of speaking about the relation between the divine and the human in Christ (for which it was to prove useful again), not about the relation between the divine in Christ and the divine in the Father and the Holy Spirit. As the encounter with Greek paganism and the conflict with heresy made

> *greater precision of thought and terminology an absolute necessity, 'Spirit' was no longer an adequate way of identifying the divine in Christ.*[4]

At Nicaea the introduction of the concept of *homousia* (*of one substance, consubstantial*) safeguarded the faith in affirming the intrinsic equality of the *ousia* (*substance*) of the Father and the Son equally. The actions of theologians like Athanasius secured the full humanity and full divinity of Jesus and drove the all-important wedge between the affirmation of an undivided and immanent Trinity and that of a coherent transcendent unity of the economic Trinity. The emphasis then fell upon the internal relationship within the Godhead and secured a coherence between the three divine persons within the all-encompassing and internal unity of *Being*. It is this distinction that lies at the heart of all Trinitarian doctrine. This God is a trinity of persons in a unity of being.

To put it another way, the Father holds nothing back but gives all δόξη (*glory*) to the Son; while the Son holds nothing back but gives all that he has to glorify the Father. God, within the mystery of the Godhead, is supreme in the order of love. Self-giving love and not transcendence, giving and not superiority, are the qualities that most mark for us true divinity. The end result was the Nicene/Constantinopolitan Creed wherein the first definitive articulation of the role and the place of the Holy Spirit to be worshiped and glorified both as the Lord and giver of life was affirmed for the first time and pronounced as catholic dogma; as one who also holds equally the place of prominence within the Godhead as the third person of the Trinity. A more fully explicated form of the creed was revised and formalized nearly sixty years later at another church council held in Constantinople in 381 CE. It was again ratified fifty years later at the third major council of Ephesus, in 431 CE, and this is the form of the creed we follow today.

The Trinitarian doctrine in Christian theology became binding in the church and was motivated primarily by the manifestation of the divine ground of being in the person of Jesus of Nazareth who is confessed to be both the pre-existent Christ and the incarnate Son of God. The Trinitarian "problem" became a part of the Christological problem, the first and basic part, as is indicated by the fact that the Trinitarian decision reached at Nicaea preceded the definitively Christological formulation that was later arrived at in Chalcedon in the following century. The Council of Chalcedon in 451 CE undertook the sizable task of reformulating the orthodox doctrine concerning the two natures of the Christ. It took its start from the doctrine of the holy Trinity espoused at Nicaea, thereby clarifying its Christological terminology on the basis that there were three *hypostases (essence or persona)* but one divine nature; otherwise there would be three gods! Chalcedon also *affirmed the bounds of a single will and a single action within the Trinity itself which fixed its understanding and its usage.* [5] Whereas

---

4. Pelikan, *The Christian Tradition*, 186.

5. Lohse, *A Short History of Christian Doctrine*. "According to the entire Hebrew tradition, and therefore also according to the New Testament, the model for understanding God in [his] activity is not the model of generation and sexual reproduction, so dear to Greek mythology, but the model of the artisan who makes and the king who governs." 71.

the Trinity addressed the inner relationship of the triune godhead, the issue of Christology addressed the inner relationship between the fully divine nature and the fully human nature in Jesus Christ. This Christology had resonated throughout the eastern churches and Chalcedon was convened to resolve any misunderstanding as to the true natures of both Jesus's full humanity and full divinity.

Bernhard Lohse marks this distinction regarding the profound meaning and the effects of the creed of Chalcedon. At Chalcedon, in the fifth-century CE, the theologians of the Western church gave their answer to the East. This sequence was historically logical, and in terms of the church's motivation to address the threats to its orthodoxy, the sequence is, in fact, reversed. It was primarily the first Christological crisis that gave rise to the Trinitarian resolution reached at Nicaea and later became more fully explicated at Constantinople. In essence, the faith of Chalcedon, when viewed through the prism of Nicaea, *became* the faith of the Christian church!

When the crisis over iconoclasm loomed large in the seventh and eighth centuries, Chalcedon came to occupy a place of prominence right alongside Nicaea as the second major buttress for the development of holy catholic dogma and church doctrine.

> No *one who examines the Chalcedonian creed against the background of the Christological controversies which preceded it can charge it with attempting to define the person of Jesus Christ or to force the inexpressible into conceptual forms. The opposite is the case. In the face of the endless discussions concerning the relationship between the divinity and humanity in Jesus Christ, the Chalcedonian creed witnesses to the historic faith of Christianity. It does this in a way that is simple and yet unsurpassably clear and striking by asserting that Jesus is one person and that he is at the same time God and man. In doing so it does not eliminate the speculative questions. What it does is to give them a direction in which alone every attempt to speak correctly about the divinity and humanity of Jesus Christ must proceed. One cannot say that with the defining of this dogma Greek speculation emerged victorious over the Christian faith. On the contrary, it is this dogma which erected a dam against speculation or, at least, against an exaggerated form of it.* [6]

When the Eastern church's claims and defense of the use of icons sought to base its case on Christological arguments, it would accuse its opponents in the west of attempting to abolish the decisions reached at Chalcedon, which had articulated the mystery of the divine dispensation in Christ with clarity and precision. Chalcedon, then, became a two-edged sword of unintended consequences thereby contributing to the eventual rupture in the eleventh century CE of Christian unity between the East and West that remains riven to this day.

It was the threat of these Christological assertions made by Arius and the Arian theologians that served as the historical context for the formulation of Trinitarian

---

6. Lohse, *A Short History of Christian Doctrine*, 94. Rohr, Ibid. "Instead of the idea of Trinity being an abstruse conundrum, it could well end up being the answer to the foundational problem of Western religion."

symbolism as espoused, first in the creedal affirmations of Nicaea/Constantinople, and then in each of the subsequent creeds. All flows from Nicaea. In the words of Arthur McGill,

> . . . *throughout all eternity the Father is communicating [this] reality to the Son; and throughout all eternity the Son is giving all glory to the Father. These are not acts which cause changes in God; they are eternal processes which makeup God's essential aliveness . . . But we, Athanasius says, believe that the Father is almighty, not because [he] keeps the Son inferior to [himself] and uses the Son to display [his] own superiority, . . . but because [he] generates the Son as true God from [his] own substance and confers all [his] glory upon the Son.*[7]

So it is that four church councils or synods would come to prominence and thus dominate the form, the shape, and the content of Christian theology down to today in the Common Era: *Nicaea, Constantinople, Ephesus,* and *Chalcedon.* All early Christian theology would be authenticated by four ecclesiastical councils. Each of them was a singularly important sequel to the development for the three hundred-year-old Christian church in that it brought final fixity to the forms of the creedal affirmation of Trinitarian theology that had been evolving over the previous centuries, even from the days of the first-century Christian Scriptures. It is this *dogma,* both of Nicaea and Chalcedon, that has been the hallmark of the Christian church for eighteen centuries.

To the ears of the modern hearer, the mere sound of the word *dogma* often has the jarring effect of grating one's fingernails across a chalkboard. It is not a friendly sounding word and therefore needs to be unpacked and placed in its appropriate context. *Dogma,* that which is *believed at a particular time and place to affirm right teaching,* is appropriately understood, then, as the formulation of certain philosophical and theological constructs, born of necessity as the result of having addressed particular historical exigencies in a specific time and place; the calling forth of a unitary response to specific challenges and questions which reflect the particular *zeitgeist* of the historical era in question.

The creedal formulations that emerged during the first 300 years of the Christian church are not to be understood solely as eternally fixed theological propositions. Rather, as is the case in all Christian theology, the creeds are the result of a continuing process of ongoing reinterpretation, reassessment and restatement of what it is the church affirms, confesses, and pronounces as the belief and the meaning of the core Christian witness and proclamation in every age.

> *The doctrine of the Trinity is ultimately a practical doctrine with radical consequences for Christian life. The reality of the indivisible Godhead, so to speak, is intrinsically relational-or, as Basil of Caesarea put it, 'God is a kind of continuous and indivisible koinonia' (Basil, Letter 38, Migne, PG 32, 332a).*[8]

7. McGill, *Suffering,* 78.

8. Lohse, *A Short History of Christian Doctrine,* 90.

The authoritative *presence* of the Holy Spirit in the Church guides and instructs the corporate community in its collective discernment of what is the truth of God's revelation. The Spirit is constantly breathing new life and vitality into the church's corporate life and mission. Both tradition and scripture will continue to shape dynamically the experience of the Church's life in the world. This vigorous reinterpretation of the scriptures and tradition in the light of new human experiences—and not a static fixity of permanence—best characterizes the role and task of the church's collective theological mind and understanding in each new day and age. Each historic moment is always pregnant with the possibility of new understanding. That which is birthed may be painful in each generation but these are the birth pangs of new life that are breathed continually into the church's midst. *New occasions teach new duties, time makes ancient good uncouth; they must upward still and onward who would keep abreast of truth* (Hymn# 519, The Episcopal Hymnal, 1940. Thomas John Williams, 1890). These past forty years in the church's life illustrate this point clearly and convincingly.

Professional theologians regularly voice their concerns that most ordinary Christians have little or no sense of the specifically Christian doctrine of God. Trinitarian theology remains at the core of all Christian truth claims. Theological language consists of a particularly nuanced vocabulary of symbols—sign posts if you will–of the expression of deeper realities. A calcified dogma, when it is adhered to only literally therefore, is doomed to the dust of death. Verbal, scribal literalism has continued to plague the church in every age down to the present day. Such static, literalistic views, particularly when appropriated in interpreting the texts of the sacred scriptures, nearly always founder on the shoals of a shallow and irrelevant *heterodoxy*, meaning that which *is contrary to or different from an acknowledged standard*.

It's not too much to suggest, then, that the earliest Christian converts, most of whom came out of the strictly monotheistic world of Judaism only to emerge into the rampantly polytheistic world of the Roman Empire, were faced with enormous challenges to their new found faith in the risen Christ of God. When questions of understanding and restating the meaning and implications of the Christian gospel began to pass from the apostolic generation to the second generation, and to the next after them, a Christian theological language slowly began forming that would confront the speculations and challenges to the faith traditions as they were being handed down from one generation of faith to the next–the dynamic equivalence of an ancient tradition that continues down to our present day. This may be gleaned as already having begun to take shape in the first century when one reads the apostolic sermons in the book of Acts.

Remarkably, it is the fourth-century CE amplification of a specifically Trinitarian *dogma*, the One God in one substance, in three personae (Gk. *hypostaseis*) which best illustrates the Christian church's attempt to position itself, both politically and theologically, between these two extremes. It is always a delicate balance, to ensure that neither of the two natures of Christ is occluded by the other. The complementarity of both survived the issuance of the 325 CE form of the creed. The Nicene-Constanti-nopolitan Creed of 381 CE, goes to considerable lengths to preserve the integrity of both. It also is rightly described as having a more fully developed *theology of glory*. Early Jewish tradition understood that the revelation of God begins with mighty acts. Early Christian tradition came to understand that the revelation of God begins with the event of the Word, the *Logos*, which is embodied in the person of Jesus Christ.

> It *is, nevertheless, the Christian adaptation of the Greek idea of the Logos for the purposes of apologetics and philosophical theology that has figured most promi-nently in the secondary literature, and for good reason. The idea of the seminal Logos provided the apologists with a device for correlating Christian revelation not only with the message of the Old Testament, but also with the glimpses of the truth that had been granted to classical philosophers. As is evident from John 1:3 and its background in Proverbs 8:30, the doctrine of the preexistent Logos was also a means of correlating the redemption accomplished in Jesus Christ with the doctrine of creation. Creation, revelation both general and special, and redemption could all be ascribed to the Logos; the presupposition for each of these activities were the transcendence of God, who 'cannot be contained, and is not found in a place, for there is no place of his rest, being his power and wisdom' was the agent through whom God had dealt with [hu]mankind], achieving [his] purpose of creation and revealing [his] will.* [9]

Indeed, John's gospel begins with the declaration of the pre-existent, eternal, and incarnate *Logos* of God and the early church quickly recognized this emphasis on the divinity of Jesus, so much so that Jesus is presented by John as being alien to this world. *Jesus said to them (the disciples), You are from below, I am from above; you are of this world, I am not of this world* (Jn 8:23 NRSV). Indeed, the language suggests how he came from beyond time into a dark place–and brought the light with him. He is, indeed, the light! It is accepted by Christian scholarship that this unique presentation of the person of Jesus at the very beginning of the fourth gospel reflects the severe conflict that existed between the Christian Jewish community and the Jewish scribal authorities. In rapid and succinct sequence, the gospel announces the arrival of the Word made flesh, the witness of John the Baptizer, the scriptures of Isaiah the prophet, the baptism of Jesus, the descent of the Spirit, and the calling by Jesus of the first dis-ciples, one of whom immediately identifies Jesus: *Rabbi, you are the Son of God! You are the King of Israel!* (Jn 1:49 NRSV) And all in the first chapter! This divine arrival in John's gospel is unlike any other in the Christian scriptures and it had practical as well as theoretical implications for the church's first theologians.

Repeatedly in modern theology today, at least in the west, theologians have again sought to bring the doctrine of the Trinity back into connection with Christian life and worship. Karl Barth, in the first volume of his Church Dogmatics (1936), inveighed against the theological tradition which starts by considering God *in the abstract* rather

9. Pelikan, *The Christian Tradition*, 187, 188.

than with the historically specific Christian experience of God as Trinity. [10]The doctrine of the Trinity, then, in our own day is not about the abstract nature of God, nor is it about God in isolation from everything other than God. It is about God's life with us and our life with each other in God. The Creed of Nicaea/Constantinople first appeared in the following form:

> We believe in one God the Father almighty,
>
> maker of heaven and earth, of all things visible and invisible;
>
> And in one Lord Jesus Christ, the only begotten Son of God,
>
> begotten from the Father before all ages. Light from light,
>
> true God from true God, begotten not made, of one substance
>
> with the Father, through Whom all things came into existence,
>
> Who because of us [men] and because of our salvation came
>
> down from heaven, and was incarnate from the Holy Spirit and the Virgin Mary
>
> and became man, and was crucified for us under Pontius Pilate, and
>
> suffered and was buried, and rose again on the third day according to the Scriptures
>
> and ascended to heaven, and sits on the right hand of the Father, and will come
>
> again with glory to judge living and dead, of Whose kingdom there will be no end;
>
> And in the Holy Spirit, the Lord and life-giver, Who proceeds from the Father,
>
> Who with the Father and the Son is together worshiped and together glorified,
>
> Who spoke through the prophets; in one holy Catholic and apostolic Church.
>
> We confess one baptism to the remission of sins; we look forward to the
>
> resurrection of the dead in the life of the world to come. Amen. [11]

Just as Christians are to grow into the fullness of who they truly are through their lives together, the relationality of God, that is, precisely who God is, is formulated in the creed. In other words, it is through the eternal loving and self-giving of one to another that each of the persons of the God-head is to be understood as a trinity of persons in a unity of being.

> *The doctrine of the Trinity is concerned with the question of the unity of God in the context of a faith which, in the same breath, asserts not only the divinity of the Father, but also that of the Son and of the Holy Spirit. Christology, on the other hand, is concerned with the question of the relation between that which is divine and that which is human in the person of Jesus . . .*[12]

The Father pours out the divine life to the Son, the Son speaks and embodies this life, and the Spirit brings both together in passionate delight and love. This divine

10. Barth, *Church Dogmatics II,* 490, 91.

11. As documented in J. N. D. Kelly, *Early Christian Creeds,* 297, 298.

12. McGill, *Suffering,* 79.

dance celebrates the life of God in our midst. Because of Jesus's death and resurrection God has graciously accepted and drawn a wayward, lost humanity into an eternal union of love. It is Christ who first embodied that love among us in the person of Jesus of Nazareth. It is the Holy Spirit who has poured that love into our hearts through the knowledge of the risen Christ and whose *presence* in the world resides in the Holy Spirit who is active in the Church as the body of Christ. This is where the Great Commission, [13]our purpose in life, enters in: to bear faithful witness to this great Good News in joyful anticipation that one-day God will be all in all. [14]

Far from being a kind of esoteric theorizing about God's inner life, with no bearing on anyone's existence here and now, the doctrine of the Trinity is rather, ultimately, a practical doctrine with radical consequences for Christian life. Instead of being a presumptuous prying into something about which we know nothing, or very little, the doctrine of the holy Trinity is the result of the church's reflecting on what it means to participate in the life of the One God, through Jesus Christ, in the power of the Holy Spirit. It was then further refined by the Cappadocian theologians (Basil, Gregory of Nazianzus, Gregory of Nyssa), and formally proclaimed at the Council of Constantinople (381 CE). Augustine of Hippo's *De Trinitate* (ca. 424 CE) was to give it its authoritative interpretation and declarative expression. This witness became the accepted position of the church at the synod of Ephesus in 431 CE.

We need constant reminding that the bible of early Christianity was the Hebrew scriptures or more precisely, *the Law and the Prophets*. Evidence begins to accumulate for the existence of many books of the Hebrew Bible in Greek from the mid-third-century BCE. By the end of the first-century CE, wider collections were in circulation among both Greek-speaking Jews and Christians, some of them revised in various ways. By the time of the first manuscripts of the Christian scriptures, most of the books of the *LXX* were already established as Scripture in the Christian churches. Most scholars believe the LXX was considered sacred by the early church.

This is what is meant when the early Christian community speaks of the *Scriptures* or when they use the quotation formula it *is written*. Alongside scripture from the beginning was a lively oral tradition which was transmitted under the authority of *the Lord*. An early oral and written tradition was comprised of select sayings of Jesus as well as short narratives concerning his life and ministry. The *words of the Lord* were not restricted to the sayings of Jesus of Nazareth alone, but they also contained the spoken words of the resurrected Christ as they appeared in the gospels. These words of the risen Lord form an essential part of the gospels' witness to the post-resurrection appearances

13. Starting with the "Baptismal Formula" of Matt. 28:19, "*baptizing them in the name of the Father, and of the Son, and of the Holy Spirit,*" Theophilus of Antioch utilized the Greek term *trias* for three-in-one-ness. This was translated by Tertullian (ca. 200 CE) as *trinitas*, explained as "three persons in one substance" and was adopted at the Council of Nicaea (325 CE).

14. "For God has placed all things under Christ's feet and has made him the head over all things for the church, which is Christ's body, the fullness of him who fills all in all" (Eph. 1:22, 23; 4:6), which is also an echo of Ps 8:6 and 110:1.

of Jesus who is now confessed as Christ. It is now beyond dispute that the sayings and teachings of Jesus as well as the stories we have about him were first circulated, not in written form, but by oral transmission. This earliest oral tradition was not due to any lack of ability on the part of the early Christians to produce written records, nor was it due to any dogmatic preference for the oral medium of transmission.[15] Rather, the interests, needs, and demands of the existential situation of the early Church, living as it did in a hostile environment, called forth those stories and writings that comprise the Christian scriptures and the dynamic traditions out of which these scriptures were to emerge.Scripture, tradition, reason and experience were to become the hallmark of the emerging Christian message of salvation.

The form and content of the tradition was thus shaped by the sociological and theological contexts which reflected the life of the early christians. This is also true, of course, for Jesus himself. The sayings, parables, and example stories of Jesus in their form are heavily dependent upon the cultural milieu of 1st century Judaism in his lifetime. It is possible to demonstrate in many instances how the different theological situations of the early Christian community after the death and resurrection of Jesus and the new cultural horizons of the early church, which soon went beyond the limits of Judaism, *provided* new molds for the reshaping of the tradition.[16]

The early Christian community's primary reliance on the LXX can be illustrated best by referencing both Paul's use in his epistles and the gospel writers use of certain psalms on the lips of Jesus. Psalm 16 is one of the psalms appealed to by the early church and parts of it are cited in all four gospels.

> *In the apostolic church, Psalm 16 was read in the light of the resurrection of Jesus . . . In the resurrection of Jesus Christ, the last limitation on the connection between the Lord and life was transcended. Now it is possible to say the psalm in the midst of life and in the face of inevitable death with a trust that matched the language of the prayer. The Lord has made known the path of life.*[17]

The gospels' authors, the evangelists, also sought to interpret the meaning of the event of Jesus of Nazareth as the Christ of God in light of both the pronouncements of the Hebrew prophets and the poets of the Psalms. Jewish Christians of the first-century CE, familiar as they were with the monotheistic declarations of their heritage and rightly, and in defiance of the dominant polytheistic culture of the Roman world, sought to make some sort of sense of the nature of the one true God, the son, Jesus Christ, and the Holy Spirit of God as evidenced in the LXX scriptures. This required a peculiar balancing act and one which demanded the full attention of the emergent Christian community. This fact is frequently overlooked and underappreciated in

---

15. Dines, *The Septuagint,* 27.

16. Kelly, *Early Christian Creeds,* 297, 298. cf. Lohse, Ibid. 71.

17. Terrien, *The Elusive Presence,* 89.

much of biblical scholarship. The *messianic psalms* lie at the heart of the earliest Christian theologians' explications and representations of Jesus as Messiah come.

While the first-century Christian community lived its life in the hope and expectation of the imminent return of the risen Christ in glory, the focus and conduct of their life together in God was not, at first, concerned with what was later to become a deeper understanding of the mysteries of God's life in their midst. Subsequent creeds were born of necessity in confronting, as they arose, particular errors and distortions of the Christian message. The interpretation of both Scriptural traditions was integral to their understanding of the nature of God, the person of Christ, the Messiah, and the *presence* and the divine activity of the Holy Spirit in the life of the church.

This understanding of the relationship between Jesus and the Psalms is especially illustrated in the earliest sermons of Peter and Paul as recorded by Luke in the book of the Acts of the Apostles. [18]God was reckoned as One in the apostolic proclamations concerning Jesus as the risen Christ of God. It would take another three centuries before the church was to determine its own understanding and develop and articulate the creedal affirmations concerning the relationship that exists between the three individuated persons of the holy Trinity. What is clear—in the early centuries—is that the church positioned itself in such a way as to affirm from its earliest writing traditions that God is One.

Paul very clearly states in I Corinthians 11, that *I received and I handed on to you the tradition I received from the Lord* (11:23, NRSV). Some scholars interpret this important text as a reference to the role of the Holy Spirit operating within the church's oral traditions to "enscripturate" what is already known and received as authoritative from the apostles. Only a few of the apostolic generation lived thirty to forty years beyond the event of the resurrection, one of them being the apostle John who probably lived well into the last decade of the first-century CE.

The early Christian writings only first began at the mid-point of that century with Paul's epistles–letters to scattered churches around the region of Asia Minor. The gospels came much later and it is unknown but also likely that the evangelists had access to the epistles, the earliest being Paul's first letter to the Thessalonians, which can reasonably be dated around 48 to 49 CE. A period of five decades (from the resurrection of Jesus), then, had passed before the writing of the first gospel of Mark. This means that Paul's letters were written without knowledge of the gospels, since each of the four gospels and the Acts of the Apostles were composed after his death in Rome, 64/65 CE.

That the four Gospel writers along with Paul and, particularly, the writer of the epistle to the Hebrews had combed the LXX scriptures, especially the Psalms for references to the Messiah, is beyond doubt. This apostolic tradition was a living and dynamic ethos that lasted for more than half a century and it preserved the memory and

18. There are around forty Old Testament quotations in the book of Acts, fourteen of which are from the Psalms. Peter's sermons are dominated by references from Psalms 2, 16, 69, 109, 110, 118, and 132. Paul's speeches also show a keen interest in Psalms 2, 16, and 89. cf. Steve Moyise, *The Psalms in the New Testament*, 66.

meaning of the life, death, and resurrection of the Lord Jesus. This is the essential basis in fact for the writing of the "New Testament" and it is therefore why it is accurate to say that the Christian scriptures are founded upon the apostles and the prophets. This close relationship between the continuity of the earliest Jewish Christians' formative understanding of Jesus and their dependence on its scriptural antecedents, is particularly relevant. Our understanding of the earliest Christians' use of the Psalms, in particular, is informed more fully by the history and subsequent development of what became the essence of Christianity's creedal formulations. Just as monotheism was a late development in Israelite religion, and was read back into the earlier centuries of its religious tradition, so it is in the Christian tradition as well.

The doctrine of the holy Trinity was called forth in controversy as was the case in most of the Church's subsequent declarations of the meaning and proclamation of the Christian faith. These were then read back into the tradition to be enshrined in the written Christian scriptures.

> *The Trinity did not become a central focus for Christian reflection until the fourth century. This troubles those who have a static view of Christian truth and who believe that such truth can only be what stands forth as self-evident in the New Testament. But such a fixed notion of truth has not prevailed throughout the history of the Christian church. On the contrary, each age penetrates and focuses on the good news in its own way . . . There is a depth and manifoldness about the revelation of God in Jesus, and the theological preoccupations of no single period in the church's history should be allowed to tyrannize the whole church. The Trinity was clearly the concern of Eastern Christians of the fourth century. What we must ask is not, Was this concern also central for the New Testament writers? But rather, is this rooted in the Biblical presentation of Jesus? Is this doctrine truly offered as a clarification and penetration of the powerfulness of God which gathers humanity into itself through Jesus?* [19]

The root of some of these traditions and their origins had already begun in the church's study of the Psalms. This witness of the Psalms was gathered from both the LXX and the Hebrew scriptures. Clearly the apostolic community valued the Psalms highly. A core theological statement on the inherent nature of the Godhead took four centuries to complete. And even then, it went through continuous reformulation and revision well into the later centuries CE. In the ebb and flow of human history in each age, just as we have traced it briefly with the emergence of the first creed of the early church, so it is with the psalmists who–for instance—took it for granted that history had meaning and purpose because the processes of history are under the sovereign control of יהוה. This is a fundamental axiom of ancient Hebrew belief and this conviction is borne and built upon throughout the entire Psalter. This brings us to the conclusion that the Hebrew poets' contributions to the early Christian church's understanding of the person and work of Jesus Christ, in her earliest writings, were enormous.

19. McGill, *Sufering*, 66, 67. cf. Pannenberg, *Jesus, God and Man*, 47–49.

Sacred Verdict

THE PSALMS GATHER TOGETHER key theological themes that are unique to the thoughts and patterns already present in ancient Israel's liturgies and communal worshiping life over a period of nearly a thousand years. The abiding refuge and a consummate trust in the *presence of* יהוה is the core thesis of this book. It is also the sacred verdict of the early Christian community. The Hebrew psalms guided the theological reflections of Israel's prophetic traditions. It is the Psalms that anticipated the fuller deliverance and redemption in the person of the Messiah of God and was to become such an essential part of the prophetic witness and declaration. The prophetic tradition of ancient Israel was first rooted in the worshiping songs of the nation. Ancient Israel's creed is articulated in the book of Psalms, and, in the words of G. W. Anderson, is *Sung, not Signed* (cf. footnote 5).

It is regarded by the Jews as axiomatic that the governance of the world rests upon the foundations of justice and righteousness; that there is a divinely ordained order; that a moral law of universal applicability is operative within the catenation of historical events; that there are positive ethical imperatives, the violation of which human beings will be held accountable; that these extraordinary biblical narratives and poetry are part and parcel of God's revelation acting within human history; that it is יהוה who dwells inside human history (immanence) and is sovereign over human history (transcendence). [1]The pursuit of this reality was key to the ancients who had less distractions then we, but who were just as perceptive, intelligent and inquisitive. Although they did not have access to our vast storehouse of technological knowledge and myriad data, their core experience bore witness to the same phenomena. The knowledge and the experience of the divine is the human quest of each successive generation.

It comes very easily to us *moderns* to sometimes have a rather condescending attitude of superiority toward the ancients. We tend to imagine ourselves as being more sophisticated and *enlightened* in this post-modern era. We view history as shaped by us, determined by us, and even perhaps, in some instances, controlled by us. We speak casually about *making history.* But the poets of the Psalter imbued the processes and the events of human history with *numinous* meaning. When Israel ceased to be a

1. Sarna, *Songs of the Heart*, 111.

nation in the early sixth-century BCE the critical reality became one of a crisis of faith. Amid the ashes of the temple and the apparent indifference and inactivity of יהוה, the poet of Psalm 74 gropes through the darkness of God's seeming abandonment and questions faith in the God of the covenant. The physical temple can be rebuilt but what of the faith in God which it represented?

> To Israel, the decades after 586 B.C.E. produced an enormous crisis of confidence as to the divine promises. Reality seemed to have delivered a massive disconfirma-tion of the content of the promises; the one-time gilt-edged securities had a market value of approximately zero in the wake of the disaster. As a result, the people experienced what we would call a crisis of faith: the experience of the absence of God and of God's silence (cf. Pss 44:1–3, 9, 23–24; 74:1, 10, 22). Doubt flourished, although no one was then tempted to question God's existence. The God-is-dead theology was never to make any headway in ancient Israel. On the other hand, the Israelites did entertain doubts as to God's ability and willingness to help.[2]

For the poet of Psalm 74, the crux of the Psalm is found in the retrospect and backward look to the horrendous damage done to the worship place and the endless scorn and contempt for the holy name, יהוה . Why does יהוה permit Israel's enemies to triumph over them? Why does יהוה withhold his *mighty arm and outstretched hand?* Why does יהוה tolerate the brutal treatment of his own people, *the flock of his own pasture,* the people of the covenant? Psalm 74 is a communal lament which is designed for use in public prayer and lamentation ceremonies and begins with a cry of distress, *Why, O God?* And concludes with a direct appeal for divine intervention: *Rise up, O God, plead your cause!"* (74:22).

The total obliteration of the sanctuary (74:3–7) and the sense of God's seeming alienation and absence is a major problem. The catastrophic dimensions of the events are vividly portrayed in verses 4–9 which describe the extent of the violence. The entire psalm as a whole is shaped by the tension between God and the enemies of God and by the perspective of God's battle against the enemies of Israel. In verses 19–21 the mortal threat to the poor comes into focus: *Do not forget the life of your poor forever. Have regard for your covenant, for the dark places of the land are full of the haunts of violence. Do not let the downtrodden be put to shame; let the poor and needy praise your name. Rise up, O God and plead your cause* (NRSV). The psalm gives no explanation of the catastrophe but attempts, in the genre of lament and of accusation, to effect the connection to God in the

> interpretive figure of a common fate linking God and [his] people in such a way that strength can be derived from this to enable the people to withstand their suf-fering. . . . The psalm resists the temptation to disengage God's divinity from the

---

2. Mettinger, *In Search of God,* 160, 161.

possibility of experiencing God in concrete history. On the contrary, it demands
that God take sides on behalf of the victims of history.[3]

Psalm 74

A Maskil of Asaph

Why, O God, do you cast us off forever?

Why blaze your anger against the sheep of your pasture?

Remember your people whom you acquired long ago,

which you redeemed to be the tribes of your heritage.

Remember Mount Zion, where you came to dwell.

Direct your steps to the perpetual ruins!

the enemy has destroyed everything in the sanctuary!

Your foes have roared within your holy place;

there they set up their emblems, their foreign emblem,

high above the upper entrance they hacked

the wooden trellis with axes.

And then, with hatchets and hammers,

they smashed all its carved work.

They set your sanctuary on fire; they desecrated

the dwelling place of your name,

bringing it to the ground. They said to themselves,

Let us utterly crush them; let us burn every shrine of

God in their land. We will utterly subdue them;

So they burned all the meeting places of God in the land.

We no longer see our emblems;

there is no longer any prophet, and there

is no one among us who knows how long it will last.

How long, O God, is the enemy to scoff?

Is the foe to revile your name forever?

Why do you withhold your hand?

Why do you keep your hand in your bosom?

3. Hossfeld and Zenger, "Psalms 2," 251.

Yet God my King is from of old,

working salvation in the earth.

You divided the sea by your might;

You broke the heads of the dragons in the waters.

You crushed the heads of Leviathan;

You gave him as food for the creatures of the wilderness.

You cut openings for springs and torrents;

You dried up ever-flowing streams.

Yours is the day, yours also the night;

You established the luminaries and the sun.

You have fixed all the boundaries of the earth;

you have made both summer and winter.

Remember this, O יהוה, how the enemy scoffs,

and an impious people reviles your name!

Do not deliver Israel, your dove, to the wild animals;

do not forget the life of your poor forever.

Have regard for your covenant,

for the dark places of the land are full of the haunts of violence.

Do not let the downtrodden be put to shame;

let the poor and the needy praise your name.

Rise up, O God, and plead your cause;

remember how the impious scoff at you all day long.

Do not forget the clamor of your foes,

the uproar of your adversaries

that rises continually.

This Asaphite poet would serve to remind יהוה that when Israel is humiliated, יהוה is humiliated. *Remember this, O יהוה, how the enemy scoffs, and an impious people reviles your name!* The form this poet's argumentation takes is to recall the great acts of God in creation; how יהוה is their God from of old, fixing the stars and the sun in their courses and ordering both night and day. For him it was not some notion of an inchoate determinism nor is he indifferent or detached. Just as he had believed יהוה was involved and immersed in the human drama so does his view of history center in the matter of being fully awake, aware, and alive to the glory/*power* that is made manifest in the twists of the human drama. Nothing less than the glory of יהוה is at stake. In particular, as Creator and Sustainer of Israel's sacred story and in general, the subject is the involvement of יהוה in and with the entire human story. The dramatic portrayal of the desecration done to the temple seeks to hold Yhwh accountable and in some sense responsible. Yhwh could have, but did not, intervene! Therein is the crisis of faith.

In some particular sense, then, all human history is regarded as God's story. In this way, the poet of Psalm 74 seems to espouse a view of history that is put in a mythic context and serves to express the realities of life in the language of human imagination in the form of mythical images.

> *The value of this language of imagination lies in its capacity to comprehend and express those realities which so often lie beyond the power of the logical constructs of the 'reasons of the mind.' In the mythical language of the Bible there is no escape from the experiences of the senses or from the actuality of historical happenings. The use of mythical language occurs when the inability to deal with the great questions of humanity with a 1+1=2 model is recognized, either explicitly or implicitly. The 'reasons of the heart' and the modes of imagination must be utilized in the upward and outward journeys which the reality of human life in God's creation requires.* [4]

The poet deals with one of the basic issues in religious thought: how do the people of God cope with disaster in the face of God's seeming absence? The answer? By hanging on to hope in God and trusting God in all the circumstances and events of life in human history. The very character and nature of God is called into question when things go badly for God's people. Israel in her own historical moment appeals ceaselessly to the acts of God not only in her life but in the life of the world. The appeal to creation is none other than the appeal to the nature of God. What does it mean to say יהוה is trustworthy in the face of history's calamities? To this question, Israel's own theology appeals to the character of God's absolute fidelity. This is not an easy poem to read. It is filled with a depth of anguish at the unspeakable things the people have seen and experienced and their anger at those who are responsible. It does not resort to noble religious sentiments. It is too real for that. In the words of Brueggemann,

> *the psalmist only wants Yahweh to feel what we feel. It is like a patriot watching the flag burned, a lover watching his beloved raped, a scholar watching the library burn-a helpless revulsion that can scarcely find words.* [5]

In this manner the psalm points to an important theological affirmation: God's love and fidelity transcend the historical moment. One could easily make the case that the constancy (חסד, *hesed*) of יהוה is the dominant theological confession of the Psalter. [6] Not only in terms of content but in terms of form, the Psalms bear witness

4. Tate, "The Interpretation of the Psalms," 255.

5. Brueggemann, *The Message of the Psalms*, 71, 72.

6. Jacobson, *Soundings in the Theology of the Psalms*, 111.

to Israel's basic confession of faith: יהוה is faithful. Israel has been elected. She has become enmeshed with a faithful God. יהוה is the God of steadfast love–חסד (*hesed*) and enduring trustworthiness אמת'(*'emet*).

The term חסד (*hesed*) is one of the great theological words in the Hebrew Bible (roughly 245 occurrences) and nearly half (127) are found in the Psalter. Although it is notoriously difficult to translate, its essence in English includes the sense of *fidelity, loyalty, loving-kindness, constancy,* and *steadfast love.* חסד (*hesed*) is a relational word conveying something of the essential internal character of יהוה. Israel's ongoing witness to God's unparalleled faithfulness is always rooted in the character of יהוה.

Likewise, the term אמת' (*'emet*) has at its root the sense of *reliance and trustworthiness* and portrays יהוה as ever faithful in deeds, trustworthy in word, and absolutely reliable in relationship. אמת'(*'emet*) occurs frequently in partnership with חסד (*hesed*) in a number of psalms. Together these two very rich and dense terms convey the essence and character of יהוה. יהוה is the One God of All who can be trusted absolutely!

Psalm 91 illustrates this nicely: *My refuge and my bulwark, Elohay (my God) in whom I will trust/*אמת'*('emet*) (verse 3), and, *Yahweh's constancy* חסד (*hesed*) *will be for you both enveloping shield and sheltering barricade* (verse 4, LW). The psalmists strove hard after faith and trust in יהוה. Rolf Rendtorff amplifies the poets' understanding by grounding the faithfulness of יהוה in creation, and even before it. He writes:

> Confidence in the unalterable faithfulness of God constitutes the ground on
> which all the rest stands, and it is deeply anchored in the past, back to the time of
> creation or even before the beginning of the world. God stands with [his] faithful
> at the beginning, before all other occurrences. At their best, they were fully alive
> to the possibilities of Yahweh, open to Yahweh's voice: the acknowledgment that
> God is good and does good and the confidence that this faithfulness exists and
> that therefore in all the future [God] will be and do good toward us.[7]

יהוה is able to conquer all the evil powers which work death and destruction on earth. יהוה is stronger than death and chaos, whose power is not limited by death. Life and death are in the hand of יהוה; and יהוה is able to give life to those who are threatened by death: *For you do not give me up to Sheol, nor let your godly one see the Pit* (Psalm 16:10, NRSV).

It is never stated *how* this deliverance takes place; it is enough to know *that* God will not deliver the psalmist's soul up to death and Sheol. Nowhere in the Psalms, it has been said, is there a reference to resurrection or eternal life. The psalmists are content to know that God is stronger than death and Sheol. They speak in terms of death and life, without spelling out their beliefs concerning the destiny of the individual soul after death, except for some general statements about Sheol, where no one can praise

---

7. Rendtorff, *Canon and Theology*. "This is what the Old Testament means by faith–firm reliance on God's historical actions in the past and firm confidence in [God's] future activity. This is the keynote of confidence in the presence and glory and faithfulness of God that dominates a great part of the Psalter; and it is precisely these psalms which have a firm place in the Christian tradition as well." 61.

יהוה. But their faith that יהוה is stronger than death provides the presupposition for an added assurance: יהוה does not leave the faithful alone in death but is present also beyond death.

> *An analysis of the references to death and the after state in the Hebrew scriptures suggests the development of the hope of personal immortality out of the belief in family and national immortality. The glimmering hope of personal immortality in the Psalms above referred to, if it exists, which I hardly believe, comes from an application to the individual of the consoling hope of national revival, or continuance of life by posterity, which we find animating the prophets in the midst of apparent national death (Ez. 37:12, Is. 53:10), and which clearly appears in the Psalms in such passages as 9:12f; 22:29–31.*[8]

The establishment of peace is assured and the clear joy of fellowship with God as it is experienced in divine protection and guidance is particularly intense. The sole answer is that there is none but יהוה, the Redeemer, with whom the psalmist longingly desires fellowship and in whom [she] assuredly entrusts [her] eternal soul.

In this confidence and armed with faith, we become more prepared to face our present existence with courage and confidence despite all of its problems and challenges. We are prepared to grow older, to experience failing health, strength and even adversity and bodily infirmities because יהוה is our intimate and reliable portion and refuge. When God's children find themselves in a world of hurt, they still know that no power is beyond God's control.

> *'Children of God,' [is] a rare expression in the Old Testament . . . [It] is a metaphor for Israel as the people of God who look to and depend on God as children do to their parent. The teacher [poet] knows and belongs to a circle of faithful souls who think of themselves in this way. His identity with them and responsibility to them is his first restraint against public cynicism. Probably they are the community for whom his confession was composed . . . he could not rescue himself from his perplexity and its accompanying bitterness and envy by the effort of his own reasoning. He tried to think it out, but the effort only brought troubled weariness. That door was closed to him also. With his concession of failure, he warns against trying to find the truth of faith in the independent work of the human intellect. Reason cannot unravel experience to supply the ground for faith.*[9]

The poet learned that trust is rooted in God's faithfulness (חסד) in acting on his behalf in the past, the present, and will likewise so act in the future. The two figurative phrases contain images that speak to us of *dwelling in the hiding-place (shelter) of Elyon* and *staying (abiding) overnight in the shadow (shade) of Shaddai*. To dwell and abide in יהוה is to live in faith and receive the rewards of faith. This is the essence of ancient Israel's descriptive metaphors (*shield, fortress, refuge, stronghold et al*). This is

8. Peters, *The Psalms as Liturgies*, 44.

9. Mays, *Psalms*, 242.

the language of faith, trust, and confidence. To dwell and abide in the *presence* of יהוה is, for some scholars, to attest to the promise of an afterlife with God.

> *The Hebrew text was finalized at a time when the official religion of Israel had no clearly formulated position on conscious survival after death in God's presence. By the time that Ps 16 was translated into Greek, after 200 BCE, Israel began to officially accept immortality–even though the temple priests, later called Sadducees, never did. Ps 16.8 reads in the Greek [LXX] ' I see the Lord before me always [throughout eternity];' A similar re-reading of Ps 16 to express the 'new' belief in bodily resurrection and personal immortality is not only found in the Dead Sea Scrolls and in the midrash . . . of the psalms but clearly in the New Testament (Acts 2:24–28).*[10]

Israel's poets have in mind primarily the sojourn to the Temple. The image of the Temple constitutes the fixed destination of the journey of faith. It is esteemed as the shelter, the place of security and these images are intended to depict the achieved peace of having found refuge by dwelling in *Elyon's* secret shelter. Dwelling in *the hiding-place of Shaddai* is meant to express the safety and peace of mind that come from the knowledge and the security of protection against all ills. Spending the night in the shadow of the Almighty is intended to express the feeling of being out of danger and springs from the confidence that there is someone else who is keeping watch. יהוה keeps watch over Israel! To position one's self within the protective love and care of יהוה is faith's fundamental thrust and attitude. יהוה is before and behind all life. For ancient Israel, this is the crux of the matter. יהוה is the life loving "life giver" and this fact of faith, which is enunciated clearly in Psalm 16, lies at the bottom of all other concerns.

> *In the contemporary world, where the fear of death often motivates frantic attempts to achieve our own security and joy, frequently through material abundance, Psalm 16 points us in an entirely different direction. Abundant life will not be something we achieve but something we receive . . . Psalm 16 is thus both a challenge to keep the Lord always before us and a promise that the experience of God's presence is its own reward: abundant life and fullness of joy.*[11]

For Israel, the faithfulness (חסד *hesed*) of יהוה is perfected in Israel's history. These mighty saving acts enable God's people to live in hope and to abide on the edge of glory. In the affirmation of the past deeds of יהוה lies the hope of an unimaginably glorious future. God's justice in life remains the hope of the godly. Even when that justice appears to have been thwarted, interrupted, or delayed, God's purposes are being realized and actualized in human history. It is the stage on which divine revelation is continually being played out. The idea of revelation as history is a fundamental premise of my approach to a theological understanding of the Psalter.

10. Stuhlmueller, *Psalms*, 119.

11. McCann, *Psalms,* The New Interpreter's Bible, Vol. VI, 738.

The God of Israel, יהוה, is active and present in the events and unfolding drama of human history. This is both a Hebrew and a Christian concept. There is nothing quite like it in any of the other world's great religions. It is this uniquely Hebraic understanding of the dimensions of the saving practice and help that is enacted by יהוה toward a people with whom an eternal covenant has been transacted. It will never be abrogated.

Salvation history is Israel's gift to the world and this lies at the heart of any right understanding of the book of Psalms. Revelation is dynamic, not static, and all human history is the stage on which the divine action and purposes are being played out. Once this concept is grasped, it can transform our own understanding of יהוה, the sacred scriptures, the pivotal role of Israel, the Christ—event, the purpose and destiny of the Church (the New Israel of God), and the eschatological hope that will be effected at the end of human history. Human history is teleological and is headed toward a consummation of all things at the end of the age.

Any theology of the Christian church that would seek to give an appropriate accounting of the reality of human suffering, sin, the fact of evil, and the gracious companionship of the Holy Spirit, guiding and dwelling within the life of the Church, must first come to a right understanding of divine revelation and the centrality of God acting in human history. The absolute sovereignty of God is affirmed both within human history, and over it. Those who long after *the glory that shall be revealed* will be rewarded ultimately by virtue of their faith. Indeed, a first century Christian hymn, Colossians, documents the true existential nature of our earthly human life with this astounding revelatory hope: It declares, *"You have died! Christ is now your life."*

> You died; and now your life lies hidden with Christ in God.
> When Christ, who is our life, is revealed, then
> you too will be revealed with him in glory. (3:4 REB)
> ὅταν ὁ Χριστὸς φανερωθῇ ἡ ζωὴ |ὑμῶν, τότε καὶ ὑμεῖς σὺν
> αὐτῷ φανερωθήσεσθε ἐν δόξῃ.

The one who trusts in God will be able to experience, amid the changes and chances of human life, the saving, protecting, strengthening fidelity of God. Psalm 90 at its heart is a commentary on the meaning of the long tramp of humanity through history. Our earthly existence is book-ended by time. We exist in time, the duration of our lives is measured by time, and we live within the boundaries and the limitations of time. God is *from eternity to eternity.* Psalm 90 is a starkly drawn depiction of human boundaries. The well-loved hymn of the Christian church, *O God Our Help in Ages Past*, is taken from the text of this potent psalm, which announces the Lord as *our place of dwelling throughout all generations.* It is in Psalm 90 that the transitoriness of human life is addressed, not as a negative rejection of human life, but as a contextual affirmation of the grace, mercy, and fidelity (חסד *hesed*) of יהוה in the midst of an awful existential reality.

The theological confirmation of this Psalm's boundaries is more fully explicated in the Christian tradition in the epistle to the Colossians. The author cites a fragment of a first century hymn of the Christian church in acclaiming the role and *presence* of the pre-existent Christ of God in creation. This is a crucial text for it traces for the early Christians their spiritual lineage and their acknowledgment of the inheritance of the promises made by יהוה to Israel and to them, as set forth in the Hebrew scriptures: The Christian writer records that, because of Christ, there now exists a new reality. Without the slightest hint of equivocation, it states that Christ is present at the creation of the cosmos; not only present but is the active agent in creation!

> In him [Christ] everything in heaven and on earth was created, not only things visible but
> also the invisible order of thrones, sovereignties, authorities, and powers:
> the whole universe has been created through him and for him. (1:16 REB)
> ὅτι ἐν αὐτῷ ἐκτίσθη τὰ πάντα ἐν τοῖςοὐρανοῖς καὶ ἐπὶ τῆς γῆς, τὰ ὁρατὰ καὶ τὰ ἀόρατα
> εἴτε θρόνοι εἴτε κυριότητες εἴτεἀρχαὶ εἴτε ἐξουσίαι

This first century CE hymn is redolent with liturgical overtones. Thematically, it is structured forcefully as a declaration of absolute power and dominance over the entire cosmos, Christ being the indelible *icon* of God. The very idea of all things is the fact that all coheres in him. This is the cosmic assertion. Christ is the pre-existent one.

> He [Christ] exists before all things, and all things are held together in him [Christ]" (1:17 REB)
> καὶ αὐτόςἐστιν πρὸ πάντων καὶ τὰ πάντα ἐν αὐτῷ συνέστηκεν

Describing God as invisible was common in Hellenistic writings and the language of the letter to the Colossians reflects this view. But such is not the case in Hebrew thought and outlook. In the language and vision of the Psalms, יהוה is never described as the *invisible God*. Rather, it is *the presence* of יהוה that is apprehended, known, and acknowledged as the glory, the radiance and the splendor of the holy.

> *The poet now turns to the elation of a constant intimacy. 'My glory is gleeful'. It may be the most ethereal aspect of his consciousness. The word 'glory' is usually applied to God, but it may be a chosen word for human honor and radiancy. The psalmist is thus able to pass from the jubilation of his terrestrial interests to a spiritual dance of [his]inner being. The current of consciousness moves from the theme of well-being in this mortal life to a life of delight beyond the grave. The permanence of the human person is a consequence of divine communion. It is not related to the Hellenistic view of the immortality of the soul. Deprived of the Presence, the self-hood of humans is not immortal by birth. It will be abandoned in the underworld. As the beloved of Yahweh, [he] will never see the lower depths of the underworld. [He] knows that love, which attaches [him] to [his] God, will*

not be ruptured by death. On account of the Presence, the prospect of annihilation in the underworld has vanished.[12]

What is always feared most by Israel–and this anxiety is expressed throughout the Psalter—is that the divine *presence* may be withdrawn. And when the *divine presence* of יהוה is withdrawn there are always negative consequences for Israel. Israel's angst is addressed forthrightly by the constant appeal to the assurance of the *presence* of יהוה. The psalmist's persistent theme in Psalm 91 is the promise of intimate joy and security–in this life— when one lives life in the close proximity of the *presence* of יהוה.

> *. . . the psalm is not concerned merely with an inner attitude of trust and a feeling of security but with a practice of trust and the reality of security that derives from the fact of God's action. In light of the focus on eternal salvation, it is important to emphasize Yhwh's declaration that we do not experience such salvation only in the future and in heaven and in the inner person. Yhwh grants it now, on earth in the body.* [13]

Nothing is more highly valued. Nothing compares with dwelling in the *presence* of God. When the *presence* of יהוה is withdrawn, all life is at risk. Perhaps this is what the psalmist is referencing when he writes of life lived in the *presence* of יהוה: *A thousand may fall on your left, myriad thousands at your right hand; but you yourself will be unscathed (LW).* The temptation inherent in this Psalm's declaration and promise is to isolate and interpret it solely in terms of individual benefits that accrue to the person apart from the community of faith. But Psalm 91 resists such an interpretation. This magnificent declaration of trust in יהוה is one which sets the *presence* of יהוה at the pinnacle of the Psalter. This poet knows the security of a life that is lived in the *presence* of the world of יהוה. We are granted a mere glimpse into what a marvelous world it is. The poet's entire being is infused with the knowledge of God and the promises of grace are beyond all measure, and beyond all human limitations. The poem is a gem of trusting faith that is brimming with hope.

One lives into faith within the broader community and each of the psalmists characterizes the blessings of life lived in connection to and with others. But when יהוה is absent, bad things happen to Israel. Only constancy and trust in יהוה are considered to be worthy of that *eternal weight of glory!* This is taken as an eternal accounting of *things not seen, for the things that are unseen are eternal* (II Cor. 4:18, NRSV). That is the sacred verdict for the poet. Our triad of psalms declares the joy and the exuberance of living life in the *presence* of יהוה.

Psalm 92, the last psalm in our triad, [14]declares: *For you, O יהוה, have made me glad by your work; at the work of your hands I will sing for joy. How great are your*

12. Terrien, *Elusive Presence*, 178, 79.
13. Goldingay, *Psalms*, Vol 3. 49.
14. Creach, *The Destiny of the Righteous in the Psalms*, "Psalms 90–92 are connected by their

works, O יהוה*! Your thoughts are very deep!* (92:4–5, REB). This is the only psalm in the Psalter entitled A *Song for the Sabbath Day!* It is a psalm of praise and confidence as the poet builds upon the deep and immeasurable security that is the theme of Psalm 91. The psalm ends on the firm foundation of "the rock!"

Psalm 92

A Psalm. A Song for the Sabbath Day

It is good to give thanks to יהוה,

to sing praises to your name, O Elyon;

to proclaim your constancy (חסד) at daybreak,

and your steadfastness all through the night,

to the music of the zither and lyre,

to the rippling melody upon the harp.

I am ecstatic with joy, יהוה, when I recall all you have done;

at the works of your hands I will sing for joy.

How great are all your accomplishments, יהוה?

the immensity of your thoughts are vexing and deep!

The faithless are not aware of this,

nor can fools ever appreciate it.

The faithless may sprout as thick as weeds

and every evildoer flourish,

but surely they are all doomed to destruction forever.

O יהוה, you are supreme above all; you dominate everything forever.

See how those who resist you perish; see how the evildoers are routed?

But you have raised my horn as if I were a wild ox;

you have poured the oil of gladness upon my favored head;

With my own eyes I have witnessed the recompense of my enemies;

my ears overheard what the faithless were whispering;

But in due time the righteous shall flourish like the palm tree;

they shall grow tall as the cedars of Lebanon.

---

common interests in the ephemeral nature of the human and the willingness of God to preserve and prolong the lives of those who trust in [Him]. On the lips of Moses, as it were, these psalms address the lament of Psalm 89 with a clear message: when mortal limits overwhelm, *trust* [italics mine] in God, the eternal Sovereign, is able to satisfy with steadfast love and make *'glad all their days'* (Ps.90:14). The Lord, who has been Israel's refuge in all generations, is held up in these psalms as the secure refuge for those who face humiliation and death (Pss. 90: 1, 9; 91:1–4, 9–12, 14–16; 92:16)." 76.

Planted in the house of יהוה, they will flourish in the courts of (my God) *Elohay*;

they will still bear fruit in old age, and so remain fresh and succulent -

All are demonstrating that יהוה is upright in all [His] deeds;

O יהוה my rock! There is not one who can find any fault in You!

Surely this psalm would have been well known to the early church as it gathered together on the sabbath for common worship, prayer and praise. Here יהוה is extolled as the One who alone is worthy of praise. The supremacy of יהוה is underscored by the language of the dominance of the rectitude of יהוה. This is the Hebrew "gospel" and the worthiness of praise and the joyful exuberance of Psalm 92 is a telling theme for this poet. The theme of praise and thanksgiving is appropriated by the early Christian community. Again, the epistle to the Colossians instructs the first century CE Christians in their liturgical life to

Let the gospel of Christ dwell among you in all its richness; teach and

instruct one another with all the wisdom it gives you. With psalms and hymns

and spiritual songs, sing from the heart in gratitude to God. (3:16 REB)

Ὁ λόγος τοῦ Χριστοῦ ἐνοικείτωἐν ὑμῖν πλουσίως, ἐν πάσῃ σοφίᾳ διδάσκοντες καὶ νουθετοῦντες ἑαυτοὺς, ψαλμοῖς ὕμνοιςᾠδαῖς πνευματικαῖς ἐν [τῇ] χάριτι ᾄδοντες ἐν ταῖς καρδίαις ὑμῶν τῷ θεῷ

It is somewhat counter-intuitive the way these three psalms function together—the eternality of God's nature is contrasted with the ephemeral nature of human life. And yet human beings are supremely valued; *You have set our iniquities before you, our secret sins in the light of your countenance* (Ps 90:8, REB). But Psalm 19:12 adds this: *But who can detect their errors? Clear me from hidden faults* (REB). Knowledge of sin is a precious gift. Human beings' sentence of death issues from the judgment of יהוה on humanity's sin.

> *Death is to be understood in the psalms, how? As a 'personal' power, or merely as a poetic personification of the common end, ordained by God, of all mortality? As far as the psalms speak of a conflict with death, the latter possibility is hardly likely. It is not the necessity of death in itself which is the enemy against whom the Psalmists seek to protect themselves, and against whom they appeal to God for help. For them it is the former 'dynamic' understanding of death which stands in the foreground; 'death' appears to them as a power separate from God, opposed to [God's] rule, and hostile, therefore, in the absolute sense a power exceeding by far the most terrible human adversaries.*[15]

The acknowledgment of human finiteness and mortality as a result of human sin may lead to an awareness and appreciation of life that is lived in each moment before the all-seeing eye of יהוה. We fear God's *wrath* because we possess knowledge of our *moral guilt*. We fear our finitude and our death because we know instinctively that we

15. Barth, *Introduction to the Psalms*, 49.

have been weighed in the balance and found wanting. God is able to conquer all the evil powers which try to work death and destruction on earth. יהוה is stronger than death and chaos, and is not limited by death. Life and death are under divine control. יהוה is able to deliver and to give life to those who are threatened by death: *'For you do not give me up to Sheol, or allow your godly one to see the Pit'* (16:10, NRSV).

> It is never stated how this deliverance takes place; it is enough to know that God will not deliver the psalmist's soul up to death and Sheol. Nowhere, however, in the Psalms is there a reference to resurrection or eternal life. The psalmists are content to know that God is stronger than death and Sheol. They speak in terms of death and life, without spelling out their beliefs concerning the destiny of the individual soul after death, except for some general statements about Sheol, where nobody can praise the Lord. But their faith that God is stronger than death provides the presupposition for an added assurance: God does not leave the pious [man] in death but is with [him] beyond death.[16]

Karl Barth lends theological cogency to the discernment of the poet's assessment of the fact of human mortality: Death is the consequence of human sin and rebellion.

> Death as it actually encounters us is the sign of God's judgment on us, the fini-tude of human life stands in fact in the shadow of its guilt. It is perhaps concealed but the very real basis of our fear of death is the well-grounded fear that we must have of God. But this is to say that at the point where we shall be at our end, it is not merely death but God who awaits us. But the God who awaits us in death and, as the Lord of death, is the gracious God. It is really true that we need not fear death, but God. We cannot fear God without finding in [him] the radical comfort which we cannot have in any other. This simply means that it is God who is our Helper and Deliverer in the midst of death.[17]

This self-reckoning is the beginning of our liberation. *Satisfy us in the morning with your* חסד *(steadfast love), so that we may rejoice and be glad all our days. Make us glad as many days as you have afflicted us, and as many years as we have seen evil* (Ps 90:14–15, NRSV). The late first century Christian proclamation in the Colossian letter, which was written more than half a millennium in the future from our psalms, declares an unimaginable and astounding truth about both humanity's serious quandary and its unimaginable hope: Action was taken by יהוה in and for us in the incarnation, death and resurrection of Jesus of Nazareth. This man of God's own choosing is accomplished fact and the psalms anticipate this event, at a specific point, in time, in human history. This is the great good news of our redemption! This portion of Colossians reads like a Christian "psalm."

> *Were you not already raised to life with Christ? Then aspire after those things that*

16. Ringgren, *The Faith of the Psalmists*, 74, 75.
17. Barth, *Christ and Adam*, 137.

are lofty, where Christ is, seated at God's right hand, and fix your thoughts on that
higher realm, not on this earthly life. You died; and your life now lies
hidden with Christ in God! When Christ, who is our life is revealed,
then you will also be revealed with him in glory. (3:1–4 REB)

οὖν συνηγέρθητε τῷ Χριστῷ, τὰ ἄνω ζητεῖτε, οὗ ὁ Χριστός ἐστιν ἐν δεξιᾷ τοῦ θεοῦκαθήμενος·
τὰ ἄνω φρονεῖτε, μὴ τὰ ἐπὶ τῆς γῆς. ἀπεθάνετε γὰρ καὶ ἡ ζωὴ ὑμῶνκέκρυπται σὺν τῷ
Χριστῷ ἐν τῷ θεῷ. ὅταν ὁ Χριστὸς φανερωθῇ (ἡ ζωὴ ὑμῶν), τότεκαὶ ὑμεῖς σὺν αὐτῷ
φανερωθήσεσθε ἐν δόξῃ.

In the light of the new reality of Christ—in the face of our mortality—our eternal home, our very human destiny, lies within the heart of a loving God's embrace. It is, then, precisely the wrath of God that *is the clearest sign to a faithful and struggling community that there is purpose in life. God's wrath is a constant and relentless pressure felt by the faithful in their lives, a presence that warns and admonishes and requires the securing of wisdom that it may be detected the better.*[18] Harrelson writes unerringly of the unrelenting pressure that is being brought to bear upon human beings in our standing before the holy and just demands, not of a wrathful God, but the God who offers us mercy and forgiveness; offers us a way out of our existential dilemma; a way out of a no-exit situation.

Mercy is the antidote to the wrathfulness of a holy God who is in no mood to let us founder on the shoals of unmitigated disasters. Living under the mercy of a just and insistent God whose only desire is to spare us–to extricate us from a self-destructive descent into the dark—is the counterpoint to what is perceived as God's backhand of judgment. But to those who are in a hopeless situation, which is all of us, mercy is offered. That we are called to live under the mercy is the radical base construct of our newly liberated lives.

These are remarkable declarations that are made under the full knowledge and acceptance of the fact that humanity is under the sentence of death.

> ... *the Psalms show their independence by their endeavor to understand the conquest of death in relationship to the faith of Israel. In the psalms 'life'means a share in the land and the promises of Israel (Ps.16), membership of the chosen people in the land of the living' apportioned to them (Ps. 27.13), and the right to live and die in righteousness, as defined by the covenant founded and ratified by Yhwh ... 'Life' for the psalms means the historical formation and appearance of the people of God, while 'death' means their sinking back into the natural existence of the heathen, fundamentally without history ... the conquest of death to which the psalms bear witness is in fact of an 'other worldly' nature. It is not based on the nature and potentialities of the world, and, within the world, of [humans], as laid down from all eternity, nor does it consist in bringing these to perfection. It is brought about by the free acts of God in [His] faithfulness,*

18. Harrelson, "A Meditation on the Wrath of God: Psalm 90," 190.

*whereby [He] calls, establishes and maintains individual [persons]–despite their
own powerlessness–as members of [His] people.*[19]

Persons of faith and persons of little or no faith live out their days—some at least
do—with the conscious awareness of their mortality; that there is an inevitability to
the fixed fact that death will visit each one of us on our last day on this planet. In
relation to this psalm, the connection between the wrath of God and the promise
of human life speaks to our existential angst concerning the purpose, meaning, and
seeming futility of our lives. In this respect, the poet of Psalm 90 instructs that God
does not leave human beings alone but comes into our lives.[20] God insists that human
life, fleeting and apparently pointless though it may seem, be a responsible life. This
fact of the "wrath" of God, then, helps us to appropriately *contextualize* our lives, so
that we may aspire to live an accurate life before God.

> *The fact that God's power brings even the dying person through death into the life
> of the new world of God–this assurance, founded on the resurrection of Christ
> Jesus, was still hidden from the people of the Old Testament. Only the power of
> unlimited trust let them hope beyond the final border. Therefore, the expressions
> of trust in the prayer songs are characterized by that unique transparency which
> then, in the pattern and witness of the certainty of the resurrection in the New
> Testament played an important role.* [21]

The poet of Psalm 91 writes: *because you have made Yhwh your refuge, and Elyon
your dwelling place, no evil shall befall you, no scourge come near your dwelling. For
Yhwh will command his angels concerning you to guard you in all your ways. On their
hands they will bear you up, so that you will not stub your foot against a stone* (Ps
91:9–11, LW). The figurative picture of *abiding within the shadow of Shaddai* is, once
again, derived from the ancient custom of the right to hospitality entrusted to the
protection of the host. In a very real sense then, it is *Shaddai* who serves as the host of
the cosmos, ever vigilant and standing watch over the whole creation.

The singular comprehensiveness and depth of trust placed in the Hebraic God is
based on the stupendous fact that יהוה, whose name humans dare utter only with awe
and reverence, is precisely the One who the individual may call–*Elohay-my God.* The
יהוה-fearing person may rise above this profane environment by the personal confession of trust in God. Invited to dare tread on the boundary of the holy, all of life is
infused with a new reality–a new relationship. It imparts to one's whole existence that

19. Barth, *Introduction to the Psalms*, 55.

20. Harrelson, Idem. cf. Patrick D. Miller, Jr. *Interpreting the Psalms*, ". . . alongside–and indeed
growing out of this conviction about God as the only context of our life—is another important dimension to the way in which the psalm speaks of our time. That is its utter *realism* about human life under
God. It reminds us in inescapable fashion that our life is clearly limited and that we must perceive it and
deal with it as such. One of the great human self-deceptions is to think of our time as unlimited when in
fact, as this psalm reminds us, our time is very short; for all of us death comes, and it is no illusion." 174.

21. Kraus, *Theology of the Psalms*, 242.

special character of respect and humility before the *presence* of the Holy in *the pursuit of God.* [22] The pursuit of God is an interior pursuit. This reorientation of the entire fact of our existence is the task and the challenge. It is, most definitely, the journey of each individual soul. [23]

It is the greatness of Israel's God who declares what are the grounds for giving thanks and praise. Israel's salvation and exaltation are not conditioned on her goodness, or even on her obedience to the covenant; Indeed, she was doomed to failure from the moment she entered into the covenant. No one could keep the covenant law–not even Moses. And no one could keep the sacrificial laws in all their complexities and demands. The wide expanse and truth of these psalms, then, is that יהוה is full aware of our human incapacitation and yet the poet can declare that *the righteous shall flourish like the palm tree, and grow like a cedar in Lebanon. They are planted in the house of* יהוה; *they flourish in the courts of our God* (Ps 92:12–13, NRSV). To flourish in life is to be planted in the promises of יהוה and to worship in the courts of יהוה—that is, to accept life as gift and dwell within the parameters of the blessings of יהוה by choosing obedience and desiring to live an accurate life before יהוה; to be open and willing to be fully known by יהוה and then to contemplate this vast reality in our lives.

From the very beginning the covenant was never based on Israel's fidelity. Rather it was always based solely on the fidelity (חסד, *hesed, faithfulness, constancy*) of יהוה. One of the distinguishing features of our three psalms is the implicit declaration of unequivocal confidence and trusting hope in יהוה. It is this certitude of trusting faith in the midst of the catastrophe of humanity's sin that binds these psalms together. These certitudes characterize the entire Psalter. This is how life is for Israel. Life actually does reside within the nature and the character of the holy God. The role of faith for the psalmists expressess itself precisely at this point. For the poet there is no higher calling then to ground one's life in the fact of חסד (*hesed, constancy, lovingkindness*) which is the very nature and the ultimate fact of יהוה.

The faith of ancient Israel is reflected in the hunger and desire for relationship with יהוה who meets Israel in her sin, her suffering and her need. Israel's *theology* is characterized primarily by its eagerness to encounter the *presence* of God in the midst of life. This is what it means to live under the mercy. The God of Israel is the Lord of all trustworthiness, constant fidelity and grace. The steadfast love (חסד *hesed*) of יהוה is the way in which יהוה is related to and invested in the life of Israel. Life that is lived under the mercy extends beyond the reach of a fearsome wrath and a dreaded rejection of all life that succumbs to this divine pressure; when all life is lived in total surrender to the will and purposes of יהוה.

---

22. cf. Tozer, *The Pursuit of God.*

23. Curtis, *Psalms,* "What the psalmist devoutly desires is a life of intimate communion with God in the here and now, a desire that can be echoed by all who repeat the psalm today, albeit that many who use the words now will also envision that communion as continuing after the death of the earthly body." 32.

Humanity's rebellion is overwhelmed by an awesome grace. It is precisely in and through this mercy that grace is experienced. All life is rooted in God. All life is precious and the life of humanity is the crown of creation. It is the basis for the psalmists' faith that it is rooted and grounded in a relationship that is shared by the whole community. The Hebrew Psalms do not know any grace apart from this. Refuge and safety mean salvation and these are the hallmarks of God's grace. It is both a free expression and a fixed relationship that binds individuals to God in covenant. Faith is rooted in promise and fulfillment. It never becomes God's duty to act. It is never arbitrary. Freedom of the will and the restriction of sin are one in God's grace.

> To learn how to trust God in the difficult and bitter circumstances is nothing short of a dangerous experiment with truth and action. It is the risky venture of every generation of believers. Like the ancient Israelites, we seek to trust God in the midst of suffering in order to find the strength not to be overwhelmed by our grief. Like our spiritual ancestry, we seek to trust God in order to find, if not all answers, then at least some comfort and reason for enduring our suffering. Again, like them, we seek to trust God in order to find the courage to stand up against those who crush us. In every generation, as reflected in the psalms of trust, all these–strength, comfort, courage–have been considered valid reasons to seek God. [24]

When life is lived under the unrestrained mercy of God's total and unconditional acceptance, the question of wrath withers and dies in the joys of a new found liberation and an unimaginable freedom. We call this salvation. God's salvation is a cauterizing love that refines, cleanses and will finally purge all human resistance. Healing and gratitude for such an overwhelming mercy have their own rewards, both in the here and now and in the longed for future life with God.

The mercy of God is not cheap. It is offered us at a costly price. For example, it is impossible to read the synoptic gospels narratives of the testing of Jesus in the wilderness without thinking of Psalm 91. In today's Church, the revised Eucharistic Lectionary appoints this psalm to be read or sung on a Sunday once every three years, the First Sunday in Lent, Year C (the gospel according to Luke). G. K. Chesterton has written of the *temptation* of Christ narrative in the Christian gospels that there are two sins against confidence and hope: *presumption* and *despair*.[25] Presumption assumes nothing is being done unless we are doing it; despair, the feeling that everything else fails when we fail. In certain of the psalms of lament this sense of despair presumes the failure of יהוה to act. This perceived failure is attributed to the inattentiveness of יהוה and becomes a recurring expression of Israel's anxiety. Upon further reflection, however, the poets place this presumed failure of יהוה in a broader and more appropriate

---

24. Pleins, *The Psalms*, 198.
25. Cf. G. K. Chesterton, *Orthodoxy*.

context.[26] Consequently, the complaints address, resolutely, the unfaithfulness of Israel and the continuing faithfulness (חסד, *hesed*) of יהוה. A confession is uttered and a vow is made toיהוי.

It is this presumption of the devil that lies at the center of the gospels' accounts of the confrontation of Jesus with the evil in the wilderness. Nikos Kazantzakis is simply wrong in referring to this as *"The Last Temptation of Christ."* It is neither the first temptation, nor the last testing of Jesus. The synoptic narrative of this face-off in the Judean desert sets the whole tone for what lies ahead. Mark's gospel, brief as usual, gives it three terse sentences, then turns the text completely on its head by stating the ministering role of angelic aides: *immediately the Spirit drove him[Jesus] out into the wilderness, and there he remained for forty days . . . He [Jesus] was among the wild beasts; and angels attended to his needs* (Mark 1: 12, 13 REB).

In the gospels of Matthew and Luke, the straight-forward designation of the tempter is simply *the devil* whereas Mark's gospel identifies the tempter as *Satan*, i.e., *the Adversary.* In this infamous use of scripture, the gospels of Matthew and Luke note how the devil employs verses 11a-12 of Psalm 91 in an attempt to corrupt Jesus and thus deter him from his appointed earthly purpose.

> *Satan placed Jesus on the pinnacle of the temple and challenged him to jump off to test God's promise that the angels would bear him up. The temptation was to take the promised protection of God into the control of his own will and act. That would have shifted the power and the promise from the free sovereignty of God to individual willfulness. Jesus saw that as a way to test God, not as the way of trust.* [27]

The devil quotes directly from the Hebrew psalm exhorting Jesus to act presumptuously; to enact the power at his disposal in the service of the devil.[28] In this vein, Psalm 91 must always be read and interpreted in the light of that wilderness encounter. In the narrative of the temptation and in preparation for his public earthly ministry, Jesus resolutely faces the powers of hell which are arrayed against him. By virtue of fasting, a chosen weakness and powerlessness, prayer, and an intense vulnerability, the Savior confronts the onslaught of a naked, crass, and corrosive evil that is absolutely destructive and demonic in its intentions and effects.

Throughout the Christian scriptures, there are ninety-three psalms quotations that are taken from more than sixty different psalms. Among the sayings of Jesus

26. Koch, "Is There a Doctrine of Retribution in the Old Testament?" "There is no place in the Old Testament where the concept of actions with built-in consequences is so obviously at work as is the case with the Psalms. This is true for so many different sections of the Psalms but particularly in the individual laments and individual songs of thanks."69.

27. Mays, Psalms, *Interpretation,* 298.

28. Holladay, Ibid. ". . . according to the testimony, it is not Jesus himself who uses the psalm but the devil! The devil is said to have quoted Ps. 91:11–12 as a temptation (Matt. 4:6; Luke 4: 10–11), and Jesus replies by citing Deut. 6:16. This is an astonishing window into Jesus' understanding of Scripture, or at least into the tradition of the first-century church about Jesus' understanding of Scripture; there is a devilish use of Scripture as well as a godly one." 116.

in the gospels there are more quotations from the book of Psalms than any other book of the Hebrew Bible. The Psalms are on the lips of Jesus. So say the gospels. The evangelists added more references, mostly as proof texts concerning Jesus' fulfillment of prophecy. In the baptism and temptation narratives, for instance, quotations from the Psalter figure prominently. In the temptation narrative the devil's use of Psalm 91 and Jesus' response to it is instructive. The fulfillment and promise of the psalm is not to be sought in Jesus' pursuit of his own mission nor in his own self-glorification. His person and will are subordinated absolutely and completely to the will of his father.

The sacred verdict is the fact that *Jesus will eventually claim the assurance contained in this psalm, but he will do so only from the cross.*[29] Quotations from the Psalms are dispersed widely throughout the gospels. Here, the devil's quotation from Psalm 91 is singularly notable. It is met by Jesus with the stern rebuke and command from scripture (Dt. 6) not to test יהוה *your God.* With single mindedness, it is the authority of the Christ (Jesus, now recognized and acknowledged by the post-resurrection community as the Messiah, the *Anointed* of God) who hurls back the lies into the teeth of the devil. It is now the resurrected Christ who confronts and rejects absolutely this purloined author- ity. Satan's power is broken and all evil will be resisted and Satan defeated. We need to learn always to read the gospels from a post-resurrection perspective.

The dimensions of Jesus' true identity and authority and power will be revealed, ultimately, to the devil, the arch-enemy of all humankind, to the Church (the Israel of God), and to the whole world. The nature of Jesus's own personhood, the purpose of his being-in-the-world and the ramifications of his public ministry, all signal a full engagement with structural and systemic evil. Jesus' response to the devil is direct: *Out of my sight! Scripture says: You are not to put the Lord your God to the test!* [Lk 4:12 REB]. This confrontation can have only one outcome: Evil will be named, it will be resisted, and it will be defeated. Peter Craigie's impressive commentary on the first fifty psalms contains the following observation:

> In the New Testament, the terminology of battle and war is consistently trans- formed into the language of spiritual warfare and the struggle against evil. Such a transformation is not new in the New Testament; it is anticipated in this and many other psalms, whose initial martial purpose had already undergone trans- formation by the time of their incorporation into the Psalter.[30]

After Jesus' life, ministry, passion, and resurrection, it is his cross that yet casts a lengthy shadow. The earliest Christians (and there is abundant evidence to sup- port this), searched diligently through the Psalter for any and all appropriations to the Messiah in order to ascertain the meaning of the suffering and death of Jesus. Within the ancient psalms of complaint/lament the most conspicuous example of this is the early church's understanding of Psalm 22 as having a particular relevance

29. McCann Jr., *A Theological Introduction to the Book of Psalms,* 165.
30. Craigie, "The Role and Relevance of Biblical Research," 75.

to the events of the first Good Friday. The glory of the resurrection of Jesus Christ as the hope of the world was first recorded by St. Paul at the mid-century mark of the first century CE and some two or more decades before the writing of the earliest gospel, Mark. The apostle provides a concluding postscript of hope for the benefit of the emergent first century community: *the last enemy to be defeated and destroyed is death—(I Cor.15, NRSV).* [31]

In the earliest gospel we find Jesus quoting from a variety of psalms.[32] This did not go unnoticed by the early Christians. Christoph Barth accentuates the causal link between the first-century Christian church's transmission of the sayings of Jesus and their relationship to the person of the Messiah in the Psalms:

> *It was not until the resurrection of Jesus, that is, until the conclusion and completion of his historical work, that it was even possible to hear and understand the message of the psalms concerning Jesus. The completion of God's redemptive work, acting in and through Christ, is the core proclamation of the apostolic church.* [33]

The Psalms (and this is also true of the Hebrew Scriptures) do not speak about the historic person of Jesus of Nazareth. The Jesus of history is not found there as a reference for these ancient texts. Rather, it is more accurate to say that these Hebrew texts speak about יהוה, the God of Israel and the world, and the way of יהוה with Israel and the world, through and in the promised coming of the Messiah of God. Only in this sense is there any implicit knowledge of the Messiah, both in the Psalms and in the Hebrew bible, generally. This fact is reflected in the first Christians' confession of Jesus as the *Anointed of God* and is appropriated in the biblical canons of both the Hebrew and Christian scriptures.

> *The quotation of Ps. 16:8–11 in Acts 2:25–29 and 13:35 raises special problems . . . Resurrection from the dead is not involved. But the statements in the Hebrew text were understood differently in Acts 2:25–28. Since the starting point is the resurrection of the one who was crucified (v.24), Ps. 16:8–11 was taken as a statement which David made about Jesus as the Messiah. Clearly a passage that announces a resurrection cannot refer to David. David is dead, and his grave can be seen in Jerusalem. Therefore, David, as a prophet who knew the promise made in 2 Sam. 7:12 13, spoke prophetically of the resurrection of Jesus Christ. It is clear that the meaning of the psalm has been transformed. Acts 2:25–29 contributed in a major way to the fact that church tradition read OT psalms, which*

---

31. Barth, *Introduction to the Psalms*, 51.

32. Four psalms, each cited or alluded to at least twice, play a major role in Mark. These are Psalms 2, 22, 110, and 118. In the Luke-Acts narratives there are fourteen quotations from Psalms; in Matthew's gospel there are five marked quotations and ten unmarked quotations–16 different psalms are quoted in the synoptic gospels. In the fourth gospel, John, there are ten identifiable quotations from the psalms. Each of the quotations is taken—most likely—from the LXX.

33. Barth, *Introduction to the Psalms*.

were really dealing with 'deliverance from death', in the light of the resurrection and interpreted them accordingly.[34]

Jesus of Nazareth is only known, recognized, and confessed as the Christ of God in the light of the cross and resurrection. This confession of faith in Jesus by the first Christians, nearly all of whom were Jews, can only be derived from the interpretation and acknowledgment of the Messiah as portrayed in the ancient Hebrew scriptures, particularly the Psalms and Isaiah. This distinction is essential and it is crucial to our understanding of the subsequent development of the early Christian church's articulation of a *Christology*. This *sacred verdict* is one of mercy and provides the basis for interpreting, from the very beginning, the meaning of Jesus' death and resurrection and its implications in light of the witness of the *messianic psalms* and the pronouncements of certain of the poets and prophets.

34. Kraus, *Theology of the Psalms*, 160.

From Eternity to Eternity

The Christian church's fuller Christology and development of the meaning of the Incarnation and the confession of the Messiah in the person of Jesus of Nazareth, took nearly five centuries and was finally and formally crafted and explicated at the council of Chalcedon in 451 CE. Understanding the distinction between the Jesus of history and the Christ of faith was first acknowledged and confessed by the earliest Christians. This only adds to and does not detract from the essential witness of the Hebrew scriptures to the promised coming of the deliverer, the redeemer, the messiah, the Anointed.

Psalm 16 is one of those psalms that held a particularly keen interest for the first-century church.

> The psalmist has understood that death could not separate him from the divine love. The early Christians found in this prayer a program of speculation when they sought to formulate the theological reflection imposed on them by their revolutionary faith in a Jesus who for them was living forever. In transcribing a reconstitution of Peter's discourse on the day of Pentecost, the Lukan editor quoted Psalm 16 in the LXX translation (Acts 2:25–28), with the subtle transfer from a terrestrial viewpoint ('at my right hand'; v.8) to that of a heavenly life ('at thy right hand'; v.11). The theologian of the nascent church had clearly discerned that an eternity of communion with God after death depended on a love that could not vanish at physical death. The God whom the poet loved is the one in whom we live and move and have our being (Acts 17:28), hence the psalmist, on the one hand, or the Christian interpreter, on the other hand, is completely at ease and at home with the perspective of this immortality.[1]

The epistles of both Paul and Peter quote the Psalms frequently in didactic as well as prophetic contexts. *For those who desire life and desire to see good days, let them keep their tongues from evil and their lips from speaking deceit; let them turn away from evil and do good; let them seek peace and pursue it. For the eyes of the Lord are on the righteous, and his ears are open to their cry. But the Lord sets his face against those who do evil to cut off all memory of them from the earth* (cf. Psalm 34:12–16 quoted in I Pet 3:10–12 NRSV). The first-century apostolic preaching and witness, proclaimed specifically in the

---

1. Terrien, *The Psalms*, 181.

post-resurrection sermons as they are recorded in the book of the Acts, take particular note of some of these psalms. Quoting from them widely and often (Psalms 16, 74, 69, and 110) indicates how early in the Christian *kerygma* [2] these psalms occupied a central role in connecting their witness to the Christ-event. This has been the position of the Christian church from its earliest days. It is noteworthy, for instance, how both Peter and Paul understood and appreciated the historical significance of Psalm 16: 8–10: *I have set* יהוה *before me at all times; with him at my right hand I cannot be shaken. Therefore, my heart is glad, and my soul rejoices; my body too rests unafraid; For you will not abandon me to Sheol, or suffer your faithful servant to see the pit (NRSV).*

This Psalm (16) is entitled *A Miktam*, one of six psalms so entitled and possibly meaning an inscription etched on a stone slab or stele, and is taken by the Christian apostles as a prophecy of Christ. [3] The apostolic generation of the early Christian church is now convinced that not merely a few isolated words, but the whole context these psalms represent speak of the Christ of God. It is important to remind ourselves that the ancient Hebrew text was only finalized after the time when the official religion of Israel had had no clearly formulated position of a conscious survival after death in God's *presence.*

> . . . all those Psalm-texts which speak of salvation from death or from the Underworld may have to be understood as testimonies of the experience of the living, of deliverance from the threat of death, back into life. This means that the Psalms make no clear and unambiguous statement concerning a life on the other side after death. The much discussed texts 16,10; 49,15; and 73, 24 do not demand a concept qualitatively different from the concept of the existence of the dead in the Underworld. Here and there we do find a hope that existence itself is not the highest possession, but rather co-existence with God; and that communion with God may possibly lessen or even overcome the loneliness of Sheol. . . . The concept of an eternal life after death was not discovered in Israel until the late Hellenistic period. [4]

By the time Psalm 16 was translated into Greek (the *LXX*, ca. 250 BCE), Israel had begun to officially accept immortality even though the temple priests, later called Sadducees, never did. Psalm 16:8, which was particularly appropriated by the apostolic community, had gone through a rather startling transformation. It now reads in the Greek Septuagint: *I see the Lord before me always [throughout eternity];* [5] Clearly, in

2. The word refers to the core proclamation by the apostolic community of the saving gospel of the risen Christ.

3. Craigie, "Psalm 29 in the Hebrew Poetic Tradition," ". . . if the word *miktam* in the title [it occurs in five other psalms titles] does indeed mean 'inscription, inscriptional poem', then it is conceivable that this psalm began its life as an inscription on a monument [stele], celebrating some specific deliverance from crisis, for which there are general analogies in Near Eastern texts." 156.

4. Seybold, *Introducing the Psalms,* 170.

5. James, *Thirty Psalmists* ". . . this saint [the poet of Ps 16] of the Old Testament has attained a height in the life with God that most of us today must acknowledge to be above us. He belongs, with

the apostolic church, Psalm 16 was read in the light of the resurrection of Jesus. In the resurrection of Jesus Christ, the last limitation on the connection between יהוה and life was transcended. Now it is possible for Christians to say this psalm in the midst of life and in the face of inevitable death with a trust that matches the language of the prayer: with trust and confidence the poet writes that the Lord has made known to me the path of life.

> *The path of life is so called, not only because of its goal but because to walk that way is to live, in the true sense of the word, already. It leads without a break into God's presence and into eternity (evermore). The joy (lit. joys) and pleasures are presented as wholly satisfying (this is the force of fullness, from the same root as 'satisfied' in 17:15) and endlessly varied, for they are found in both what [He] is and what [He] gives—joys of [His] face (the meaning of presence) and of [His] right hand. The refugee of verse 1 finds [himself] an heir, and [his] inheritance beyond all imagining and all exploring.* [6]

The author of this confident prayer is an individual who openly and obviously trusts in the inherent goodness and reliability of יהוה. That יהוה has been very gracious and generous throughout his life is the psalmist's personal experience of God's guidance and protection. Although the Hebrew is scrambled in verses 3 and 4 and the meaning uncertain, the following terms *portion, cup, lot, boundaries, and heritage* imply that the one whose disposition toward life is prayerful becomes the recipient of the manifold blessings of יהוה. Indeed, יהוה is the guarantor of blessing! This poet clearly has eternal values in view. This psalm is cited by Peter in his resurrection speech in the Christian Testament (Acts 2:25–28) and is referred to additionally by Paul in defense of the resurrection faith in Acts 13:35.

Psalm 16

A Miktam of David

Protect me, O God, for in you I take refuge.

I say to יהוה, *"You are my God;*

I have nothing good apart from you."

You have placed in my heart a wondrous love.

As for the holy ones in the land,

they are the noble ones

---

the Author of Psalm 73, to those purest souls who fly to God as the moth to the flame. God to him is not a background, not something added to life, not merely one among many interests; [He] is all. His mystic communion with God is toughened and made vigorous by the stern ethical sense which chastens and disciplines his mind; nor is its joy thereby dimmed, for in this very 'counseling' of God he finds his supreme reason for thanksgiving." 155.

6. Kidner, *Psalms 1*, 86.

in whom is all my delight.

Those who choose other gods multiply their sorrows;

their drink offerings of blood I will not pour out

or take the names of the faithless upon my lips.

O יהוה, it is you who are my chosen portion and my cup;

you are the guarantor of my lot.

The boundaries have fallen for me in pleasant places;

Indeed, I have a goodly heritage.

I will bless יהוה who gives me counsel;

in the night also my heart instructs me.

I will keep יהוה in view at all times;

because he is at my right hand, I shall not be moved.

Therefore, my heart rejoices, and my soul is glad;

even my body will rest secure.

For you will not abandon my soul to the dead,

nor let your beloved one see the Pit.

יהוה has made known to me the path of life.

In your presence there is fullness of joy;

at your right hand are unimagined glories forevermore.

A similar re-reading of Psalm 16, to express the "new" belief in bodily resurrection and personal immortality, is not only found in the Dead Sea Scrolls and in the midrash of the Psalms but clearly in the Christian Scriptures (Acts 2:24–28). Following the completion of Jesus' earthly life and ministry, it was very soon recognized by the apostles that these psalms had something more to say–a whole lot more to say about the one who is to come at the end of human history and reign as King of Kings and Lord of Lords. Of the early Christian community's use and application of various psalms, Christoph Barth says plainly that there can be no doubt of the

> *conscious uprooting of single words or whole phrases from their psalmic context, far less of the willful alteration of the meaning of a text of scripture from the sense in which it was accepted. Anyone who explores the nuances of the ways in which the Old Testament Psalms are used in the New Testament will be amazed at the ways in which Israel's songs of prayer and praise were alive and present in the early church.* [7]

7. Barth, *Introduction to the Psalms*, 69.

The primary significance of the text of Psalm 16 lies in the confidence of the psalmist in the face of his physical mortality. His relationship with יהוה will not end in death. David, to whom the psalm is attributed, died; but we are confident that in his death he too enjoyed the *presence* of יהוה in some special sense. For Peter and Paul, the text speaks of the resurrection. They appropriately argued that since David died and did not rise from the grave, the psalm received a special significance in view of Jesus' death and resurrection. Jesus, as the Son of David, was raised up from death by God, *because it was impossible for death to keep its hold (grip) on him.* (Acts 2:24 REB). In the progressive unfolding of God's revelation, Peter, in Acts, saw a prophetic/messianic meaning in the psalm. The resurrection of Jesus gives us ground for confidence since we too will not suffer annihilation. The Father will crown [his] beloved ones with a larger life beyond this life. This is the vision of God which is beyond our ken.

God is concerned with the whole being, and therefore the body is included in the renewal of life. Israel's יהוה is Jesus' father too! Along with their witness to the history and reality of Israel, the apostolic community bore witness to the life and work of Jesus wherever the people of God gathered.

> The apostles are convinced that not merely a few isolated words, but the whole context which they represent, taken in what to the best of their knowledge was its proper meaning, speaks of Jesus, the Messiah. The identification of Jesus as the promised Messiah of God is everywhere affirmed throughout the Psalter by the apostles. They become convinced that Jesus' story and the story of the Psalms belong together and so they comb the Psalmic text for an abundance of references that speak of the servant of God. The antecedents to Jesus Christ in the Psalms is fundamental to the Church's proclamation that the salvation and redemption of the world is rooted in the Hebrew scriptures, most especially in the Book of Praises. Christians can no longer read the Psalms without making the connection between the two. [8]

This psalm reveals the meaning of Jesus' life and work. By making evident the close and essential similarity between the history of Israel and the life of Jesus, the Psalter shows us that Jesus and Israel belong together. *Their respective histories cannot be understood apart from each other. They show, in fact, that they are one and the same.* [9]Here, then, is the remarkable record of God's dwelling with this particular people, or to put it the other way around, the dwelling of this people with their particular God— יהוה. Such is the extent to which the psalmists place their trust and commitment, both

---

8. Barth, *Introduction to the Psalms*, 70.

9. Barth, *Ibid.* "Here the understanding of the [Hebrew] scriptures are not an aim in itself, but an indispensable means toward the understanding of the life and historical acts of Jesus, which otherwise would be altogether incomprehensible: only through the witness of the scriptures (John 5.39) is Jesus recognized . . . It is certainly not sufficient to answer that the psalms *predicted or foretold* His life—in broad outline or even in specific detail. Actually, they speak of the history and reality of *Israel.*" 69.

in the community of faith, of which they are a part, and to that community's God to whom they are wholly committed. It is true to say that Israel's

> *trust is monotheistic, not pluralistic. The psalmist's commitment to the Lord [YHWH] is exclusive. [He] enacts the first commandment in [his] life. For [him], there is no other God. . . . this trust is the confidence of life in the face of death. All three dimensions of the psalmist's being– heart, soul, and mind–participate in this joyous security. It infuses his entire being.*[10]

Here the distinction is drawn sharply between Jesus of Nazareth and the Christ of faith with significant implications. Jesus is confessed as *the Christ* in the early church's post-resurrection proclamation of the gospel, the *good news*. The resurrection of Jesus is fully embraced by the earliest Christian writing at the midpoint of the first century. In this earliest Christian scripture, the resurrection is the central focus of the proclamation. Paul, in his first letter to the church at Thessalonica, which is the earliest epistle and scripture in the Second Testament writes: *Everyone is spreading the story of our visit to you: how you turned from idols to be servants of the true and living God, and to wait expectantly for his Son from heaven, whom he raised from the dead, Jesus our deliverer from the retribution to come* (I Th 1: 9–10 REB), and to the latest writings at the far end of the century, probably the Petrine epistles: *Praised be the God and Father of our Lord Jesus Christ! In his great mercy by the resurrection of Jesus Christ from the dead, he gave us new birth into a living hope* (1 Peter 1:3 REB).

These writings that emerged out of the community of resurrection faith span a period of roughly fifty years. The witness of the Christian scriptures to Jesus of Nazareth as the risen Christ is uniformly coherent and internally consistent. This story and this confession are only brought to fruition, to fulfillment, with the apostolic witness to the resurrection of Jesus Christ. It is this confession in resurrection faith that now becomes, for the Christian church, the full complement of the witness that they found in the Psalms.[11]

The Hebrew mind-set considered the human body to be sustained and kept by God in the midst of the realm of death in life. God's power brings the dying person through death into the life of the new world of God. This is the Christian assurance. It is founded on the resurrection of Jesus from the world of the dead. This actualized hope in resurrection was hidden from the people of God in the world of the Psalms. It is the fact of their uncompromising trust that led them to dare to hope at all beyond death as the final border. There are to be sure glimmers of some kind of hope in the

---

10. Mays, "A Commentary on the Psalms," 86, 87.

11. Ollenburger, "If Mortals Die, Will They Live Again? The Old Testament and Resurrection." *Ex Auditu*, 41.

ongoing life of the faithful that do find expression in the Psalms, particularly in Pss 16, 49, 56, 68, and 73.[12]

These five psalms when taken together seem to imply a vision of life that extends beyond earthly life, beyond Sheol, beyond death! Scholars for the most part are reluctant to appropriate these texts as indicating a formed Hebrew belief in life beyond the barrier of death. Yet when viewed from the perspective of the trust and confidence psalms, there is more than a slight inference or suggestion of a developing, burgeoning belief in an afterlife. It is impossible for us Christians to read the Psalms as they are written without viewing them through the prism of our resurrection faith. To be mindful of this fact will allow us more and more to differentiate between the meaning these psalms now have for us, and discipline us to read them as they actually were written. The Hebrew text must be allowed to speak for itself if we are to rightly appreciate the burden of its message.

Psalm 139 reverses the consideration of life after death, now to focus on life before birth. A darkness envelops each of these two periods of sacred time. There is a confidence in God's tender care of the embryo in the mother's womb and this psalm links with Psalm 22:8–11: *Commit your cause to* יהוה ; *let him deliver–let him rescue the one in whom he delights! Yet it was you who took me from the womb; you kept me safe on my mother's breast. On you I was cast from my birth, and since my mother bore me you have been my God. Do not be far from me.* For the prophet Jeremiah and the secret place of one's life, the *presence* of God is self-sustaining. *Now the word of* יהוה *came to me saying, 'Before I formed you in the womb I knew you, and before you were born I consecrated you; I appointed you a prophet to the nations'.* (Jeremiah 1:4,5 NRSV). Jeremiah very clearly articulates his belief that his life was begun in the deepest mysteries of eternity. This is an affirmation of one's life being hidden in the counsels of Yhwh. Clearly a number of psalms seem to affirm an afterlife–what it is we now celebrate as the Christian hope. This theology of God in the Psalter gives further evidence to a developing and emerging creed within Israel's ancient and continuing faith formation. Some specific expressions of trust in יהוה are characterized by what Dahood understands as a unique transparency of hope.

> *The version proposed here is a statement of belief in the beatific vision in the afterlife; . . . The vision of God mentioned here is doubtless that of Pss xvi.11; xvii.15; xli. 13; lxxiii. 26, which suggest a belief in an afterlife in the presence of Yahweh. If perfect justice is not attained in this life, it will be in the next; this seems to be the ultimate motive for the psalmist's confidence.*[13]

12. *"For you do not give me up to Sheol, or let your faithful one see the Pit (Ps 16:11); But God will ransom my life; he will snatch me from the grasp of death (Ps 49:15); For you have delivered my soul from death, and my feet from falling, so that I may walk before God in the light of life (Ps 56:13); Our God is the God of our salvation; and God is the Lord, by whom we escape death (Ps 68:20); Yet I am always with you; you hold me by my right hand. You will guide me by your counsel, and afterwards receive me to glory"* (Ps 73:23–24). NRSV.

13. Dahood, *Psalms*, 71.

It is this transparency that informed the poetry of ancient Israel. It also found voice in some of the prophets, most particularly Jeremiah, Isaiah and Ezekiel, and is especially invoked here in the words of the poet of Psalm 139.

Psalm 139

To the leader. Of David. A Psalm.

O יהוה, you search me and you know me,
you know my resting and my rising,
you discern my thoughts from far away.
You search out my path and my lying down,
and are acquainted with all my ways.
Even before a word is on my tongue
you know it, O יהוה, completely.

You hem me in, behind and before, you surround me,
you lay your hand upon me.
Too marvelous for me is your knowledge;
it is so high I cannot possibly attain it.
O where can I go from your spirit?
O where can I flee from your face?

If I ascend to highest heaven, you are there;
if I make my bed in the grave, you are there as well.
If I take the wings of the morning
and settle at the farthest bounds of the sea,
even there your hand shall lead me,
and your right hand holds me fast.

If I say: *"Surely the darkness will hide me*
and the light around me become night,"
even darkness is not dark to you;
the night is as bright as the day,
for dark and light to you are both alike.

For it was you who fashioned me in my inward parts;
and knit me together in my mother's womb.
I will praise you, for I am fearfully and wondrously made.

TRUSTING YHWH

How wonderful are your works; this I know very well.

Already you knew my soul
when my body was made in secret;
intricately woven into the depths of the earth
was I being molded in secret.
Your eyes gazed upon my unformed substance,
your eyes saw all my actions,
they were all written in your book;
every one of my days was decreed
when none of them as yet existed.

To me how weighty are your thoughts, O God!
The sum of them is vast and they are innumerable!
Were I to count them—they are more than the sand;
Were I to come to the end, I am still with you.

O God, would that you destroy the wicked!
Keep the bloodthirsty evildoers far from me.
They speak with deceit and rebel against you;
they rise up arrogantly and speak maliciously against you.
Do I not hate those who hate you, יהוה,?
and loathe those who rise up against you?
I hate them with a perfect hatred
and count them as my adversaries.

O search me, O God, and know my heart,
O test me and know my thoughts.
See that I follow not the wrong path
and lead me a right to life eternal.

The poet of Psalm 139 muses on the inescapable God. The poet contemplates the infinite boundaries of the eternal. Life, his life, begins in the secret place where God dwells—before conception, before birth, before time. His life is viewed as having begun in the mystery of God's inconceivable *presence*. The eternity of God is juxtaposed to the ephemeral characteristic of human life. Life that is completely surrounded by the life-giving, life-loving יהוה sets the stage for the poet's consideration of the mystery of divine discernment–that everything about the psalmist, even the innermost thoughts, are not a mystery to יהוה. Such knowledge of the ways of God comes from the deeply interior way that יהוה discerns and knows the poet completely.

His innermost thoughts have to do with commitment to the ways of יהוה and come from God's searching and testing in order to discern the poet's inclination of heart and mind. There is no escaping the *presence* of יהוה in all of creation, including one's own individual and personal creation which is the specific action that lies hidden in the mind of God.

The psalms of trust emphasize repeatedly that the one who knows יהוה can live a reasonably joyful, hopeful, and confident life. In Psalm 139, knowledge of יהוה leads one to hope and trust in all that comprises life. This is the singularly clearest message to all who long so much to live in hope and confidence. In theological discourse, this is known as the *apprehension of the knowledge of God.* In acquiring this knowledge, the ancients' recognition and acceptance of that knowledge are directly identified with the Name of this self-revealing God. To confess the Name יהוה is tantamount to knowing God! Israel not only knew that God has a name. They knew and they loved the Name! יהוה.

Apart from the *Elohistic Psalter,* the name יהוה is the most common reference to the God of Israel in the book of Psalms. It is the name of self-communication and covenantal love. The name יהוה assumes covenantal perfections even as the stinging repudiation of Israel's failure to abide by the dictates of the covenant is cruelly enunciated. The covenant established between the people and Yhwh their God has timely consequences for good and ill. Israel in her humanity fails to abide by the covenantal requirements and so is marked both for blessing and judgement. The ephemerality of her mortal existence does not go unappreciated by her God, who only desires what is best for her as a covenant partner.

> יהוה *passed before Moses, and proclaimed,* 'יהוה, יהוה, *God merciful and gracious, slow to anger, and abounding in steadfast love and faithfulness, keeping steadfast love for the thousandth generation, forgiving iniquity and transgression and sin, yet by no means clearing the guilty, but visiting the iniquity of the parents upon the children and the children's children, to the third and fourth generation* (Ex 34:6–7, LW).

The pattern and the witness of the poets is that they know their conversations with יהוה have an eternal dimension. They ruminate in the *presence* of the eternal and the holy scriptures, of which the Psalms are a central part, and bear witness to their willingness to embrace incredulous promises and vows made to them by יהוה. We Christians come to this mystery of things seen and unseen with something quite different in mind. But in doing so, Christians stand on the shoulders of these poets who have traversed the landscape of a daring faith and a lively hope in the trustful ways of יהוה. We too, like them, live from faith to faith, from hope to hope, from eternity to eternity.

The hope of the resurrection to eternal life is the central focus in the Christian scriptures. But understanding scripture's witness is never an aim in itself. Rather, it is for Christians an indispensable means to contextualizing the life and the historical work of Jesus which would, otherwise, be altogether incomprehensible and abstruse to us.[14]

> *The Psalms raise the issue of hope even in the face of pain, and hope can lead one through hardship and trial. The Psalms are honest pilgrimage songs of faith and thus deal with all of life, including despair and hope. Hope is not always at hand, but the Psalms persevere in the journey through crisis toward hope's light and liberation.*[15]

The subsequent promise and fulfillment of the vows made to them by יהוה are continually affirmed in Israel's sacred story: *I will take you as my people, and I will be your God. You will know that I am* יהוה *your God, who has freed you from the burdens of the Egyptians. I will bring you into the land that I swore to give to Abraham, Isaac, and Jacob; I will give it to you for a possession. I am* יהוה (Ex 6:7 REB). The people of יהוה felt the closeness of their God, even as יהוה had promised to be their God and adopt them as [his] children. They knew יהוה by name.

> *Did Israel recognize the existence of other gods than YHWH? It is surely true that she called her God by names other than YHWH. Now whether these differ-ent names were thought to denote different gods, at least in the earliest period, is difficult to say. When Exod 6:2 tells us that YHWH is El Shaddai, it is reasonable to suspect that there had been cause to think otherwise. In the deep prehistory of this verse may lie an effort to subsume El Shaddai into YHWH. Henceforth, these words are treated as two names for the same God . . . but the idea that YHWH is the only God appears, unambiguously, many times in the Hebrew Bible . . .*[16]

They prayed in the name of יהוה and they addressed their thanksgivings to that Name. They loved the meaning of the Name for it bound them in covenantal love to the purposes of יהוה for them, and through them to the whole world and all cre-ation. Though we ourselves are not certain of the precise pronunciation, we adopt a

---

14. Westermann, *The Living Psalms,* "The message of Jesus' resurrection takes its place in the earliest apostolic preaching. Just as in the psalms, the praise of God's saving act in Christ has within itself the impulse to widen out to the furthest distance." 114. cf. Kraus, Ibid. "The body of [man] is sustained and kept by God in the midst of the realm of death. The fact that God's power brings even the dying person through death into the life of the new world of God–this assurance, founded on the resurrection of Christ Jesus, was still hidden from the people of the OT. Only the power of unlimited trust let them hope beyond the final border. Therefore, the expressions of trust in the prayer songs are characterized by that unique transparency which then, in the pattern and witness of the certainty of the resurrection in the NT, played an important role." 241.

15. Bellinger, *Reading and Studying the Book of Praises,* 141. Note: cf. Jurgen Moltmann, *Theology of Hope.* Moltmann, who was imprisoned in one of the Nazi concentration camps during World War II, developed the theme of hope as a theological organizing principle in this important book published in the late 1960's—yet another example of "theologizing" one's understanding of the faith when born of the extremity of human experience.

16. Levenson, *Sinai and Zion,* 58.

common form of the Name's love, joy, and tenderness of יהוה expressed so beautifully in many psalms. In Psalm 7:17, the psalmist uses several references: *to the Holy One I will give thanks to יהוה because of [his] righteousness and will sing praise to the name of יהוה Most High* (Elyon). Psalm 47:2, a Korah hymn, stresses the vindicating nature of Yahweh's character: *For יהוה Most High (Elyon) is awesome; יהוה is the great king over all the earth.* And again, in Psalm 97:9, the poet acclaims the title *Elyon* as applicable to יהוה and asserts [His] dominance and distinctiveness: *For you, יהוה, are Most High (Elyon) over all the earth. You יהוה are lifted far above all gods (LW).*

This exaltation and reverence of the Name יהוה lies at the heart of psalmic spirituality. The poet's use of appellatives for the divine name in the beginning strophe (91:1–2), and their powerful resonance with the images of refuge and safety, demonstrate Israel's emergent understanding and her conscious choice to risk all in her submission to the One God of the eternal covenant. This God is יהוה. These questers after the *elusive presence* of יהוה intended to dwell–in silence, if necessary–within the shadow of Shaddai! Here the poets of Israel contemplate the mystery of the silence of Yhwh.

> *The theme of silence is Hebraic as much as common to later forms of disciplinary contemplation of the infinite. This may astonish those who mistakenly identify the Word (which is also an act) with the Platonic logos. The God who creates and acts is also the God who remains silent and refuses to act . . God's silence informs the silence of human trust. The psalmist is acquainted with [the] practice of the art of theological silence . . . and experimented with the 'non-word' that prefigures and precedes the contemplation of Beingness.* [17]

To learn to live in that holy space of silence before the mystery of God is the task of a disciplined faith that will lay claim to the promises of God and hold onto them no matter what. This is the way of יהוה with us and it is our chosen *path of life*. It is this path that is our immense journey from eternity to eternity.

17. Terrien, "The Numinous, the Sacred, and the Holy Scripture," 101.

The Path of Life

As was noted earlier, the primary image that is used to express life's course and conduct in the Psalms is the metaphor *the path of life* (ארח חיים) No other image is more richly textured and manifold, none more precise in nuance and connotation. The path of a man was the way he followed through life, the direction of his going, and the manner of his walking. It was a good word because it was drawn from the vicissitudes of daily life, from a land of many roads and paths in which walking was the usual manner of going from one place to another. It was a good symbol because it involved beginning and end and the intention which prompted the journey. What makes this terminology important in Israel's manner of thinking is that it is applied to יהוה, Israel's Leader, who goes on before, as the *Shepherd of Israel* leading [his] flock, and showing the people how to walk the *path of life*.

> *What makes this terminology of supreme importance in Israel's manner of think-ing is that it is applied to God. [He] is Israel's Leader, who goes on before, as a shepherd before [his] flock, and shows [him] the path of life (Ps. 16:11) . . . . a [man's] way and a [man's] deed is one and the same. Obedience is walking in the way of the commandments of God . . . the divine requirements or commands are the divine ways . . . It is God who determines the right way; it is [he] who points the way a [man] should go. Without [his] leading, Israel does not know the way to take. [He] is always confronted with the choice between the good road and the bad, the straight road and the crooked. The good road is the way of life and well-being.*[1]

The images of the *way of life* and the *path of life* are not identical. The *way of life* designates the course of human existence, the way of existential striving from birth to death. The *way of life* is existential and temporal. The *path of life* precedes birth and leads to life eternal. Obedience is walking in the way of the commandments of יהוה. The divine requirements or commands are the divine way. It is יהוה who determines the right path; it is יהוה who points the way a person should go. Without the leading of יהוה, Israel does not know the pathway to take. Israel is always confronted, as are we, with the choice between the good road and the bad, the straight road and the crooked.

---

1. Muilenburg, "Psalm 4:7," 34, 35.

The *path of life* is the way of life and well-being: *You will show me the path of life; in your presence there is fullness of joy, and in your right hand are unimaginable glories for evermore* (Psalm 16:11, LW).

> *Thanks to the deepening of his faith, the poet envisages the marvel of happiness forever: 'Thou wilt show me the path of life'. Many exegetes find in this sentence the conviction that Yahweh will reveal a code of conduct for the remaining years of the poet's mortal existence rather than the vision of eternal life. A certain doubt may persist; yet an analysis of every word supports the traditional interpretation.[2]*

The phrase *the path of life,* is rooted in the Deuteronomy exhortation: *I have set before you life and death . . . Choose life, that you and your descendants may live* (Deut. 30:19, NRSV). It is undeniable that this path of life is intended to be understood as Israel's highway to God. The covenant entered into between יהוה and Israel will never be abrogated! This is Israel's destiny and, as Psalm 16 instructs, it is her hope and her salvation.[3] The covenant entered into with Israel, by יהוה, has been extended to all humanity. This is the universality of purpose and promise that has become the hope of humankind.

The journey of the Psalms, then, is from lament to praise, from the temporal to the eternal, from the particular to the universal. יהוה is Israel's One God of All and there is none other. It is יהוה who personifies the near, the personal, and the immanent and simultaneously transcendent God. This confidence and trust in יהוה is both a necessity and a virtue. It is a necessity because the absence of trust leads to a disintegration of life into fear and anxiety; it is a virtue because it leads to the fullness of life which God intended with the granting, in the first place, of God's first and best gift—the gift of life itself.

Such trust is never based upon an assessment of the self. It is rooted in the conviction that it is יהוה who draws us into a loving relationship. It is grounded in the nature and character of God. יהוה is the One who actively seeks out Israel and speaks the divine oracle, the word of the promise of salvation to Israel. יהוה always takes the initiative; יהוה always responds; יהוה will, whether on behalf of the people of God, or, in spite of them, act. יהוה speaks: *I will be a bulwark of safety; I will lift you up because you acknowledge my name. When you cry to me, I will answer; when in dire straits, I will be with you and raise you to a place of honor; I will save* (91:13,14, LW).

---

2. Terrien, *The Elusive Presence*, 179.

3. Boers "*Psalm 16 and the Historical Origin of the Christian Faith*," "Psalm 16 knows that Yhwh is the God of this life and not just the future life nor just of religious life, and provides for this life in abundance. It is one of the reasons why people should stay faithful to Yhwh. The psalm thus refuses us the right to confine God to the realm of Christology, eschatology, or religious experience and dissociate questions of our relationship with God from questions about land and food. Psalm 16 belongs not just to Christ or to the future or to religious life but also to material life now. The psalm does not treasure a relationship with God more than the gifts of life, but it assumes that the one is the key to the other." 107.

To all who long after the plenitude of redemption, יהוה reveals God's self and communes with us; reveals truth to us (and the truth about us), which is of ultimate consequence. It is God who is always seeking to draw us into a relationship that finds the full measure of its unfolding grace in the communion of abiding *presence*, communion, and answered prayer. At the end of the day, Israel knows herself to be known by יהוה–fully, completely, intimately. This knowledge of God is rooted in Israel's experiences and encounters with the holy. יהוה chooses to draw near, especially in times of disorientation and dislocation, and in times of discouragement and despair.

We all are familiar with these experiences of life. It is out of our human need and dislocation that the perplexed and troubled soul is most available to seek out the *presence* of the holy. יהוה is the God of promise who assures us that all who seek after [him] with their whole heart will find and be found by [him]. To find and to be found by יהוה is to traverse the *path of life*. What is most critical to the psalmists' thinking is the quality of their lives with God now, in this life. They rest any future afterlife in the hands of יהוה.

> "... all those Psalm-texts which speak of salvation from death or from the Underworld may have to be understood as testimonies of the experience of the living, of deliverance from the threat of death, back into life. This means that the Psalms make no clear and unambiguous statement concerning a life on the other side after death. The much discussed texts 16,10; 49,15; and 73,24 do not demand a concept qualitatively different from the concept of the existence of the dead in the Underworld. Here and there we do find a hope that existence itself is not the highest possession, but rather co-existence with God; and that communion with God may possibly lessen or even overcome the loneliness of Sheol." [4]

Each of these Hebrew poets has expressed the truth of these affirmations in the face of real life experience. The sting of suffering and the ugliness of evil do not obviate the poets continued conviction that יהוה hears their cries and is not unmoved by their deepest concerns and their cries from out of the depths. Post-modern people know something of the heights and the depths of human experience; the shallow disorientation and the oft times depressing idiosyncrasies of this life. Irrespective of the stunning advancements made in science and the manifold complexities of modern technology, all of which have been witnessed in the last half century, the competing vision for the transformation of the world into a new order has only intensified. Post-modern humanity in the western world is, in the main, largely ignorant and skeptical of the spiritual resources, disciplines and visions of the ancients. There may remain a lingering fascination with the Bible. But confidence in the idea of a self-revelatory deity has unquestionably waned over the past three centuries. Today, its nearly wholesale obliteration by a voracious secular culture shows to what extent we are all still children of the Enlightenment.

4. Seybold, *Introducing the Psalms*, 170.

In the mid seventeenth-century CE, Rene Descartes proposed that all reality con-sisted of both mind and matter. Mind represented the human sphere and everything nonhuman was embraced under *matter*. Matter was the realm of the rational order, open to scientific inquiry and empirical examination. The rise of science has had some very beneficial effects for the study of the Bible, not the least of which is the historical-critical method that forced biblical scholars of the nineteenth century to take account of a whole host of inconvenient truths. There are those who resist the salient truths of new realities in every age. But the overall results of looking at the biblical record in new and exciting ways cannot be ignored. Science too is God's gift to the critical mind.

The significance of this is obvious: Whatever is not human is, by extension, em-pirically observable and scientifically verifiable as *matter*. Such is the nature of our inheritance over the previous three and a half centuries. Living a life of faith and trust in a personal God, who inspires in us the hunger for relationship, is increasingly for-eign to the ways in which the modern, rational world seeks to inspire itself. The life of faith and trust is fraught with challenges, disappointments and defeats; but it is also the path of life that leads to fullness, joy and wholeness. The way of the wisdom tradi-tion of the ancients and their sapiential (wisdom) spirit is present in a few particular psalms. [5]Herein lies the paradox of Israel's faithful obedience to the call of יהוה in the crucible of human experience; and the goodness of יהוה in the face of catastrophic and persistent evil. This is the philosophical problem of theodicy.

> . . . *certain psalms do belong together because of the similarities in the religious problems they examine. These are Psalms 37, 49, and 73. . . the theological prob-lem addressed in all three psalms is what we have learned to call a theodicy [Theodicy refers to the attempt to pronounce God innocent of the evil that befalls human existence. The word originates with Leibniz in the early 18th C.E. but the concept is old as millennia]. How can one justify God's ways in the face of ap-parent evidence to the contrary? Psalm 73 achieves fresh insight into the resolu-tion of this vexing problem. It suggests that the issue has been stated falsely, and therefore the author restates the problem. In essence the psalmist contends that the goods of this world are wholly irrelevant to the matter of God's justice. Proof of God's goodness rests in divine presence, not in material prosperity*[6]

The psalmists remind us over and again what are the greatest threats to the path of life. We learn from the Psalms that the path of a life traveled with יהוה can be pock-marked with the inflicted wounds of weakness and suffering. This is the path יהוה apparently chooses to sojourn with us as well.[7]The saints down through the age

5. Crenshaw, *The Psalms*, 139.

6. Ibid.

7. *New Interpreter's Study Bible*. ". . . there is the belief articulated throughout the Psalter that 'the path to God lies within.' Only one psalm says, *'Create in me a clean heart, O God, and put a new and right spirit within me'* (51:10). By contrast, references abound to the righteous who rejoice and follow justice on account of the disposition of their hearts. . . .While we may believe that God wants

of the Christian church bear witness to the struggles and difficulties that confront us in our earthly pilgrimage. They confirm that it is not easy but the path of life is the only way worth traveling. The image of the *path* and the use of various metaphors for journeying and pilgrimage is employed judiciously by the ancient poets.

As we have already seen, Hebrew existentialism is a dominant theme in Psalm 90. It also arises frequently within other psalms of the Psalter. In the sight of יהוה vast expanses of time such as eons, the detailed events of which humanity cannot take in at a glance, shrink and *are as yesterday when it is past, or as a watch in the night,* the smallest unit of time measurement in Old Israel. Our human perspective shrinks further when measured by such a standard. Using the picturesque images of Hebrew speech the poets endeavor by means of comparisons to make this thought as clear as possible.

Human life is like a breath, the like of which יהוה, as it were, *sweeps away*; or like sleep which has no more significance when one looks back on it in the morning; finally, it is like the grass that quickly changes its form: *all flesh is grass! It flourishes in the morning and at evening it withers and it is gone(LW)*. What is being described by the poet in Psalm 90 is not the product of a gloomy pessimism, which we may often feel, but rather the result of a comprehensive and sober realism. It is the conundrum of human existence: we live, we suffer, we die. The poet sees things as they really are, though certainly he does not measure them by a standard that is commonplace and superficial, but rather sees them from the divine perspective of eternity. And for this poet, perspective is all. Can humankind, in its existential quandary, only pine...

> Is suffering, nothing but suffering, the answer which God gives to those who seek [him] with a pure heart? Is trouble, nothing but trouble, the portion which God allots to those who do not plunge into the stream of power and fame, wealth and success? Why do the faithless prosper and the faithful suffer hardship? How intolerable that perspective is! How terrible the consequences of such a contrast! The despairing conclusion is that 'All is in vain'![8]

For these poets, life without יהוה is meaningless: suffering instead of happiness, impotence instead of power, failure instead of success. Doubt and despair are

---

contrition and repentance, only one psalm holds this prerequisite: 'The sacrifice acceptable to God is a broken spirit; a broken and contrite heart, O God, you will not despise' (51:17). More usually, God aspires to teach the heart what it needs ... Wholeness comes as God instructs the heart to know, reorienting understanding as needed, so that the psalmist is confident. As a matter of the heart, the psalmists follow a way that leads to God." 829.

8. Kraus, *Theology of the Psalms*, 196. cf. Tillich. On the Transitoriness of Life, in *The Shaking of the Foundations*. "That is the mood of ancient [mankind]. Many of us are afraid of it. A shallow Christian idealism cannot stand the darkness of such a vision. Not so the Bible. The most universal of all books, it reveals the age-old wisdom about [man's] transitoriness and misery. The Bible does not try to hide the truth about [man's] life under facile statements about the immortality of the soul. Neither the Old nor the New Testament does so. They know the human situation and they take it seriously. They do not give us any easy comfort about ourselves. We must read the 90th Psalm in this light" [293–310].

hallmarks of the human journey.[9] But what is intolerable to the psalmist is to lose the grasp on faith; to be overwhelmed by a multiplicity of life's tragedies and hardships—and then, to succumb to them!

There are several key psalms that trace the movement from doubt to trust in considerable detail. One of the finest examples, as we have referred to before, is Psalm 73[10] where the psalmist begins to doubt the traditional belief in the inherent goodness of יהוה toward the upright.

> The psalm begins and ends with statements about the goodness of God, but how that goodness is experienced and understood undergoes a profound recasting in the course of the psalm. Verse 1 is a proverbial statement of the teaching that is basic to the faith of the psalmist . . . God's goodness is a sure blessing for the pure in heart among God's chosen people because they are the ones who respond to the election of God with a singleness of devotion (24:4). Purity of heart is to will one thing, the love of God (Kierkegaard). It is the love of God that answers the free choice of God to have a people and opens the self to the will of God to be with them. Hidden in the proverb is the implication that it is God [himself] who is the goodness given those [he] chooses to be 'with'.[11]

יהוה at the very least, appears to be utterly unresponsive. Psalm 73 is particularly significant in that it is not only speech *to* יהוה but also goes over into speech *about* יהוה, meditating on [his] being and work. For this reason, it is considered by some commentators to be a *wisdom psalm*. But this does not seem correct; meditative speech about יהוה and [his] work is not of itself indicative of a background in wisdom, and the psalm as a whole is too strongly influenced by the structure of the individual lament for this to be likely. There is an even more important conclusion for all theology to be drawn from Psalm 73. In an indirect way it is a prayer for counsel that rests on the bedrock of trust. But this trust can erode in the face of the seeming success of the faithless and arrogant. What is needed is a new and fresh perspective on the ways of יהוה which come from outside the poet. He is being acted *upon*!

> . . . the psalmist testifies to his intimate trust in Yahweh and expresses confidence (a kind of indirect prayer) that the offenders will be destroyed by Yahweh, from whom they have gone astray. The language is especially appropriate for the king: he is perpetually beside God, who has taken hold of his right hand. God conducts him by the agency of his 'counsel', which is here rather like the personified word

9. Zimmerli, *Man and His Hope in the Old Testament,* observes incisively that "faith, assailed by its inability to comprehend God's 'order' in the experiences of everyday life, finds its way to the bold confidence which confesses that it will cleave to God as its 'portion' even when heart and body fail." 165.

10. Hayes, *Understanding the Psalms,* "Ancient Israelites not only experienced crises which threatened their general well-being but they also experienced crises of faith. Psalm 73 can be understood as the thanksgiving psalm of one who had undergone a severe crisis of faith during which he was tempted to forsake his religious heritage." 93.

11. Mays, *Psalms,* 210.

and the covenant-graces which assist in guidance. 'Counsel' itself is commonly associated with kings and their political affairs. Parallel is the remarkable assurance that God will take him up in glory; Verse 25 again implies a very close relationship: God is 'for' him and 'with' him. The relationship is 'forever'; God is 'the rock of my heart' and 'my portion'.[12]

Speaking *to* יהוה comes before speaking *about* יהוה. Psalm 73 opens *Book III* and helps shape the direction of the entire Psalter.[13] Most notably does it pick up words and themes from Psalms 1 and 2 and develops the point of Ps. 1:6— *for* יהוה *watches over the way of the righteous, but the way of the faithless is doomed*—exploring how יהוה watches over the righteous, and how the wicked perish when things seem to go so well for them.

Psalm 73 also recalls Psalms 42–43 at the beginning of Book II where David feels far from God . . . *How deep I am sunk in misery . . . I shall wait for God . . .* In this psalm, God's goodness and nearness are explored in light of the question put forth by the faithless, *'How can God know?'* (v. 11). In both psalms God is the poet's refuge (43.2; 73.28) but while in Psalms 42–43 God's nearness will lead David to God's dwelling . . . *Send out your light and your truth to be my guide; let them lead me to your holy hill, to your dwelling place. Then I shall come to the altar of God, the God of my joy and delight* (43:3–4, NRSV); in Ps. 73.17 (*until I went into God's sanctuary*) the faith experience opens up before the poet in an entirely new dimension, in the midst of his wavering, and leads him to a new orientation and understanding of God's nearness and *presence*.

The deepening of the poet's faith and understanding matches the development in thinking about sacrifice. Sacrifice in this context has to do with what is ultimately prized and considered to be of the highest value. Sacrifice implies costliness and that which is of special significance to the suppliant is *nearness to* יהוה. Both developments are related in the context of the relation of wealth to piety (Pss. 49.7–9, 16–20; 73.2–12) and both resolutions involve a change in the heart of the faithful. *The sacrifice acceptable to God is a broken spirit; a broken and contrite heart, O God, you will not despise* (51.17 NRSV). It is a matter of the "heart" and the word appears seven times in the psalm. These connections with earlier psalms and the movement within Psalm 73 allow the poet to move from Torah (Psalm 1) toward praise (Psalms 145 to 150), while at the same time maintaining a balance between the two. Fundamentally, Psalm 73 is about the heart; note how it recurs repeatedly. Here is this critically important psalm which details the crisis of faith for one vexed poet.

---

12. Eaton, *Kingship and the Psalms*, 70.

13. McCann, *Great Psalms of the Bible*, "The significance of Psalm 73 as a 'highpoint' or 'peak text' may be reinforced by its placement within the book of Psalms. It is the opening psalm of Book III; and probably not coincidentally, it recalls Psalm 1, in which the wicked are also prominent characters, and also Psalm 2. In a real sense, Psalm 73 rehearses the message a reader of the Psalter would have learned by first reading Psalms 1–2 and then continuing through Psalms 3–72—that is, true happiness or goodness does not derive from physical or material prosperity but rather involves the experience of God's enduring presence in all circumstances, including life's worst." 94.

Psalm 73

A Psalm of Asaph

Assuredly God is good to Israel!
To those who are pure in heart
But as for me, my feet came close to stumbling,
and my steps had almost slipped,
for I was jealous of the arrogant
when I saw the peace and prosperity of the faithless.

For they suffer no pangs,
their bodies are sleek and perfectly sound.
They are not troubled like the rest of humanity,
nor plagued like other people.
They adorn their pride as a necklace,
they clothe themselves in violence.

Their eyes bulge out of indulgence
and the haughtiness of their heart overflows.
They mock and dissemble evil,
speaking of oppression from above.
They set their mouth against the heavens
and their tongue struts through the earth.

So His people turn towards them,
drinking in their words to the full.
And they say: *How can God know?*
Does the Most High (Elyon) take any notice?

Look! Such are the faithless,
always at ease and growing in power!"
Surely I have kept my heart clean for no good purpose
and washed my hands continually in innocence.
For I am tormented all day long,
I am anxious morning after morning.
Yet if I had said, '*I will speak thus!*'
I would have betrayed a generation of your children.

TRUSTING YHWH

For when I strove to understand what all this meant
it was always too difficult for my mind to grasp.
Until I entered into the sanctuaries of God;
then and there I began to finally understand
what becomes of the faithless.

Surely You have set them on a slippery path,
and hurl them into utter ruin.
How they are suddenly destroyed,
wiped out, utterly swept away by terrors.
Like a dream to one suddenly awake, O Lord,
You despise these phantoms when You arise.

When my heart grew embittered
and I was pierced with inner pain,
I was stupid and did not know;
I acted like a dumb beast before You.

But now, as for me, I see I am always in your *presence*;
You have taken me by my right hand.
You will guide me with Your counsel
and afterwards you will lead me to glory.

Whom else have I in heaven but You?
And having You, I want nothing on earth.
My flesh and my heart may waste away
but you are the rock of my heart;
and my possession forever is God.

For now, I see how those who are far from You perish.
You put an end to those who are faithless.
But as for me, to be near God is my glee.
I have made יהוה God my refuge,
that I might tell of all your marvelous works
at the gates of the city of Zion.

Psalm 73, a psalm of Asaph, is one of the great texts of the Bible and represents a major turning point in the Psalter. The transition from doubt to faith is a process as old as life itself. Now the poet is drawn into a new relationship in the sanctuary where

> provision was made for individuals to bring their laments or emergency prayers, somewhat like Hannah at the Shiloh sanctuary in 1 Sam 1:10–11. It was customary for the sufferer to receive from the temple personnel a response in God's name, and doubtless at least such a response is presupposed as the basis for the ensuing note of confidence.[14]

The psalm specifically raises the question of why the ungodly prosper and the seekers after יהוה suffer unjustly. The problem of human suffering, as a theme in our psalms of trust, is never treated by the poets of the Psalms with a wink and a nod. Rather it is always subsumed under a pronouncement and an acknowledgment of the mercy and the *presence* of God in the midst of the misfortunes and randomness of human life. For our poets all suffering is redemptive. That is to say, the poets cannot imagine a situation of hopeless, meaningless suffering that is unreachable to the mercy, grace, and love of God. That vows are made in anticipation of God's deliverance reflects the stalwart faith of these ancient poets, who dare to risk all in the firm confidence that it is יהוה who sees, knows, and acts on behalf of the human sufferer.

> 'afterward thou wilt receive me to glory:' (v. 24). This familiar phrase presents considerable difficulties in its interpretation, but there is no need to think that the text is corrupt. The real problem is whether it refers to this life or to the life after death; commentators are divided on this point. The Israelite view of after life is characterized by the shadowy Sheol existence which was largely negative. It was only in the late post-Exilic period that a different idea of life after death was gradually formulated. Had the author of this Psalm believed that the afterlife provided for a final judgment of God, he would have found little difficulty in explaining the prosperity of the wicked and that misfortune of the righteous. Therefore, it seems that he also must have shared in the common Sheol belief. On the other hand, Psalm 73 may represent a tentative venture to go beyond the then current beliefs, although the result would be a glimpse rather than a firm faith. If this was the case, then it is understandable why the Psalmist remained content that God was his portion forever (v. 26) without giving a more definite shape to his hope.[15]

There is a recognition among these ancient word-smiths that suffering is endemic to human life and experience. This is a given reality. But bolstered by the sense of the saving help of יהוה, new insight is gained into the meaning of *being near God*. Similarly, the poet of Psalm 91 comes to realize that nothing else in all of creation can compare with the awareness and experience of the near *presence* of יהוה. The apprehension of

14. Allen, "Psalms 101–150," 6.
15. Anderson, *Psalms II.*, 535.

the *presence* of יהוה in the midst of life is all! Psalm 73 traces the journey of one devout person from doubt to a new and refined faith in the goodness and mercy of יהוה.

The starting-point of course, for theology as discourse about God, is not the intellectual question: "What can we say about God?" "What sense does it make to speak of God?" Much more does theology begin by speaking *to* God and so here in Psalm 73, reflection on God develops from speaking *to* God. In this psalm what is in question is existence in relation to God, the quest for God in the hopelessness of all that the poet encounters in this challenge to faith and a continually trusting heart—the edges of human existence when pushed to its limits. Resolution for the poet begins with his confession:

> The psalmist confesses that he almost betrayed the people of God by envying the prosperity enjoyed by wicked persons, until he went into God's sanctuary and saw their fate. While we cannot be sure what transpired in this setting, we can only note that he suddenly realizes the fleeting character of riches, and he then takes the further step toward cherishing God above all other treasure. [16]

Theology is born and first grows not from thought but from life. The perceived unavailability or the absence, or the apparent lack of connection to יהוה, is frequently expressed throughout quite a few psalms, but none more so than here in Psalm 73. They are reconciled, eventually, by the poet's eventual statements of trust, which are followed by a renewal of vows and praise to יהוה. *But as for me, to be near God is my highest joy. I have made the LORD God my refuge, that I might tell of all Your works at the gates of the city of Zion* (Ps 73:28, REB). For this poet, trust in יהוה is the great equalizer.

In this manner, the Psalter offers us a clean distinction from the emphasis on the futility and meaninglessness of human life as expressed overtly in the book of *Ecclesiastes,* a Latin transcription of the Greek translation of the Hebrew קהלת (*Qoheleth),* frequently rendered *Preacher* (following a tradition from Luther) or *Teacher.* Qoheleth appears resigned to the irrelevance of יהוה because life is *all emptiness and a chasing after the wind* (Ecclesiastes 1:14, REB). In Psalm 73 the problem of evil and the suffering of the righteous lurk just beneath the surface. That human existence does not always seem purposeful and meaningful is unquestionably on the mind of the poet. However, what remains unstated and what is always being anticipated is that יהוה, despite all appearances to the contrary, will surely vindicate and deliver the poet out of the hands of all enemies. [17] For our trusting poets, all their affairs are surrendered into the hands of the God who holds them as in a love that will not let them go!

16. Crenshaw, *Old Testament Wisdom,* 183.

17. Crenshaw, *The Concept of God in Old Testament Wisdom in In Search of Wisdom.* "Psalm 73 traces the movement from doubt to trust in great detail. At first the psalmist begins to doubt traditional belief in God's goodness toward the upright, for experience presents far too many examples of prosperous villains. Conscious of teetering on the brink of folly, the psalmist makes a concerted effort to purify such thoughts, receiving support in the assembled congregation of the faithful. Here the psalmist recognizes the insubstantiality and ephemerality of the success enjoyed by the wicked, but, more importantly,

Do these enemies include the ultimate end of human existence in death? Is the descent to the realm of the *Pit*, or the *underworld, Sheol*, the murky, shadowy, formless void of an afterlife where there is no conscious praise of יהוה, the Hebrews eternal destiny? Or is there a movement that can be traced within the Psalter toward a formative belief in the resurrection to eternal life? Such an emergent belief came later in the Hellenistic era with the rise of the apocalyptic literature, and the book of Daniel in particular. It is juxtaposed, starkly, to the dour picture drawn in Ecclesiastes, the *indifference* of God, which reflects the failures that haunt the "wisdom school" tradition. To maintain that ancient Israel had no conscious awareness or hope for life after death is simply not accurate. The longing and hope for life beyond the boundary of death is implanted deep in the human heart.

Resurrection from the dead, never to die again, is unknown until Jesus of Nazareth is raised by God from death and exalted as the Christ of God. But one can still hear the yearning, the longing for glory expressed in some key texts. For the poet in Psalm 73, the experience of being a person of faith in the world while maintaining loyalty to יהוה no longer corresponded to the way of human experience.

A new way forward must be sought. The psalm closes with a contrast between alienation from and refuge in God (vv.27, 28). Psalm 73 confronts the difficulties and concludes that nothing in heaven or on earth can compare with being near God. In this respect, one thinks of Paul's matchless oration on the unsurpassing love of God in Romans 8. This is indeed the highest good. The poet does hesitate on the threshold of belief in personal immortality, introduced by piety rather than by doctrinal discourse. He acknowledges that those who are removed from God die!

> *Those distant from God die. Autonomy is a harlotry that does not work. That autonomy leads to perishing is an insight very old in the tradition of Israel . . . The psalmist is now unabashedly a companion of Yahweh and without apology. The nearness of the speaker is contrasted with the distance of the others. As distance leads to death, so nearness leads to 'good.' Psalm 73 ends with a sense of well-being. One who ventured out has discovered how pleasing is the haven of God's fellowship. It is striking that only here in verse 28 is the name of Yahweh finally uttered. It is as though it has been withheld and must not be sounded until the right moment, the moment of happy resolution and serious fidelity.*[18]

The poet admits life's unfairness and puts the question squarely before God, as did Jeremiah (12:1). This theme appears frequently in wisdom reflections which examine the uncertainties of experience and the mysteries of the preponderance of evil in the midst of human life. Like Job, the poet is skeptical about God's ways and has a firm grasp

---

acquires a fresh awareness of divine nearness. Bolstered by a sense of God's touch and leadership, the psalmist realizes that nothing else in all of the universe quite compares with God's *presence*. That nearness alone confirms the accuracy of the original credo, and it now becomes permissible to entertain the bold thought that even death's power may yield to a greater force, the God of glory." 15, 16.

18. Brueggemann, *Message of the Psalms,* 120, 121.

of reality. In the end God's *presence* does not solve the problem but it gives an assurance which intelligence alone cannot grasp. In Israel's traditions the school of wisdom held that the just would be appropriately compensated in this life and justifiably rewarded, while the unjust and the faithless would be dealt with in proper kind—in this life!

Ancient Israel struggled mightily with the problem of the suffering righteous and the self-aggrandizing, avaricious wicked. The psalmists begged, exhorted, pleaded and cajoled יהוה to set things right—now, in this life. This theme of the imminence of relief in the face of injustice pervades the Psalter and appears frequently in the wisdom reflections which examine the uncertainties of human experience and the mysteries of life. When a person surrenders control in prayer, there arises a new perception of reality. The personal encounter with God supercedes all else.[19]

Simply put there is ample evidence in the Psalms of prosperous villains and human perfidy seemingly triumphing over the faithful ones of יהוה. John Goldingay, in his stirring commentary on the Psalms, describes the complementarity of the activity of God in the midst of the human struggle; it is an issue of both awareness and knowledge; between a committed faith and the realities of human experience.

> The *faithless may grant that God 'knows,' that there is 'knowledge' with [Elyon], but 'yada' and 'da'at' more likely indicate that God does not take any notice of what goes on. The point is underlined by the terms for God, el and elyon. Both suggest the might and power of God: surely this exalted deity does not bother with ordinary this-world affairs. But such a view deconstructs. The might of God means that God can and will not only know but will also do something about it.* [20]

The poet in Psalm 73 is fully conscious of an impending catastrophe. He is aware that he is teetering on the brink of a disastrous unbelief. Now the poet wonders aloud and questions his concerted efforts to purify such thoughts, but his entire experience of God's world is being called into question.... *the trouble is not so much a question of survival as a problem of faith!*[21] He protests: *Surely I have cleansed my heart in vain; how utterly useless it has been for me to continually purify my hands in innocence* (73:13, REB). He finds himself in great distress, unable to reconcile in his own mind *the way of* יהוה in a wicked and perverse generation, that is, *BUT THEN I went into the sanctuaries of God; then I understood.* (73:17, NRSV)[22] Another version puts it as follows: *Accordingly, I went into God's sanctuary and my understanding was renewed* (REB).

19. Schaefer, *Psalms*, Berit Olam, 181. cf. Ackroyd, *Doors of Perception.*

20. Goldingay, *Modes of Theological Reflection in the Bible*, 407.

21. Mays, *The David of the Psalms*, 241.

22. Smith, "A Crisis in Faith," in *Restoration Quarterly*. 17.3 Some have even argued that "the troubled poet resorts to visiting the desolate ruins of one of the illegitimate pagan shrines and there discovers anew the uselessness of idols and the eternal value of communion with God." 178. n.95. cf. T. D. Alexander, "The Psalms and the After Life," *Irish Biblical Studies* (1987) 2–17.

What is clear in the text is that there is this fundamental shift that is at once both dramatic and pronounced. Within the community of the faithful, the psalmist gains revelatory insight into the problem that has so vexed his spirit. It is then that the poet recognizes the unsubstantial and ephemeral success of the wealth and power enjoyed by the ungodly especially those who were once faithful, but who now have abandoned the way of יהוה. The poet, having come to his senses, now realizes anew that only life and peace are to be found in obedience *to* and trust *in* יהוה. Having reoriented himself to the ancient path of life anew, he continues on in trust and confidence despite all appearances to the contrary.

> Here an individual, in whose fate numerous human ills combine, recounts how he was in danger of wandering from the fullness of the goodness of his God, and why this came about. . . . The account related, 'My feet had almost stumbled' . . . 'Almost!' This anticipates the outcome. De facto it did not happen. God's servant was in the greatest danger, but God did not permit him to fall[23]

Psalm 73 speaks for us in our own time, not because it gives a theological answer but because it portrays realistically the situation in which new theological understanding must be found. Today we know, even more radically than did the wisdom psalmist, that theological formulations which appeared in a previous era are often no longer viable in facing the harsh realities of contemporary human experience. How can we talk about the 'happiness' of the God-fearing in a world where six million Jews were incinerated in Nazi ovens; where today many millions of people are doomed to live out their lives on the economic margins; where the threat of nuclear annihilation or biological warfare hangs over every military adventure; where radical Islamic jihadists terrorize the planet?

Theology that is vital always stands on the boundary between the old views, the old theology, which has been systematized, and the new theology, which must be reformulated. We somehow know this intuitively—that if a theology cannot carry the freight then it is doomed to irrelevancy–as well it ought. If a person's intellect is to be brought into the sanctuary of God, this standing on the boundary between the old and the new is imperative. The text of Psalm 73 bears out this truth convincingly. [24]The speaker, the poet, is perplexed by the prosperity of the faithless. Resolution, however, is reached within the hallowed walls of the temple, where the poet has discerned the fate of the wicked. Whether through a vision or through a dream, or simply by being

23. Kraus, *A Continental Commentary*, 170.

24. Goldingay, *Psalm II*. "To say 'God is good' can be a routine statement. Such a statement of 'orientation' can be one made in untested, rather unthinking and shallow faith. But in this context it is more than routine. The conviction is one that has been sharply tested by what the suppliant can see going on in the community. Here it is uttered as a statement of 'renewed orientation' after an experience of 'disorientation' such as the one the psalm will recount, and it thus gains a new depth. With spiritual bravery, the Midrash goes as far as to count the afflictions of which the psalm speaks as themselves gifts of God's goodness. They are good because they contribute to the purifying of the heart." 401.

awestruck by the temple's grandeur, the speaker becomes convinced that God's punishment of the wicked is imminent, that their fate is sealed. But by whatever means, it is there in the sanctuary, in *"nearness to God"* that the speaker finds an answer.

The temple is, for these ancient poets, the locus of revelation. This revelatory encounter is a profound one in the Psalter. It gives us a glimpse into the transition that is taking place between the traditional *orthodox* understanding of the nature of evil and suffering, and introduces a burgeoning development within the faith community of ancient Israel that seeks a new understanding of the faithfulness and abiding *presence of* יהוה in the midst of the experiences of severe suffering and loss and the paradoxes that are implicit in one's assessment of the troubles of life when contrasted with the worshiping faith in יהוה. It is in the communal experience of worship that one may begin to gain mastery over thoughts of futility and a not so benign attitude of despair.

This disjunction that ever occurs in human life is part of the paradox that is faced by persons of faith in seeking to reconcile the vast chasm that often exists between *one's declared faith and one's personal life experience of suffering, grief, and loss; the space between tragedy and triumph.* [25]The psalmists come to grips with this reality, particularly in the psalms of trust. These are not indifferent to the demands of faith in יהוה and they sometimes voice their complaints bitterly and openly to יהוה. The egregiousness and the apparent successes of the unbelieving wicked, especially in the face of the Psalmists' long-suffering and despair are readily acknowledged openly, and sometimes with an evident rage against יהוה to act on their behalf and reconcile the irreconcilable! Konrad Schaefer notes the sad truth about belief how, not infrequently, sadly,

> people just seem to get bored with God, above all when disappointment, disillusionment, and prolonged silence challenge the faith and tempt them to look elsewhere. The psalmist questions the value of practicing the faith. The temptation to disregard God is real. But to relinquish faith would betray that community of the devout. What prevents the psalmist from defection is the sense of obligation to the community.[26]

A fresh awareness and a revelatory experience of the nearness of יהוה envelopes the poet when he enters the *sanctuaries* (the plural is explicit in the Hebrew). It is there the poet's discouragement, disillusionment and despair are transformed into confidence, acceptance, and hope. A new vision of the involvement and action of יהוה in the midst of life is acquired, but it has been gained at considerable cost. It is this transformation to a faith that is internalized, cherished, and acted upon by the poets of the Psalter that is so evident. This is the gift of יהוה. They choose to dwell in close proximity to יהוה and their destination is glory! *Nevertheless, I am continually with [Yhwh]; Yhwh grasps my right hand, guides me with instruction, and afterward will*

---

25. Cf. Goulder, *The Psalms of Asaph*, 52, 53.

26. Schaefer, "Psalms," 179. Note: There is no mystery to unbelief. It comes quite naturally to us.

receive me in/to/with glory (73:22,23, LW).[27] The preposition in Hebrew is imprecise and here it could mean any of the three with differing interpretations. I opt for the traditional form, "to".

Another tender insight into this hope is found in Psalm 116:15 where the Hebrew reads, *precious in the sight of* יהוה *is the death of the godly ones* literally, *their blood will be precious in [his] eyes.* The point is not that יהוה is bloodthirsty, or delights perversely in the death of the faithful. Not at all. The psalmist, who has been delivered from death, affirms that the life-threatening experiences of the followers get the direct attention of יהוה, just as a precious or rare object would catch someone's eye. Psalm 72:14 also breathes a similar expression of such conviction whereby יהוה is cast as the redeemer of those in peril, death or otherwise. *From harm and violence* יהוה *will defend them;* יהוה *will redeem their lives.* The verb *redeems* casts יהוה in the role of a leader who protects members of [his] extended family in times of need and crisis. And Psalm 19:14 adds this: *May my words and my thoughts be acceptable in your sight, O* יהוה, *my rock and my redeemer (LW).* And again in Psalm 69:18, *Come near me and redeem me! Because of my enemies, rescue me!* The poet writes: *draw near unto my life and redeem it.*

The verb *redeem* is used in conjunction with the noun *life* and conveys the saving, delivering activity of יהוה on behalf of those precious and valued in the sight of יהוה. In all, the poets know that being continually with יהוה is the only good. *Psalm 73 is a highpoint in the Psalter. Like Job it courageously and spiritually insists on maintaining faith in a God who is active in the present, not just an afterlife, and a God who is active in the visible world, not just in an invisible inner life.*[28]

To be redeemed is to be *with Yhwh* and this introduces another peculiarity of the Psalms when taken as a whole. Here the reader interacts with the words of a psalm as a participant in the authorship of that psalm; what is meant is that the reader so completely *identifies* with the text to such a degree that, even though the reader is fully aware that the words of the composition may belong to an ancient poet, they have become one's own words in prayer. This is altogether extraordinary! James Kugel writes of this phenomenon:

> It [a particular psalm] may have been written by an ancient Levite, but at the moment of its recitation, its words become the worshiper's own; they speak on his or her behalf to God. There are few other cases I can think of in which such a total adoption of a text takes place. This seems to me a remarkable phenomenon, precisely because what is crucial are not the words themselves, but the mind of the worshiper who utters them. The very attitude of prayer pushes to the background

---

27. Eaton, *The Psalms,* "The differing interpretations of this psalm's hope, call attention to the peculiarity of classical Old Testament religion, in that it mostly sees no clear hope of life beyond death, yet ever returns from sorrows to trust and contentment in the goodness of the Lord of life. However, a full faith in a resurrection-life beyond death was at last attained, it was not found easily!" 200.

28. Goldingay, *Psalm II,* 419.

the historical circumstances of the psalm's composition. The true author is now the worshiper himself. [29]

Such an experience is not an uncommon phenomenon when one engages the Psalter as the vehicle of prayer. These very particular words are able–or, at the very least–have the inherent capacity to pull out of the human soul the words and the sighs that range far beyond our own stilted prayer vocabulary. The psalms of confidence, the songs of trust, seem to be specifically suited to the kind of prayer that requires a non-verbal vocabulary. They go beyond words to the depths of their arresting images and to the core of their affirmations.

> *In the midst of it all the psalmist finds a stillness toward God. Before the almighty Lord, his soul is a still centre. And the meaning of this silence of the spirit is trust–profound and decisive acknowledgment that power belongs to God, and in [Him] alone is salvation; [He] is faithful, and the source of all true hope. Perhaps it is on the way toward this stillness that wavering people are counseled to 'pour out' their heart before God. As they lay all their fears and doubts at [His] feet, they too will be granted that stillness which is the best prayer for the mighty deeds of the Saviour.*[30]

Our look at another song of trust is a psalm of David, Psalm 27. This song of the faithful one is the basis for a prayer for help in the face of baseless false accusations. Here the poet expresses trust in יהוה against all enemies and an eagerness–a hunger–to dwell in the divine *presence*. Here the tone set forth by the poet reflects an ebullience of confidence that, right from the start, alerts the reader that יהוה is clearly in charge of the affairs of this person's life. There is sheer delight with which the poet goes about the business of describing the path of life lived in the *presence* of יהוה. The light of salvation penetrates the darkness and illumines the path of the trusting poet so as to eliminate the fear of all that his enemies may be conspiring against him. Fearless now, he presses on, confidently, serenely.

The opening of the psalm (27:1–6) is a statement of confidence which is characterized by three metaphors: *light, salvation,* and *refuge.* The first metaphor, *light,* signals a force that dispels the darkness (here representing the poet's enemies) and is reminiscent of Psalm 23:4 in which fearlessness is expressed despite the dark shadow of the unknown (*even though I walk through the valley of deep darkness I will fear no evil*). The poet is expressing his own fearlessness which is also implied by similar language in Psalm 18:29 (*It is you who light my lamp;* יהוה *my God, lights up my darkness*). Second, יהוה is also the God of *salvation* (victory or deliverance) and the emphasis is on the power of יהוה to counter any force waged against the suppliant. The third term, *refuge,* is here ambiguous but it may refer to *stronghold or high tower.*

29. Kugel, *How to Read the Bible: A Guide to Scripture,* 473.

30. Eaton, *The Psalms,* 234.

The language certainly applies to a military context and connotes a place of military advantage. Actually all three metaphors may be associated with a military situation where the king as commander-in-chief against Israel's enemies, is supported by the power and will of יהוה. Opponents against the king are likewise the enemies of יהוה. So this psalm is clearly a royal liturgy and its stirring ring of confidence is marked by one of the most single-minded statements to be found anywhere in the Hebrew scriptures: *One thing I have asked of* יהוה, *one thing will I seek after; to live in the abode of* יהוה *all the days of my life* (Ps 27:4, LW).). The expression has no parallels among the biblical numerical sayings.[31]

Such is the nature of the confidence and trust in יהוה which is exclaimed in this bold statement of the king. Here is an instance of a psalm that has strong Davidic overtones amid its broader application to a royal liturgy.

Psalm 27

Of David

יהוה is my light and my salvation; whom shall I fear?
יהוה is the stronghold of my life;
of whom shall I be afraid?

When evildoers assail me to devour my flesh—
my adversaries and foes—
they stumble and fall.
Though an army should encamp against me,
my heart shall not fear;
though war rise up against me,
yet I will be confident.

One thing have I asked of יהוה,
one thing will I seek after; to live in the house of יהוה
all the days of my life,
to gaze upon the fair beauty of יהוה
and to inquire in [his] temple.
For [יהוה] will hide me and shelter me
in the day of trouble;
[יהוה] will conceal me under the cover of [his] dwelling
and establish me securely high upon a rock.

---

31. Craigie, *Psalms 1–50*, 232.

Now my head is lifted up above my enemies all around me,
and I will offer in [his] dwelling-place sacrifices with
shouts of joy; I will sing and make
music for יהוה.
O יהוה, hear my voice when I call;
have compassion and answer me.

Of you my heart has spoken: "*Seek God's face.*"
It is your face, O יהוה, that I seek;
Do not hide your face from me.
Do not dismiss your servant in anger;
you who have been my constant help.
Do not abandon me or forsake me,
O God of my salvation.

When father and mother may forsake me,
יהוה will lift me up.
Teach me your way, O יהוה,
and on a level path lead me.

When the wicked lie in ambush do not give me up
to the will of my adversaries, for false witnesses rise
up against me and are breathing threats of violence.
I believe that I shall see the goodness of יהוה
in the land of the living.
Wait for יהוה! Hold firm and take heart.
Have courage. Hope in יהוה.

Here is a psalm brimming with the confidence of a faithful poet and is the basis
for a prayer for divine intervention in the face of false accusations. Hebraic faith is
the faith of salvation. This poet sets out with the firm declaration that fullness of life
in יהוה is about light and salvation and refuge. The ancient poets also valued their
reputations in being faithful and obedient to יהוה; but when their righteousness and
their fidelity are impugned; they take it as requiring the immediate attention of יהוה.
This is a theme that is also common throughout the psalms of complaint–justice in
the face of false accusations; vindication by יהוה in the face of evil and treacherous
remarks–confidence and hope in the midst of all threats and all dangers.

The poet expresses trust in יהוה against all enemies, foreign and domestic, and is
ever eager to stay and to dwell within the *presence* of יהוה. *It is your face, O יהוה that I
seek.* As we have seen in our previous psalms, the desire to dwell in the *presence* of יהוה

is all-encompassing. This is the great good of faith–to be known by יהוה as faithful and to seek to position one's life in that secret and covert hiding place where there is life with God. When we come to know and have our being in יהוה we are untouchable by the enemies and evildoers and adversaries of this life. Schleiermacher in his sermon on prayer, reminds us that *the sustained prayer of a fervent believer is necessary to an understanding of the "book of prayer" for we live and move and have our being under the watchful eye of the Most High*. There is a transcendent quality to salvation, the like of which lifts the poet up on a high rock of security and safety where God dwells in all glory and light. The path of life binds the poet to יהוה and guarantees that the *presence* of יהוה will encompass and surround the faithful one all the days of his life.

Psalm 27 also represents a firm and resolute declaration of trust that comes at the very end of the psalm: *I am sure I shall see the goodness of יהוה in the land of the living. In יהוה, hold firm and take heart. Hope in יהוה!* (Ps 27:13–14, LW). Psalm 56 also echoes this same vow of unyielding belief: *O God, you have rescued my soul from death, you have kept my feet from stumbling so that I may walk in the presence of God and enjoy the light of the living* (Ps 56:14 NRSV). Dahood even goes so far as to assess this language as referring to the afterlife, although most scholars do not follow him in this particular regard.[32] But the individual reader cannot escape the joy and confidence which surrounds the poet in his acknowledgement of the divine *presence*.

That יהוה is both the journey and the destination of a vibrant faith is a continuing theme in the Psalter as well. The graciousness and favor of יהוה is highly to be prized. It is not often that we think of God's desiring our friendship. What comes through again and again in these songs of trust is how desirous is יהוה in having [his] loved ones gathered together in that place of *presence*. One poet puts it of יהוה: *My joy is gleeful!*

Throughout this book, the word *presence* has been highlighted in italics. The reason for this is intentional. It is to take note of the fact that the path of life is both our destiny and our destination. This is the place of the meeting with God, face to face. Remember that there is no Hebrew word for *presence*; that it is a reference to the face of יהוה being turned toward the suppliant. Living one's life in the *presence* of יהוה is to live with God's face turned toward us; this is an appropriate goal and an attuned value of the journey of faith. In the words of Bonhoeffer: "*No blessing is greater in its rewards than that which comes from doing the will of God.*"

That God, too, values and enjoys our companionship is reflected over and again in these psalms of confidence. That we are precious to יהוה is also a conviction that is born out of the crucible of a lived faith amid the challenges and confrontations of this life. To seek the face of יהוה at every moment of our lives is to traverse the *path of life*–that is the challenge. The promised rewards are unfathomable and the *presence* of יהוה is continuously being interpreted to us by love.

---

32. Dahood, *Psalms I*, 170.

Interpreted by Love

PSALM 91 IS A sturdy companion to the person who is seeking a relationship of divine companionship. Its boldness and unbroken courageous witness to יהוה have enabled many persons down through the centuries to rise above all sorts of temptations, anxieties, doubts and despairs. By virtue of the soaring energy of its unqualified trust and confidence in יהוה, it leaves behind every earthly fear, every human doubt and all qualifying and inhibiting considerations, and lifts one up above the depressing realities of life to the hopeful certitude of a faith which is able, not only to endure life, but to master it. The mastery of life with all its inherent ambiguities and hazards is witnessed to by the poets. Psalm 73 is a prime example where the poet anticipates his deliverance ("יהוה *will receive me*"). For this poet יהוה will always have the last word.

> *In the Old Testament context, it is an unexpected word, and it is put in cryptic terms. Essentially it is a statement of confidence in God, a declaration of trust that God will not let death cancel the relation to him that the faithful have in life. There is no valid immortality strategy for mortals, but with God it is a different matter. God is more powerful than the power of Sheol. God will pay the ransom that liberates the teacher and those who identify with him from the death penalty. Here the legal idiom is a metaphor: There is no payment and no court, the focus is on the actor and the result. How the deliverance will take place is said only in the mysterious 'he will take me' (NRSV, 'receive me'). The expression points to the reception of Enoch and Elijah from life into the divine presence as analogies (see Pss. 16:10–11 and 73:24). In many psalmic contexts, the divine rescue from death is help that delivers from the dangers of death. But in the context of this psalm, with its emphasis on the eventual death of all, such a salvation word would mean little. Here the hope is that God, not Sheol, will be the final hope of the souls who trust in him.*[1]

What is most remarkable about Psalm 73 is the security and assurance believers can enjoy in the midst of dire threats. No peril to the poet is too severe for יהוה. These psalms which are meant to lead us into such experiences that are only possible with יהוה, were also encountered first-hand by the early Christians. The poet's trust

---

1. Mays, *Psalms*, 193.

in Israel's God requires a further readiness to submit to the will of God, particularly when one is completely unsure what that divine will might entail. Stanley Jaki provides us with a vivid example from the early history (third-century CE) of the Christian church. With the beginning of state sanctioned persecution of Christians in Imperial Rome in the third century under the emperor Decius, the first wave struck very hard.

> *When Decius' persecution came and all the foundations of a growing Christian world appeared to collapse, Cyprian, bishop of Carthage, went into hiding at the urging of his own flock, only to remain in his post when the second wave came. He now truly took his refuge in the Lord alone. This in spite of the fact that he could not guess how close at hand was the demise of Decius himself, who, next to Diocletian, was the most cruel persecutor of Christians during pagan Imperial times. Cyprian could not guess the kind of 'barbed arrow,' a sudden early death on the battlefield, which God was preparing for the one, who—Cyprian was to record this—had a sharp perception of the strength of the Christian (movement).*[2]

Theologian Arthur McGill in his magnificent little book, reflects on this interrelatedness between suffering and justice and the rewards or retributions that characterize psalmic theological perspectives. In ancient Israel's communal experience of suffering and God's apparent absence there is still the witness to divine *presence*, blessing and renewal. In the end, it is this experience of nearness that ultimately confirms the accuracy of Israel's original confession of faith in יהוה. With the confirmation of that confession, what now becomes possible is the heretofore unthinkable: the anticipation that even death's power, the ultimate human boundary, may yet yield to a greater force, the God of grace and glory, the interpreter of love!

> *The Psalms express hope in a variety of ways. The laments move from despair to hope . . . Note the association of the sanctuary with hope. The Psalms also associate hope with the faith community; there one encounters hope firmly based in the faith tradition that demonstrates God's trustworthiness (Ps 11). So the Psalms raise the issue of hope even in the face of pain, and hope can lead one through hardship and trial. The Psalms are honest pilgrimage songs of faith and thus deal with all of life, including despair and hope. Hope is not always at hand but the Psalms persevere in the journey through crisis toward hope's light and liberation.*[3]

The poets' experiences signal a major shift in the theology of ancient Israel and mark a new perspective and re-orientation. Their understanding and recognition of the ways of יהוה in the face of chaos, the disintegration of the moral order, the universal scope

2. Jaki, *Praying the Psalms*, 53. cf. Cyprian, however, was to die a martyr in the next wave of persecution under Valerian on 14 September, 258 CE when he held fast to the faith unto death. It would be another sixty years before the brutality toward, and torture of, Christians as a matter of state sponsored terrorism, would be brought to an end by the emperor Constantine. By the time of the early fourth century the Christian church had already weathered many storms before the emperor Constantine issued the Edict of Toleration (Milan) in the early fourth-century CE.

3. Bellinger, *Psalms: Reading and Studying the Book of Praises*, 141

and reality of unimaginable human suffering, and the matrix of cosmic evil, represent a quantum leap forward in Israel's developing self consciousness and theological discourse. What was perceived earlier as Yahweh's rejection and seeming absence from the people of God in the midst of their human struggles, is now revealed as the knowledge of the holiness, grandeur, and infinite love of יהוה for the whole world. Israel's troubles are the troubles of all humanity. Israel's God, יי, is the God of all humanity. Israel's promised deliverance and redemption mark the universal salvation of all humanity.

The poet is encouraged by simply reflecting on who יהוה is. His whole being receives consolation from the conviction that יהוה is sufficient. יהוה can give "rest" to all who are looking for quietness of heart. יהוה is the source of "salvation" and is the strength of [his] people. Salvation signifies the whole process of redemption extending to vindication and the enjoyment of covenantal privileges. יהוה alone will save, because [he] alone is faithful and able. יהוה is faithful in giving love (*hesed*) and rewards, and is also able in that [he] is strong as a "rock" and a "fortress" (lit., "high place"); the poet's confidence rests ultimately in יהוה.

Resting in יהוה requires waiting and patience. *Declare that יהוה is just: my rock, in whom there is no unrighteousness* (Ps. 92:15, LW). *Rest in יהוה, wait patiently for [him].* Even though he may have many reasons to fear, the psalmist's faith rises to a new height in believing the promise of יהוה that the righteous *"will never be shaken"* (Ps 125:1). יהוה is entirely capable of defending the poets from any threat, any danger, any foe, any time. In this citing of our last psalm, the pilgrim poet of Psalm 125 knows this to be the case. He knows it with assurance. The expressions of confidence and trust in יי are striking in the first three verses and they sum up the promises of God to the faith community.

Psalm 125

A Song of Ascents

Those who put their trust in יהוה
are like Mount Zion which will never be shaken;
but stands forever.

Jerusalem! Even as the mountains surround her,
so יהוה surrounds [his] people,
from this time forth and forevermore.
For the scepter of the faithless shall not rest on the land
allotted to the faithful,
so that the righteous might not stretch out
their hands to do wrong.

Do good, יהוה, to those who are good,

to those who are upright in heart.

But as for those who turn aside to their own crooked ways,

יהוה will drive them away.

On Israel, peace!

In contrast to his profound confidence in יהוה, the poet has little faith in the king-dom of humanity. Humanity that is in opposition to יהוה is destructive, selfish, and deceitful. Yet faith in the knowledge of יהוה overcomes the strongest opposition.[4] The poet of Psalm 125 expresses in a communal prayer God's safekeeping of the people of God in a post-exilic setting. It provides us with valuable insights into the faith as it is expressed in the post-exilic Judean community.

> *It reveals a society struggling with the pressures upon it and represents the en-deavors of its religious leaders to hearten it with encouragement and prayer. Zion theology and Deuteronomy and sapiential teaching are harnessed to the task of supporting the people's faith. Yahweh's protective power and faithfulness to [his] promises concerning the people and land are theological factors used to bring comfort and hope to the faithful and to encourage moral perseverance . . . The discrepancy between traditional faith and contemporary experience is chan-neled positively into ardent, polarized prayer.*[5]

The land allotted to Israel refers to the granting of the land of Canaan to Israel for all time. יהוה is the God of promise and rewards the people of God when they are faithful to the covenantal demands laid down at Sinai. Why then does יהוה allow evil to prosper and, conversely, the godly to suffer, despite their living lives of faithfulness and obedience to יהוה? The psalm closes with a priestly benediction in response to the prayer (cf. I Sam 1:17) and suggests the calling forth of the blessing of יהוה upon the faithful yet, troubled people. Again it is Psalm 73 that confronts the difficulties and challenges and concludes that nothing in heaven or on earth can compare with יהוה. The psalm hesitates on the threshold of belief in personal immortality, introduced by piety rather than by doctrinal discourse. The poet admits life's unfairness and puts the question squarely before God on behalf of the post-exilic community!

This theme appears frequently in the various wisdom reflections which examine the uncertainties of experience and the mysteries of life. In the end God's *presence* does not solve the problem but it gives an assurance which intelligence alone cannot grasp. The answer to the wisdom problem withdraws into contemplation. Failure was necessary for the poet to perceive reality differently, as a gift of יהוה. When a person relinquishes control in prayer, יהוה expands the perception to a new level. The highest value to be prized is a personal encounter with יהוה which outweighs everything. The

4. Tozer, *The Knowledge of God*, 45.

5. Allen, "Psalms 101–150," 169.

wicked assail heaven and earth, which in the end does not even matter in the poet's new view of things.

The cry goes on but the heart stands firm. *"How then is one to live?"* is the question that lies at the heart of the psalms of trust. Despite everything, the ancient poets declare that it is trust in the absolute fidelity of יהוה that will win out in the struggle with and against the irreconcilable paradoxes of human life. Together with Psalms 90 and 92, Psalm 91 is a mightily impressive and towering poem of absolute confidence and unshakable trust in the face of unmitigated dangers and imminent disasters. Indeed, the poet's very existence is bound up in this stubborn trust in אלהי (*Elohay*), who is *my God*.

Life for our poets is the great adventure of negotiating the shoals and tracking the elusive *presence* of יהוה, the One who will never abandon him. True confidence in God will never be in vain. Faith has its own rewards. Boldness of faith is not naive belief.

> *There is a realism about the Psalms that should commend them to a generation which with some justification accuses the church of turning a blind eye to the actualities of human life and failing to integrate experience and faith. The Psalter comes face to face with human experience and does not shrink from verbalizing it and relating it to a kaleidoscope of divine truth. The measure in which Christians find the blatancy of the laments embarrassing is the measure by which they must judge their own openness to life. The Psalms function as honest gauges of human experience. Whatever a person's lot, he or she can read a group of psalms with which to find rapport and a route to God[6]*

The external difficulties are insignificant in comparison with the poets' deepest desire to experience more fully the *presence* of יהוה. This is the goal of the life of faith. In the *presence* of יהוה fear is banished. The longing for the temple of יהוה expresses the intensity of the psalmists' seeking after יהוה. The inexpressible joy of God's *presence* assures the evident goodness and love of יהוה. The poets' desires of the heart are to dwell in the *presence* of יהוה for the rest of their lives. The temple was the visible expression of the *presence* of יהוה and was sought after by the godly. It was the depth, the height, and the breadth of this boldness of faith that resulted in their daring claims and unshakable confidence. In the final analysis, the psalmists teach us to place our trust in the sure promises of יהוה. The desire and heart-felt longing for God's *presence* always arises out of a fundamental human need. The human need is ever for friendship with Yhwh!

The psalmist is not an escapist, for he wants to hang on to יהוה until he is fully assured of the glorious *presence*. With this assurance, he knows that he is in the protective hands of יהוה. Characteristically, the poet does not keep his faith to himself. He looks forward to proclaiming aloud the great acts of יהוה. While these words were first addressed as an encouragement to his own heart, they had the intended effect of encouraging each and every godly person to draw courage from them and instill trust and confidence in יהוה. Indeed, our pilgrim poet utters a final doxology: On Israel,

6. Allen, *Word Biblical Themes: The Psalms*, 40.

peace! Adopting a personal commitment of trust in God enables one to make this sort of firm declaration. It is forged and tempered in the embers of testing and all is tried in the furnace of a settled resolve over the course of a lifetime. *The clean heart struggles through all inward and outward contradictions to reach the place where God is present, waits for [his] message, and submits to [his] counsel and guidance.*[7]

When life is on the line, as happens to all of us, here is the sole recourse needed: *My refuge, my fortress, my God in whom I trust.* Such a one–in fact already dwells in the shelter of Elyon, the Most High; is already safely ensconced within the shadow of Shaddai, the Almighty; is thus positioned and situated in life and able to declare that it is יהוה alone who saves and delivers. Only from this perspective of trusting faith can one's life be lived in the face of all obstacles and threats to the contrary. Faith is always actively and vitally invested and interested both in the realization and in the actualization of the divine help–and is played out continuously over the contours of human life. Saving faith is the stalwart witness to the superintendence that lies behind these varied and sometimes disparate compositions.[8]

One may place one's trust in this witness to God's self-revelation both in the written texts of sacred scripture and in the particular events of one's human history. Both lend credence to the inherent authority and the comforting realization of divine self-disclosure. The Psalms have a defining and astounding relevance for us in today's world. Today's Christian church needs to appropriate these psalms in their regular corporate worshiping life and fails to do so at its peril. They are indeed the ground of all praise and thanksgiving and the burden of their message is particularly relevant in today's world of a banal cynicism and unbelief. People need the radical experience of salvation–the root experience of God active and alive in their daily lives; what is not needed in today's church is simply more information *about* God. Salvation is intended to bring faith to the fore and let all else dissipate. It is the saving actions of Yhwh that continue to draw men and women into the divine embrace.

In the final pages of Gerhard von Rad's opus on Old Testament theology, there is a moving description of the tragic situation of *Israel before Yahweh* and the subsequent promise of the coming of the Christ. With the knowledge and awareness of the Psalms, and its movement from complaint to trust and praise, he writes how it is that

> the great moments of Israel's history brought the nation a faith awareness in which it was always on pilgrimage . . . a stranger in time; these were the archetypes of mighty predictions; with the passing of time Israel increasingly swelled Yahweh's promises to an infinity, so that in the sacred texts expectations kept

7. Kraus, *Theology of Psalms*, 170.

8. Keel, *The Symbolism of the Biblical World*, "What really liberates [the psalmist] however, is not the knowledge that 'sin does not pay', but the experience of the 'nearness of God.'" Only that is a sure defense against despair. This nearness means 'life'. The life offered by God on Zion is manifested in the broad forecourts . . . In them is manifested the living, life-loving God [himself]. With [him] is the 'fountain of life' and it lies within [his] power to permit one to take the ' path of life' (Ps 16:11) and to dwell in the ' land of the living.'" 186.

mounting up to vast proportions. Left to itself without this ancient witness . . .
the Hebrew Bible becomes a baffling enigma, . . . because if it has no sequel, its
unbounded expectation points straight into the void.[9]

But rather than being left to peer into the void with no sequel, we are left with something quite completely different: the abiding legacy of trusting יהוה as it has been bequeathed us by ancient Israel. It is, in the final analysis, this *enigma* that exposes us to the Psalms. And in turn the Psalms expose ancient Israel's kindred confession and promise of a revealed faith to the Christian church. The Psalms first appeared to Christians, from their earliest beginning, as triumphal songs of fulfillment. We Christians believe the book of Psalms bears witness to the promises of God's Savior Messiah. This is only possible because the ancients continue to speak from the deep personal reservoirs of their encounters with the Holy over the course of three millennia. This is their precious legacy to us, which is as real and relevant to us as it was when these remarkable poems were first composed and sung in the temple over three-thousand years ago:

First, we come to know that we are not alone! From all eternity, we are known and accepted, favored and cherished, forgiven and free! We are ultimately safe, held, and loved from before time and forever. This is the heart of the psalmists' message and likewise the heart of the Christian gospel. God's love will win out in the end!

Second, God's word is all faithfulness and constancy, and absolutely trustworthy. It is over the course of a lifetime that we learn to live, fearlessly, in faith. Third, having practiced these principles throughout our earthly sojourn, we are finally able to die, fearlessly, in faith.[10] The early Christians very quickly appropriated the witness of the Psalms to Jesus Christ. This is confirmed throughout the witness of the Christian Bible. This ought not surprise us. These last words—in the divine oracle—accurately summarize the promise of the world's Savior to us–the eternal promise of *shalom*. It is a good thing indeed that it is יהוה who speaks the final word of salvation to us in the divine oracle concluding Psalm 91:

> [יהוה speaks] *"Hear this: I will rescue the one who yearns after me;*
> *I will be a bulwark of safety;*
> *I will lift you to a high place because you have acknowledged my name.*
> *To the one who calls for me, I will answer; when in dire straits,*
> *I will be there and I will raise you to a place of honor; I will save.*
> *I will fill your days full with contentment;*
> *I will demonstrate my saving power to you for a lifetime." (LW)*

9. Gerhard von Rad, *Old Testament Theology,* II, 319–320.

10. *Schottenstein Edition of the Hebrew Bible* "When people refer to events as being either good or bad, they are usually describing their perception of these events rather than the nature of the events themselves. But the Psalmist declares: *nearness to God is my good!* When I am loyal and faithful to God and [He] is thus near to me, all events are good. Whatever [He] metes out to me–reward or chastisement–is truly for my benefit" 201, 202.

Appendix

Psalm 90 *Prayer—Of Moses, the man of God*

Adonai, you have been our dwelling place in all generations.
Before the mountains were brought forth,
before the earth and the cosmos were born,
even from eternity to eternity, you are *God*.

You turn humankind back into the dust, and say:
"*Back to what you once were, mortals.*"
To you, a thousand years are but a single day,
and yesterday, now over and gone, is but a watch in the night

You sweep humanity away; all of you but a dream,
like grass that sprouts and flowers in the morning,
yet it withers and dries; and before dusk it is gone.

We too are consumed by your anger;
we are are terrified by your fury;
having summoned up our sins, everything is made
manifest in the light of your countenance-

so it is that all our days dwindle before your wrath;
we bring our years to an end like a sigh.
Our lifetime is so brief—seventy years,
or if we are strong, perhaps eighty –

but they only add up to boisterous anxiety and stormy troubles;
they are soon gone with the wind, and we with them.
Who is it who has felt the the full force of your anger?
Your wrath is as great as the fear that is due you.
Teach us to be mindful of the brevity of our days,

that we may gain hearts full of wisdom.
O YHWH—how long until you turn your face toward us?
We beg you to have compassion on your servant (Israel)!

Satisfy us in the morning with your steadfast love,
    so that we may sing and be happy all our days;
    make our future as bright as our past was sad,
for we remember those years you were correcting us.

Let your servants show forth your wonders;
    O, let our children see your glorious power.
YHWH , our God! Be upon us; prosper our handiwork -
O [YHWH], we implore you—make the work of our hands succeed.

Psalm 91

The one who dwells in the hiding place of *Elyon (Most High)*,
and who passes the night within the shadow of *Shaddai (the God of Heaven)*, speaks:

"I will say to YHWH, 'You are my refuge and my bulwark,
You are Elohay (my God) in whom I put my trust'."

Surely YHWH is the One who will rescue you from the snare of the fowler,
and from the lethal pestilence that rains down ruinous destruction.
[Yhwh] will cover you beneath a feathering cloak,
and will conceal you in a covert refuge.
The constancy of YHWH will be for you both enveloping shield and sheltering
barricade;

You will fear nothing—neither the terrors abroad in the night,
nor the arrow that flies by day;
neither the plague that stalks in the dark,
nor the scourge that wreaks havoc at high noon.

A thousand may fall on your left, myriad thousands at your right hand;
but you yourself will remain unscathed.
Make no mistake! You will see it all—
gazing intently with your eyes wide open.
You will witness what has become of the faithless–rotting corpses all.

Because you are the one who has made YHWH "my refuge,"
and *Elyon (Most High)*, "my haven of fastness,"
No disaster shall overtake you;
no calamity shall approach your dwelling place.

YHWH will command angels who will guard your going out and your coming in;
gentle aides will lift you up in the hollow of their hands,
so as not to stub your foot on a stone and stumble.

You will stand astride the cub and viper;
you will trample under foot the lion and serpent.

[YHWH speaks] *"Hear this: I will rescue the one who yearns after me;*
I will be a bulwark of safety;
I will lift you to a high place because you have acknowledged my name.
To the one who cries for me, I will answer; when in dire straits,
I will be there–and will raise you to a place of honor; I will save.
I will fill your days full with contentment;
I will demonstrate my saving power to you for a lifetime."

Psalm 92 *A Psalm. A Song for the Sabbath Day*

It is good to give thanks to YHWH,
to sing praises to your name, O *Elyon (Most High);*

to proclaim your constancy at daybreak,
and your steadfastness all through the night,
to the music of the zither and lyre,
to the rippling melody upon the harp.

I am beside myself with joy, YHWH, when I recall all you have done;
at the works of your hands I will sing for joy.
How great are all your achievements, YHWH,
the immensity of your thoughts are vexing and deep!

The stupid are not aware of this,
nor can fools ever appreciate it.
The faithless may sprout as thick as weeds
and every evildoer flourish,
but surely they are all doomed to destruction forever.

O YHWH, you are supreme above all ; you dominate everything forever.
See how those who resist you perish; see how the faithless are routed?
But you have raised my horn as if I were a wild ox;
you have poured the oil of gladness upon my favored head;

With my own eyes I have witnessed the recompense of my enemies;
my ears overheard what the faithless were whispering;
But in due time the righteous shall flourish like the palm tree;
they shall grow tall as the cedars of Lebanon.

Planted in the house of YHWH, they will flourish in the courts of *Elohay (my God);*
they will still bear fruit in old age, and so remain fresh and succulent -
All are demonstrating that YHWH is upright in all [His] deeds;
O [YHWH] my rock! There is not one who can find any fault in You!

Bibliography

Achtemeier, Elizabeth. "Preaching from the Psalms." *Review and Expositor* (1984) 437-449.
———."The Use of Hymnic Elements in Preaching." *Interpretation* 39 (1985) 46-59.
Ackroyd, Peter. *Doors of Perception: A Guide to Reading the Psalms.* London: SCM, 1983.
———. "Some Notes on the Psalms." *Journal of Theological Studies* (1966) 392-399.
Albertz, Rainer. *A History of Israelite Religion in the Old Testament Period: Volume I: From the Beginnings to the End of the Monarchy.* Translated by John Bowden. Old Testament Library. Louisville: Westminster John Knox, 1994.
Albright, William Foxwell. *The Biblical Period from Abraham to Ezra.* New York: Harper & Row, 1963.
———. *Yahweh and the Gods of Canaan.* Garden City, NewYork: Doubleday, 1968.
Alexander, T. D. "The Psalms and the After Life." *Irish Biblical Studies* (1987) 2-17.
Allen, Leslie C. "Psalms 101–150." *Word Biblical Commentary* 21(eds.) Glenn L. Barker and David A. Hubbard. Nashville, Tennessee: Nelson, 1987.
Anderson, A.A. *Psalms.* 2 vols. New Century Bible Commentary. Grand Rapids: Eerdmans, 1972.
Anderson, Bernhard W. "The Bible in a Postmodern Age." *Horizons in Biblical Theology* (2000) 1-16.
Anderson, Bernhard W., with Stephen Bishop. *Out of the Depths: The Psalms Speak for Us Today* Fourth edition. Louisville: Westminster John Knox, 2004.
Anderson, G. W. "Enemies and Evildoers in the Book of Psalms." *Bulletin of The John Rylands Library* 48 (1965/1966) 18-29.
———. "Israel's Creed: Sung, Not Signed." *Scottish Journal of Theology* (1963) 277-85
———."A Note on Ps 1:1." *Vetus Testamentum* (1974) 233.
———."'Sicut cervus': evidence in the Psalter of private devotion in ancient Israel." *Vetus Testamentum* 30 (1980) 388-97.
Alter, Robert. *The Art of Biblical Poetry.* New York: Basic Books, 1985.
———. *The Book of Psalms: A Translation with Commentary.* New York: W. W. Norton, 2007.
Balentine, Samuel E. "A Description of the semantic field of Hebrew words for 'hide.'" *Vetus Testamentum* 30 (1980) 137-53.
———. *The Hidden God: The Hiding of the Face of God in the Old Testament.* New York: Oxford, 1983.
———."Prayers for Justice in the Old Testament: Theodicy and Theology," *Catholic Biblical Quarterly* 51 (1989) 597-616.
Barre, M. "Hearts, Beds, and Repentance in Psalm 4,5 and Hosea 7, 14." *Biblica* (1995) 53-62.
Barth, Christoph. *Introduction to the Psalms.* New York: Charles Scribner's Sons, 1966.
Barth, Karl. *Christ and Adam: Man and Humanity in Romans 5,* Philadelphia: Fortress, 1966.

————. *Church Dogmatics. Vol. 1.* Philadelphia: Fortress, 1963.

————. *Church Dogmatics: A Selection with Introduction.* (ed) by Helmut Gollwitzer. Louisville, Kentucky:Westminster John Knox, 1994.

————. *Dogmatics in Outline.* New York: Harper and Row, 1959.

————. *The Resurrection of the Dead.* Translated by H. J. Stenning. New York: Fleming H. Revell, 1933.

Beattie, D. R. G. and P. R. Davies. "What does *Hebrew* Mean?" *Journal of Semitic* Studies 56.1 (2011): 71-83.

Beckwith, R.T. "The Early History of the Psalter," *Tyndale Bulletin* .1 (1995) 1-27.

Bellinger, William. "The Interpretation of Psalm 11."*Evangelical Quarterly* 56 (1984) 95-101.

————. *Reading and Studying the Book of Praises.* Grand Rapids: Eerdmans. 2006.

Beuken, W. "Psalm 39: Some Aspects of the Old Testament Understanding of Prayer." *Heythrop Journal* 19 (1978) 1-11.

Blenkinsopp, Joseph. *Wisdom and Law in the Old Testament: The Ordering of Life in Israel and Early Judaism.* Oxford: Oxford University Press. 1995.

Boer, P. A. H. de. "The Meaning of Psalm LXXIII 9." *Vetus Testamentum* (1968) 260-264.

————. "Psalm CXXI:2." *Vetus Testamentum* 16 (1966) 287-292.

Boers, H. W. "Psalm 16 and the Historical Origin of the Christian Faith." *Zeitschrift für die neutestamentliche Wissenschaft* (1969) 105-110.

Boling, Robert G. "'Synonymous' Parallelism in the Psalms." *Journal of Semitic Studies* 5 (1960) 221-55.

Bonhoeffer, Dietrich. *Psalms: The Prayer Book of the Bible.* Philadelphia: Augsburg, 1974.

————. *Meditations on Psalms.* Translated by E. Robertson. Grand Rapids: Zondervan, 2002.

Booij, Th. "The Hebrew Text of Psalm 92,11." *Vetus Testamentum* (1988) 210-213.

————. "Psalms 120-136: Songs for a Great Festival." *Biblica* 91.2 (2010): 241-255.

————. "Psalm 90, 5-6: Junction of Two Traditional Motifs." *Biblica* (1987) 393-396.

————. "Psalm 116, 10-11: The Account of an Inner Crisis."*Biblica* 76 (1995) 388-395.

Bosma, Carl. "Discerning the Voices in the Psalms: A Discussion of the Two in Psalmic Interpretation." *Calvin Theological Journal* (2009) 155-172.

Botterweck, G. and Ringgren, H. (eds). *Theological Dictionary of the Old Testament.* Grand Rapids: Eerdmans, 1974.

Bowker, J. W. "Psalm CX." *Vetus Testamentum* 17 (1967) 31-41.

Bradshaw, Paul F. *The Search for the Origins of Christian Worship.* New York: Oxford University Press, 1992.

Braude, W. G. *The Midrash on the Psalms,* 2 Vols. New Haven: Yale University Press, 1959.

Brennan, J. P. "Psalms 1-8: Some Hidden Harmonies." *Biblical Theology Bulletin* (1980) 25-29.

Brettler, Mark Zvi. *God is King: Understanding an Israelite Metaphor.* Journal for the Study of the Old Testament Press, 1989.

————. "Judaism in the Hebrew Bible? The Transition from Ancient Israelite Religion to Judaism," *Catholic Biblical Quarterly* (1999):448-60.

Bright, John. *A History of Israel.* Third Edition. Philadelphia: Westminster, 1981.

Brown, William. P. *Seeing the Psalms: A Theology of Metaphor.* Louisville: Westminster John Knox,2002.

————. Psalms In *Interpreting Biblical Texts.* Nashville: Abingdon, 2010.

Broyles, Craig C. *The Conflict of Faith and Experience in the Psalms: A Form-critical* and *Theological Study*. Journal for the Study of the Old Testament Supplement 52. Sheffield: Academic Press, 1989.

———. Psalms. *New International Biblical Commentary*. Peabody, MA: Hendrickson, 1999.

Brueggemann, Walter. *Abiding Astonishment: Psalms, Modernity, and the Making of* History. Louisville, Kentucky: Westminster/John Knox Press, 1991.

———. " Bounded by Obedience and Praise: The Psalms as Canon." *Interpretation* (1991) 63-92.

———. " The Crisis and Promise of Presence in Israel." *Horizons in Biblical Theology* 6 (1979) 47-85.

———. " From Hurt to Joy, From Death to Life." *Interpretation* 28 (1974) 3-19.

———. *The Message of the Psalms: A Theological Commentary*. Philadelphia: Augsburg, 1984.

———. "A Shape for Old Testament Theology, II: Embrace of Pain." *Catholic Biblical Quarterly* 47 (1985) 395-415.

———. *The Spirituality of the Psalms*. Minneapolis: Fortress , 2002.

Brunner, Emil. *The Christian Doctrine of God*. Vol. I. Translated by Olive Wyon. Philadelphia: Westminster, 1950.

Buber, Martin. "The Heart Determines: Psalm 73," In *Theodicy in the Old Testament*. (ed.) James L. Crenshaw. Issues in Religion and Theology No 4. (109-118) Philadelphia: Fortress, 1983.

———. *Right and Wrong: An Interpretation of Some Psalms*. London: SCM, 1952.

Bullock, C. H. *Encountering the Book of Psalms: A Literary and Theological Introduction*. Grand Rapids: Academic, 2001.

Buss, M. J. " The Psalms of Asaph and Korah." *Journal of Biblical Literature* (1963) 382-392.

Campbell, A. F. "Psalm 78: A Contribution to the Theology of Tenth-Century Israel." *Catholic Biblical Quarterly* 41 (1979) 51-79.

Carney, S. "God Damn God: A Reflection on Expressing Anger in Prayer." *Biblical Theology Bulletin* 13 (1983) 116-20.

Cashmore, Gwen, and Joan Puls." Thirsty in a Thirsty Land." *Ecumenical Review* 2 (1994) 204.

Ceresko, Anthony R. "Psalm 121: A Prayer of a Warrior?" *Biblica* 70 (1989) 496-510.

Chester, D. K. " The Theodicy of Natural Disasters." *Scottish Journal of Theology* (1998) 485-505.

Childs, Brevard S. *Introduction to the Old Testament as Scripture*. Philadelphia: Fortress, 1979.

———. "Psalm Titles and Midrashic Exegesis." *Journal of Semitic Studies* 16 (1971) 137-150.

Clines, David J. A. "Psalms Research since 1955. I. Psalms and the Cult," *Tyndale Bulletin* 18 (1967)103-126.

———. "Psalms Research since 1955. II. The Literary Genres," *Tyndale Bulletin* 20 (1969) 105-25.

Clouda, Sheri L. "The Dialectical Interplay of Seeing and Hearing in Psalm 19 and Its Connection to Wisdom," *Bulletin of Biblical Research* (2000): 181-95.

Cohen, A. *Psalms: Hebrew Text, English Translation and Commentary Digest*. Revised Edition. Surrey, UK: Soncino, 1992.

Cohen, Moshe S. *Our Haven and Our Strength: The Book of Psalms*. New York: Aviv, 2004.

Cooper, A. M. "The Life and Times of King David according to the Book of Psalms," In *The Poet and the Historian: Essays in Literary and Historical Biblical Criticism* (ed.) Richard E. Friedman.Chico, California: Scholars, 1983.

Cole, Robert. "An Integrated Reading of Psalms 1 and 2." *Journal for the Study of the Old Testament* 98 (2002) 75-88.

Cook, Stephen L. *The Social Roots of Biblical Yahwism*. 8. Atlanta: Society of Biblical Literature, 2014.

Countryman, L. William. *Living on the Border of the Holy: Renewing the Priesthood of All*. New York: Morehouse, 1999.

Craigie, Peter C. "Hebrew Thought about God and Nature and Its Contemporary Significance."*Canadian Journal of Theology* 16 (1970) 3-11.

———. "Psalm 29 in the Hebrew Poetic Tradition." *Vetus Testamentum* 22 (1972) 142-51.

———. Psalms 1-50.(Second Edition with Supplement by Marvin Tate & Dennis Tucker) *Word Biblical Commentary* 19. Nashville, Tennessee: Nelson, 2004.

———. "The Role and Relevance of Biblical Research." *Journal for the Study of the Old Testament* 18 (1980) 19-31.

Creach, Jerome F.D. "Like a Tree Planted by the Temple Stream: The Portrait of the Righteous in Psalm 1:3 " *Catholic Biblical Quarterly*. no. 1 (1999) 43-46.

———. *The Destiny of the Righteous in the Psalms*. St. Louis: Chalice, 2008.

———. *Yahweh as Refuge and the Editing of the Hebrew Psalter*. Journal for the Study of the Old Testament Supplement 217. Sheffield: Academic Press, 1996.

Crenshaw, James L. " The Concept of God in Old Testament Wisdom." In *In Search of Wisdom* (1-18) (eds.) Leo G. Perdue, Bernard B. Scott and William J. Wiseman. Louisville: Westminster/John Knox, 1993.

———. *Defending God: Biblical Responses to the Problem of Evil*. Oxford: University Press, 2005.

———. " Impossible Questions, Sayings, and Tasks." *Semeia* 17 (1980) 19-34.

———. *The Psalms: An Introduction*. Grand Rapids: Eerdmans, 2001.

———. "In Search of Divine Presence." *Review and Expositor* . 3 (1977) 353-69.

———. " Theodicy," *Anchor Bible Dictionary*, Vol. 6. ed. David Noel Freedman. (444-47) New York: Doubleday, 1992

———. *A Whirlpool of Torment: Israelite Traditions of God as an Oppressive Presence*. Overtures to Biblical Theology vol. 12. Philadelphia: Fortress, 1984.

Crim, Keith R. *The Royal Psalms*. Richmond: John Knox, 1962.

Crollius, Ary A. R. " 'Derek' in the Psalms." *Biblical Theology Bulletin* (1974) 312-17.

Cross, Frank Moore. *Canaanite Myth and Hebrew Epic: Essays in the History of the Religion of Israel*. Cambridge: Harvard University Press, 1973.

———. "Notes on a Canaanite Psalm in the Old Testament." *Bulletin of the American Schools of Oriental Research* 117 (1949) 19-21.

———. " Yahweh and the God of the Patriarchs." *Harvard Theological Review* 55 (1962) 247-69.

Curtis, Adrian. *Psalms*. Revised English Bible. Epworth Commentaries. London: Epworth, 2009.

Curtis, Edward M. " Ancient Psalms and Modern Worship." *Bibliotheca sacra* (1997) 285-96.

Dahood, Mitchell. *Psalms: A New Translation with Introduction and Commentary*. The Anchor Bible 3 vols. Garden City, New York: Doubleday, 1965 to 1970.

Daly-Wenton, M. "David the Psalmist, Inspired Prophet: Jewish Antecedents of a New Testament Datum." *Australian Biblical Review* (2004) 32-47

Davidson, Robert. *The Vitality of Worship: A Commentary on the Book of Psalms*. Grand Rapids: Eerdmans, 1998.

Davies, Phillip R. "The Origin of Biblical Israel." *Journal of Hebrew Scriptures* (2005): 1-14.

Davis, Eli. "The Psalms in Hebrew Medical Amulets." *Vetus Testamentum* (1992): 173-78.

Davis, Ellen F. "Psalm 98: Rejoicing in Judgment." *Interpretation* 46 (1992): 171-175.

Davis, Thomas. *Shifting Sands: The Rise and Fall of Biblical Archaeology.* Oxford: Oxford University Press, 2004.

Davison, Lisa W. " 'My Soul is like the weaned child that is with me': The Psalms and the Feminine Voice." *Horizons in Biblical Theology* 23 (2001) 155-67.

Day, John. *Psalms.* Old Testament Guides. Sheffield: Academic Press, 1972.

———.(ed.) " How Many Pre-exilic Psalms are there?" (225-49) In *In Search of Pre-Exilic Israel.* Journal for the Study of the Old Testament Supplement 406. London: T&T Clark, 2004.

Dead Sea Scrolls Translated: The Qumran Texts in English. Translated by F. Garcia Martinez. Leiden: Brill; Grand Rapids: Eerdmans, 1996.

deClaisse-Walford, Nancy. *Reading from the Beginning: The Shaping of the Hebrew Psalter.* Macon, Georgia: Mercer, 1997.

Dines, Jennifer M. *The Septuagint.* Michael A Knibb. London: T & T Clark, 2004.

Drijvers, Pius. *The Psalms: Their Structure and Meaning.* London: Burns & Oates, 1965.

Eaton, John H. "The King as God's Witness." *Annual of the Swedish Theological Institute* (1970) 25 -40

———. *Kingship and the Psalms.* Studies in Biblical Theology (2) No. 32. SCM, 1976.

———. "Problems of Translation in Psalm 23: 3f." *The Bible Translator* 16 (1965) 171-76.

———. "Psalm 4: 6-7." *Theology* 67 (1964) 355-57.

———. *Psalms: A Historical and Spiritual Commentary with an Introduction and New Translation.* New York and London: T&T Clark International, 2005.

Eliade, Mircea. *Cosmos and History: The Myth of the Eternal Return.* Princeton, New Jersey: Princeton University Press, 1954.

———. "Theodicy," *The Encyclopedia of Religion*, Vol. 14, (ed.) Mircea Eliade (430-41). New York: Macmillan. Columns, 1987.

Encyclopedia of Archaeological Excavations in the Holy Land.(ed.) M. Avi-Yonah. Oxford: Oxford University Press, 1975.

Encyclopedia Judaica. Vol. 13. (ed.) "The Book of Psalms," (13-22). New York: Macmillan. Columns, 1971.

Emerton, J. A. "The Biblical High Place in the Light of Recent Study." *Palestine Exploration Quarterly* (1997) 116-32.

Endres, John C, SJ. "Psalms and Spirituality in the 21st Century." *Interpretation* (2002) 143-54.

Engnell, I. " Planted by the Streams of Water: Some Remarks on the Interpretation of the Psalms as Illuminated by a Detail of Ps. 1. " *Studia Orientalia* (1953) 85-96.

———. " Problems of Translation in Psalm 23: 3f." *The Bible Translator* 16 (1965) 171-76.

Eissfeldt, Otto. *The Old Testament: An Introduction.* Translated by Peter R. Ackroyd. New York: Harper Row, 1965.

———. "El and Yahweh," *Journal of Semitic Studies* 1 (1956): 25-37.

———. "Psalm 76," *Theologische Literaturzeitung* 82 (1957): 801-8.

Estes, Daniel J. "Like Arrows in the Hand of a Warrior," *Vetus Testamentum* 41 (1991): 304-11.

Fackre, Gabriel. "I Believe in the Resurrection of the Body." *Interpretation* (1992) 42-52.

Evans, Craig A. *From Jesus to the Church: The First Christian Generation*. Philadelphia: Westminster John Knox, 2014.

Feininger, Bernd. "A Decade of German Psalm-Criticism," *Journal for the Study of the Old Testament* 20 (1981) 91-103.

Finkelstein, Israel and N. A. Silberman, (eds). *The Bible Unearthed: Archaeology's New Vision of Ancient Israel and the Origin of the Sacred Texts*. New York: Simon and Schuster, 2002.

———. *David and Solomon: In Search of the Bible's Sacred Kings and the Roots of the Western Tradition*. New York: Free, 2006.

Flint, Peter W. "The Book of Psalms in the Light of the Dead Scrolls." *Vetus Testamentum* (1998) 453-72.

———. *The Dead Sea Scrolls and the Book of Psalms*. Leiden: Brill, 1997.

——— and Patrick D. Miller, Jr., (eds.) *The Book of Psalms: Composition and Reception* Leiden: Brill, 2005.

Floysvik, Ingvar. *When God Becomes My Enemy: The Theology of the Complaint Psalms*. St. Louis: Concordia, 1997.

Flynn, Shawn W. *YHWH: The Development of Divine Kingship in Ancient Israel*. Leiden: Brill, 2014.

Fontaine, Carole. "Arrows of the Almighty." *Anglican Theological Review* 66 (1984) 243-48.

Franken, H. J. *The Mystical Communion with JHWH in the Book of Psalms*. Leiden: Brill, 1954.

Fredericks, Daniel C. " A North Israelite Dialect in the Hebrew Bible? Questions of Methodology."*Journal of the National Association of Professors of Hebrew* 37(1996) 7-20.

Freedman, David N. "The Real Formal Full Personal Name of the God of Israel," In *Sacred History, Sacred Literature*. (ed.) Shawna Dolansky, (81-89) Winona Lake, Indiana: Eisenbrauns, 2008.

———. and Pam Fox Kuhlken. *What are the Dead Sea Scrolls and Why Do They Matter*. Grand Rapids: Eerdmans, 2007

Freehof, Solomon B. *The Book of Psalms: A Commentary*. Cincinnati: The Union of American Hebrew Congregations, 1938.

Fretheim, Terence E. "Nature's Praise of God in The Psalms." *ExAuditu* (1987) 16-30.

———. *The Suffering of God: An Old Testament Perspective*. Philadelphia: Fortress, 1984.

———. " Theological Reflections on the Wrath of God in the Old Testament." *Horizons in Biblical Theology* 24 (2002) 1-26.

Frost, S. B. "The Christian Interpretation of the Psalms." *Canadian Journal of Theology* 5 (1959) 25-34.

Futato, Mark D. *Interpreting the Psalms: An Exegetical Handbook*. Grand Rapids: Kregel, 2007.

Garfinkel, Yosef. "The Birth and Death of Biblical Minimalism." *Biblical Archaeology Review*, Vol. 27, No. 3. (2011) 47-53.

Gelander, Shamai. "Convention and Originality: Identification of the Situation in the Psalms." *Vetus Testamentum* 42 (1992) 302-16.

Gerstenberger, Erhardt. S. "Psalms," In *Old Testament Form Criticism* (179-224). ed. J.H. Mayes. Austin, Texas: Trinity University Press, 1974.

———. *Theologies in the Old Testament*. Translated by John Bowden. Minneapolis: Fortress, 2002.

Gillingham, Susan E. " The Exodus Tradition and Israelite Psalmody," *Scottish Journal* of *Theology*, 52.1. (1999) 19-46.

———. *The Poems and Psalms of the Hebrew Bible.* London: Oxford Press, 1994.

———. *Psalms through the Centuries* Vol. I. Oxford: Blackwell, 2008.

Goldingay, John. "Diversity and Unity in Old Testament Theology." *Vetus Testamentum* (1984) 153-68.

———. "The Dynamic Cycle of Praise and Prayer in the Psalms." *Journal for the Study of the Old Testament* 20 (1981) 85-90.

———. "Modes of Theological Reflection in the Bible." *Theology Today*(1991) 199-237.

———. "Psalm 4: Ambiguity and Resolution." *Tyndale Bulletin* (2006) 161-72.

———. Psalms. 3 vols. *Baker Commentary on the Old Testament.* ed. Tremper Longman, III. Grand Rapids: Baker Academic, 2006 to 2008.

———. "Repetition and Variation in the Psalms." *Jewish Quarterly Review* (1978) 146-57.

Goulder, Michael D. " David and Yahweh in Psalms 23 and 24," *Journal for the Study of the Old Testament* 30 (2006) 463-73.

———. " The Fourth Book of the Psalter," *Journal of Theological Studies* 26 (1975) 269-89.

———. "Psalm 8 and the Son of Man," *New Testament Studies,* 48.1. (2002) 18-29.

———. *The Psalms of Asaph and the Pentateuch.* Journal for the Study of the Old Testament Supplement. 233. Sheffield: Academic Press, 1996.

———. *The Psalms of the Sons of Korah.* Sheffield: JSOT, 1982.

Grabbe, Lester. *Ancient Israel: What Do We Know and How Do We Know It?*New York: T&T Clark, 2007.

Gray, John. " The Kingship of God in the Prophets and Psalms." *Vetus Testamentum* (1961) 1-29.

Gruenthaner, Michael J. "The Future Life in the Psalms." *Catholic Biblical Quarterly* 2 (1940) 57-63.

Gunkel, Hermann H. *Introduction to Psalms.* Completed by Johann Begrich. Tr. J. D. Nogalski. Macon, Georgia: Mercer, 1998. (*Die Psalmen. Gottinger und kommentar zum Altes Testamentische*), 1929.

Guthrie, Harvey H., Jr. *God and History in the Old Testament.* New York: Seabury, 1960.

———. *Israel's Sacred Songs: A Study of Dominant Themes.* New York: Seabury, 1967.

Habel, Norman C. "He Who Stretches out the Heavens." *Catholic Biblical Quarterly* (1972) 417-30.

Halkin, Hillel." Can the Bible Be Trusted? " *Commentary* (1999, July) 39-45.

Hanson, R. P. C. *Studies in Christian Antiquity.* Edinburgh: T&T Clark, 1985.

Harkness, Georgia. *The Providence of God.* Nashville, Tennessee: Abingdon, 1960.

Harper Collins Study Bible. The New Revised Standard Version with the Apocryphal/Deutero-canonical Books. New Annotated Edition by the Society of Biblical Literature. (General Editor) Harold W. Attridge. New York and San Francisco: Harper Collins, 2006.

Harrelson, Walter. "A Meditation on the Wrath of God: Psalm 90," In *Scripture in History and Theology* (eds.) Arthur L. Merril and Thomas W. Overholt. Pittsburgh: Pickwick, 1977.

Hays, Christopher M. and Christopher B. Ansberry (eds.) *Evangelical Faith and the Challenge of Historical Criticism.* Grand Rapids: Baker Academic, 2013.

Hayes, John H. " The Tradition of Zion's Inviolability." *Journal of Biblical Literature* (1963) 11-26.

———. *Understanding the Psalms.* Valley Forge, PA: Judson, 1976.

Hebrew and English Lexicon of the Old Testament. 1907. Translated by Edward Robinson. (eds.) F. Brown, S. S. Driver, and C. A. Briggs, 1907. Fifth Edition. Reprinted with corrections. London: Oxford University Press, Amen House, 1957.

Hengel, Martin. *The Septuagint as Christian Scripture*. Transl. by Mark E. Biddle. Edinburgh: T & T Clark, 2002.

Hobbs, T. R. and P .K. Jackson. "The Enemy in the Psalms." *Biblical Theology Bulletin* 21 (1991) 22-29.

Holman, J. "The Structure of Psalm CXXXIX." *Vetus Testamentum* 21 (1971) 298-310.

Holladay, William. *The Psalms through Three Thousand Years: Prayer Book of a Cloud* of *Witnesses*. Minneapolis: Augsburg, 1993.

Hopkins, Denise Dombrowski. *Journey through the Psalms*. Revised. St Louis: Chalice, 2002.

Hossfeld, Frank- Lothar, and Erich Zenger. "Psalms 2. 51-100 and Psalms 3.101-150." *Hermeneia- A Critical and Historical Commentary on the Bible*. Minneapolis: Fortress, 2005 and 2012.

Howard, David, M., Jr. "Editorial Activity in the Psalter: A State-of-the-field- Survey." *Word and World* 9 (1989) 274-85.

Hunter, Alastair. *An Introduction to the Psalms*. New York: T&T Clark. A Continuum imprint, 2008.

———. Psalms. *Old Testament Readings*. London: Routledge, 1999.

Hunter, J. H. "Theophany Verses in the Hebrew Psalms." *Journal of the Old Testament Society of South Africa* (1998) 255-70.

Hyatt, J. Philip. "Yahweh as 'the God of my father.'" *Vetus Testamentum* 5 (1955) 130-36.

Jacobson, Rolf. "The Costly Loss of Praise." *Theology Today* 57 (2000) 375-85.

———. (ed.) *Soundings in the Theology of Psalms: Perspectives and Methods in Contemporary Scholarship*. Minneapolis: Fortress, 2011.

Jaki, Stanley. *Praying the Psalms: A Commentary*. Grand Rapids: Eerdmans, 2001.

James, Fleming. *Thirty Psalmists*. New York: George P. Putnam's Sons, 1938.

Jinkins, Michael. *In the House of the Lord: Inhabiting the Psalms of Lament*. Collegeville, Minn.: Liturgical Press, 1998.

Joffe, Laura. " The Answer to the Meaning of Life, the Universe and the Elohistic Psalter." *Journal for the Study of the Old Testament* 27 (2002) 223-35.

Johnson, Elizabeth A. "Does God Play Dice? Divine Providence and Chance." *Theological Studies* (1996) 3-18.

Johnson, William Stacy. " Rethinking Theology: A Postmodern, Post-Holocaust, Post-Christendom Endeavor." *Interpretation* 55 (2001) 5-18.

Kaminsky, Joel and Anne Stewart. "God of All the World: Universalism and Developing Monotheism in Isaiah 40-66." *Harvard Theological Review* (2006) 139-63.

Keel, Othmar. *The Symbolism of the Biblical World: Ancient Near Eastern Iconography and the Book of Psalms*. New York: Seabury, 1978.

Kelly, J. N. D. *Early Christian Creeds*. Third Edition. New York: Longman, 1981.

Kidner, Derek. Psalms. 2 Vols. *Tyndale Old Testament Commentary*. Downers Grove, Illinois: Inter-Varsity, 1973 to 1975.

Kirkpatrick, A.F. *The Book of Psalms*. Cambridge Bible for Schools and Colleges. Cambridge: University Press, 1910.

Knierm, Rolf. "Old Testament Form Criticism Reconsidered." *Interpretation* 27 (1973) 449-68.

Koch, Klaus. "Is There a Doctrine of Retribution in the Old Testament?" In *Theodicy in the Old Testament. Issues in Religion and Theology*, No. 4. James L. Crenshaw, (ed.) Philadelphia: Fortress, 1983.

Koester, Helmut. *History and Literature of Early Christianity*. New York: Walter De Gruyter, 1982.

Koehler, Ludwig. "Psalm 23." *Zeitschrift für die alttestamentliche Wissenschaft* 68 (1956) 227-34.

Kolbet, Paul R. " Athanasius, the Psalms, and the Reformation of the Self." *Harvard Theological Review* 99 (2006) 111-75.

Kraus, Hans- Joachim. *The Psalms, A Continental Commentary*. 2 vols. Minneapolis: Fortress, 1989 to 1993.

———. *Theology of the Psalms*. Minneapolis: Augsburg, 1986.

Kruger, Thomas. "Psalm 90 und die Verganglichkeit des Menschen," *Biblica* (1994) 91-119.

Kselman, John S. "A Note on Psalm 4,5." *Biblica* (1987) 103-05.

Kugel, James L. *The God of Old: Inside the Lost World of the Bible*. New York: Free, 2003.

———. *How to Read the Bible: A Guide to Scripture, Then and Now*. New York: Free, 2007.

Labuschagne, C. J. *The Incomparability of Yahweh in the Old Testament*. Leiden: Brill, 1966.

Lampe, G. W. H. *The Holy Spirit in the Writings of Luke*. Birmingham:University of Birmingham,1955.

LeMon, J. M. "Yahweh's Winged Form in the Psalms: Exploring Congruent Iconography and Texts", In *Orbis biblicus et orientalis*. Fribourg: Academic; Gottingen: Vandenhock and Ruprecht, 2010.

Leslie, Elmer. *The Psalms: Translated and Interpreted in the Light of Hebrew Life and Worship*. New York: Abingdon, 1949.

Levenson, Jon D. *Creation and the Persistence of Evil*. San Francisco: Harper & Row, 1988.

———. *Sinai and Zion: An Entry into the Jewish Bible*. New York: Winston, 1985.

Limburg, James. "The Book of Psalms," *Anchor Bible Dictionary*, Vol. 5. ed. David Noel Freedman. (522-536). New York: Doubleday, 1992.

———. "Psalm 121: A Psalm for Sojourners." *Word and World* (1985) 180-87.

Loewenstamm, Samuel E. "The Lord is My Strength and Glory." *Vetus Testamentum* (1969) 464-70.

Lowry, Richard. "The Dark Side of the Soul: Human Nature and the Problem of Evil in Jewish and Christian Traditions." *Journal of Ecumenical Studies* (1998) 88 – 97.

Lundbom, Jack R. " Psalm 23: Song of Passage." *Interpretation* 40 (1986) 5-16.

Lohfink, Norbert. *In the Shadow of Your Wings*. Collegeville, Minn.: Liturgical, 2003.

Lohse, Bernhard. *A Short History of Christian Doctrine*. Third Printing. Translated by. F. Ernest Stoeffler. Philadelphia: Fortress, 1985.

Macintosh, A. A., " Psalm XCI 4 and the Root rhs." *Vetus Testamentum* 23 (1973) 56-62.

Magonet, Jonathan. *A Rabbi Reads the Psalms*. London: SCM, 1994.

Marttila, M. "Collective Reinterpretation in the Psalms: A Study of the Redaction History of the Psalter." In *Forschungen zum Alten Testament*, 2. Reihe, 13. Tubingen: Mohr Siebeck, 2006.

Mays, James Luther. "The David of the Psalms." *Interpretation* (1986) 143-56.

———. *Psalms*. Interpretation. Louisville: Westminster/John Knox, 1994.

———. "The Language of the Reign of God." *Interpretation* 53 (1993) 117-26.

———. "The Place of Torah-Psalms in the Psalter." *Journal of Biblical Literature* (1987) 3-12.

———. " 'In a Vision:' The Portrayal of the Messiah in the Psalms." *Ex Auditu* (1991) 1-8.

McCann, J. Clinton Jr., "Psalm 73: A Microcosm of Old Testament Theology" (247-57). In *The Listening Heart: Essays in Wisdom and the Psalms*. Journal for the Study of the Old Testament Supplement 58. Sheffield: JSOT, 1987.

———. "The Psalms as Instruction." *Interpretation* 2 (1992) 117-28

———. *The New Interpreter's Bible*. Vol. 4 Psalms. Nashville: 2003.

———. "Righteousness, Justice, Peace: Contemporary Theology of Psalms." *Horizons in Biblical Theology* 23 (2001) 111-31.

———. (ed.) *The Shape and Shaping of the Psalter*. Journal for the Study of the Old Testament Supplement 159. Sheffield: JSOT, 1993.

———. *A Theological Introduction to the Book of Psalms*. Nashville: Abingdon, 1993.

McCarthy, M. C. " 'We Are Your Books': Augustine, the Bible, and the Practice of Authority." *Journal of the American Academy of Religion* 75 (2007) 304-41.

McCarter, P. Kyle Jr. "The Historical David." *Interpretation* 46 (1986) 117-29.

McFall, Leslie. "The Evidence for a Logical Arrangement of the Psalter." *Westminster Journal* (2000) 223-56.

McGill, Arthur C. *Suffering: A Test of Theological Method*. Philadelphia: Geneva, 1968.

McKay, John W. "Psalms of Vigil." *Zeitschrift für die alttestamentliche Wissenschaft* (1979) 229-47.

———. *Religion in Judah under the Assyrians*. Studies in Biblical Theology No. 26. Naperville, Illinois: Alec R. Allenson, 1973.

McKeating, Henry. "Divine Forgiveness in the Psalms." *Scottish Journal of Theology* (1965) 69-83.

McKenzie, J.L. "A Note on Psalm 73 (74) 13-15." *Theological Studies* 11 (1950) 275-82.

Meek, T. J. *Hebrew Origins*. York: Harper Torchbooks, 1960.

Mendenhall, George. *The Tenth Generation: The Origins of the Biblical Tradition*. Baltimore: Johns Hopkins University Press, 1972.

Merril, A.L. "Psalm 23 and the Jerusalem Tradition." *Vetus Testamentum* (1965) 354-60.

Mettinger, Terence N. D. *In Search of God: The Meaning and Message of the Everlasting* Names. Translated by Frederick Cryer. Philadelphia: Fortress, 1988.

Milgrom, J. "Israel's Sanctuary: The Priestly 'Picture of Dorian Gray.'" *Revue Biblique* (1976) 390-99.

Miller, Patrick D, Jr. " Dietrich Bonhoeffer and the Psalms." *Princeton Seminary Bulletin* 15 (1994) 34-54.

———. "Enthroned on the Praises of Israel: The Praise of God in Old Testament Theology." *Interpretation* 39 (1985) 3-19.

———. *Interpreting the Psalms*. Philadelphia: Fortress, 1996.

———. *The Lord of the Psalms*. Louisville: Westminster/John Knox, 2013.

———. " In Praise and Thanksgiving." *Theology Today* 2 (1988) 180-89.

———. "Synonymous-Sequential Parallelism in the Psalms." *Biblica* (1980) 256-60.

———. "Trouble and Woe: Interpreting the Biblical Laments." *Interpretation* 37 (1983)32-45.

Miller, R. D., II. "Yahweh and His Clio: Critical Theory and the Historical Criticism of the Hebrew Bible." *Currents in Biblical Research*. 2 (2006) 149-68.

Mitchell, David C. "'God Will Redeem My Soul from Sheol': The Psalms of the Sons of Korah." *Journal for the Study of the Old Testament* 30 (2006) 365-84.

———. "Lord, remember David: G. H. Wilson and the Message of the Psalter." *Vetus Testamentum* (2006) 526-47.

Moltmann, Jurgen. *Theology of Hope*. New York: Harper & Row, 1967.

Morgenstern, Julian. *The Fire Upon the Altar*. Chicago: Quadrangle, 1963.

Mowinckel, Sigmund. *The Psalms in Israel's Worship*. Two Volumes. Oxford: Basil Blackwell, 1962.

Moyise, Steven and Maarten J. J. Menken, (eds). *The Psalms in the New Testament*. New York: T&T Clark, 2004.

Muilenburg, James. "Form Criticism and Beyond." *Journal of Biblical Literature* 88 (1969) 1-18.

———. "Psalm 4:7." *Journal of Biblical Literature* 63 (1944) 235-56.

———. *The Way of Israel*. Religion Perspectives. New York: Harper & Row, 1961.

Muller, Mogens. *The First Bible of the Church: A Plea for the Septuagint for the Study of the Old Testament*. Supplement No. 206. Sheffield: Sheffield Press, 1996.

Morgenstern, Julian. "Psalm 11." *Journal of Biblical Literature* (1950) 221-31.

Murphy, Roland. "The Faith of the Psalmist." *Interpretation* 34 (1980) 229-39.

———. *The Gift of the Psalms*. Peabody, Mass.: Hendrickson, 2000.

Nelson, Richard D. *Historical Roots of the Old Testament (1200-63 BCE)*. Biblical Encyclopedia. Atlanta: Society of Biblical Literature, 2014.

New International Standard Bible Encyclopedia. Vol. 3. (eds.) Geoffrey W. Bromiley, Peter C. Craigie and Herman Ridderbos, "Psalms," (1029-1040). Grand Rapids: Eerdmans, 1999.

New International Version Archaeological Study Bible. Grand Rapids, Michigan: Zondervan Publishers in collaboration with Gordon-Conwell Theological Seminary, South Hamilton, Massachusetts: 2005.

New Interpreter's Study Bible. New Revised Standard Version. (ed.) Walter J. Harrelson. Nashville, Tennessee: Abingdon, 2003.

Niebuhr, H. Richard. *Radical Monotheism and Western Culture: With Supplementary Essays*. New York: Harper Collins, 1972.

Niebuhr, Reinhold. *The Nature and Destiny of Man*. New York: Charles Scribner's Son, 1949.

Nock, Arthur Darby. *Early Gentile Christianity and Its Hellenistic Background*. New York: Harper Torchbooks, 1962.

Norris, Kathleen. *The Cloister Walk*. New York.: Riverhead, 1996.

———. *The Psalms with Commentary*. New York: Riverhead, 1997.

Noth, Martin. *The History of Israel*. Second Edition. Edinburgh: R. & R. Clark, 1960.

———. "History and the Word of God in the Old Testament." In *Bulletin of The John Rylands University Library* 32 (1950) 194-206.

———. "The 'Re-presentation' of the Old Testament in Proclamation." *Evangelische Theologie* (1952) 6-14.

Oberman, J. "The Divine Name YHWH in the Light of Recent Discoveries." In *Journal of Biblical Literature* 68 (1949) 301-23.

Old, Hughes. "The Psalms of Praise in the Worship of the New Testament Church." *Interpretation* 39 (1985) 20-33.

Ollenburger, Ben C. "If Mortals Die, Will They Live Again? The Old Testament and Resurrection." *Ex Auditu* 9 (1993) 29-44.

Otto, Rudolph. *The Idea of the Holy*. New York: Oxford University Press, 1958.

Oxford Study Bible. Revised English Bible with the Apocrypha. (eds.) M. Jack Suggs, Katherine Doob Sakenfeld and James R. Mueller. New York: Oxford University Press, 1992.

Pannenberg, Wolfhart, et al., (eds.) *Revelation as History*. New York: Macmillan, 1968.

Pannenberg, Wolfhart. *Jesus, God and Man*. Philadelphia: Westminster, 1973.

Parke-Taylor, G. H. *Yahweh: The Divine Name in the Bible*. Waterloo, Ontario: Wilfrid Laurier University, 1975.

Pelikan, Jaroslav. *The Christian Tradition: A History of the Development of Doctrine*. Vol. 1. The Emergence of the Catholic Tradition. Chicago: University Press, 1971.

———. The Spirit of Eastern Christendom (600-1700) In *The Christian Tradition*, Vol.2. Chicago: University Press, 1971.

Pemberton, Glenn. *After Lament: Psalms for Learning to Trust Again*. Abilene, Texas: Abilene Christian University Press, 2014.

Perdue, Leo G., et al., (eds.) *In Search of Wisdom*. Louisville: Westminster/John Knox, 1993.

Peters, John P. *The Psalms as Liturgies*. New York: Macmillan Company, 1922.

Petersen, David L. "Portraits of David: Canonical and Otherwise." *Interpretation* 40 (1986) 130-42.

Pittenger, Norman. *Picturing God*. London: SCM, 1982.

Pleins, J. David. *The Psalms: Songs of Tragedy, Hope, and Deliverance*. Maryknoll, New York: Orbis, 1993.

Ploeg, J. M. W. van der. "Le Psaume XCI dans une recension de Qumran." *Revue Biblique* (1965) 210-17.

Prevost, Jean-Pierre, ed. *A Short Dictionary of the Psalms*. Collegeville, Minnesota, Liturgical, 1997.

Pritchard, J. B., ed. *Ancient Near Eastern Texts Relating to the Old Testament*. Third Edition. Princeton, New Jersey: Princeton University Press, 1969.

Prothero, Roland. *The Psalms in Human Life*. New York: E. P. Dutton & Company, 1905.

Provan, Iain W., V. Philips Long and Tremper Longman III. *A Biblical History of Israel*. Louisville: Westminster/John Knox, 2003.

Psalms. (*The Revised Grail Psalms: A Liturgical Psalter*) A New Translation from the Hebrew arranged for singing to the Psalmody of Joseph Gelineau. Prepared by the Benedictine Monks of Conception Abbey. Collegeville, Minn.: Liturgical, 2010.

Rabin, Elliott. *Understanding the Hebrew Bible: A Readers Guide*. City, New Jersey: KTAV, 2006.

Rad, Gerhard von. *God at Work in Israel*. Nashville, Tennessee: Abingdon, 1980.

———. *Old Testament Theology*, 2 Vols. Nashville, Tennessee: Abingdon, 1968.

Renckens, Henricus. *The Religion of Israel*. New York: Sheed and Ward, 1966.

Rendsburg, G. "Additional Notes on 'The Last Words of David.'" *Biblica* 70 (1989) 403-08.

———. *Linguistic Evidence for the Northern Origin of Selected Psalms*. New York: Journal of Biblical Literature, 2004.

———. "The Northern Origin of 'The Last Words of David' (2 Sam 23,1-7)." *Biblica* (1989) 113-21.

Rendtorff, Rolf. *Canon and Theology*. Edinburgh: T&T Clark, 1994.

———. *God's History: A Way through the Old Testament*. Philadelphia: Westminster, 1969.

———. "The Impact of the Holocaust on German Protestant Theology." *Horizons in Biblical Theology* 15 (1993) 154-67.

Richardson, R.D. "The Psalms as Christian Prayer and Praises." *Anglican Theological Review* (1960) 326-46.

Ringgren, Helmer. *The Faith of the Psalmists*. Minneapolis: Fortress, 1963.

Roberts, J.J.M. "The Davidic Origin of the Zion Tradition." *Journal of Biblical Literature*. (1973) 329-44.

———. "God's Imperial Reign according to The Psalter." *Horizons in Biblical Theology* 23 (2001) 211-21.

———. "The Hand of Yahweh." *Vetus Testamentum* 21 (1971) 244-51.

Rogerson, John W. *The Psalms in Daily Life*. Oxford: Oxford University Press, 2004.

———, and J. W. McKay. *Psalms*. 3 vols. Cambridge Commentary on the New English Bible. Cambridge: Cambridge University Press, 1977.

Rosenberg, Abraham J. *Psalms*. 3 vols. New York: Judaica, 1991.

Rosenberg, Roy A. "The God Sedeq." *Hebrew Union College Annual* (1965) 161-67.

———. "Yahweh Becomes King." *Journal of Biblical Literature* (1966) 297-307.

Russell, David S. *From Early Judaism to Early Church*. London: SCM, 1986.

Ryrie, Alexander. *Deliver Us From Evil: Reading the Psalms as Poetry*. London: Darton, Longman & Todd, 2004.

Sabourin, Leopold. *The Psalms: Their Origin and Meaning*. Second Edition. New York: Alba House, 1974.

Sanders, James A. *The Monotheizing Process: Its Origins and Development*. Eugene, Oregon: Cascade, 2014.

———. *The Psalms Scroll of Qumran Cave 11*. Ithaca, New York: Cornell University Press, 1969.

———. *Torah and Canon*. Philadelphia: Fortress, 1972. Reprint: Eugene, Oregon: Wipf & Stock, 1999.

Sarna, Nahum M. *Songs of the Heart: An Introduction to the Book of Psalms*. New York: Schocken, 1993.

Schaefer, OSB, Konrad. "Psalms." In *Berit Olam: Studies in Hebrew Narrative and Poetry*. Collegeville, Minnesota: Liturgical, 2005.

Schleiermacher, F. D. W. *The Christian Faith*. 2 Vols. New York: Harper Row, 1972.

Schuller, E. M. *The Dead Sea Scrolls: What Have We Learned?* Louisville: Westminster John Knox, 2006.

Segal, M. H. "El, Elohim, and YHWH in the Bible." *Jewish Quarterly Review* (1955) 89-115.

Seybold, Klaus. *Introducing the Psalms*. Edinburgh: T&T Clark, 1990.

Shepherd, Massey H. *The Psalms in Christian Worship*. New York: Seabury, 1976.

Sheppard, Gerald T. " Theology and the Book of Psalms." *Interpretation* 46 (1992) 143-55.

Shophar Tehillim. The Book of Psalms. The Schottenstein Edition. (ed.) Rabbi Menachem Davis. New York: Mesorah, 2005.

Skinner, J. *Prophecy and Religion: Studies in the Life of Jeremiah*. New York: Harper Row, 1984.

Slomovic, Eliezer. "Toward an Understanding of the Formation of Historical Titles in the Book of Psalms." *Zeitschrift für die alttestamentliche Wissenschaft* (1979) 350-80.

Sloyan, Gerard S. *The Three Persons in One God*. Englewood Cliffs, New Jersey: Prentice-Hall, 1964.

Smith, Mark S. *The Early History Of God: Yahweh and the Other Deities in Ancient Israel*. The Biblical Resource Series. Grand Rapids: Eerdmans, 2002.

———. "The Levitical Compilation of the Psalter." *Zeitschrift für die alttestamentliche Wissenschaft* 103 (1991) 258-63.

———. "The Psalms as a Book for Pilgrims." *Interpretation* 46 (1992) 156-66.

———." Seeing God in the Psalms: The Background to the Beatific Vision in the Hebrew Bible." *Catholic Biblical Quarterly* 50 (1988) 171-83.

———. "Setting and Rhetoric in Psalm 23." In *Journal for the Study of the Old Testament* (1988) 61-66.

Smith, Terry L. "A Crisis in Faith: An Exegesis of Psalm 73." In *Restoration Quarterly* 17.3 (1974) 162-84.

Snaith, Norman H. *The Distinctive Ideas of the Old Testament*. London: Epworth, 1944
———. *Studies in the Psalter*. London: Epworth, 1934.

Soden, John Mark. "Whom Shall I Fear? Psalm 27." *Exegesis and Exposition* (1988) 1-24.

Soggin, J. Alberto. *Israel in the Biblical Period: Institutions, Festivals, Ceremonies, Rituals*. Edinburgh: T&T Clark, 2001.

Sonne, Isaiah. "Psalm Eleven." *Journal of Biblical Literature* 68 (1949) 241-45.

Soskice, J.M. *Metaphor and Religious Language*. Oxford: Clarendon, 1985.

Steussy, Marti J. *David: Biblical Portraits of Power*. Columbia, South Carolina: University of South Carolina Press, 1999.

———. *Psalms*. Chalice Commentaries. St. Louis: Chalice, 2004.

Stuhlmueller, Carroll. *Psalms*. 2 vols. Old Testament Message, No. 22. Wilmington, Delaware: Glazier, 1983.

———. *The Spirituality of the Psalms*. (eds) C. Dempsey and T. Lenchak. Collegeville, Minnesota: Liturgical, 2002.

Swenson, Karen M. *Living through Pain: Psalms and the Search for Wholeness*. Waco, Texas: Baylor University Press, 2005.

Tappy, Ron E. "Psalm 23." *Catholic Biblical Quarterly* (1995) 255-80.

Tate, Marvin E. "The Interpretation of the Psalms." *Review and Expositor* (1984) 363-76.

———. Psalms 51-100. *Word Biblical Commentary* Vol.20. Waco, Texas: Baylor University Press, 1980.

Terrien, Samuel. *The Elusive Presence: Toward a New Biblical Theology*. New York: Harper, 1978.

———. "The Numinous, the Sacred and the Holy in Scripture." *Biblical Theology Bulletin* 12 (1982) 99-108.

———. *The Psalms: Strophic Structure and Theological Commentary*. Grand Rapids: Eerdmans, 2003.

———. "Towards a New Theology of Presence." *Union Seminary Quarterly Review* (1969) 22-77.

Theological Dictionary of the Old Testament. Volumes I-XIV. (eds.) G. Johannes Botterweck, Helmer Ringgren and Heinz-Josef Fabry. (Translation by John T. Willis, Douglas W. Stott and David E. Green). Grand Rapids: Eerdmans, 1975 to 2005.

Theological Lexicon of the Old Testament. 3 Volumes. (ed.) Ernst Jenni with assistance from Claus Westermann. (Translation by Mark E. Biddle). Peabody MA: Hendrickson, 1997.

Thompson, Thomas. *The Mythic Past: Biblical Archaeology and the Myth of Ancient* Israel. New York: Basic, 1999.

Tillich, Paul. "The Divine Name." *Christianity & Crisis* 20 (1960/61) 55.

———. *Systematic Theology*. 3 volumes. Chicago: University of Chicago Press, 1963.

Tomback, Richard S. "Psalm 23:2 Reconsidered." *Journal of Northwest Semitic Languages* 10 (1982) 93-96.

Toorn, Karel van der. *Scribal Culture and the Making of the Hebrew Bible*. Cambridge, MA: Harvard University Press, 2007.

Tozer, A.W. 1989. (reprint). *Faith Beyond Reason*. (ed. G. B. Smith) Camp Hill, Pennsylvania: Christian, 1959.

———. *The Knowledge of the Holy*. New York: Harper Collins, 1961. Reprint: 1981.

———. *The Pursuit of God*. New York: Harper Collins, 1957. Reprint: 1997.

Tsevat, Matitiahu. "Psalm XC 5-6." *Vetus Testamentum* (1985) 115-17.

———. "A Study of the Language of the Biblical Psalms." *Journal of Biblical Literature Monograph Series* Vol. IX. Philadelphia: Society of Biblical Literature, 1955.

Vander Kam, James C. *The Dead Sea Scrolls Today*. Grand Rapids: Eerdmans, 1994.

VanGemeren, Willem A. *Psalms,* The Expositor's Bible Commentary. Vol. 5. Grand Rapids: Zondervan, 2008.

———. "Psalm 131:2 –*kegamul* The Problems of Meaning and Metaphor." *Hebrew Studies* 23 (1982) 51-57.

Vaux de, Roland. *Ancient Israel: Its Life and Institutions*. 2 Vols. 1. Social Institutions; 2. Religious Institutions. New York: McGraw-Hill Paperback Edition, 1965.

———. *The Early History of Israel*. Translated by J. D. Smith. Philadelphia: Westminster, 1978.

Vawter, Bruce. "Postexilic Prayer and Hope." *Catholic Biblical Quarterly* (1975) 460-70.

———. "Yahweh: Lord of the Heavens and of the Earth." *Catholic Biblical Quarterly* 48 (1986) 461-67.

Vervenne, Marc. "Do We Use Them as a Form, or as the Voice of Our Hearts? Exegetical Reflections on the Psalms of Israel." *Questions liturgiques* 71 (1990) 162-90.

Vos, C. J. A. *Theopoetry of the Psalms*. London: T&T Clark, 2005.

Vriezen, Th. C. *The Religion Of Ancient Israel*. Philadelphia: Westminster, 1967.

Wagner, J. Ross. "From the Heavens to the Heart: The Dynamics of Psalm 19 as Prayer." *Catholic Biblical Quarterly* 61 (1999) 245-61.

Wallace, H. N. *Word to God, Word from God: The Psalms in the Prayer and Preaching of the Church*. Burlington, Australia: Ashgate, 2005.

Wallace, Robert E. *The Narrative Effect of Book IV of the Hebrew Psalter*. Sheffield: Academic, 1994.

Waltke, Bruce K. "Superscripts, Postscripts, or Both?" *Journal of Biblical Literature* (1991) 583-96.

———. *The Psalms as Christian Worship: A Historical Commentary*. Grand Rapids: Eerdmans, 2010.

Watts, John D. W. "Psalms of Trust, Thanksgiving, and Praise." *Review and Expositor* 71 (1984) 395-406.

———. "YHWH-Malak Psalms." *Theologische Zeitschrift* 21 (1965) 341-48.

Weaver, David. "From Paul to Augustine: Romans 5:12 in Early Christian Exegesis." *St. Vladimir's Theological Quarterly* 27.3 (1983) 187-206.

Weiser, Artur. *The Psalms*. Old Testament Library. London: SCM, 1962.

Weiss, Johannes. *Earliest Christianity,* Vol. II. Translated by Frederick C. Grant. New York: Harper, 1959.

Westermann, Claus. "God and His People: The Church in the Old Testament." *Interpretation* 17 (1963) 259-70.

———. *The Living Psalms*. Grand Rapids: Eerdmans, 1989.

———. *Praise and Lament in the Psalms*. Atlanta: John Knox, 1981.

———. *The Psalms: Structure, Content & Message*. Minneapolis: Augsburg, 1980.

———. *A Thousand Years and a Day*. Louisville:Westminster/John Knox, 1996.

Whitley, Charles Francis. "The Semantic Range of Hesed." *Biblica* (1981) 519-26.

———. "The Text of Psalm 90,5." *Biblica* (1982) 555-57.

Wifall, Walter. "El Shaddai or El of the Fields." *Zeitschrift für die alttestamentliche Wissenschaft* (1980) 24-32.

Williams, Ronald J. "Theodicy in the Ancient Near East." *Canadian Journal of Theology* 2 (1956) 14-26.

Willis, John T. "A Cry of Defiance–Psalm 2." *Journal for the Study of the Old Testament* 47 (1990) 33-50.

——. *Insights from the Psalms.* 3 vols. Abilene, Texas: Biblical Research, 1974.

——. "Psalm 1–An Entity." *Zeitschrift für die alttestamentliche Wissenschaft* 9 (1979) 381-401.

Willis, Timothy M. "A Fresh Look at Psalm 23: 3(a)." *Vetus Testamentum* 37 (1987) 104-06.

Wilson, Gerald H. *The Editing of the Hebrew Psalter.* Chico, Calif.: Scholars, 1985.

——. "Evidence of Editorial Divisions in the Hebrew Psalter." *Vetus Testamentum* 34 (1984) 337-52.

——. *The Psalms.* Vol. 1. *The NIV Application Commentary.* Grand Rapids: Zondervan, 2002.

——. "The Qumran Psalms Manuscripts and Consecutive Arrangement of Psalms in the Hebrew Psalter." *Catholic Biblical Quarterly* 45 (1983) 377-88.

——. "The Qumran Psalms Scroll Reconsidered: Analysis of the Debate." *Catholic Biblical Quarterly* 47 (1985) 624-42.

——. "The Shape of the Book of Psalms." *Interpretation* 46 (1992) 129-42.

Wolverton, Wallace I. "The Psalmists' Belief in God's Presence." *Canadian Journal of Theology* 9 (1963) 82-94.

Wright, N. T. "One God, One Lord, One People," *Ex Auditu* 8. (1992) 12-33.

Wurthwein, Ernst. *The Text of the Old Testament: An Introduction to the Biblia Hebraica.* Translated by Errol F. Rhodes. Grand Rapids: Eerdmans, 1995.

Yeivin, Israel. "The Division into Sections in the Book of Psalms." *Textus* VII (1969) 76-102.

Zenger, Erich. "The Composition and Theology of the Fifth Book of Psalms, Psalms 107-150." *Journal for the Study of the Old Testament* 80 (1998) 77-102.

——. *A God of Vengeance? Understanding the Psalms of Divine Wrath.* Louisville: Westminster/John Knox, 1996.

——. "New Approaches to the Study of the Psalms." *Proceedings of the Irish Biblical Association* 7 (1994) 27-54.

Zevit, Ziony. "Psalms at the Poetic Precipice." *Hebrew Annual Review* (1986) 351-66.

——. "Three Debates about Bible and Archaeology." *Biblica* 83 (2002) 1-27.

Zimmerli, Walther. *Man and His Hope in the Old Testament.* Naperville, Illinois: Alec R. Allenson, 1968.

Zyl, A. H. van. "Psalm 23." *Oudtestamentische Studien* 13 (1963) 64-83.

Author Index

Scripture Index

Early Christian Writings